THE GREATEST
CONSPIRACY

BUT YOU CAN RIGHTLY DIVIDE THE WORD OF TRUTH

This book is a guide to the scriptures of the
King James Version Bible

JESSIE DUNSON

THE GREATEST CONSPIRACY
Copyright © 2025 by Jessie Dunson

ISBN: 979-8894792316 (hc)
ISBN: 979-8894792293 (sc)
ISBN: 979-8894792309 (e)

The Reading Glass Books
1-888-420-3050
www.readingglassbooks.com
fulfillment@readingglassbooks.com

Contents

CHAPTER 1

THE MILK OF THE WORD

After you read this first paragraph, I want you to ask God to reveal the TRUTH of His word to you. As you read this book, I want you to get your Bible and look up every scripture mentioned in this book. As you search the scriptures for the TRUTH, you will be studying God's word. You can study God's word for thirty minutes and accomplish more than simply reading it, until you are blue in the face. I don't want you to just take my word for it—I want you to seek God for the TRUTH in His word. In God's word, God is referred to as Jesus, the Father, the Son, and the Holy Ghost, and Melchisedec. The New Testament spelling is Melchisedec, and the Old Testament spelling is Melchizedek, but both are the same person, and later in this book, Jesus is going to teach you from John chapter 8, who Melchisedec was and is. In John 14:26, Jesus says that the Holy Ghost is our teacher. If you learn anything from this book by comparing it with the Bible, it will be Jesus teaching you. If you continue reading this book, and look up and read every scripture that I share with you from your King James Version Bible. And start claiming everything you learn is TRUTH from God's word. Jesus will be your personal tutor. If you don't already know, later you will learn that Jesus is the Living Word and He truly knows how to teach about Himself. If you continue and seek Jesus for TRUTH, He will begin turning up the Light of your understanding. You can have Ephesians 1:17-18 come alive in you, and your family's lives. Simply ask Jesus every day for TRUTH. The word of God is TRUTH, but there are TRUTHS in God's word that only Jesus can reveal to us. Come on, and let's get off the first page, and allow Jesus to write His word in your mind and heart.

Now, it is time to ask Jesus to teach you His TRUTH. You don't have to go into a long drawn-out prayer, unless you want to. Just simply ask Jesus to open up your heart and mind so you can understand and obey His word. If you can understand His word, most likely, you will obey what you learn, because you will know that it is from God.

I am Jessie Dunson, a servant of Jesus Christ and my fellow man. I want to share with you a part of what Jesus has taught me. I read and study God's word every day. I am seeking and learning God's word so I can obey it and become a friend of Jesus and be a part of His Bride. To all who read this book that know the TRUTH and to all who desire to receive this TRUTH with us, grace and peace will be multiplied unto you through the knowledge of Jesus, our God. Here is a passage of scriptures that everyone who reads and studies God's word should know. Read Matthew 13:1–23. Now, I want you to read 1 Corinthians 3:1–9. In your mind and heart, I may be sowing God's seed (word) or I may be watering the seed (word) that you have already received, but as you now know, God is the one that is going to increase your knowledge. Read Matthew 11:27, and you will learn that this knowledge comes by revelation only.

This book RIGHTLY DIVIDES the scriptures, but not particularly in this order, referring to where and when the New Testament church started and how to be born-again. We are also going to find out what is TRUTH and what is false. This book is an example of how a person can RIGHTLY DIVIDE the word of God and find the TRUTH about a certain subject. When you RIGHTLY DIVIDE the word of God, it is God giving you a clear understanding and the correct interpretation of His word. We are also going to find out who wrote the Bible and what authority they have to tell us how we are to live.

In this chapter, we are going to find out how and why God's word can and has been falsely interpreted over the past two thousand plus years. We are not supposed to add or take away from God's word. You can clearly see in Revelation 22:18–19 that God will add or take away from any person that does not use His word correctly. I have never found in the Bible where we can multiply God's word. But in 2 Timothy 2:15, we can find division.

The key words in this scripture are all of them, but let us look at these two key words—RIGHTLY DIVIDE. When someone does not RIGHTLY DIVIDE God's word, they will be getting a false interpretation. The scripture in 2 Timothy 2:15 is where I got the last part of the title of this book. The first part of the title came from knowing the TRUTH about how Satan has deceived the false churches of the world. I will explain that last statement a little later in this book.

Remember that Jesus tells us in John 14:26 that the Holy Ghost is our teacher, which is God living and walking inside us every day. If we ask God for knowledge and wisdom of His word, He will give them to anyone who hungers and thirsts after righteousness and is willing to obey His word as they learn. If we don't have the wisdom and understanding of His word, let us read what Apostle Peter said will happen. Read 2 Peter 3:15–16. Verse 15 says that Paul wrote with the wisdom given to him. Verse 16 says as also in all epistles, Paul wrote of some things hard to be understood, "which they that are unlearned and unstable wrest, as also the other scriptures." In the New Oxford American Dictionary, the word wrest has a few definitions. I am going to list two of them that coincides with these scriptures. The first definition is twist. The second is distort the meaning or interpretation of something to suit one's own interest or views. The end of verse 16 says that they wrest not only Paul's letters but also the other scriptures. Peter was referring to what the other apostles and prophets wrote, and he says it will be unto their own destruction.

In the first chapter of Galatians, Paul is writing to the church in Galatia. In Galatians 1:6–9, Apostle Paul is warning them and us (the church) about what Peter said would happen if a person doesn't have the wisdom and understanding of God's word and tries to teach someone. Apostle Peter said that unlearned and unstable people will wrest (twist or change) the gospel. Here in these scriptures, I understand that there is one true gospel, and it has and will be changed again.

I said a little earlier that we would learn who wrote the Bible and about their authority to tell us how we are supposed to live. In verse 8, Paul wrote, "Though we, or an angel from heaven." Before I go any further, I want to explain these three words; and they are we, our, and us. When you read we, our, or us in the New Testament, 99.9 % of the time, it is referring to the apostles, because they wrote the New Testament.

As far as the angel from heaven goes, I believe Paul was saying that we should not listen to any angel that teaches something contrary to what they have already written. In chapters 2 and 3, you will learn how both of these religious groups were deceived by Satan using angels. I am going to write verse 8, but I'm going to paraphrase a little. Paul says in verse 8, "We, or an angel from heaven, do not have the right to preach any gospel other than what we have preached."

Jesus wanted everyone to understand what Paul was saying in verse 8 so much, and I mean on the high end of so much, that He had Paul repeat it again in verse 9. But in this scripture, Paul added the word "any." That means no one is allowed to add or take away from God's word. Even Jesus Himself is not going to change the gospel. EVER! Remember that the Holy Ghost is our teacher, and His name is Jesus. You must ask Jesus for the TRUTH, and He will teach you the TRUTH because He is TRUTH.

I want to share with you another set of scriptures that also teaches us about someone else that has the authority to teach us how we are supposed to live. Read Ephesians 2:19–22. Now, you know that Jesus, the apostles, and the prophets have the authority to tell us how to live here on earth. In 1 John 4:6, John says it, as clear as it can be said. In this scripture, John uses these two words—we and us. In this scripture John was referring to the church, and sinners because if someone has not obeyed the apostle's teachings, this is how we know the Spirit of TRUTH and the spirit of error.

I just wrote in a previous paragraph that the apostles wrote the New Testament, but that is not completely true. I should have said apostles/disciples, because as far as I know, three of Jesus' disciples wrote a part of the New Testament. And they are Mark that wrote the gospel of Mark, and Jude. Jesus' Brother that wrote Jude and Jesus other brother, John that wrote the gospel of John and Luke. Luke wrote one of the gospels, and he also wrote the book of Acts. As I read Luke 1:1–4, I came to understand a part of why the Lord had Luke write some of His words. Luke was one of the Lord's disciples from the beginning. Luke writes in Luke 1:3, "It seemed good to me also, having had perfect understanding of all things from the very first, to write unto thee in order, most excellent Theophilus."

Referring to when Luke wrote the gospel of Luke, he writes,

> The former treatise have I made, O Theophilus, of all that Jesus began both to do and teach. Until the day in which He [Jesus] through the Holy Ghost had given commandments unto the apostles whom He [Jesus] had chosen. (Acts 1:1-2)

Just as Luke acknowledges that Jesus chose His apostles, I know that Jesus chose Luke to write these two books in His word, or they would not be there. If I know that Luke was chosen to write these books, I must learn and obey what he says in his writings, just as if it were any of the apostles or Jesus, Himself.

I will admit I'm neither the sharpest nor the brightest tool in the workshop. As I was writing chapter 6 about the milk and meat of God's word, I realized that I have put the cart in front of the horse. As I thought about what I was writing in chapter 6, I realized that chapters 4, 5, 6, 7, and 8 of this book are going to be hard to swallow (accept) for most of you who read this book. I felt that I should come back and write this to inform you (the reader) that you are going to find in these chapters the meat of God's word. You are going to find filet mignon, but this filet mignon is going to be as tough as round steak, because most likely, it will go against most everything that you have learned from God's word. Chapters 2 and 3 are going to be hard for some to accept; but chapters 4, 5, 6, 7, and 8 are going to be downright tough, for most of you. First, you need for your faith to grow in Jesus, so when it's time, you will be able to receive the meat of God's word. Read Luke 17:5 and also Romans 10:17.

For a lack of a better word, I must put the horse back in front of the cart. I suggest that you go and strengthen your faith by reading the four gospels— Matthew, Mark, Luke, and John. These books teach us about Jesus' life. I believe you need to read the scriptures that teach how, when, and where Jesus was born. As you read the four gospels, your faith in Jesus will grow. The four gospels are the biography of Jesus. These books teach us about the birth and life of Jesus. They also teach us about His death, but there is something else they teach that is more important—His resurrection!

While reading and studying the gospels, you are going to learn something in the gospel of John that is essential for your (and everyone's) salvation. I have already mentioned this before, and the term that I used comes from God's word, and it is born-again. Jesus teaches us about being born-again in John 3:1–8. After you are born-again and the Lord lives inside you, these scriptures will be clearer to your spiritual ears.

Jesus plainly tells us in John 3:3, "Verily, verily, I say unto thee, except a man be born-again, he cannot see the Kingdom of God." In verse 4, Nicodemus asked the Lord. "How can a man be born when he is old? Can he enter the second time into his mother's womb, and be born?" Then, Jesus tells Nicodemus, "Verily, verily, I say unto thee, except a man be born of water and the Spirit, he cannot enter into the Kingdom of God." Jesus makes a really clear statement about this plan of salvation in verse 7. He says, "You must be born again."

As you read this book, you are going to hear a few times about being born-again. As I write about the false teachings that are in the world, most of the time, I mention God's TRUTH about being born-again. Ever since Adam and Eve sinned, Jesus was the only baby born that was not born a sinner. No matter how good our parents raise us, there comes a day when the Lord wants His chance to teach us. When a person is born-again, they truly become a newborn baby. If you will allow the Lord, He will teach you His ways through His word and life's experiences as you walk and talk with Him. If you will try, the Lord will teach you.

You are going to learn from God's word that when you are baptized in the name of Jesus and filled with His Spirit, you are born-again, just as our brothers and sisters before us. Jesus says in Acts 1:8, "But you shall receive power after that the Holy Ghost is come upon you." When you are born- again, you will have God's Spirit living inside of you. At that time, you will have God's power to withstand Satan's power and to accomplish anything that your heart desires. Just remember that you must do your part, and I promise you, Jesus will do His.

Read 1 Peter 2:1–2. As you learn these things about Jesus from the four gospels, you will find yourself inside the milk jug of God's word. These are the first things you need to learn from God's word. As you read the four gospels, you will see Jesus' love for the sinner. It's not that He loves people who sin, but He is looking at the saint, which they can become. When you realize that Jesus loves you, you will have gotten off to a good start in this race. If you don't know, let me tell you how much Jesus loves you. Sure, Jesus says in His word that He loves us many times, but He did something greater than that. He put His words into action, and you know, actions always speak louder than words.

I am speaking to myself here also. Our actions should speak louder than our words. Here is what the Lord has done for us all. God came to earth and made Himself a body. He came to earth to find Himself a Bride. He was born of a virgin; then, God grew from a baby into a man and walked this earth. I know with such a statement, I might have just lost some of you, so let God's word explain. Read Isaiah 9:6, and you will see and hear what God's word says about who the baby Jesus was (is). When Jesus came to the end of His life as a man, He took upon Himself the sins of the whole world. Jesus was crucified on the cross and died a brutal death for you and me. But it was far from being over. On the third day, Jesus was resurrected, and He is alive forevermore, and He has given us the opportunity to live forever with Him in heaven as His bride. That is how much Jesus loves us. In John 15:13, Jesus tells us, "Greater love hath no man than this, that a man lay down his life for his friends." I believe these things are what the Lord would call the milk of the word.

Here is something everyone should know. Most Bible believers know that after Jesus' trial, the Roman leaders had Him beaten before He was crucified on the cross. What the world (ungodly people) didn't know is the beating that Jesus took was for our healing. The word plainly teaches that the stripes He took that day were so we could be healed of any sickness or disease through faith. Read Isaiah 53:1–5. In these scriptures, Isaiah was prophesying (foretelling the future) and teaching us how the Lord was going to accomplish the redemption of mankind. Also, in these scriptures, the Lord lets us know that our healing has already been paid for. Read and remember 1 Corinthians 6:18–20.

I'm going to write about all the scriptures from God's word that teaches how the Lord healed everyone who asked Him. I just remembered that there is one the Lord didn't heal. Truly, the one He doesn't heal is one of His greatest miracles. I will explain when I get to those scriptures. As you begin studying the word of God, you will learn the need to ask Jesus for everything. You may not ever need the Lord to heal you, but sooner or later, you will ask Him to heal someone you love. You are about to learn in this chapter that Jesus is the GREAT PHYSICIAN. The Lord made us, and He knows how to fix us.

Would you rather have an earthly doctor or the Lord operate on your heart? I only know what I have seen and what I have experienced. I have seen that an earthly doctor cut you wide open to operate on your heart. I have experienced the Lord removing my heart of stone and given me a new fresh heart in which He could write His word upon.

I have pulled up my shirt many times in the past thirty years as I witnessed to show that I don't even have a scar—none, nothing, not even a scratch. I am so thankful to the Lord Jesus because He revealed to me that He is the GREAT PHYSICIAN. I want to say at this time while the Lord and Satan are listening to what I'm thinking and writing, I will never allow anyone or anything, especially Satan, to change my mind. Jesus is the GREAT PHYSICIAN.

This thought just came to me about the first operation on earth. You can read about it in Genesis 2:18–25. Verses 21–22 tell us, "The Lord caused a deep sleep to fall upon Adam, and he slept: and He took one of his ribs and closed up the flesh instead thereof, and the rib, which the Lord God had taken from man, made He a woman, and brought her unto the man." This scripture says that the Lord closed up the flesh. That lets me know the Lord literally opened up Adam and took his rib. Now, this is just my opinion, but I don't believe the Lord used staples or needle and thread. I believe the Lord pulled Adam's flesh back together and then fused his flesh together, without leaving a scar. I just believe that is the way the GREAT PHYSICIAN would do it.

Later, you are going to learn in this book how Satan rebelled against God and how he was kicked out of heaven. You are also going to learn that when Jesus was born, Satan tried to destroy Him. But first, as we learn from the four gospels how Jesus heals, we can learn some important lessons in Matthew 4:1–11. Later in this book, we are going to learn some other important lessons from these scriptures, but now, we need to learn about fasting.

In Matthew 4:1–11, you will find Satan coming against the Lord again. This time, Satan catches the Lord at His weakest, or so he thought. Jesus had fasted for forty days and forty nights, He was weak in His body, but spiritually, He was strong. Satan will come against the Lord two more times before this world ends. I am referring to when Satan tries to destroy the Lord in the last two world wars. After the end of the Last World War, Satan is thrown into HELL, and I believe at that time, he will never be heard from again.

Here, I am preaching to myself also. We need to fast as we continue our walk with the Lord. We will find that fasting will be one of the most important acts that help us continue our race all the way to the end. When we fast, we bring our bodies under subjection unto the Lord. When we don't allow our bodies to eat, I believe we are showing the Lord that we can control our bodies and not allow it to be in control.

I can't even imagine fasting for forty days and forty nights. The longest I have ever fasted was for four days and four nights. And believe me, when I walked into a store, everything looked good enough to eat. Even the pictures on the packages were tempting. There is an old saying, "try it, you'll like it," and in this case, I believe it will be true. So I tell you—try fasting, you'll like the results. When we get to Matthew chapter 17, you will learn from the Lord's own mouth how effective fasting can be.

Your faith will grow as you read in the gospels how Jesus heals people no matter what kind of sickness they may have. You truly need to get this next scripture in your heart and mind. Hebrews 13:8 says, "Jesus Christ the same yesterday, today, and forever." Jesus has not changed, and He has not stopped healing. Not only should we ask the Lord to heal us, but also we must learn how to ask the Lord for everything, and we must ask in the name of Jesus. As you study His word, Jesus will teach you how to communicate with Him.

This is what Jesus teaches us in Matthew 7:7–11 "Ask and it shall be given you: seek and ye shall find: knock and it shall be opened unto you." This is not my first time to do this, but at this very moment, I find myself turning around from my computer and grabbing my Bible. Before I began to knock, tears began flowing down my face. To you who read this book, try knocking and feeling the warm tears as they flow down your face, and Lord willing, you will know how I feel (unspeakable joy and full of glory) right now. The Bible teaches that the Lord knows the number of hairs that is on your head. And I believe He is also keeping an account of our tears.

I don't even know how long it has been since I began knocking, because I could not knock without praising and worshiping Jesus for His TRUTH that He has shared with me. You men who think crying is for babies—just try it! When you give your heart to Jesus, He will unstop those dried-up tear ducts. I'm not ashamed to say that my eyes are still full of tears, and I can barely see to type. But I will try again to write what Jesus promised us in Matthew chapter 7. Jesus says that if we ask,

It shall be given to you: seek and ye shall find: knock and it shall be opened unto you. For every one that asketh receiveth; and he that seeketh findeth; and to him that knocketh it shall be opened. Or what man is there of you, whom if his son ask bread, will he give him a stone? Or if he ask a fish, will he give him a serpent? If ye then, being evil, know how to give good gifts unto your children, how much more shall your Father which is in Heaven, give good things to them that ask Him? (Matthew 7:7–11)

Before I go any further, I must tell you, that I got a chance to edit my book. And this is where Jesus allowed me to add to this story, so He could shine more light on this TRUTH, and I know that this is filet mignon steak, being mixed with God's milk of His word, but easy to understand even for beginners. Jesus cooks a filet mignon just right! You be the judge of how He cooks (teaches!)

I want to share with you something I have learned about having your prayers answered. You can learn what I have learned about praying in 1 Kings chapter 8. I have already written about 1 Kings chapter 8 later in this book, but at this time, we are seeking God's word trying to find out how to connect with His ear and heart.

Knowing the consequences, of the claim that I am about to make, I am not afraid to say, that BILLIONS of people before us never knew, and BILLIONS of people after us will never know, this SECRET GOLD NUGGET, that Jesus is allowing us to learn here. And I promise you, that you are going to find plenty of GOLD NUGGETS from God's word, as you continue studying, by RIGHTLY DIVIDING God's TRUTH.

You need to read and study this chapter, but for now, I want to bring your attention to something really important that you need to start doing. In 1 Kings chapter 8, you will read how one of the wisest men that ever walked this earth prayed for us and gave us a secret to getting our prayers answered. Read 1 Kings 8:22–60 and learn to pray toward Jerusalem and the temple. You may say that Solomon was not talking about us (the Gentiles), but I believe you need to read verses 41-43 again, and just know that we are strangers of Israel, until we are born-again. Later in this book you will learn, what I just wrote about being connected with Israel. And you know, that we live in a far country. The Lord can answer every prayer from His people, all at one time but, just listen in 1Kings chapter 8, how the LORD listens and watches over Jerusalem and His Temple, DAY AND NIGHT, (24/7) ready to answer your prayer. Jesus acknowledges your faith as you pray towards Jerusalem, and His Temple. Jesus gave me this TRUTH to share with His Bride to be. I hope that you obey Solomon, because it is for you too!

In 1 Kings 8:22-60 Solomon prays, and gives eight different scenarios, and whatever scenario you find yourself in, start praying towards Jerusalem, because Solomon ask our Creator to help us, if we will obey God's word. SIMPLE! Just start praying, facing Jerusalem!

A perfect example of what I have been writing about can be found in the book of Daniel. Read Daniel chapter 6, and you will hear a story of a great man of God. If you don't know, this chapter is about Daniel being thrown into the lion's den. Daniel had read about Solomon's prayer, as he dedicated the new Temple to the LORD. Daniel knew that the Lord would answer Solomon's prayer, so in Daniel 6:10, Daniel let them know what he thought about their decree. You must read the whole chapter to see what happens to Daniel. You know that old saying, "he came out of it smelling like a rose," but he was blessed so much more than that.

I want you to read Daniel 6:10 again, and pay close attention to the last four words of that scripture which are, (as he did aforetime.) This tells me, that Daniel had learned about praying towards Jerusalem, the city that is called by God's name and God's Temple. Just like Solomon had taught Daniel, Shadrach, Meshach, and Abednego.

And all four young men were very wise, to listen to the third wisest man, that ever walked this earth.

Later in this book, I reveal the two wisest men, and they were the same. How can that be? You will learn about them later in this book. I always remember what the angel tells Mary, Jesus' mother, in Luke 1:37. "For with God nothing shall be impossible." They will be explained later and it is a great revelation, how they are the same, but two different people. This is one of the MYSTERIES of God's word that Jesus taught me, and He will reveal it to you also, if you ask Him.

Read 1 Kings 8:46-50, because it sounds like Solomon, gave one of his scenario just for Daniel, Shadrach, Meshach, and Abednego in his prayer. Let me share with you, what the Lord taught me about how Shadrach, Meshach, and Abednego prayed. Because it is conjecture, and we MUST read between the lines to find this TRUTH, but I believe, that Jesus will teach you as you continue reading God's word. You are about to chew on some meat of God's word. But very soon you can start drinking the milk of God's word again.

Let's read between the lines of God's word in Daniel 2:1-19. As you read, you will learn that King Nebuchadnezzar had a dream, and in verse 1 he said that "…and his sleep brake from him." which means in Mississippi, he woke up and couldn't go back to sleep. And the dream that he had he forgot it, and now he is going to butcher all the magicians, and the astrologers, and the sorcerers, and the Chaldeans, if they can't tell him the dream, and the interpretation of the dream, and they could not! Now look at verse 13 and you will hear that they began looking for Daniel and his fellows, which are Shadrach, Meshach, and Abednego.

As soon as Daniel heard, that the King was mad, he goes to the King in verse 16, and asked the King for some time, to seek the Lord for his dream, and interpretation of it. And in verse 17 says, that Daniel went to his house. And just look who he found in his house, which was Hananiah, Mishael, and Azariah, which are Shadrach, Meshach, and Abednego. The Prince of the eunuchs changed their names. But Daniel made the thing known to them in verse 18, because Daniel needed them to help him pray and "… desire mercies of the God of Heaven concerning this secret…" I was raised up around gambling and I only have two of these, but I would bet my left , that they all prayed together facing Jerusalem. Now that, is how to dig or RIGHTLY DIVIDE God's TRUTH from His word.

Since I am writing about Shadrach, Meshach, and Abednego. I want to share with you, how the Lord showed me in details, how He saved them, when they were thrown into the fiery furnace. Again, I got a chance to edit my book and add this story, because it is something that was just revealed to me in April 2023, and I am so glad to get the opportunity, to share it with you. You just wait and see, what you are going to learn from this book, guiding you to the scriptures of God's word. I have read and studied my book ever since I wrote it, and I am on my eleventh time reading it, and I will continue reading it until I go home, because Jesus taught me so much that I never knew before, and I never want to forget. I hope and pray, that you read and study it multiple times too, and obey what you now know is TRUTH.

To start this story (TRUTH) about Shadrach, Meshach, and Abednego. We must first find out what the scriptures say God is. Hebrews 12:29 says "For our God a consuming fire." You can find in Daniel chapter 3, why Shadrach, Meshach, and Abednego were thrown into the fiery furnace. Read the entire chapter and then come back here, and I want to share with you what Jesus taught me about this situation, that they had to endure.

This TRUTH started coming to me, sometimes in April of 2023, after I read Hebrews 12:29 "For our God a consuming fire" that I have read a hundred times before. But this time, God's word began speaking to me. And I began thinking about Shadrach, Meshach, and Abednego, when in Daniel 3:19, Nebuchadnezzar "…commanded, that they should heat the furnace one seven times more than it was wont to be heated." And you will learn from chapter 7 of this book, that when Nebuchadnezzar said "heat the furnace seven times hotter," he spoke God's number of completion, and invited the Lord inside the furnace with Shadrach, Meshach, and Abednego. And verse 22 teaches us, that the God flame slew (or consumed) those soldiers, as they opened the door to the furnace. Remember "For our God a consuming fire" Verse 20 says that Nebuchadnezzar commanded the most mighty men in his army, and the God part of the fire killed those mighty solders immediately, and simultaneously God speaks to the regular fire, and commands it in verse 27 powerless, and tells it don't singe a hair on their heads! Don't damage their coats! And don't even put your smell on them! WOW! What a mighty God we serve. I can feel this TRUTH as TRUTH about our Lord, the consuming fire. I will take this to the grave with me as TRUTH that Jesus taught me.

I want to share a couple more scriptures, before we leave this TRUTH, from Daniel. In Daniel 3:25 Nebuchadnezzar said "that he sees four men loose, walking in the midst of the fire, and it don't even hurt them, and the form of the fourth is like the Son of God." Now read Revelation 1:12-15, and you will learn that when John turned to see the person that spoke to him, and John said in verse 14 that "His head and hairs white like wool, as white as snow; and His eyes as a flame of fire." Verse 15 says "and His feet like unto fine brass, as if they burned in a furnace." Jesus was the fourth man in the furnace.

Read, learn, and believe Hebrews 13:8 "Jesus Christ the same yesterday, and today, and forever." Jesus can and will answer your prayer, if you will obey His word as you learn it. And as I am writing these words, Jesus is revealing to me these words and they are, that I do not believe that when Jesus walked this earth with His Apostles with "His head and hairs" (were not) "white like wool" (which I believe is Jesus' hair and beard) and, I don't believe Jesus went around with "eyes as a flame of fire." Jesus' outward appearance has changed, but, He is our Creator, and that is what makes "Him the same yesterday, and today, and forever." Wow that is good teaching! Thank you Jesus…

Listen to this scripture how powerful. I believe one of the most powerful scriptures from God's word, and it is found in Hebrews 4:12. I am going to quote it, and just listen to every word. "For the word of God quick, and powerful, and sharper than any two edged sword, piercing even to the dividing asunder of soul and Spirit, and of the joints and marrow, and a discerner of the thoughts and intents of the heart." Powerful!

These scriptures that you are about to read are not just what Matthew wanted to write. You need to realize that Matthew wrote his gospel so we would have this history (TRUTH). Matthew was an eyewitness to what you are about to read. Read what Matthew saw Jesus do in Matthew 4:23–24. According to Matthew,

> Jesus went about all Galilee, teaching in their synagogues, and preaching the gospel of the Kingdom, and healing all manner of sickness and all manner of disease among the people. And His fame went throughout all Syria, and they brought unto Him all sick people that were taken with divers diseases and torments, and those which were possessed with devils, and those which were lunatic, and those that had palsy, and He healed them.

For your faith to grow, we are going to go through the four gospels and the book of Acts and read about all the healings that Jesus and His apostles did. You need to get more familiar with God's word, so I am going to let you look up and read most of these scriptures for yourself. Read Matthew 8:1–4 and Matthew 8:5–13. In these next scriptures, Matthew tells the story about when Jesus comes to Peter's house and heals his mother-in-law.

And when Jesus was come into Peter's house, and saw his wife's mother laid, and sick of a fever. And He touched her hand, and the fever left her, and she arose, and ministered unto them. When the even was come, they brought unto Him many that were possessed with devils, and He cast out the spirits with word, and healed all that were sick, that it might be fulfilled which was spoken by Isaiah the Prophet, saying, Himself took our infirmities, and bare sicknesses. (Matthew 8:14–17)

Peter confirms in his writings what Isaiah prophesied would happen concerning the Lord's death. If you know anything about the Bible, you should know that Peter was an apostle. He was an eyewitness of Jesus' adult life and death and life (referring to after His resurrection). Read 1 Peter 2:24. Peter was writing these scriptures to whoever will read and understand that he has seen the fulfillment of Isaiah's prophecy. If you can believe that Jesus was crucified on the cross and died for our sins, you should be able to believe that Jesus took that beating so we can be healed. The secret to being healed is to ask Jesus to heal you. Believe that Jesus will heal you and receive your healing by thanking Jesus for your healing. Truly, it is as simple as that.

These next scriptures found in Matthew are not about Jesus healing anyone, but they do speak of His mighty power, and I think you should hear them. Read Matthew 8:23–27, 8:28–34, and 9:1–8.

And it came to pass, as Jesus sat at meat in the house, behold, many publicans and sinners came and sat down with Him and His disciples. And when the Pharisees saw, they said unto His disciples, Why eateth your Master with publicans and sinners? But when Jesus heard, He said unto them, they that be whole need not a physician, but they that are sick. (Matthew 9:10– 12)

If you are sick, you truly need the GREAT PHYSICIAN.

As you continue reading these scriptures, you will see that there is no sickness or disease the GREAT PHYSICIAN can't cure. Jesus put you here on this earth because He wants you here. You're not a mistake. Always remember that He made your body, and He can heal your body.

You are about to hear something in the next set of scriptures that goes far beyond healing someone.

> While He spake these things unto them, behold, there came a certain ruler, and worshipped Him, saying, my daughter is even now dead. But come and lay thy hand upon her, and she shall live. And Jesus arose, and followed him, and His disciples. (Matthew 9:18–19)

The first thing you need to understand is that this man came worshipping Jesus and just listen to the faith he has in Jesus. After he tells Jesus that his daughter is dead, his faith began to shine ever so bright. He simply says to Jesus, "Come and lay thy hand upon her, and she shall live."

As you can see in these scriptures when Jesus saw and heard his faith, it moved God into action, and when God gets into action, anything is possible.

In verses 20–22, you are about to read how Jesus healed a woman on His way to raise the girl from the dead. According to the scripture, while Jesus was on His way to raise the dead,

> A woman, which was diseased with an issue of blood twelve years, came behind, and touched the hem of His garment.
>
> For she said within herself, if I may but touch His garment, I shall be whole. But Jesus turned Him about, and when He saw her, He said, daughter be of good

comfort, thy faith hath made thee whole. And the woman was made whole from that hour.

Now, this woman thought that if she could just touch Jesus' garment, she would be healed. But Jesus lets her know that it was her faith that made her whole. And when you reach out to Jesus with your faith, you will be healed of any sickness or disease.

As soon as Jesus finished healing the woman who had the blood disease, He continued on His way to help the family that had the deceased daughter.

> When Jesus came into the ruler's house, and saw the minstrels and people making a noise, He said unto them, give place: for the maid is not dead, but sleepeth. And they laughed Him to scorn. But when the people were put forth, He went in, and took her by the hand, and the maid arose. And the fame hereof went abroad into all that land. (Matthew 9:23–26)

Read Matthew 9:27–31 and you will see how Jesus healed two blind men. In Matthew 9:32–33, you will read how Jesus cast out a devil from a man who was possessed. You also need to read Matthew 9:35–38. Jesus says in verse 37 that there are plenty of souls that need saving, but there are only a few soul winners (paraphrased). And then He says in verse 38 that we need to pray to the Lord that He would send forth laborers into His harvest. I want to challenge you to ask the Lord to send you (the reader) to be a soul winner. I dare you. I asked the Lord to allow me to be a soul winner. As you can see, He is helping me write a book to help populate heaven. I can only imagine what the Lord is going to do for you. Whatever the Lord does for you, it will be a blessing. Read Ephesians 3:14–21.

Read Matthew 10:1–8 and you will see how the Lord gave men on earth power to heal the sick, cleanse the lepers, raise the dead, and cast out devils. Jesus says in Acts 1:8, "But ye shall receive power, after that the Holy Ghost is come upon you." I want to challenge you again. I want you to ask the Lord for His Spirit (the Holy Ghost) to live inside you so you can have this power working in you.

As we go through the book of Matthew, we will come across chapter 11, and in this chapter, we are going to learn about John the Baptist. As John studied the Old Testament, he read and learned from the Prophet Isaiah. The reason I want you to know what John learned from the Prophet Isaiah is that we are going to read in the scriptures how Jesus reminded John of the TRUTH he learned. The scriptures that John learned are in Isaiah 35:3–6.

Verse 4 says that God (Jesus) is going to come and save us. "Then the eyes of the blind shall be opened, and the ears of the deaf shall be unstopped. Then shall the lame leap as a hart [deer], and the tongue of the dumb sing: for in the wilderness shall waters break out, and streams in the desert" (verses 5– 6).

If you don't already know about this, you will learn in just a few pages what John knew—Jesus was on His way, while they both were still in the womb. Read John 1:19–34 and you will learn that when John the Baptist saw Jesus coming, he acknowledges Jesus as "the Lamb of God, who takes away the sin of the world." Even though John knew that Jesus had come, he began to doubt when he was put in prison.

In Matthew 11:2–5, you will learn how John the Baptist's faith was revived, as he heard what Jesus was doing.

> Now when John had heard in the prison the works of Christ, he sent two of his disciples, And said unto Him, Art thou He that should come, or do we look for another? Jesus answered and said unto them, Go and shew John again those things which ye do hear and see: The blind receive their sight, and the lame walk, the lepers are cleansed, and the deaf hear, the dead are

raised up, and the poor have the Gospel preached to them. (Matthew 11:2–5)

While in prison, the question that John wanted answered was, "Are you the Lord from heaven who is supposed to come and save us that I read about in Isaiah chapter 35?" When Jesus says to John's disciples, "Go and show John again these things, which you do hear and see," what Jesus was saying to John's disciples is, "When John hears of My actions, he will remember what he learned about Me from the prophets. John will know I am God, and I have come to earth to bring salvation." I believe when John's disciples began telling him, "Jesus told us to tell you this. The blind receive their sight and the lame can walk, the lepers are cleansed, and the deaf can hear," I believe at that very moment, John had a reality check like no other.

Let me tell you what I don't believe. I don't believe that God had Isaiah write this prophecy in Isaiah 35:3–6 just for John. I believe this TRUTH was written for anyone who can receive it. If this is the first time you ever RIGHTLY DIVIDED these scriptures, and you didn't know who Jesus is, I hope and pray that you have the same reality check that John had.

What I'm about to write in this paragraph is mostly speculative, but it sounds really good. When John's disciples began telling him what Jesus told them to say, I believe John began to say,

> I know. I know now. I know who Jesus is.
>
> Now, let me tell you who Jesus is. Remember when I said, "I indeed baptize you with water unto repentance, but He that cometh after me is mightier than I, whose shoes I am not worthy to bear. He shall baptize you with the Holy Ghost, and with fire."
>
> He is here, boys. He is here. God has come to earth to save His people. All those years being raised with my

cousin Jesus, I could always see that He was blessed of God, but I had no idea until now. It's hard to swallow (believe) that my cousin could be God Almighty, but I believe the prophets. And above that, my Spirit bears witness with His Spirit. Believe me, and teach this TRUTH to the whole world. Jesus is that baby that Isaiah prophesied about in Isaiah 9:6.

Matthew 12:9–15 teaches us how Jesus healed a man who had a withered hand. I have never seen a withered hand, but I believe it would be wrinkled and deformed-looking. I was going to ask you if you believe the Lord could heal him, but after all the miracles that you have seen with your ears, you too should know that Jesus is the GREAT PHYSICIAN and He can heal any sickness or disease. As you know, surely, the man's hand was restored. Verse 13 says that his withered hand was restored, just like his other hand. Verse 15 says that when Jesus knew the Pharisees plotted to destroy Him, "He withdrew Himself from thence; and great multitudes followed Him, and He healed them all." If you believe that Jesus made you, you must believe that He can heal you.

In Matthew 12:22, Matthew tells how he saw Jesus perform three miracles on one man. While reading this scripture, you will find that this man was possessed with a devil. Also, you will find that this man was blind and dumb. I want you to really look at this scripture, and you will see Satan will devour anyone if they allow him to.

But that day when Jesus came by was this man's blessed day. Not only did the man get freed from Satan, but also he was healed so he could see and speak. If you could speak with that man today, there is no way that you could convince him Jesus doesn't heal. At this time, you need to read Hebrews 13:8 again.

In Matthew 14:14, Jesus has attracted another multitude of people. And this scripture details that He was moved with compassion toward them, and He healed their sick. If you will continue reading Matthew 14:15–21, you will see another miracle Jesus did for this multitude. After the Lord had finished healing their sick, Jesus' disciples came to Him and informed Him that the multitude was hungry and that He should send them away to find food. But as you will find out, Jesus had other plans.

Here in these scriptures, you can clearly see how the Lord can easily provide for you and your family.

In verses 16–17, Jesus says, "They need not depart; give ye them to eat. And they say unto Him, we have here but five loaves, and two fishes." And as you should now know, the Lord says, "Bring them here to me." The Bible says in verse 19 that after the Lord had commanded the multitude to sit down on the grass, "He took the five loaves, and the two fishes, and looking up to Heaven, He blessed, and brake, and gave the loaves to the disciples, and the disciples to the multitude." This is something you should know and do every time before you eat. Read and study 1 Timothy 4:1–6. In these scriptures, you are going to find that BIG word IF two times.

"And they did all eat, and were filled: and they took up of the fragments [leftovers] that remained twelve baskets full" (Matthew 14:20). The scriptures never gave a complete number that was in this multitude, but verse 21 notes, "They that had eaten were about five thousand men, beside women and children." I don't know how many people was there that day, but there could have been a few more thousand women and children. The number of the multitude that day doesn't really matter. What really matters is if you believe that Jesus can—and does—feed your family each day. Read and study Matthew 6:25–34.

These next set of scriptures are not about healing, but they do again let us see the mighty power of the Lord. Matthew 14:22–33 tells us the story about how Jesus walked on water. The part of this story I want to bring your attention to is in verses 28–31. As you read these scriptures, you will see that Peter says to the Lord, "Lord, if it be you, let me come unto thee on the water." Notice what the Lord tells Peter in verse 29. Jesus simply says, "Come." "And when Peter was come down out of the ship, he walked on the water, to go to Jesus. But when he saw the wind boisterous, he was afraid; and beginning to sink, he cried, saying, Lord, save me" (Matthew 14:29–30).

Peter did walk on water for a short period. But when he took his eyes off the Lord and began to look at all the wind and waves, he started to sink. But look how fast the Lord helped him, when Peter cried out, "Save me." Verse 31 details that Jesus immediately stretched out His hand and caught him. Then, Jesus began scolding Peter, saying. "O thou of little faith, wherefore didst thou doubt?" If Peter would have kept his eyes on the Lord, he could have walked across the sea. So now as you walk with the Lord and find yourself sinking, just remember—fix your eyes on the Lord and say, "Lord, help me." Before you can say the "p" in help, the Lord will be there.

According to Matthew 14:34–36, after they had gotten into the ship, they crossed over the water. "And they came into the land of Gennesaret. And when the men of that place had knowledge of Him [Jesus], they sent out into all that country round about, and brought unto Him all that were diseased; and besought Him, that they might only touch the hem of His garment; and as many as touched the hem, were made perfectly whole."

I'm about to get partly off the message, but it will be edifying if you can hear (understand) it. In Matthew chapter 15, you are going to hear the Lord say something that will surprise you. As this person approaches Him for help, He calls her a DOG, just because she was not a Jew. I know it was surprising to me when I first read it. Read Matthew 15:21–28 and hear for yourself what Jesus says to this woman. This woman that came from Canaan was a Greek (Gentile).

Here are a few scriptures for you to read to help you understand a little why Jesus would say such a thing about any human being. When Jesus first started His ministry, He was focusing on the Jewish people. Read John 1:11 and you will see that John says, Jesus "came to His own [the Jews], and His own received Him not." We have already read these scriptures, but here, they need repeating. This time, only read Matthew 10:5–6. In the first few verses of Matthew chapter 10, Jesus commanded His disciples to go and preach the gospel and to heal the sick. But notice in verses 5–6 what Jesus commands His disciples. Jesus says, "Go not into the way of the Gentiles, and into city of the Samaritans enter ye not. But go rather to the lost sheep of the house of Israel."

Just as you and me and our forefathers before us had a different time dispensation, it was just not the Gentiles and Samaritan's time YET. But when the Lord heard her faith speak out, He could not deny her request. I want you to see how the Lord reaches all the way around the Jew's time dispensation and meets her need. She already knew what she was in His eyes, but look what she does as soon as He calls her a DOG. In Matthew 15:27, "she said, TRUTH, Lord: yet the dogs eat of the crumbs which fall from their Master's table." In verse 28, "Jesus answered and said unto her, O woman, great thy faith: be it unto thee even as thou wilt."

As you can see in the scriptures you have read, the Lord started not to help her because she was not Jewish. But now, we can all come to the Lord and seek Him for our needs. While I am writing about the different time dispensations of the Jews, Gentiles, and the Samaritans, I want to tell you the TRUTH that I know. It is as simple as this. A Jew is a Jew. A Gentile is a person that is not Jewish. Now, it's not as simple to find out who the Samaritans are. To find the TRUTH about the Samaritans, you must study their history. When I wrote chapter 9, how the Samaritans were born-again, I will explain what I learned in my studies about them.

You just read how Jesus came to His own and His own rejected Him in John 1:11. As you are about to find out, it is a bad thing to reject the Lord. Read John 12:48. When the Lord was rejected, He countered with a rejection for the most part. Let me explain. You will need to read and study Romans chapter 11 to find out about the Jews in part (most) being blinded (rejected).

I want you to read Romans chapter 11 for yourself, but I am going to explain verse 25. Paul starts off in verse 25 by saying that he doesn't want the brethren (the church) to be ignorant of this mystery. Paul finishes that verse by saying, "Blindness in part is happened to Israel (the Jews), until the fullness of the Gentiles be come in" (Romans 11:25). This scripture lets me know that some Jews will be saved during our time dispensation and a last Gentile is going to be saved.

I believe when the last Gentile is saved ("when the fullness of the Gentiles be come in"), the Lord is going to turn His ear again to His people (the Jews). I also have written about this later in the book in greater detail, but it wouldn't hurt to hear a little about it now. The scriptures that teach us about the Lord turning back to save the Jews are found in Revelation chapter 7. These scriptures teach us that there will be 144,000 Jews saved during the tribulation period. I could continue writing about this because there is so much to write about. But at this time, I must get back to writing about how Jesus heals.

Matthew 15:29–31 shows us what Jesus did after He had cast out the devil from the daughter of the woman who He called a DOG.

> And Jesus departed from thence, and came nigh unto the Sea of Galilee; and went up into a mountain, and sat down there. And great multitudes came unto Him, having with them lame, blind, dumb, maimed, and many others, and cast them down at Jesus' feet; and He healed them. Insomuch that the multitude wondered, when they saw the dumb to speak, the maimed to be whole, the lame to walk, and the blind to see: and they glorified the God of Israel.

As you read Matthew 15:32–39, you will see that Jesus has compassion on this multitude also. This time, the menu will be just about the same as last time. Jesus asks His disciples, "How many loaves have ye? And they said, seven, and a few little fishes" (verse 34). Verse 36 shows us that the Lord "took the seven loaves and the fishes, and gave thanks." That is truly what the Lord wants to hear from us. I believe when we say, "I'm sorry," to the Lord, it is music to His ears. But I also believe thanks would be right up there with the things that pleases God's ears. Remember what you read in 1 Timothy 4:1–6; if not, read it again. This multitude of people that the Lord fed was four thousand men, besides the women and children. This time, I want you to put in your two cents about the number that was in the multitude. I want you to answer this to yourself. If there were 50,000 people in this multitude, do you believe that there would be some that didn't get to eat?

In Matthew 17:14–20, you will find a man seeking the Lord for help for his son. In verses 15–16, the man asked the Lord,

> Have mercy on my son, for he is lunatick, and sore vexed: for oftentimes he falleth into the fire, and oft into the water. And I brought him to thy disciples, and they could not cure him.
>
> Then Jesus answered and said, O faithless and perverse generation, how long shall I be with you? How long shall I suffer you? Bring him hither to me. And Jesus rebuked the devil; and he departed out of him: and the child was cured from that very hour.
>
> Then came the disciples to Jesus apart, and said, Why could not we cast him out?
>
> Then Jesus said unto them, Because of your unbelief: for verily I say unto you, If ye have faith as a grain of mustard seed, ye shall say unto this mountain, Remove

hence to yonder place; and it shall remove; and nothing shall be impossible unto you. (Matthew 17:17–20)

In verse 21, Jesus gives us the answer we are looking for. Jesus says, "Howbeit this kind goes not out but by prayer and fasting." The Lord has just told us the secret to getting our prayers answered. Earlier in this chapter, I said that fasting would be an important part in our walk with the Lord. As you can see, the Lord says here that if we will combine our prayer and fasting, nothing shall be impossible for us to accomplish.

Matthew 19:1–2 says, "And it came to pass, when Jesus had finished these sayings, He departed from Galilee, and came into the coast of Judea beyond Jordan; and great multitudes followed Him; and He healed them there." Now, let's go to Matthew 20:29–34, and we will find the Lord healing two blind men. As you read these verses, you will see sometimes that it's okay to get loud with the Lord.

When these two men heard that Jesus was coming by, they cried out and said, "Have mercy on us." Now, we can only imagine how loud the multitude was that day. But these two men were louder than the multitude. As the blind men began to get louder than the crowd, the multitude began to rebuke them. They told the blind men to hold their peace. But these two blind men truly needed the Lord, so they got even louder, saying, "Have mercy on us." By now, you should know the rest of the story (how the Lord healed them). The Lord can actually hear your thoughts; there is nothing wrong with His hearing. If you ever find yourself getting loud when talking with the Lord, it's okay.

"And the blind and the lame came to Him in the temple; and He healed them" (Matthew 21:14). As you have read God's word, I want to ask you this—have you seen Jesus turn anyone away and deny them of their need? As I have stated at the beginning of this book, there is going to be one. But as you are going to find out, it is one of Jesus' greatest miracles.

In Matthew 21:17–22, Jesus confirms what He said in Matthew 17:20 with an example. Remember what you read in Matthew 17:20—Jesus said, "For verily I say unto you, if ye have faith as a grain of mustard seed, ye shall say unto this mountain, remove hence to yonder place; and it shall remove; and nothing shall be impossible unto you."

Referring to Matthew 21:14, after Jesus heals the blind and lame, He leaves the temple. In Matthew 21:17–22, Matthew records,

> And He left them and went out of the city into Bethany; and He lodged there. Now in the morning as He returned into the city, He hungered. And when He saw a fig tree in the way, He came to it, and found nothing thereon, but leaves only, and said unto it, Let no fruit grow on thee henceforward forever. And presently the fig tree withered away.
>
> And when the disciples saw, they marveled, saying, How soon is the fig tree withered away! Jesus answered and said unto them, Verily [truly] I say unto you, if ye have faith, and doubt not, ye shall not only do this to the fig tree, but also if ye shall say unto this mountain, be thou removed, and be thou cast into the sea: it shall be done. And all things, whatsoever ye shall ask in prayer, believing, ye shall receive.

You need to realize that Jesus spoke to this fig tree and He said that we could also speak to a mountain, and it would listen to our command. Here is that BIG word IF again. God's word teaches us this fact—IF a person has faith and does not doubt in what they are trying to accomplish, anything is possible, because God is God, and He honors faith. I want you to hear what Jesus has to say about a mustard seed-sized faith. In Matthew 13:31–32 Jesus teaches us, "The kingdom of heaven is like to a grain of mustard seed, which a man took, and sowed in his field. Which indeed is the least of all seeds: but when it is grown, it is the greatest among herbs, and becometh a tree, so that the birds of the air come and lodge in the branches thereof."

In Luke 17:6, you will find that Jesus gives us another example of how our mustard seed faith will work. Again, Jesus teaches us, "If ye had faith as a grain of mustard seed, ye might say unto this sycamine tree, Be thou plucked up by the root, and be thou planted in the sea: and it should obey you." The Lord is teaching us that He will answer our prayers IF we will believe and not doubt.

In Luke chapter 17, the Lord began giving His apostles commandments. Read verses 1–4, and hear what the Lord told His apostles to do. Then you will know why they asked Him to increase their faith in verse 5. In this war, every Christian must fight against Satan. I am here to tell you that if we will do His will, God will not send His people into war without the armor of God.

Read Ephesians 6:10–17 and you will hear what Apostle Paul teaches us about putting and keeping on the armor of God. As you read these scriptures, you will see that Apostle Paul is teaching us how to stand against Satan. We must put on the whole armor because Satan is going to come after you. But at this time, I want to bring your attention to verse 16. Paul starts by saying, "Above all, taking the shield of faith, wherewith ye shall be able to quench all the fiery darts of the wicked."

God's word teaches us that He has given everyone a measure of faith. Read Romans 12:3. But we must all ask the Lord to increase our faith and help it to grow into a large shield. At this time, I want you to do a simple experiment. I want you to understand and learn about the mustard seed-sized faith. I want you to hold a pencil up in front of you as your shield of faith. Now, I want you to get someone to throw a few items at you. With your small shield of faith, I want you to see that you will be lucky if you can stop any of those fiery darts, which the devil is throwing at you. Now, I want you to get a book and hold it up in front of you. As they (Satan) throw the fiery darts, it will be so much easier to block the darts with a book-sized faith. Now, I want you to go outside and get the garbage can lid. I believe I have made my point. Sure, a little bit of faith in God will go a long way, but the Lord never said that He wants our faith to stay small, as a mustard seed. The Lord wants all of His people's faith to grow.

Now, we are about to read how Mark experienced (saw) Jesus heal the sick and needy. I'm not going to write about all the healings from Mark's book, because he recorded most of the same miracles that Matthew recorded. I'm also not going to comment on every miracle, because I believe you need to read and study your Bible for yourself. But I will have to comment on some of the miracles, because I just can't help myself.

I want you to read Mark 6:1–6, and see how Jesus' own friends and family felt about this miracle worker. Read Mark 6:54–56. In Mark 7:31–37, Mark tells us how Jesus healed a man who was deaf and had an impediment in his speech, and they asked the Lord to lay His hands on him.

> And he [Jesus] took him aside from the multitude, and put His fingers into his ears, and he [Jesus] spit, and touched his tongue. And looking up to Heaven, He sighed, and saith unto him, Ephphatha, that is, be opened. And straightway his ears were opened, and the string of his tongue was loosed, and he spake plain. And he [Jesus] charged [instructed] them [the crowd] that they should tell no man: But the more He charged them, so much the more a great deal they published [told]. (Verses 33–36)

Believe you me, as soon as you see the Lord heal someone such as this, you will tell everyone you come in contact with.

I know that I have shared with everyone who will listen to what I have seen the Lord do. Later in this book, you will hear me say that the Lord has spoken to me seven (7) times in thirty-two years. Now, the Lord has spoken to me many more times as He taught me His word. But when I say seven (7) times, I mean that He spoke to me out loud in English and told me specific things to do.

One of those times when the Lord spoke to me is what inspired me to write this book. I want you to know that it took me sixteen years to start writing this book. It took a while to start, but as you can see, I did write. Later, you will find in this book what the Lord taught me that day that inspired me to write. You are also going to find out how Satan has deceived the people of this world in the past, present, and even in the future.

In Mark 10:46–52, you will find that Jesus heals another man who has a loud mouth. These scriptures are about a blind beggar, named Bartimaeus. And it's not that he has a big mouth, but he just had to get the Lord's attention. This crowd also tried to shut him up, but he too got louder than the crowd, just enough that Jesus heard him. And as you should know, the Lord told him to come to Him. In verse 51, Jesus asked him, "What wilt thou that I should do unto thee? The blind man [Bartimaeus] said unto Him, Lord, that I might receive my sight." Then Jesus tells him in verse 52, "Go thy way, thy faith hath made thee whole. And immediately he received his sight, and followed Jesus in the way."

Now, we will see some other miracles that Jesus did through the eyes and hand of Luke. You need to start by reading Luke chapter 1. I want you to go and read this chapter so you can have a better understanding, because truly, that is what we are trying to accomplish. In chapter 1, you are going to learn how the Lord blessed a priest named Zacharias and his wife Elisabeth with a son. And this is truly a blessing because this baby is none other than John the Baptist.

You are about to hear again how the GREAT PHYSICIAN does His perfect work. The scriptures say that they had no child because

Elisabeth was barren (unable to have children), and they both were "well stricken in years." Unable to have children and being very old are two giant obstacles in their lives. But sometimes prior to the time that the angel came and spoke with Zacharias, he had prayed to the Lord and asked Him for a son. God's word never said what I'm about to say, but as you read these scriptures, you will know what I'm saying is TRUTH. Now, just imagine all the things that the Lord had to do to prepare her body to give birth.

I believe, first, the Lord healed her womb. Then, I believe the Lord made her strong and a youthful-feeling body so she would have the strength to carry and to raise their child. Zacharias might not have been able to even throw a ball, but I believe Elisabeth could. In no way am I trying to say anything negative about Zacharias. Truly, Zacharias fulfilled his part in all of this. I believe Zacharias would be one of the first in line to tell you that his God is a miracle worker and the GREAT PHYSICIAN.

While writing about Jesus, it's hard to stop mentioning Him as the GREAT PHYSICIAN, because that is what He is. I know that if you get to heaven, you are not going to think of such things as this, but if you asked Elisabeth about the operation of her womb, I believe she would say that the Lord did it, and He didn't even leave a scar. I don't just believe—I know that Elisabeth will tell anyone that Jesus is the GREAT PHYSICIAN.

I'm about to write and share with you some meat of God's word. I am going to briefly mention this because it just feels right to speak of it now. Did you hear in these scriptures why the Lord chose Zacharias and Elisabeth to be the parents who brought John the Baptist into this world? You have got to look way beyond the words that are written on these pages, and you can only learn this from the Lord. In the beginning (foundation of the world), the Lord could see through the portals of time, and He saw Zacharias and Elisabeth as they were going to be during that time. According to Luke 1:6, "And they were both righteous before God, walking in all the commandments and ordinances of the Lord blameless." I can tell you in one word why the Lord chose them to be John's parents, and that word is predestination.

Now, don't stop reading just because you hear this word. I do explain the TRUTH about this later in this book. But I will give you this hint at this time, the Book of Life. Most people don't know when the Book of Life was written. But if you will continue reading, you will find out according to the scriptures. Zacharias and Elisabeth were chosen at the foundation of the world to be John the Baptist's parents. Later, when you learn about the Book of Life and when it was written, then you will know what you have just read is the TRUTH.

Now, for what I believe was the greatest miracle that is written in God's word—it would have to be how the birth of our Lord took place. The story starts in Luke 1:26. According to the scriptures, the same angel (Gabriel) who came to Elisabeth also came to Mary in the sixth month. As you read these scriptures, you will hear how Mary was chosen by God to bring Himself into this world.

In verses 27–37, you will see how the angel came "to a virgin espoused to a man, whose name was Joseph, of the house of David; and the virgin's name Mary. And the angel came in unto her, and said, Hail, highly favored, the Lord with thee." Then, he tells her that she is blessed among women. Now, when she saw the angel,

> She was troubled at his saying, and cast in her mind what manner of salutation this should be. And the angel said unto her, fear not, Mary: for you have found favor with God.
>
> And, behold, thou shalt conceive in thy womb, and bring forth a son, and thou shalt call His name Jesus. He shall be great, and shall be called the Son of the Highest; and the Lord God shall give unto Him the Throne of His father David. And He shall reign over

the house of Jacob for ever; and of His Kingdom there shall be no end.

Then Mary asked unto the angel [the obvious question], How shall this be, seeing I know not a man? (Verses 29–34)

Then the angel begins explaining to her how the Holy Ghost shall come upon her and how the power of the Highest will overshadow her. Then, Gabriel tells her that holy thing that shall be born of her shall be called the Son of God.

Verse 36 lets us know that Elisabeth and Mary are cousins. As you can see, this family was a spiritual family, so spiritual that the Lord chose them to be His pathway to earth. Gabriel also tells Mary that Elisabeth too has "conceived a son in her old age, and this is the sixth month with her, who was called barren." Just as Gabriel wanted Mary to hear this, I want you to hear it too. Gabriel told this not only to Mary but also to everyone who would listen with spiritual ears. In verse 37, Gabriel says, "For with God nothing shall be impossible." As soon as Mary heard those words, which Gabriel spoke, she said, "Behold the handmaid of the Lord; be it unto me according to thy word." As soon as Gabriel acknowledged that she had accepted her role as the mother of the Lord, he departed.

We can only imagine how Mary felt when Gabriel came to her that day and also not only about her good news but also about Elisabeth's news of her son. I know that Mary read and studied the book of Isaiah. I believe that when Mary heard the words of Gabriel, her mind reflected back to what she had learned from God's word. I believe the scripture in Isaiah 7:14 flashed back into her mind. This godly young woman who was a virgin could see that Isaiah's prophecy was being fulfilled in her. Read Isaiah 7:14, and see for yourself what it says.

According to Luke 1:39–40, "Mary arose in those days, and went into the hill country with haste, into a city of Juda; and entered into the house of Zacharias, and saluted Elisabeth." The scriptures say,

> When Elisabeth heard the salutation [greeting] of Mary, the babe leaped in her womb; and Elisabeth was filled with the Holy Ghost. And she spake out with a loud voice, and said, blessed thou among women, and blessed the fruit of thy womb. And whence this to me, that the mother of my Lord should come to me?
>
> For, lo, as soon as the voice of thy salutation sounded in mine ears, the baby leaped in my womb for joy. (Luke 1:41–44)

According to this scripture, John the Baptist knew that Jesus was on His way, while they both were still in the womb.

According to verse 56, Mary stayed with Elisabeth for about three months. If I were a betting man, I would bet that Mary and Elisabeth stayed awake on the first night, referring back to the scriptures. I can hear with my spiritual ears how Mary and Elisabeth went to the Old Testament and found the scriptures (prophecies) concerning their sons. Mary was probably telling Elisabeth to read Isaiah 40:3, because Isaiah spoke of her son coming into the world many years ago. Isaiah said, "Your son John would be the voice that comes crying in the wilderness, preparing the way for [my] son." Isaiah also said that John was going to "make a straight highway for our God in the desert."

In Matthew chapter 3, you will find the fulfillment of Isaiah's prophecy concerning John and Jesus. John the Baptist was born to be the forerunner for Jesus (God) to help get His ministry started here on earth. As you read Matthew chapter 3, I want you to read verses 9–10 a couple of times. Then, I want you to make the connection with the scriptures in Galatians 5:22–23. When you read Matthew

3:9, you can see the Lord doesn't have to have you or me. He can raise His church from the stones of the earth. But what He really wants is for us to obey and serve Him by helping our fellow man. Don't ever forget what Gabriel told Mary in Luke 1:37: "For with God nothing shall be impossible."

I believe, as Mary was expressing her joy about Elisabeth's son, Elisabeth had to say, "I truly am blessed of the Lord. But you, Mary, are being used to bring our Savior to earth. You are that virgin that Isaiah spoke of in Isaiah 7:14. And, Mary, you and I know that the interpretation of Immanuel is God with us. And, Mary, flip the page to Isaiah 9:6. And you will see more clearly. God tells Isaiah to describe your baby as Wonderful, Counselor, the Mighty God, the Everlasting Father, the Prince of Peace. And as I have said and will say again, you are blessed among women, and blessed is the fruit of thy womb."

Elisabeth could have even asked Mary a question like this, "Do you remember when you were a young girl, and we went to the synagogue to hear God's word? I have told you all of your life to serve the Lord that He would keep you and bless you. But, Mary, even I didn't expect blessings of this magnitude. To everyone who knows us, they have watched our walk with the Lord, and they have seen our devotion. Now, they also know if they serve the Lord, He will keep them and bless them also."

I know most of what I just wrote is speculation. But I just can't believe Mary and Elisabeth would sit around talking about the weather after receiving such great news from God. If Gabriel came and told me certain things were going to happen in my life, I would not be able to keep my mouth shut. I would tell anyone and everyone who would listen.

This next set of scriptures is not about healing, but they do teach us about a miracle that Jesus did.

Luke 5:1–11 is where you can hear about this miracle. Verse 1 tells us, "And it came to pass, that, as the people pressed upon Jesus to hear the word of God, He stood by the lake of Gennesaret." As Jesus stood there, He saw two ships that were unattended. Jesus saw that the fishermen had gone to wash their nets.

Then, verse 3 tells us that Jesus went aboard Simon's ship and asked him to go out a little from the land. So Jesus "sat down and taught the people out of the ship." As soon as Jesus finished speaking, He tells Simon, "Launch out into the deep, and let down your nets for a draught [catch]." Then, Simon says unto Him, "Master, we have toiled all night, and have taken nothing. Nevertheless at thy word, I will let down the net."

As soon as Simon Peter let down the net, they caught a great multitude of fish, so much so that their nets began to brake. Then, Peter had to call his partners who were in the other ship so that they would come help them. And they came and filled both ships so much so that they began to sink. When Simon Peter saw how the fish came to the net, he fell down at Jesus' knees, saying, "Depart from me; for I am a sinful man, O Lord. For he was astonished, and all that were with him, at the draught of the fishes which they had taken" (verses 8–9).

The two sons of Zebedee—James and John—who were partners with Simon were also astonished after seeing the catch they had made. Then, Jesus says unto Simon, "Fear not; from henceforth thou shall catch men. And when they had brought their ships to land, they forsook all, and followed Him" (verses 10–11).

That day, not only did these three men saw with their eyes, but also they saw with their hearts. When you begin to look with the eyes of your heart at all the miracles that Jesus has done, you too will forsake all and begin following Him. When I started writing about this story, I said that it was not about healing, but I was wrong. When I got to this point, I realized that there had been at least three hearts that were healed. Notice that God's word doesn't speak of anyone else following Jesus that day. I believe we all must learn to hear the unwritten words from God's pages. If you study and obey what you learn, you will learn how someday.

In Luke 5:12–15, you will find that Jesus goes to a certain city, and there, He finds a man full of leprosy. When this man, who was full of leprosy, saw Jesus, he fell down and begged Jesus, saying, "Lord, if thou wilt, thou canst make me clean [you can make me clean]" (verse 12). And then Jesus touched him and said, "I will: be thou clean. And immediately the leprosy departed from him. And He [Jesus] charged him to tell no man: but go, and shew thyself to the priest, and offer for thy cleansing, according as Moses commanded, for a testimony unto them. But so much the more went there a fame abroad of Him: and great multitudes came together to hear, and to be healed by Him of their infirmities" (verses 13–15).

My daughter Chasity came over to our house the other night. As we sat around and talked, she was asking questions, trying to find out why she had this rash. And as you can see, I'm right in the middle of writing about how Jesus heals. So naturally, I began explaining to her what I have been writing about and how Jesus can heal any kind of sickness or disease. Here comes that big word IF. If a person has faith and believes that Jesus will heal them, He will.

I told her the same thing as I am telling you. Read the first five books of the New Testament so your faith will grow. I told her that in Romans 12:3, the Lord gives every person a measure of faith. But we need to nourish our minds by reading and studying God's word so our faith will grow. I told Chasity that night that a rash would be a simple task for the Lord. I told her how the Lord had opened the blinded eyes, made the lame walk, and cleansed the leprous.

I even mentioned the story of how Jesus raised Lazarus from the dead. I'm going to write about Lazarus in greater detail when we get to the gospel of John. But for now, you who don't know, Lazarus was a friend of Jesus. But to show the power of God, Jesus allowed Lazarus to die before He went to him. When Jesus got to where Lazarus was buried, his sister Martha says to Jesus, "Lazarus has been dead four days, and he stinks by now. I believe that his body has started to decay." But with the Lord, it doesn't matter what condition you're in when you call on Him. Nothing could stop the Creator from raising that dead body. Never forget what Gabriel told Mary—"For with God nothing shall be impossible" (Luke 1:37). I told my daughter that night if the Lord could put life back into a dead body that had started decaying, her rash was nothing.

Luke 6:17–19 tells us, "And He [Jesus] came down with them, and stood in the plain, and the company of His disciples, and a great multitude of people out of all Judea and Jerusalem, and from the sea coast of Tyre and Sidon, which came to hear Him, and to be healed of their diseases. And they [the people] that were vexed with unclean spirits: and they were healed. And the whole multitude sought to touch Him: for there went virtue out of Him, and He healed all."

In Luke 7:11–16, you are going to find the Lord raising a young man from the dead. Now, I want you to read Luke 10:1–20. Here, you will see how the Lord sent seventy of His people to minister to the needy. He tells them to go in peace and to share their peace. Jesus also told them to heal the sick and to tell them that "the kingdom of God is come nigh unto them" (verse 9).

> And the seventy returned again with joy, saying, Lord, even the devils are subject unto us through thy name. And He [Jesus] said unto them, I beheld Satan as lightning fall from heaven. Behold, I give unto you power to tread on serpents and scorpions, and over all the power of the enemy: and nothing shall by any means hurt you. (Luke 10:17–19)

Now, my interpretation of these scriptures is that Satan is weak and he has already lost the war and God has given us (the church) His Spirit so we can live a victorious life with Him over Satan.

I have already mentioned earlier about the Book of Life, and I'm about to mention it again. The reason I am speaking about the Book of Life is because I am planting a seed now so when you read later in this book about the Book of Life, you will have some knowledge of it. We all need to know the TRUTH about the Book of Life.

In Luke 10:20, Jesus speaks about the Book of Life. Jesus says to the seventy when they returned unto Him, "Don't rejoice just because the spirits are subject unto you, but rejoice because your names are written in heaven." Later in this book, you are also going to learn that the Lord has an eraser, and He has been erasing names from the Book of Life since man began to reject Him. Read Revelation 20:15. Later, you will also learn about the word "blot."

Now, in Luke 13:10–17, you will find Jesus healing a woman who had a problem with her body for eighteen years. Read about that healing and see what you get out of it. Luke 17:11–19 teaches us how Jesus healed ten lepers. As you read, you will find that only one came back to thank the Lord for his healing. Jesus asked the one who once was a leper, "Were there not ten cleansed? But where the nine?" (verse 17). I believe when the Lord does something for us, no matter what it is, we should always give Him thanks. As I have said earlier in this book, I believe giving thanks to the Lord is like when someone repents—referring to it being music to His ears. As you can see, the Lord wanted to hear thanks from the other nine that were healed.

If you read Luke 18:1–8, you will learn how to get the Lord to answer your prayers. Jesus spoke to the people here by using a parable (a story). Jesus starts the story in verse 2.

> There was in a city a judge, which feared not God, neither regarded man: And there was a widow in that city; and she came unto him, saying, Avenge me of mine adversary. And he would not for a while: but afterward he said within himself, Though I fear not God, nor regard man;

yet because this widow troubleth me, I will avenge her, lest by her continual coming she weary me. (Verses 2–5)

Now, that was the end of Jesus' story. In verses 6–7, the Lord lets us know why He told us this story. Listen close to what these scriptures say. He says, "Hear what the unjust judge saith" (verse 6). Jesus wants us to hear from this story how this widow keeps bugging the judge. Jesus also wants us to hear these words from the judge—"She comes to me every day with her problems, and to tell you the TRUTH, I am getting tired of her. I will help her so she will leave me alone."

Jesus is not like that judge. He will never get tired of hearing from us, and He does not want us to leave Him alone. As a matter of fact, look at what the Lord says in verse 7: "And shall not God avenge [help] His own elect [the church], which cry day and night unto Him." In other words, "Bug me!" If you will make time and cry day and night unto the Lord, read verse 8 and you will see what the Lord promises He will do for you.

At this time, I want to share with you how these scriptures (Luke 18:1– 8) came alive in my family's life. There is no way to know how many times I have read these scriptures. For thirty-two years, I have read and studied God's word. But at the beginning of 2006, I heard what the Lord wanted me to hear from these scriptures. Look how the Lord blessed my family because I believed these scriptures and how I used them as the Lord told me to.

Back in 1996, my sister-in-law (Gracie) and I purchased a ten-acre tract of land in Olive Branch, Mississippi. And the asking price was $25,000. But me being so brilliant and using my peabrain, let me tell you what I did. I wrote four sentences telling the owners why I didn't want to buy the property, along with our counteroffer. And to our surprise, they agreed and knocked off $2,000 per sentence, and we purchased the ten acres for $17,000. At that time, I knew the Lord was blessing us, but I didn't know how much.

Being an outdoor person, I went to the land and worked on it, as often as I could. I spent ten years working and clearing that land with a weed eater, a chainsaw, and a double-bladed axe. As soon as I heard what Jesus said in Luke 18:1–8, I talked to Gracie about selling the property. I told her that I was always at the land working and that I believed that the Lord and I could sell it. So we hired a man with a bulldozer, and he helped me clear the front of the property.

Every day while I worked on the land, I would ask (bug) the Lord to sell the property for us. Let me tell you that the Lord was waiting on me and my faith. When the Lord chose who to purchase our property, He didn't just choose anyone. Within a month of asking (bugging) the Lord for help, the Lord sent North Central Electric Company. Then, the negotiations began. I'm not going to get into all of that, but I will tell you that the Lord helped us sell that property for over $200,000 just like He said He would do in verse 8 (speedily).

Since the Lord was so good finding us a buyer for that property, I went back to Him with another request. I told the Lord that since He was so good with our last project, I needed Him to be in control of selling the Coldwater house. To you who don't know, the Coldwater house is located in Coldwater, Mississippi. The Coldwater house was purchased by my wife's Grandpa (C. J. Holland) in 1965.

This is where I met my wife forty-four years ago. I'm sure that the old house had some sentimental value to every member of the family. We have visited and spent many holidays in that old house. Most people who have gone to the Coldwater house would comment how they loved the old house. Grandpa spent most of his life doing construction. I too have spent most of my life doing construction, and when I see something that I want to spend time building or refurbishing, that is just what I do. So I believe when Grandpa first saw the old house, he wanted to make a home for his family, so he did. This big home (almost 4000 square feet) was a hundred years old and cost a lot of money to maintain.

When Grandpa died, he left the old house to my wife's mother (Helen Cummins), who was one of Grandpa's daughters. Helen took care of both Grandpa and Grandma, until they died. I believe Grandpa gave Helen the house so she would always have a place to live. But I also believe that in Grandpa's mind, he knew that Helen, out of ten siblings, was going to take care of him and his wife for the rest of their lives. And she did.

I wrote most of that to say this—after Grandpa and Grandma died, Cindy and I moved in with Helen and Gracie into the old house. Now, it was our turn to take care of Helen. We stayed for a year or more in Coldwater, but none of us was happy living in Coldwater. After we sold the land, we finally had the money and could afford that old house, but we knew that we needed a more energy-efficient home.

So we decided to run an ad in the local newspaper to sell the house, and we decided to sell it for $75,000. Notice that I wrote in the last sentence that we decided. We were about to mess up and not allow the Lord to put everything in order to sell the house. So I went back to the Lord with my request for Him to sell the house.

Within a couple of weeks, the Lord had a real estate agent call me. She believed that she could get us more money, so she put it on the Internet. The first couple came to look at the house about a week after posting it online. They immediately said that they wanted the house, but as you know, without a contract, we had to keep showing the house.

The first couple came back to look at the house the next day, but there was another couple there looking.

The first young lady says to us in tears, "Why are these people here looking at my house? I told you that I wanted this house." A few days later, the Lord had them write us a check for $89,500. Now, that is what the Lord did for us just because I asked Him a few times, and I believe that He would help us. In selling the land and the house, the Lord blessed us with almost $300,000, and He did it speedily, just as He said He would. It sounds like I'm boasting, and I am, but I am boasting about the Lord. I want you to try this for you and your family. Study Luke 18:1–8, and then believe and BUG the Lord just as He tells us to. If you try this, you are going to find that the Lord will be there when you need Him.

I just had to share with you how the Lord blessed my family by allowing His word to come alive in our lives. But now, it is time to get back to God's word and find out what else Jesus did for the people, when He walked this earth. In this next scripture, Jesus doesn't heal anyone, but He does make a bold statement in Luke chapter 19. I believe if this statement, which Jesus made, were to happen, it would be as equal to healing someone as far as miracles go.

As Jesus was entering Jerusalem, with a loud voice, the whole multitude of the disciples began to rejoice and praise God for all the mighty works they had witnessed. In Luke 19:38, they cried, "Blessed the King that comes in the name of the Lord. Peace in Heaven, and glory in the highest."

Verse 39 tells us, "And some of the Pharisees from among the multitude said unto Him, Master, rebuke thy disciples." In verse 40, Jesus responded, "I tell you that, if these should hold their peace, the stones would immediately cry out." There is no doubt in my mind that if they had stopped praising the Lord, we would be reading how God put mouths on the rocks from the streets of Jerusalem.

I'm going to quote David and the Giants a couple of times in this book, and here is one of them—"Here is one less stone" I (Jessie Dunson) will never allow a rock take my place from praising my Lord.

We will have to read from Matthew, Mark, Luke, and John for our next miracle (healing) to find the TRUTH about what took place in the garden when Jesus was betrayed, because they all tell the story of what happened that night, as they remember it. Mark gives the most basic account of what happened that night. In Mark 14:32–50, Mark simply tells how Jesus was betrayed by Judas and how the mob laid their hands on Jesus and took Him. And one of them who stood by drew a sword and smote a servant of the high priest and cut off his ear.

In Luke chapter 22, he records how Jesus heals the man that Mark wrote about by attaching the ear back onto his head. Let's begin reading in Luke 22:35–38. As Jesus spoke to His disciples one night, He says,

> When I sent you without purse, and scrip, and shoes, lacked ye any thing? And they said, Nothing. Then said He [Jesus] unto them, But now, he that hath a purse, let him take it, and likewise scrip: and he that hath no sword, let him sell his garment, and buy one. For I say unto you, that this that is written must yet be accomplished in me, And he was reckoned among the transgressors: for the things concerning me have an end.
>
> And they [the disciples] said, Lord, behold, here two swords. And He [Jesus] said unto them, It is enough.

Now, Jesus knew what was about to happen, and He knew that two swords were enough to accomplish what He wanted to show them (all of us) that night.

Jesus taught His apostles to love, make peace, and have compassion with their fellow man. But, as you read the rest of Luke chapter 22, you will see in verse 49 that the disciples were ready to kill for the Lord. Luke tells us in verse 50 that it was the right ear that was cut off. Now, I don't know this for sure, but I believe when this man's ear was cut off, it fell to the ground. I also believe that Jesus bent over, picked up the man's ear, and placed it back on the side of his head. Now, that is what I believe happened, because the GREAT PHYSICIAN was there.

Now, let's read and see what Matthew recorded about this night. In Matthew 26:52, Jesus says to the disciple who cut off the ear,

"Put up again thy sword into his place. For all they that take the sword shall perish with the sword" (verse 52). Then, in verse 53, Jesus continues, "Thinkest thou that I cannot now pray to my Father, and He shall presently give me more than twelve legions [72,000] of angels?" Jesus was just letting His apostles know that they were not going to war at this time.

The apostles knew Jesus as the Lamb of God, but what they didn't know is that this same Jesus would reign one day, and He would rule with a rod of iron (vengeance). When Jesus walked this earth with His apostles, He was spreading love and peace as the Lamb of God. But the war that they thought was going to happen would not take place for more than two thousand years later. You will learn later in this book that when Jesus comes back for His Bride, He will begin ruling with a rod of iron. The word teaches us that when Jesus opens the fifth seal in Revelation chapter 6, Jesus' disciples will be there at this war to see their blood avenged.

When Jesus comes for His church and He destroys the enemy (not Satan), there will be another world war one thousand years later. This last world war is commonly called the Battle of Armageddon. Through the years, there have been so many misconceptions of these last two wars. Most people that I know have been taught that there is one war. But I'm here to tell you that there are two end-time world wars, and they are one thousand years apart. But later in this book, the TRUTH will be revealed about all of this.

Now, in John chapter 18, John gives his recollection of that night. In John 18:1, he lets us know where the garden was. Also in verse 2, he lets us know that Jesus and His disciples often went there. In verses 4–6, John tells us something else that happened that the other apostles didn't mention.

> Jesus therefore, knowing all things that should come upon Him, went forth, and said unto them, Whom seek ye? They answered Him, Jesus of Nazareth.

Jesus saith unto them, I AM. And Judas also, which betrayed Him, stood with them. As soon then as He had said unto them, I AM, they went backward, and fell to the ground.

I don't know about you, but if I had been there that day and He knocked me off my feet down to the ground, I believe I would have turned around and left Him alone.

In verse 10, John informs us who did the cutting that night. According to the scripture, it was Simon Peter who drew the sword and cut off the servant's right ear. The scriptures don't teach this, but I believe Peter was trying to split the servant's skull. I believe Peter was trying to kill him, but the Lord only allowed the sword to cut off his right ear. After all, you have read about Jesus healing, you know as well as I do that if Peter would have cut off the servant's head, the Lord would have just as easily placed it back on his shoulders and said the same thing, "Put up that sword." Also, in this scripture, John tells us the name of the servant who temporarily lost his ear, and his name was Malchus.

2 Timothy 2:15 is the scripture that I used for a part (RIGHTLY DIVIDING THE WORD OF TRUTH) of this book's title, because it is true. We must RIGHTLY DIVIDE God's word to find the TRUTH. As you now know, it took reading all four gospels to find the TRUTH of what happened the night Jesus was betrayed. Before you finish reading and studying this book, you will learn more about RIGHTLY DIVIDING God's word.

Now, let's read about the miracles found in the gospel of John. If you read John 4:46–54, you will hear about how Jesus did a long-distance miracle. Listen really closely to the scriptures, and you will learn that if you will just believe God's word and show some faith in Jesus, the Lord will answer your prayers. Remember Hebrews 13:8—Jesus is the same yesterday, today, and forever. If you are in Mississippi, Jesus can and will heal someone in New York City.

Also remember this—God is not limited in any way because He is omnipresent. When He is in Mississippi, He is also in New York City.

The next miracle that we are going to read about is found in John 5:1–9. Now, this miracle involves a pool of water, and as you are about to find out, this pool is a miracle in itself. The scripture starts off by telling us that there was a feast of the Jews, taking place in Jerusalem. Verse 2 describes that this pool was over by where they kept their sheep. According to the Bible, this pool of water was called in the Hebrew tongue Bethesda that had five porches. If I had to guess I would say that the porches wrapped around the pool.

I don't know what happened to this pool, but during the time Jesus walked this earth, there was a pool of water in Jerusalem wherein a person could be healed of any sickness or disease, but only if that person goes into the water first after the water was stirred by the angel. Verse 3 tells us that on these porches "lay a great multitude of impotent folk, of blind, halt, withered, waiting for the moving of the water." Then, verse 4 explains, "For an angel went down at a certain season [due season] into the pool, and troubled [stirred] the water: whosoever then first after the troubling of the water stepped in was made whole of whatsoever disease he had."

In verse 5, you can find where the next healing begins to take place. As Jesus walked by this pool of water, He saw a man there who had an infirmity for thirty-eight years. "When Jesus saw him lie, and knew that he had been now a long time, He saith unto him, Wilt thou be made whole? The impotent man answered Him, Sir, I have no man, when the water is troubled, to put me into the pool: but while I am coming, another steppeth down before me" (verses 6–7).

Jesus' response to that was, "Rise, take up thy bed, and walk." Verse 9 details, "And immediately the man was made whole, and took up his bed, and walked."

When this man said to Jesus, "Sir, I have no man, when the water is troubled, to put me into the pool. While I am coming, another steps down into the pool before me." As you now know, this man didn't have to get into the water to be healed. He was taken from last place and brought to the front of the line to be healed.

Read the scriptures in John 5:10–18, and Philippians 2:5–8. These scriptures will help you to understand what I'm about to say. This statement is hard for most people to accept (understand), but it is true. Before you finish reading this book, you too will know that this statement is true. This man who was lying beside the pool that day at first didn't know he was talking to the Creator (inventor) of this pool. He was lying there talking and soon to be standing before God Almighty. Please don't stop reading! If you continue reading this book and comparing it with the Bible, you will find out who Jesus really is.

As I was driving home from the land today, I was praying and worshiping the Lord. I began thinking over what I had written a little earlier about how Jesus healed the man at the pool of Bethesda. I want to tell you what I believe happened that day.

As you read this book, you will see throughout that I put in my two cents when I think I have something to contribute. I will never on purpose add or take away from God's word, but I will let you know what I believe. So here I go putting in my two cents again. As you now know, every time a multitude of sick people came in contact with Jesus, He healed them all. I don't believe that that day would have been any different. I know that Jesus was the inventor of compassion. It's not recorded, but I believe Jesus healed all of them who were around the pool that day. That is just the kind of GREAT PHYSICIAN He is.

I want to bring something to your attention that is written in John 5:4. According to this scripture, "An angel went down at a certain season into the pool, and troubled the water." Now, this is what I believe about this certain season. You have heard of the four seasons—spring, summer, fall, and winter. But I want to inform you of the fifth season that is mentioned in God's word a few times. I believe that this certain season mentioned in John chapter 5 is the fifth season.

I believe the fifth season is the best season of them all. As you are about to find out, during the fifth season, all things are possible. The fifth season is called due season. The due season is used by God to bless His people (Christians) who obey Him. I also believe that the due season only belongs to God's people. As you read the scriptures that I'm about to share with you, you will know that when God's people obey Him, He blesses them in due season. What I like about the due season is God's blessings and that it can come in any of the other four seasons. I want you to read for yourself about the due season. The first set of scriptures you need to read is in Leviticus 26:1–46. In these scriptures, the Lord lets us know what He will do for us if we will obey Him. He also lets us know what He will do to us if we don't obey Him. To find this TRUTH about the due season, you must read this entire chapter of Leviticus.

At this time, I want to share something with you that happened to me the other day. It says in Leviticus 26:36 that the Lord will cause a shaken leaf to chase them. Some who have read these scriptures may ask, "How can a shaken leaf chase someone?" Well, let me tell you what just happened to me a few days before I read this chapter in Leviticus. As I was working on the land the other day, there was a great burst of wind. But the wind only rushed through one tree that was full of dead leaves. Now, I have worked outside in the woods all of my life, and never before has this happened to me. That day, when the wind rushed through that tree, it scared me. For a second, I didn't know what was coming upon me. I truly believe if this would have happened at night, I would have run. Now, I know personally the Lord can frighten someone with a shaken leaf.

Let's read some of the other scriptures that teach us about due season. If you will read Deuteronomy chapter 11, you will find more TRUTH about due season. These scriptures pretty much say what you just read in Leviticus. They say that if you obey the Lord, He will bless you in due season. I want to comment on verses 26–28. The Lord says that He has given us two different lives to choose from. "Behold, I set before you this day a blessing and a curse. A blessing, if ye obey the commandments of the Lord your God, which I command you this day. And a curse, if ye will not obey the commandments of the Lord your God." In these scriptures, the Lord is plainly telling us how to achieve due season and how not to receive it.

Read Galatians 6:7–9 so you can hear what Apostle Paul has to say about due season. This is a fact.

Whatever kind of seed you sow into the ground is what you will receive at harvest time. That is the way the Lord has designed this life here on earth—seed, time, and harvest. Having been raised on a farm, I know about seed, time, and harvest. A farmer must plant the seed, then he has to allow time for the Lord to help it grow, and finally, he can harvest. Verse 9 tells us that we are not to "be weary in well doing: for in due season we shall reap, if we faint not." I have seen and lived in due season for many years, and it is wonderful to be blessed by the Lord. If I were you, I would ask the Lord to teach me His word and help me to obey it, so I could live in due season.

As you read your Bible, you are going to see that sometimes, the Lord uses a different terminology. He uses the words due time, which I believe is the same as due season. I just wanted to share with you what I believed about due season.

The next miracle that we are going to read about is found in John 9:1–41.

> And as Jesus passed by, He saw a man, which was blind from birth. And His disciples asked Him, Master, who did sin, this man, or his parents, that he was born blind? Jesus answered, Neither hath this man sinned, nor his parents: but that the works or God should be made manifest in him. (Verses 1–3)

Before I go any further, yes, the Lord healed this blind man. The Lord could have simply said, "You're healed," but He chose to spit on the ground and make some clay for his eyes. Then, the Lord sent him to wash in the pool of Siloam. There is no set way how the Lord heals. I believe that you think like I do. If you were blind, I know that you wouldn't care if the Lord spit in your eye if that is the way He chose to heal you. To tell you the TRUTH, it doesn't really matter how the Lord heals us because He knows what is best for us.

There are all kinds of miracles that Jesus did while He walked this earth. John 21:25 says and there are also many other things which Jesus did, the which, if they should be written every one, I suppose that even the world itself could not contain the books that should be written. But the miracle that you are about to hear—I believe—is the greatest of all except for the born- again experience. You will find this story in John 11:1–45. This story is about Lazarus and his two sisters, Mary and Martha. Verse 5 tells us that Jesus loved all three of these people.

Jesus had spent time with this family and eaten with them at their house. Read John 12:1–7 and you will learn that Mary was the lady who anointed Jesus' feet with spikenard, a very expensive ointment. And then, she wiped His feet with her hair. As you read and study God's word, you will find that Mary, Martha, and Lazarus was like family to Jesus.

And I would bet that she was at His trial, she watched Him take the beating for our healing, and she was there to comfort Jesus' mother when He was crucified. In Acts 1:14, you can bet that she was one of the women who were on the first day of the New Testament church with Jesus' mother and His siblings. As you study God's word, you can see that Mary was very thankful toward Jesus for Him bringing her brother back from the dead. Mary's actions spoke louder than her words.

As you read the story about Jesus' friends in John chapter 11, you will see that after Jesus heard that Lazarus was sick, He stayed where He was for a few more days. Reading between the lines, Jesus knew that Lazarus was going to die, so He delayed His coming to him until Lazarus' death. Jesus did this so He could show God's power and glory here on earth.

As Jesus got to the town where Lazarus and his sisters lived, He found out that Lazarus had been dead for four days. Verses 20–21 tell us that as soon as Martha heard He was coming, she went and met Him. Immediately, Martha showed her faith in Him. She told Jesus, "If you had been here, my brother would not have died." But in verse 23, Jesus tells her, "Thy brother shall rise again." If you will continue reading, you will hear Martha's reply in verse 24: "I know that he shall rise again in the resurrection at the last day." Please hear what Jesus says to Martha in verses 25–26:

> Jesus said unto her, I am the resurrection, and the life: He that believeth in me, though he were dead, yet shall he live: And whosoever liveth and believeth in me shall never die. Believest thou this?
> She saith unto Him, Yea, Lord.

Then, Martha leaves and goes to Mary and informs her, "The Master is come, and calleth for thee [He wants to see you]" (verse 28). As you can see in the scriptures, Mary didn't waste any time. She got up hastily and went to where the Lord was. When Mary saw the Lord, she "fell down at His feet," and she also showed her faith in Him. She said exactly what Martha said, "If you had been here, my brother would not have died."

When Jesus saw Mary and her friends weeping, "He groaned in the Spirit, and was troubled." Then, Jesus asked her, "Where have you laid him?" Just in case you don't know, John 11:35—"Jesus wept"—is the shortest scripture found in God's word as far as I know. If you will continue reading your Bible from verse 35, you will learn about how Jesus raised Lazarus from the dead. As Jesus wept, the Jews who were there that day made this statement, "Behold how He loved him!" (verse 36).

As Jesus approached the grave, He groaned in himself again. The grave "was a cave, and a stone lay upon it" (verse 38). Jesus said, "Take ye away the stone." Speaking up, Martha tells the Lord, "By this time, he stinketh for he hath been four days." Jesus saith unto her, "said I not unto thee, that, if thou wouldest believe, thou shoul-dest see the glory of God?"

So they removed the stone in front of the grave. And Jesus looked up and prayed to the Father. Now, when He had finished praying, He cried with a loud voice, "Lazarus, come forth" (verse 43). Notice that the Lord specifically called Lazarus' name. If the Lord would have just said, "Come forth," I believe every grave in that cemetery would have been emptied.

Now, you have seen what the Lord can do—even to the extent of raising a man from the dead, who had been in the grave for four days. Most of you who read this book do not have this kind of problem. But just in case, now you know the Lord can do anything you ask Him. If you live for God and just believe in Him, then you will see God's power and glory in your family's life. Once you have experienced the power that is in the name of Jesus, you will call on Him often.

Paul says in Colossians 3:17, "Whatsoever you do in word or deed, all in the name of the Lord Jesus, giving thanks to God and the Father by Him."

In John 14:12–14, Jesus says,

> Verily [truly], verily [truly], I say unto you. He that believeth on me, the works that I do shall he do also; and greater than these shall he do; because I go unto my Father. And whatsoever ye shall ask in my name, that will I do, that the Father may be glorified in the Son. If ye shall ask any thing in my name, I will do.

As you read God's word, you will find the scriptures are full of His promises to the believer.

Soon, we are going to read from the book of Acts and see how the Lord gave man power to do His work for Him when He went to heaven. But first, we need to read the scriptures that teach us what Jesus told His apostles just before He goes to heaven for the second time. These scriptures are commonly called the Great Commission and confirm the TRUTH about how Jesus gave us (the saints) power over sickness and even death.

In Mark 16:15–18, Jesus tells His followers,

> Go ye into all the world, and preach the gospel to every creature. He that believeth and is baptized shall be saved; but he that believeth not shall be damned. And these signs shall follow them that believe; In my name shall they cast out devils; they shall speak with new tongues; they shall take up serpents; and if they drink any deadly thing, it shall not hurt them; they shall lay hands on the sick, and they shall recover.

Verse 20 tells us, "And they went forth, and preached every where, the Lord working with, and confirming the word with signs following. Amen."

Here is another set of scriptures that teach us the Lord gave His people (the church) the power to lay hands on the sick, and the Lord will heal them. Listen really closely to what I just wrote—it is the Lord that does the healing. In James 5:14–16, James says, "Is any sick among you? Let him call for the elders of the church; and let them pray over him, anointing him with oil in the name of the Lord." In the following verses, I will emphasize the key to getting healed. "The prayer of faith shall save the sick...and if he have committed sins, they shall be forgiven him. Confess faults one to another, and pray one for another, that ye may be healed. The effectual fervent prayer of a righteous man availeth much". If you are born-again and live right, God will answer your prayers.

If you continue reading James 5:17–18, you will see how the Lord answered the prayer of Elias (Elijah). After you read James 5:17–18, you need to read 1 Kings chapters 17–18. In these two chapters, you will find out how the Lord used and demonstrated His power through Elijah. You will also learn how these people were blessed because Elijah believed (had faith) in God. Chapter 17 begins with how the Lord stopped the rain and then in chapter 18 how the rain returned. After reading these two chapters, you should see that God can and will take care of you if you have faith in Him.

Listen to what Apostle Paul teaches us in 1 Corinthians 2:1–5. He says,

> And I, brethren, when I came to you [the Corinthians], came not with excellency of speech or of wisdom, declaring unto you the testimony of God. For I determined not to know anything among you, save [except] Jesus Christ, and Him crucified. And I was with you in weakness, and in fear, and in much trembling. And my speech and my preaching not with enticing words of man's wisdom, but in demonstration of the Spirit and of power: That your faith should not stand in the wisdom of men, but in the power of God.

When we study the book of Acts you will see (hear) how Apostle Paul lives what he tells us to do throughout his teachings. He demonstrates God's power through the Spirit of God.

Going against Satan without having the power of God's Spirit is something you should never try or do. Acts 19:13–16 is a perfect example of what I'm talking about. Luke recorded this lesson, teaching us not to go against Satan without God's Spirit. In verse 13, Luke begins by saying, "Then certain of the vagabond Jews, exorcists, took upon them to call over them which had evil spirits the name of the Lord Jesus, saying, We adjure you by Jesus whom Paul preacheth."

Luke continues in verses 14–16, "And there were seven sons of Sceva, a Jew, chief of the priests, which did so. And the evil spirits answered and said, Jesus I know, and Paul I know; but who are ye? And the man in whom the evil spirit was leaped on them, and overcame them, and prevailed against them, so that they fled out of that house naked and wounded." As you can see, these evil spirits were even being sarcastic with the seven non-Christians. If you don't already know, you will learn through God's word that Satan is a SUPER POWER in our world.

In 2 Corinthians 4:4, Apostle Paul calls him the god of this world, and so he is. God is the SUPER POWER, and without God's Spirit, Satan will take over you, and you will spend eternity in HELL. We need to continue seeking and learning God's word so Satan will not have any power over us.

There is another book in God's word that has milk in it that you must read, and it is the book of Acts. The book of Acts is the fifth book in the New Testament. In Acts, you will learn how, when, and where the church was started by the actions of the apostles. Not only should you read, but also study the book of Acts and seek the Lord for His plan of salvation. Only in the book of Acts can you find out how our brothers and sisters before us were born-again. Here is another fact—if you are not born-again in the same manner as they were, you are born-again. I will let you fill in the blank.

After you learn God's TRUTH about who He is and the TRUTH about His plan of salvation, you will be able to hear when someone tries to teach you a false doctrine. I wrote about God's TRUTH throughout this book, but a big part of this book is about the false teachings that come to us daily. As you continue reading, you will learn that Satan is in control of the false doctrines of this world. This is why we need to know the word of God.

In the last chapter of this book, I'm going to write about God's plan of salvation and who Jesus is. If you read this entire book, I believe you are hungry for God's TRUTH. And the Lord will see your desire for His TRUTH, and He will reveal Himself to you. Some will say that the TRUTH is not hidden, and I can read God's word, so it's not hidden from me. This is why I'm writing this book because it is hidden. I believe you will know it is hidden through this question—why are there so many different kinds of churches in the world? The answer to that question is they are not RIGHTLY DIVIDING God's word.

For most of you who read this book, you will find out that you didn't know God's TRUTH. This may not, but I believe that this is a good example of what I'm trying to convey to you. A couple of years ago, there was a commercial, and it was about a man who found out there is a better ice tea than what he had been drinking. On this commercial, he says, after tasting the tea, "This is gooood." I wonder what else I have been wrong about.

If you have seen this commercial, maybe you will have a better understanding of what I'm saying. I'm here to inform you that the tea (teaching) that you have been consuming is only part TRUTH. We all need to know the whole TRUTH. If you continue reading this book, you will find out that the majority of people don't understand God's word. Most of the time, the majority of people are correct, but in this case, the minority is, and they know God's TRUTH.

God's word is hidden from most of the world (people), because it is spiritually discerned. Pray for the Lord's guidance, and read 1 Corinthians 2:6–16 and also Ephesians 3:1–5. The Lord has hidden the TRUTH, and Satan has used man to wrest (change) the TRUTH. So this lets me know that I must seek the Lord for His TRUTH, because He is TRUTH. Jesus says in John 14:6, "I am the way, the TRUTH, and the life."

You are going to hear a few times in this book John 8:32: Jesus says, "And ye shall know the TRUTH, and the TRUTH shall make you free." Most of the world has heard this scripture misquoted for most of their lives. If you will read this scripture again, you will see (hear) that it says make you free, not set you free. There is a big difference. To set something free is an immediate action. To make you free is an ongoing process. Believe me that growing in God is an ongoing process. Today is August 13, 2014, and I have been growing in the Lord for thirty-one years now. On August 11, 1983, I started this race toward heaven, and I have grown a lot; but there is so much more I need to learn. But most of all, I need to do what I know to do, because I know the TRUTH.

I want you to know before you look at these pictures I'm not boasting of myself, but I am boasting in Jesus of how He has taught me. This is how I found God's TRUTH. This first picture is the front cover of my Bible. I paid $100.00 for this Bible, and it is made of leather, and as you can see, it is almost worn out. Oh, by the way, this is my second Bible. The first one was not made of leather, but it was in a much worse shape than this one.

This second picture is a side view. When I purchased this Bible, it was about 1½ inches thick, and now, you can see that it is swollen from me reading and studying it.

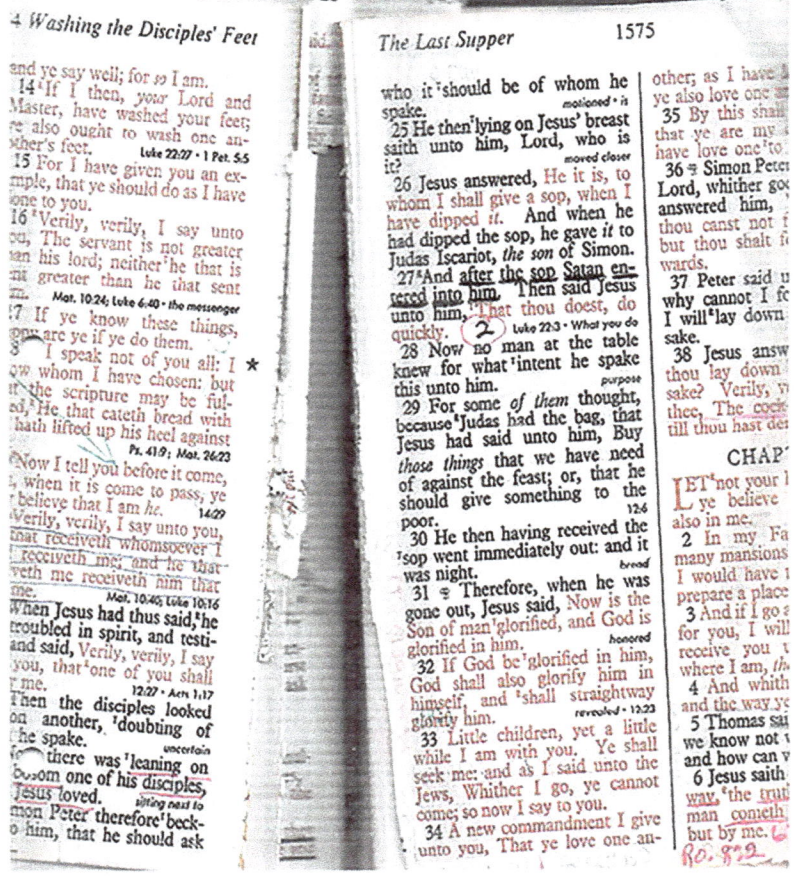

This third picture shows how my Bible is falling apart from the inside.

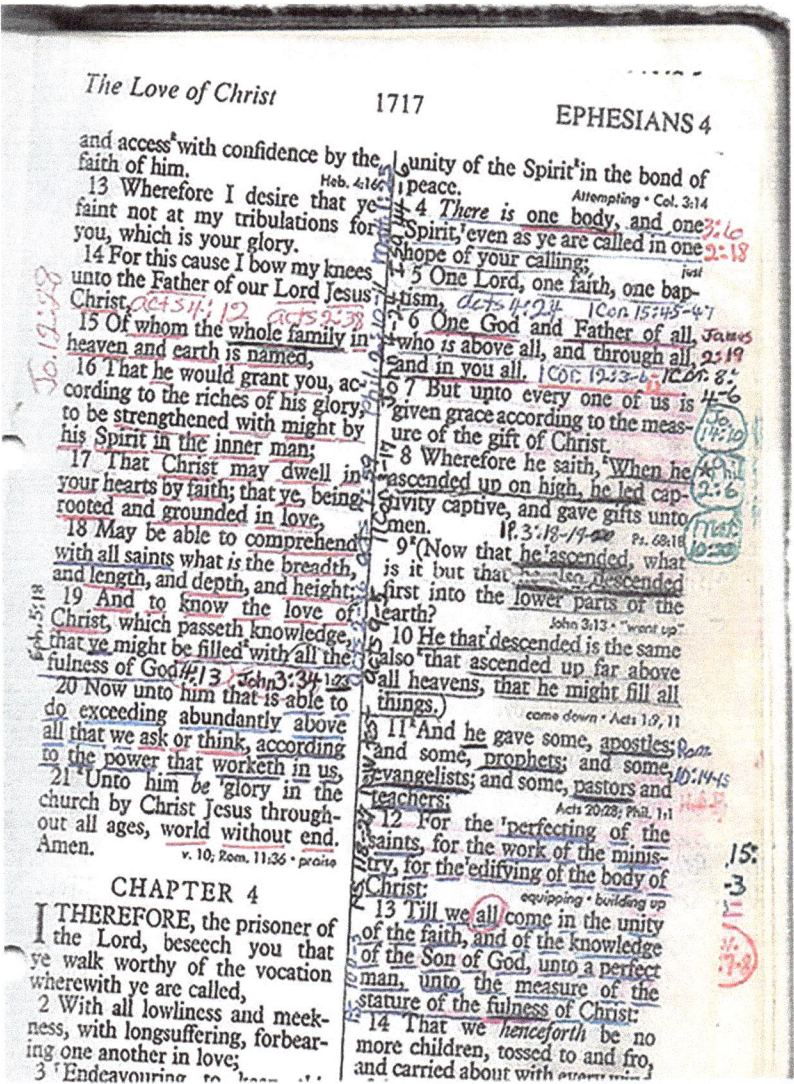

This fourth and last picture should show you the importance that I saw in certain words. And as you can see, I made other scripture references as I studied God's word. Feel free to look up any or all of those scriptures.

I want to say again that I'm not boasting about myself. But I am boasting about what the Holy Ghost (Jesus) has taught me. Jesus showed my family the TRUTH back in the summer of 1983, and these pictures show my desire to know more about Him and His TRUTH. Very few people have found gold just lying on top of the ground. As I have said, God hid His TRUTH from the wise and prudent, and Satan has used man to wrest God's TRUTH. Believe me—we must dig deep into God's word to find His gold mine that He wants to share with us.

As you can tell by these pictures, I have been digging deep into God's word. I am so blessed to have found all the gold nuggets that the Lord has shared with me from His word. And the Lord knows that I'm not a selfish person, but I do want more TRUTH. God's word teaches us that if we will receive these gold nuggets (God's TRUTH) and do them, we will get to live with Him and walk on the golden streets of heaven. I can only share with you what the Lord has shared with me. After you learn the TRUTH that I have written in this book, it will be up to you to seek the Lord to show you where to find more gold nuggets. Just remember to share what you learn from God's word with others.

The $100.00 that I paid for my Bible was the best $100.00 that I have ever spent. If you will go and purchase yourself a Bible and begin reading and studying it, you too will be blessed by God beyond measure. Always remember to ask the Lord for the TRUTH, and He will teach you His TRUTH. Never forget, and read John 14:26 often.

Now, let's get back to the scriptures and find more TRUTH. Here is something that I want to share with you, and it is the timeline of Jesus' ascension to heaven and His descent back to earth. Let's read some scriptures and confirm and find out about this timeline. In John chapter 20, you can find out about the day Jesus was resurrected. To set the scene, I want you to remember how Mary Magdalene loved Jesus, because Jesus had cast seven devils out of her. Read

Mark 16:9. As you read John 20:1, you will see that Mary was the first person to go to the grave site. After she could not find the Lord there, verse 2 tells us that she ran and came "to Simon Peter, and to the other disciple, whom Jesus loved [John], and saith unto them, They have taken away the Lord out of the sepulcher, and we know not where they have laid Him."

As you continue reading John 20:1–19, you will see that Peter and John went back to their homes, but Mary stayed at the grave site. Verse 11 tells us, "But Mary stood without at the sepulcher weeping: and as she wept, she stooped down, into the sepulcher." When she went into the grave, she saw "two angels in white sitting, the one at the head, and the other at the feet, where the body of Jesus had lain" (verse 12). I pray that you heard what I just wrote; if not, I will say it again—where the body of Jesus HAD LAIN. As she talked with the two angels, "she turned herself back, and saw Jesus standing, and knew not that it was Jesus" (verse 14). Now, you must remember that Mary was a close friend of Jesus and was only a few feet from Him, but she did not know the man she was talking to.

In verse 15, Jesus says to her, "Woman, why weepest thou? Whom seekest thou?" Even though she was face to face with Jesus, she didn't know that it was the Lord she was talking to. The scriptures tell us that she believed Him to be the gardener. In verse 16, Jesus calls her by her name. When He said, "Mary," she knew that it was Jesus because she called Him Rabboni (Master). I wrote all of that to show you this TRUTH about the timeline of Jesus going to heaven for the first time.

In verse 17, Jesus tells Mary, "Touch me not: for I am not yet ascended to my Father: but go to my brethren, and say unto them, I ascend unto my father, and your Father; and my God, and your God." Then, Mary did as the Lord told her to do; she went and told the disciples that Jesus has gone to heaven.

We can find the TRUTH about when Jesus came back to earth in verse 19. John tells us, "Then the same day at evening, being the first of the week [Sunday]." After Mary left Him that Sunday morning, according to the scriptures (John 20:17), Jesus went to heaven.

In Luke chapter 24, he gives us his recollection of the day Jesus was resurrected and returned to earth. According to Luke 24:13, "Two of them went that same day to a village called Emmaus." The scriptures tell us that they went their way, and Jesus met them on the road and went with them. Both of these men knew Jesus. "But their eyes were holden that they should not know Him" (Luke 24:16). Then, Jesus began to teach from the scriptures the things concerning Himself. Verse 31 tells us, "And their eyes were opened, and they knew Him; and He vanished out of their sight." As these two men told the apostles what happened on the road a little earlier, Jesus came into where they were gathered and said, "Peace unto you."

Remember that Jesus told Mary not to touch Him, because He had not yet ascended to the Father. Notice in Luke 24:39 when Jesus tells them to "behold my hands and my feet, that it is I myself: handle me." This scripture lets me know that Jesus has gone to heaven and returned back to earth. Verses 44–45 detail that Jesus taught them from the scriptures things concerning Himself. "Then opened he their understanding, that they might understand the scriptures" (verse 45). Read Ephesians 1:18. Just as the Lord had to open their understanding, we need him to open up our understanding also.

In the next four scriptures, you will hear what Jesus tells His disciples about where to go and what to expect when they get there. In verses 46–49, Jesus tells His apostles,

> Thus it is written, and thus it behooved Christ to suffer, and to rise from the dead the third day. And that repentance and remission of sins should be preached in His name among all nations, beginning at Jerusalem. And ye are witnesses of these things. And, behold, I send the promise of my Father upon you: but tarry ye in the city of Jerusalem, until ye be endued with power from on high.

If you don't know, you are about to learn that Jesus was telling His apostles to go to Jerusalem and start the New Testament church. If you will read verses 50–51, you will see that Jesus was taken up to heaven. This was the second time that Jesus went to heaven since He came to earth in the flesh.

Now, let's read from the book of Acts and learn about the birth of the church. In Acts 1:1–2, Luke tells us that he wrote about "all that Jesus began both to do and teach." In that scripture, Luke was talking about when he wrote his gospel according to what he remembered Jesus doing. In verse 2, he says, "Until the day in which He was taken up, after that He through the Holy Ghost had given commandments unto the apostles, whom He had chosen." In this verse, Luke was referring to Luke chapter 24, when Jesus told His apostles to go to Jerusalem until they were "endued with power from on high." In Acts 1:3, Luke tells us, "To whom also He shewed Himself alive after His passion by many infallible proofs, being seen of them [the apostles], forty days, and speaking of the things pertaining to the kingdom of God."

In verse 4, Jesus assembled together with "commanded them that they should not depart from Jerusalem." Notice that the apostles are in Jerusalem forty days after He commanded them to do so, in Luke chapter 24. Just as Jesus told them in Luke chapter 24, He tells them again in Acts 1:4–5: Jesus "commanded them that they should not depart from Jerusalem, but wait for the promise [receiving the Holy Ghost] of the Father, which ye have heard of me. For John truly baptized with water; but ye shall be baptized with the Holy Ghost not many days hence [from now]."

This is when Jesus tells His apostles in Acts 1:8, "But ye shall receive power, after that the Holy Ghost is come upon you: and ye shall be witnesses unto me both in Jerusalem, and in all Judaea, and in Samaria, and unto the uttermost part of the earth." When Jesus says, "Unto the uttermost part of the earth," He was referring to places like Little Texas or Seven Mile Mississippi. Even if there is only one family that lives there, Jesus wants somebody who has His Spirit to go and tell them about His plan of salvation.

Verse 9 tells us, "When He had spoken these things, while they beheld, He was taken up; and a cloud received Him out of their sight." And as far as I know from the scriptures, Jesus returned to earth in a bodily form a few more times. He appeared before Apostle Paul and Apostle John in the book of Revelation. But He did return as the Holy Ghost. He came to live inside of us to give His people who are called by His name power over Satan and his deceiving ways. Read the entire chapter of Romans 6:1–23; it is a good teaching from Apostle Paul about living a sin-free life if you can hear him.

Acts 1:13 informs us that when the other people came in, they went in where the eleven apostles were assembled in an upper room. The reason why there were only eleven apostles in the upper room that day is because Judas— the twelfth apostle—killed himself, because he had betrayed the Lord. If you will read verses 16–26, you will learn how Jesus got His thirteenth apostle. As you read from the book of Acts, you will learn how Paul became the fourteenth apostle.

"These all continued with one accord in prayer and supplication, with the women, and Mary the mother of Jesus, and with His brethren. And in those days Peter stood up in the midst of the disciples, and said, (the number of names together were about an hundred and twenty)" (Acts 1:14–15). Now, the scriptures don't say this, but when Jesus told them to go to Jerusalem, there could have been a great multitude there that day. But only 119 or 121 people showed up for church that day. The reason I said 119 or 121 people is because Peter said about an hundred and twenty. That is just how I believe God's word.

Before I leave Acts chapter 1, I want to bring something else to your attention. Notice that verse 14 tells us that Mary was there in the upper room, with the followers of Jesus. Mary also had to be a follower of her Son because she knew who Jesus was from the beginning. For the last few years, I have heard this song "Mary Did You Know" around Christmas time. To tell you the TRUTH, I believe that this song is the best song of all time.

I truly believe the writer of this song knew who Jesus was, as He walked this earth. A part of the lyrics of this song goes like this, "Mary did you know that…this child that you've delivered, will soon deliver you." If you have never heard of this song, it will do you good to download it and listen to it a few times. In Acts chapter 2, you will see and hear how Jesus delivers His mother from sin.

You had better believe this—if Jesus' mother had to be born-again, so should you. I can only believe that as Jesus sat around the house and ate with His parents, He told them, "You must be born again," just as He told Nicodemus, in John chapter 3.

Read Acts 2:1, where you will start learning about the day of Pentecost, which means fiftieth day. Now, you already know that Jesus had spent forty days with His apostles before He went to heaven to stay. On the fortieth day, He tells them to stay in Jerusalem and that they "shall be baptized with the Holy Ghost not many days hence." Acts 1:12 tells us that as soon as Jesus went to heaven, "Then returned they unto Jerusalem from the mount called Olivet, which is from Jerusalem a Sabbath day's journey." I don't really know how far that would be, but it can't be very far, because God's laws concerning the Sabbath are strict. So these scriptures that we have been reading allow us to know the timeline from Jesus' resurrection until He pours out His Spirit upon the church.

Now, I want you to read for yourself what happened on the first day of the New Testament church. I want you to read Acts chapter 2 and then come back here so we can go over what you have read. I'm going to talk about some of the scriptures now, but in chapter 9, I will explain what happens on this day by using other scriptures that will help us understand more TRUTH.

Now, please hear this. If your church doesn't teach this same plan of salvation that you see and hear in Acts chapter 2, it is time to leave and find one that does. Always remember to ask Jesus for the TRUTH, and He will teach you the TRUTH, because He is the TRUTH. If you seek Jesus for the TRUTH, He will help you find the right church so you can be fed with His word.

Acts 2:1–4 teaches us that the 119 or 121 people that came to church "that day were ALL filled with the Holy Ghost and began to speak with other tongues, as the Spirit gave them utterance." At this time, I want you to make this connection with a couple of scriptures. I want you to read these two scriptures together so you can hear God's TRUTH. Hold your place in Acts 2:2–4, and flip back and read John 3:7, where Jesus tells Nicodemus, "You [all of us] must be born again."

When you RIGHTLY DIVIDE these scriptures, you will find a big part of God's plan of salvation for the entire world. So far, in Acts 2:1–4, you have seen and heard a major part of the born-again experience. As you read Acts chapter 2, you will hear that Apostle Peter was the preacher on the day the church was born. Let's read Acts 2:36–41. In verse 36, Peter starts by saying, "Therefore let all the house of Israel know assuredly, that God hath made that same Jesus, whom ye have crucified, both Lord and Christ. Now when they [the multitude] heard this, they were pricked in their hearts, and said unto Peter and to the rest of the apostles, Men, brethren, what shall we do?" They had just asked the billion-dollar question to find out how to be born-again.

In verses 38–39, Peter tells them (us) ALL three steps to salvation. In verse 38, "Peter said unto them, Repent, and be baptized every one of you in the name of Jesus Christ for the remission of sins, and ye shall receive the gift of the Holy Ghost." That day, God's chosen preacher says a whole lot in verses 38–39, but there are four words in verse 38 that you had better hear, and they are *every one of you.*

In verse 39, the Apostle Peter says another mouthful. As I explain verse 39, I'm going to paraphrase a little because I'm going to read between the lines and tell you what I believe Peter did and said that day. First, I want to tell you what I didn't see him doing. I didn't see the Apostle Peter sitting in a recliner and preaching to a multitude of people in one of the hottest church services that I have ever heard of. I see Peter up on his feet, walking around and pointing his fingers, and speaking with boldness of the Spirit, but speaking the TRUTH in love.

As you read verse 39, you will see that Peter says, "For the promise." Peter was confirming what Jesus said when He promised to give His Spirit to the believers. I believe, Peter points at the multitude and says, "For the promise is unto you." Then, he lowers his finger and eyes to the children's level and says, "And to your children." Then, I believe, he points over their heads and says, "And to all that are afar off, as many as the Lord our God shall call." Peter probably didn't know who he was referring to when he said, "As many as the Lord our God shall call." But he was speaking of the 144,000 Jews that will be born-again during the tribulation period. The reason I mentioned this because the scriptures don't teach us about anyone being born-again during the millennium (thousand year) reign. At this time, I want you to go, to the last page of this book, and read (My Personal Warning) because I believe, the Lord is allowing me to even reach out to some people during the millennium while the Church is in Heaven. PLEASE DON"T BELIEVE THE LIE that Jesus is going to set up His Kingdom here on this earth. BECAUSE IT IS A LIE! Jesus went to Heaven to prepare His Bride a place to live. Read John 14:1-3. You will learn God's TRUTH about all this later in your Bible.

Then, in verse 40, he tells them, "Save yourselves from this untoward generation." While in verse 41, Apostle Peter says another mouthful, "Then they that gladly received his word [heard God's plan of salvation] were baptized; and the same day there were added about three thousand souls." Here, I'm reading between the lines again. If you will hear what Peter didn't say, you will hear him say that there were some that day that didn't receive God's plan of salvation.

A scripture keeps coming to my mind, so I must make a comment on what Peter says at the end of verse 39: "As many as the Lord our God shall call." I kept thinking about what Jesus said in Matthew 20:16: "For many be called, but few chosen." I don't know what this scripture says to you, but here is what it says to me, "For many be called, but few chosen."

If we don't do His word, we will not be chosen. In Matthew chapter 7, Jesus gives us the only two scenarios there are. Read Matthew 7:24–29. Jesus has that right (righteous judgment) to choose His Bride. If you believe that Jesus has called and chosen you, you had better chose Him back and obey His TRUTH. If you really want to know what Jesus expects of us, stop reading this book at this time, and read Matthew chapters 5, 6, and 7. I don't care if you have read these chapters a dozen times, you need to read them a few more dozen times, and then, read them again.

If you claim to be saved (born-again), and you achieved your salvation some other way than God's plan, it is wrong. Do you remember what Jesus said in John 8:32? Well, here it is again—"And ye shall know the TRUTH and the TRUTH shall make you free." Once you are born-again, you have begun the race, but there is one more step you must do to be saved, and that is to live God's word as you learn it.

I want to tell you what I believe about all of this. I believe God's salvation is neither milk nor meat, but the cream of the crop, for without His salvation, we could not achieve what Paul teaches us in Galatians 5:22–23. Therefore, we could not live in the perfect law of liberty that Apostle James teaches us about in James 1:16–27. As I have said, we will look a little deeper in these two chapters (Acts chapters 1 and 2), when you get to chapter 9 of this book. Now that you know God's plan of salvation, it's up to you to do it and to share it with your friends and family and to whomever the Lord leads you to. To be able to share God's TRUTH, you must know what you are teaching. Before you try teaching God's word, I suggest reading and studying the book of Acts, until you know it, and then ask the Lord to send you to be a soul winner.

After you receive the Holy Ghost, you will have a power greater than any power that can come against you. Jesus gives us His power to serve Him and to be able to resist Satan's influences. I want to be really clear about this—it's the Lord in us that does the healing. It is our faith in the name of Jesus that makes miracles happen. Read Acts chapter 3, and you will learn about one of these miracles. In Acts 3:1–16, you will learn that it is not just having faith or using the name of Jesus. But miracles happen when someone uses Jesus' name through faith in His name.

If you continue reading from Acts 4:1–31, you will hear the rest of this story (TRUTH). In chapter 4, you will also learn how the religious leaders of that time tried to stop the apostles from doing the Lord's work. As you read, you are going to find out they could not stop the apostles. And as you can see through the words I have written more than two thousand years later, God's TRUTH is still being spread throughout the world. In Acts 4:12, the Apostle Peter tells us again, "Neither is there salvation in any other: for there is none other name under heaven given among men, whereby we must be saved." Using the name of Jesus, mixed with faith in His name, is so important.

You must hear what I'm about to say. When a person is baptized in the name of Jesus and baptized by God's Spirit, they are born in the family of God. But more than that, I believe that when you are baptized in Jesus' name is how the Bride takes on His name. I believe that this is a good time to read Ephesians chapter 3.

I want to bring something else to your attention, from Acts chapter 3. Most so-called Christians believe that it is wrong to worship God in church loudly, especially in jumping around or dancing. In your mind, I want you to put yourself at church in a wheelchair.

I'm here to tell you that if the Lord came over you and healed you, there is no way you would stay in that wheelchair. You would be all over that church just as this man was, leaping and shouting to the roof of that church so that your voice will be heard in heaven. Not only is this okay to worship God in this manner, but also I believe it's required of us.

As I write about these miracles, which other men accomplished through faith in His name, it makes me ashamed of myself that I call myself a Christian. At this moment, I just don't feel so powerful. Now, don't get me wrong, I still have God's power in my hands and my lips, but I just don't feel so powerful at this moment. I believe we all will experience these feelings of being powerless, as we walk with the Lord. I believe that, but I know this. This is why we all must go to Jesus in prayer and be renewed in the Holy Ghost.

I have experienced the Lord healing or helping someone, because I had faith in His name. But these miracles are so few and far between. It's good to remember and talk about those miracles of the past. But I want to be able to tell someone about what the Lord did yesterday or even today. I will make this promise to you the reader, to myself, and to God. I will try harder to see God's Spirit move in the lives of my fellow man.

To learn about the gifts of the Spirit, you need to read and study 1 Corinthians chapter 12. While reading and studying these scriptures, you will learn how the Lord shares His gifts with the church. When you read verse 31, you are going to hear the Apostle Paul say something, and you need to find the answer. What better way to find out is by reading 1 Corinthians chapter 13.

As you read and study God's word, you will learn that all of the church didn't go around healing. God has given these gifts of the Spirit to whom He will. But IF—there is that BIG word IF again—you are born-again, you have the power of God inside of you. I'm not telling you anything new here, but when you get the Lord's attention, by using your faith in His name, you can accomplish anything.

Jesus plainly teaches us in Matthew chapter 18, and He uses the word "anything." Listen to what Jesus has to say in Matthew 18:18–20 about us using our faith.

> Verily I say unto you, Whatsoever ye shall bind on earth shall be bound in heaven: and whatsoever ye shall loose on earth shall be loosed in heaven. Again I say unto you, That if two of you shall agree on earth as touching any thing that they shall ask, it [anything] shall be done for them of my Father which is in heaven. For where two or three are gathered together in my name, there am I in the midst of them.

As you can clearly see in Jesus' own words, we have an easy access to God's Spirit. When you have another person who believes with you about anything, God will answer your prayer.

Now, let's find out about Jesus teaching us how and how not to pray. You can find this TRUTH in Matthew 6:5–8. In verse 5, the first thing Jesus teaches us is how not to pray. Jesus tells us, "When thou prayest, thou shalt not be as the hypocrites: for they love to pray standing in the synagogues and in the corners of the streets, that they may be seen of men." At the end of verse 5, Jesus makes a strong statement against those hypocrites, who want to be seen, "Verily I say unto you, They have their reward." Then, Jesus tells us how to pray in verse 6, "But thou, when thou prayest, enter into thy closet, and when thou hast shut thy door, pray to thy Father which is in secret; and thy Father which seeth in secret shall reward thee openly."

In verses 7–8, Jesus warns us again about being like the heathen. He says, "But when ye pray, use not vain repetitions, as the heathen: for they think that they shall be heard for their much speaking.

Be not ye therefore like unto them: for your Father knoweth what things ye have need of, before you ask Him." Please hear what Jesus said in that last statement. Even though He knows what we need, the Lord still wants us to ask Him in prayer. My prayer closet is my bathroom and bedroom, but everyone has to find their own prayer closet. Your prayer closet simply means your place to be alone with your Creator. When you begin praying and talking with the Lord about His will for your life, you will find that you will have to lose your life to find it. Read Matthew 10:39.

The next story is not about someone being healed, until the people saw death come to a family for lying to God. As you finish reading the last few scriptures of Acts chapter 4, they are a prequel (events that precede) of the story in chapter 5. Read Acts 4:32–37 and then Acts 5:1–10, and you will learn a very important lesson—never lie to the Lord.

Acts 5:11 tells us that when the church heard of these deaths, great fear came upon all of them. In these scriptures, you will find, just as there are today, believers and non-believers. Paraphrasing verse 13, the non-believers dared not to join the church. As it was that day, it's still a mistake not to join the church. Then in verse 14, "And believers were the more added to the Lord, multitudes both of men and women." Now, let's read and find out how the believers were blessed by the Lord that day. Verse 15 explains, "Insomuch that they brought forth the sick into the streets, and laid on beds and couches, that at the least the shadow of Peter passing by might overshadow some of them."

The scriptures never mention that the Lord healed anyone by Peter's shadow passing over them. But I believe that there were some who were healed that day as Peter's shadow passed over them because of their faith. When you read these scriptures, you will see that to these people that day, having faith in the name of Jesus became more important than anything else in their lives. As I read these scriptures, I can see faith oozing out from them. As God's

Spirit moved and healed that day, there was so much faith flooding God's throne; everyone who called on the name of Jesus were healed. Verse 16 says, "There came also a multitude of the cities round about unto Jerusalem, bringing sick folks, and them which were vexed with unclean spirits: and they [the believers] were healed every one."

In verse 17, you will find jealousy once again from the religious leaders. As you read Acts 5:17–42, you will see that the religious leaders didn't have the power of the Holy Ghost in them. Verse 18 tells us that those religious leaders took the apostles and put them in the common prison. What they didn't realize is that they were fighting against God. In verses 34–39, you will see that Gamaliel tried to warn those religious leaders that if this teaching were from God, there is no way to win that battle.

The scriptures (19–20) tell us that an angel of the Lord came and opened the prison doors. Then, this angel commanded the apostles, "Go, stand and speak in the temple to the people all the words of this life." The religious leaders tried to stop the apostles and God's message, but they couldn't. When you read the last two scriptures of chapter 5, you will see what the apostles thought of non-believers trying to stop them from preaching the gospel in Jesus' name.

As you read about these next miracles, you will be able to see how the Lord was working through Philip, one of the Lord's apostles. As I read these scriptures, I believe that Philip had the gift of healing. But if not, God was mightily still working through him. I could write what these scriptures say, but I believe you should read them for yourself from the Bible. Read Acts 8:5–7.

I believe you should read as much as you can from your Bible and become familiar with it, because it is our road map to the golden streets of heaven. I believe you too want to know where you're going. And nothing is as important as finishing the race, which is ahead of us. Read Matthew 24:13. To you who will listen, read, but most of all study our road map (the Bible). Read Matthew 7:13–14. There is no way to go to an unfamiliar place without studying the road map.

And you had better believe this—there is no way to go to heaven without studying God's word and living it as you learn.

At this time, I want to share with you how my brother Emmett learned God's TRUTH. Emmett was a riverboat pilot, and he was gone for six months. He would work one month on and one month off. But every time he came home, we would be together, until he had to go back to work. Emmett moved in with us in 1979, soon after our son Jason was born. When my wife's younger sister Sandra turned eighteen, she also moved in with us. As best as I can remember, she moved in with us in 1980. Since the mid-1970s, she had her eyes on Emmett from the time she was a young girl. When she was about twelve years old, she said that she was going to marry Emmett.

In August 1983, he left for the month, like he has been doing for years. But when he returned in September, we were not the same, because my family had started going to church. My wife and I were baptized in Jesus' name on August 14, 1983, and were seeking the Holy Ghost. When Emmett came home, he was ready to smoke some weed, because he didn't get to smoke that much out on the river. The month earlier, I was smoking an average five to ten joints (if that is the way you spell joints) a day. But when he came home, me and my wife started explaining to him how we quit smoking pot and also cigarettes. We also told him what we had learned from God's word. Now, we didn't know very much, but we told him about God's plan of salvation in Acts 2:38–39 that the Lord had revealed to us.

Now, it has been thirty-three years ago, and it's hard to remember every detail. But I remember him being the same. I could tell that he was uncomfortable in his own home. In the fall of 1983, Emmett came home and began telling us that he had found a lump under his arm. A month or so later, he went to the hospital and had it removed, and the mass was analyzed, and the results came back malignant. So he started treatments for cancer.

We all would help Emmett in any way we could, but Sandra did the most; she stayed by his side to the end. What I'm about to say is saying a lot, but I believe Sandra took care of Emmett as good or better than our mother could have. The Lord brought Emmett and Sandra together just at the right time. Most people have heard that God works in mysterious ways. I know He has worked mysteriously in my family.

I believe it was around February 1984 when Emmett and Sandra moved to their own home. They bought a double-wide in Abbeville, Mississippi, and it needed a little work done to it, so I helped fix what I could. As we worked on their house, I could not help myself from talking about the Lord. I already knew what Emmett believed, because we were raised together. I also knew that I was speaking God's word in another light than he had ever heard.

As a new convert, I'm sure I said some things and did some things that he could not understand. But let me tell you how he saw God's TRUTH. I don't remember what day or month, but I do remember getting into bed one night and God's Spirit filling my bedroom. So naturally, I got out of bed and went on my knees to pray. As I talked with God, I began telling Him what I thought about Emmett, but I was not telling the Lord anything that He didn't already know, but He wanted to hear me say it.

Now, what I'm about to say will be hard for some to believe, unless you believe. Just as the Lord is going to change our bodies, at the last trumpet sound, in a moment, and a blink of an eye, He took (teleported) me to their house in Abbeville, Mississippi. I should remember every moment of that night, but I don't, although I do remember standing in their bedroom and watching them sleep. I don't know how long I was there, but in a moment and a blink of an eye, I was back home in my bedroom. In my mind or in my body, I don't know. I only know what I know, and besides that, I don't know.

I'm in no way trying to compare myself with the Apostle Paul. I believe he's more a man of God than I will ever be. I can only pray to be close to what he was in the Lord. But I want you to read 2 Corinthians 12:1–3. We will come back and read a few more of these scriptures a little later.

I don't know how significant it was for me to go to their house that night, but the Lord allowed me to do so. I do remember this—it did not take the Lord long at all to put in Emmett's heart the desire to know His TRUTH. The next morning after I went (was teleported) to their house, I heard a knock on the door. When I opened the door, there stood Emmett. The first thing that came out of his mouth was, "Can you show me the scriptures that you have been talking about?" As I turned to go get my Bible, Emmett sat down on the steps of our front porch.

When I came back, I sat down beside him and opened my Bible to Acts chapters 1 and 2. I believe the only scripture that Emmett knew at that time was John 3:16. So I began telling him how, when, and where the New Testament church started. And I also told him that there is one God and His name is Jesus. We sat there on the steps and read Acts chapters 1 and 2. As we read, I would ask him if he understood what he was reading. He would just nod his head and say yes.

I told him as I'm telling you now—listen closely to these next few scriptures. Peter says in Acts 2:36–39,

> Therefore let all the house of Israel know assuredly, that God hath made that same Jesus, whom ye have crucified, both Lord and Christ. Now when they heard, they were pricked in their heart, and said unto Peter and to the rest of the apostles. Men, brethren, what shall we do? Then Peter said unto them, repent, and be baptized every one of you in the name of Jesus Christ for the remission of sins, and ye shall receive the gift of the Holy Ghost. For

the promise is unto you, and to your children, and to all
that are afar off, as many as the Lord our God shall call.

When we got through reading verse 39, Emmett said to me, "I
don't see why everyone can't understand that."

I asked him, "Do you remember how you were baptized when
you were a teenager?"

He replied, "Yes, and I was baptized wrong."

I said to him, "You have just seen God's TRUTH for the first
time. You have been chosen to see [understand] what billions before
you could not see."

I didn't have to tell him, but he said, "I must get into the water
and be baptized right."

I should know this also, but I don't remember how long it
took him to get baptized correctly, although it wasn't long, maybe
a week or two.

Now, Emmett and Sandra were still just living together, and
God's Spirit was truly working on both of them. When God's Spirit
begins convicting you of anything, most people obey Him. Again,
I don't know how long it took them, but it was not long, and they
were married. Now, Emmett was also my brother-in-law, and Sandra
was my sister-in-law both ways. Sandra was also Cindy's sister and
sister-in-law, and Emmett was Cindy's brother-in-law both ways.

That morning when we were sitting on our porch, I told Emmett
the same thing that I taught our two children and now their children.
And IF you will hear this TRUTH, which is in Acts chapters 1 and 2,
you will hear what I have taught and will teach my entire Christian
life. I tell everyone who will listen that God's salvation plan has not
changed and will not change. I don't know why someone could be,
but I'm not ashamed of the gospel of Christ. As a matter of fact,
I'm proud to be a believer in the name of Jesus.

Emmett died back in the winter of 1985. He had only been
in church about a year or so. And a couple of days before he died

(came alive), he said to me from his hospital bed, "I don't know why the Lord has blessed me so, because I don't know very much about His word."

I immediately replied, "Emmett, you know more about God's word than billions of people. God revealed to you His TRUTH, and you obeyed His TRUTH, when you were baptized in Jesus' name and received God's gift of the Holy Ghost."

Not only was Emmett an older brother or brother-in-law, but also he was a friend to me and my wife and a father figure to our two children. I remember one day in the hospital, the nurse asked him, "Are these your children?"

He replied, "No, they are my brothers, but they are just like mine. They are probably the only two kids that I will ever have."

A couple of days before he passed away, he told to me, "I have to tell you something that you don't know. When Jason [our son] was little, I took him to Arkabutla Dam and swam out to the buoys, with him on my back. And on the way back to the beach, I caught a cramp and almost drowned us both."

What could I say, but, "It's okay. You saved him."

I know that the Lord had his hands on them that day. But ever since the day he told me that, I believe that it was Jason who saved Emmett that day, because he knew he had to get Jason back on the beach. Without any doubt in my mind, Emmett was the type who would have given his life for my family, and in many ways, he did. I had been studying God's word for a year or so, and I knew more about God's TRUTH than he did. But I don't believe I will ever be the man he was. I am sixty-one years old now, and I still stand by my last statement.

The day before he passed away from this life, he began speaking out of his head, as some family members said. But I believe, he knew what he was saying. He would begin describing things in heaven and looking up at the ceiling, as if he was looking through it into heaven. He would even ask, "Do you see it?" I'm not trying to pass judgment, but I believe Emmett has been in heaven for the past thirty-two years, waiting for Jesus to open the fifth and sixth seals. We will learn about the Lord opening the fifth and sixth seals later in this book.

When I went to Emmett and Sandra's house, was the first time, the Lord has taken me on such a journey. I know that I have started talking about myself, but let me explain. Like I said earlier, if you believe, a year or so later, I had an encounter with Satan as I awoke one morning. I'm not going to go into all this story, but if you ever see me in person, I will be glad to fill in the blanks that I'm leaving. Early one morning, I was having a dream, and when I woke up, Satan (an evil spirit) was in my bedroom. I immediately began calling on Jesus. You will find as you run this race, Jesus is the first name to call when you are in trouble. My mind just thought about "Jesus Take the Wheel," if you know what I'm talking about.

I wanted answers to the dream I had about Sister Jackson and why Satan was in my bedroom when I woke up. As soon as I asked the Lord those two questions, the Lord said, "Come on." I only remember a small part of the dream about Sister Jackson. And after I woke up, I remember Satan being in my bedroom, and I remember talking with the Lord and asking Him the two questions, and Him telling me to come on. There are two other things that I remember about that morning. When the Lord said, "Come on," I remember putting my arm around my wife and began explaining to her where I was going. I don't know if she was even awake, but I remember telling her that I was leaving my body and that only lasted for a few seconds. I'm ashamed of what I'm about to say, but the last thing I remember is that I told the Lord, "I can't handle this." I immediately was back home in my bed, wide awake and confused.

I believe this happened in 1985, but I'm not sure of the exact time. Later that day, I called Sister Jackson, and she thanked me for calling her and told me that it was her birthday. Before we ended our talk, she asked me and Cindy to pray for her and her family, and I asked her to do the same. My biggest regret was not being able to help her and inform her what the Lord had showed me about her family. Brother Jackson was the first pastor that my family went to church under. I'm about to speak for my family, and I believe that I'm speaking the TRUTH. My whole family loved the Jackson family.

I have always believed the Lord was going to allow me to prophesy to her, but my immaturity in God stopped me. The Jackson family moved on to another church, and as time went by, we would hear about them. I'm not going to write about what we heard. But every time I heard something that happened to them, I would always remember what I didn't do for them. Even today as I sit here writing, it bothers me, and I can't even explain how I feel at this moment. I guess I just feel ashamed of myself because I couldn't help them in their troubles. If any of the Jackson family ever reads this book, all I know to say is, "Forgive me for being so weak back then."

In the past thirty years, the Lord has not carried me on another journey, and I can't blame anyone or anything, especially not God. I can't even blame Satan, but myself. I heard my own mouth tell the Lord, "I can't handle this." I'm not trying to make myself the victim, even though I am, but I really blew it that day. I know that both families plus lost that day, and it's my fault. Only God knows how many lives were changed because I told the Lord these four simple words (I can't handle this). Evidently, the Lord knew that I could not handle it, because He completely erased from my mind the journey He took me on that day. We all need to be careful with the words that we speak, especially the words we speak to our Lord. Believe me, you will get what you ask for.

If the Lord ever trusts me again and tries to use me in that way, I believe I will keep my mouth shut, except asking Him for help to hear what His Spirit is saying to the church. I will try to never quench the Spirit of God again. To tell you the TRUTH, I'm tired of beating myself up, because the Lord has forgiven me, and

I truly believe the Jackson family will forgive me also. I hope I get the chance to talk with them about this one day, because I will ask them for their forgiveness. Do you remember what I believe about repentance? I believe saying I'm sorry is music to God's ears also.

Food for thought: I write about this later, but I want to mention this now, so you can hear and see what you think about it. A thousand plus years from now, Jesus is going to destroy this earth and in Revelation 21:1-2 teaches us, that "we are going to have a new heaven, and a new earth for the first heaven and the first earth were passed away; and there was no more sea." Here I want you to think about our new world. There will be no cars or trucks or motorcycles I don't believe. And no airports. Ever since Jesus teleported me twice, I have believed, that is the way we will travel on our new earth. Matthew 5:5 Jesus says: "Blessed the meek: for they shall inherit the earth." Our new earth will be our Kingdom and Jesus' Bride will inherit the new earth.

I have gotten off the main subject of healing, but I'm about to continue writing how the Lord heals through man. But before I do, I want to say something about Emmett, Sandra, and the Jackson family. I don't really know why I wrote about them, but while I wrote, I had a few good memories, but the bad memories outweighed the good ones. It's not that I have more bad memories than good ones, but it's just I was writing more about the bad memories of that time period. Even though it was thirty-two years ago, it truly took a lot out of me to relive those days again in my mind. As I am writing these words, my hands are shaking, and my eyes are full of tears because of some of those bad memories. But I know when I go to Jesus in prayer, He will strengthen me again. As a matter of fact, as I think about it, the shaking hands and tearful eyes are strengthening me already to keep on running this race so I can make it home (to heaven).

When we read from Acts chapter 2, we only read a part of the story. Paul Harvey is one of the most well-known commentators of my generation. He was known as the man who said, "And here is the rest of the story." And I too will tell you the rest of the story from Acts chapter 2, when I write the last chapter of this book, about being born-again.

Soon, we are going to learn about the conversion (change of heart) of Saul. And you will learn that Saul has his name changed. Before you learn about Saul's conversion, you need to read Acts 7:51–60. As you start reading, you will hear Stephen preaching a hard sermon for them to swallow. In verse 58, you will see that Saul was there at the stoning (killing) of Stephen. If you will continue reading in Acts chapter 8, you will learn a little more about Saul. Read verses 1–4. In these scriptures, you will learn that at that time, Saul was one of the main persecutors of the church. After the death of Stephen, Saul continued his persecution on the church. In Acts 9:1–2, Luke teaches us about Saul's eagerness to stop what he believed to be a false teaching.

He was brought up to believe in one God (Jehovah). You are about to find out that Saul was fighting against God as he persecuted the church. Gamaliel had already warned the religious leaders about going against the apostle's teachings. Saul was one of the religious leaders at that time. I believe Saul was at that meeting when Gamaliel warned them. But Saul believed that he was serving God by rejecting the apostle's teachings, just as most do today. I'm here to tell you that the apostle's teachings were true then, and they are still true today (2,016 years later).

If you don't know, you are about to find out that no one can stand against the Lord. What Saul didn't know was that he was put on this earth for God's purpose. Saul was chosen by the Lord, while God was laying down the foundation of this world. Saul was to be God's mouthpiece of what he was fighting against. Saul (Paul) would be one of the most influential apostles the Lord chose to spread His message.

Now, we are going to find out about Saul's conversion and what it took to get Saul's attention toward the TRUTH. To find out about his conversion, we need to start in Acts 9:3. I'm going to write these scriptures because I want to bring out certain points as you read. Verses 3–4 say, "And as he [Saul] journeyed, he came near Damascus, and suddenly there shined round about him a light from heaven. And he fell to the earth, and heard a voice saying unto him, Saul, Saul, why persecutest thou me?"

This next verse is one that I want to explain. In verse 5, Saul asked the Lord a very direct question, when the Lord asked him, "Why persecutest thou me?" Saul asked, "Who art thou, Lord?" As you read this, I want you to remember this—Saul didn't believe in Jesus. He was working for Jehovah, trying to stop this imposter (Jesus) and His message. When Saul asked the Lord, "Who art thou, Lord?" he was asking, "Are you Jehovah God?" Here is what you need to learn. The Jehovah God of the Old Testament says, "I am Jesus whom thou persecutest." Here, Saul was about to learn that the God of the Old Testament came to earth as a human to redeem His people from this evil world. I believe the greatest mystery in God's word is that the God of the Old Testament became a man. Most people that have lived in this world have believed in the trinity or some other strange god. But I'm here to tell you that there is only one God, and His name is Jesus.

At the end of verse 5, Jesus says, "Hard for thee to kick against the pricks [ox goads]." For those of you who don't know what an ox goad is, it is a sharp pole used to drive animals. As they drove their animals, they would stick them with the goad to make them move. The ornery animals would sometimes kick in retaliation to being stuck, and that is what the Lord was saying to Saul—"You are kicking against the point."

Jesus was teaching Saul that the Old Testament teachings were just what they were. Old! Jesus is teaching Saul that he is fighting against the new and better way. Paul writes about this later in his life, as he writes the book of Hebrews. If you what to know the TRUTH about this, read Hebrews chapter 8. As you read God's word, just remember the words testament and covenant mean the same thing, and they both mean agreement.

As you are about to learn that after Saul's conversion, he immediately teaches about this New Testament, or agreement, that God has with His people. And he is still teaching us today that God's new name is Jesus. As you read this book, you will hear me use some of the same scriptures a few times. I hope you understand I'm trying to help you find the TRUTH. I will write about this later in this book, but I believe I should mention it now. I found all of God's names that were used in the entire Old Testament. Just in case you don't know, the Old Testament is about four times the size of the New Testament. God's name was recorded only a dozen or so times in the entire Old Testament. In the New Testament, God's name (Jesus) was mentioned 975 times. You have just heard the TRUTH, so on judgment day, you will have no excuse for not knowing His name.

We all need to learn to ask this question that Saul asked the Lord in Acts 9:6—"What wilt thou have me to do?" Then, the Lord says to Saul, "Arise, and go into the city, and it shall be told thee what thou must do." I hope you heard the last two words (must do) of the last sentence.

Verse 8 says, "And Saul arose from the earth, and when his eyes were opened, he saw no man, but they led him by the hand, and brought into Damascus." Verse 9 tells us, "And he [Saul] was three days without sight, and neither did eat nor drink."

In verse 10, the scriptures let us know who will be God's Christian contact that is going to help Saul come to the knowledge of the TRUTH. Ananias was the man that Saul needed to go and see to hear God's salvation plan. As you can see in these scriptures, God's plan for Saul's Christian life was beginning. I also want you to notice in these scriptures how Jesus communicated with Saul and Ananias to bring Saul into God's will.

In verses 11–12, the Lord tells Ananias where to find Saul in the city. In verses 13–14, Ananias tells the Lord, "I have heard by many of this man, how much evil he hath done to thy saints at Jerusalem. And here he hath authority from the chief priests to bind all that call on thy name." In verses 15–16, the Lord begins to inform Ananias that Saul is very important for His ministry. Jesus says to Ananias, "Go thy way: for he [Saul] is a chosen vessel unto me, to bear my name before the Gentiles, and kings, and the children of Israel. For I will shew him how great things he must suffer for my name's sake."

When the Lord told Ananias "to go thy way," what the Lord was saying to Ananias was "to go and do what I told you to do concerning Saul." You are about to see from the scriptures that Ananias did just as the Lord told him. Verse 17 tells us, "And Ananias went his way, and entered into the house; and putting his hands on him said, Brother Saul, the Lord Jesus, that appeared unto thee in the way as thou camest, hath sent me, that thou mightest receive thy sight, and be filled with the Holy Ghost."

As you can see in the last scripture, God heals Saul and then let him know through Ananias that he needed to be filled with God's Spirit. Verse 18 says, "Immediately there fell from his eyes as it had been scales, and he received sight forthwith, and arose, and was baptized." If you will continue reading Acts 9:19–31, you will learn how Saul grew in the Lord and spoke boldly in the name of Jesus. And just as the Jewish leaders had Jesus killed because of His message, they were going to try to kill Paul for that same message. I'm going to start writing Paul from now on because that is his new name. Read Acts 13:9. From that scripture forth, Saul was known as Paul.

In Acts 9:18, Luke says that Paul's eyes were healed, and he arose and was baptized. That scripture never says how he was baptized. You need to read Acts 22:16 to find out how Ananias told Paul to be baptized. In Acts 9:17–18, Ananias tells Paul to be filled with the Holy Ghost and to be baptized. Ananias tells Paul the same thing Apostle Peter told the Jews on the day of Pentecost—you must be born-again. Now, let's read Paul's testimony. You can find his testimony in Acts chapter 22. If you will read Acts chapter 22, it will help you understand what you read in Acts chapter 9 about Paul's conversion.

At this time, I want to tell you something that I believe about Apostle Paul. I'm going to say what the scriptures says and let you make up your own mind. First, I want you to read Philippians 3:3–6 and hear Paul's testimonial. Paul begins by saying in verse 3, "For we are the circumcision [Jews], which worship God in Spirit." In this verse, Paul claims to be a Jew.

In verses 5–6, Paul describes his lineage and his dedication to what he was brought up to believe about God. One of the commandments of God to the Jewish people is circumcision. That is why most of the writers of God's word referred to the Jewish people as the circumcision. Paul starts off in verse 5 by saying, "Circumcised the eighth day, of the stock of Israel, the tribe of Benjamin, an Hebrew of the Hebrews." Now, that was his lineage.

Now, you are about to see Paul's devotion toward what he had been taught as a young man. At the end of verse 5, Paul says, "As touching the law, a Pharisee." Just in case you don't know, a Pharisee is the strictest sect of the Jews concerning the law. In verse 6, Paul says, "Concerning zeal, persecuted the church." Then, he goes on to say, "Touching the righteousness which is in the law, blameless." I hope you will read the rest of chapter 3 in Philippians (7–21), and you will learn a lot more about Apostle Paul. Now, you have learned from God's word that Paul had been fighting against the new teaching in which he would become one of God's most valuable sowers of His word.

You just read in Philippians and heard Apostle Paul say that he was a Jew. Now, I want you to go back to Acts chapter 22 and find out what Paul asked one of the soldiers as they bound him with thongs. In verse 25, Paul says to the soldier who stood by, "Is it lawful for you to scourge a man that is a Roman, and uncondemned?"

Verse 26 says that when the centurion heard, he went and told the chief captain, saying, "Take heed what thou doest, for this man is a Roman."

Verse 27 says that the chief captain came and asked Paul, "Tell me, art thou a Roman?" Then, Paul answered him, yea. Then, the chief captain says to Paul in verse 28, "With a great sum obtained I this freedom." Then, Paul tells him, "But I was born." I have heard preachers (Franklin Gram) say that Apostle Paul was a Roman citizen.

And I know that Mr. Gram is way smarter than me in a lot of ways. And Apostle Paul might have been a Roman citizen, but I believe what Paul was saying in Acts 22:28 that he was born a Roman. As you can see, by what you have read, Paul has declared himself to be a Roman and a Jew. I started telling you about Paul by saying that I was going to share with you what I believed about him. There is only one way for Paul to be a Roman and a Jew. I believe that Paul was a mix breed between a Jew and a Gentile. I have come to believe, that Paul was a Samaritan. I will explain later. I have written what I know about the Samaritans in chapter 9.

As you can see by my writings, I don't care about Apostle Paul's lineage. This is what I know—God chose him and said to Ananias, "He is a chosen vessel unto me." And that is all I need to know. I'm just giving you my opinion about him. The TRUTH is I want to know what Apostle Paul taught so I can obey it and keep my name in the Book of Life. Paraphrasing Romans 2:16, Paul writes, "On judgment day, the people will be judged according to my [Paul's] gospel." Not only are you to learn God's word, but also you have got to obey the word. Obeying God's word is what keeps your name in the Book of Life.

I wrote and shared with you what I believe about Apostle Paul. As you study God's word, you will find that Apostle Paul was one of God's greatest men of the New Testament era. But now, we must continue learning about how Jesus heals through man. As you continue reading Acts chapter 9, you will find Apostle Peter being used by the Lord again to heal someone. Read Acts 9:32–35, and you will see how the Lord used Apostle Peter to heal a man named Aeneas. And not only did the man get healed, but also the scriptures say that after the man was healed, all that dwelt at Lydda and Saron saw him and turned to the Lord. As you can see, not only were the sick blessed that day, but also all who saw the miracle turned to the Lord. Notice what Peter says in verse 34, "Jesus Christ maketh thee whole." Apostle Peter knew who the GREAT PHYSICIAN is.

In Acts 9:36–42, you will find Apostle Peter being used by the Lord again to raise the dead. It says in verse 42 that this miracle "was known throughout all Joppa; and many believed in the Lord." Just imagine if this was your mother or sister that was brought back to life. I believe everyone who knew her would know that it was a miracle from God, and just like those folks, many would turn to the Lord. You included! When people see Jesus do a miracle such as this, most who see it wants to learn more about Jesus and will turn to Him. In the last chapter of this book, you will learn that Peter didn't just come to Joppa by chance. The Lord led him there so he could open the door for us Gentiles to God's plan of salvation. We will study this later in Acts chapter 10.

This next healing that I want you to read about is in Acts chapter 14. You will find the Lord using Apostle Paul to heal a crippled man, who was crippled from birth. You can find this story in verses 8–15. When you find yourself in a similar situation and God has used you to lay hands on and heal someone or just simply witnessing on your job, I want you to remember what Paul and Barnabas did when the people began to lift them up and even wanted to sacrifice unto them.

Verses 14–15 tell us that when Paul and Barnabas heard that the people were going to do a sacrifice unto them, they tore their clothes and ran among the people and cried out, "Sirs, why do ye these things? We also are men of like passions with you, and preach unto you that ye should turn from these vanities unto the living God, which made heaven, and earth, and the sea, and all things that are therein." If you can learn this, you will have learned one of the most important lessons to becoming a saint. It's Jesus—period. You can't do anything without Him. If you will always remember that and obey God's word, you will live with God throughout eternity.

Read Acts 16:16–18, and you will find Apostle Paul casting out an unclean spirit (devil) from a young woman. Verse 19 says, "When her masters saw that the hope of their gains was gone, they caught Paul and Silas, and drew into the marketplace unto the rulers." As you continue reading verses 20–33, you will see how the Lord allowed His servants to be thrown into prison. When you give yourself to the Lord, you never know where you will have to go to win a soul. As you read this story, remember that the Lord can do anything.

In verse 25, you will see how Paul and Silas witnessed to all the prisoners by praying and singing praises to their God. I also want you to see from these scriptures how the Lord shook this prison with an earthquake. And as you will see (hear), God shook the prison so hard that it opened all the doors that kept the prisoners secure. The Lord then shook loose everyone's bonds from their feet. Now, that's a miracle in itself, but nothing compared to what the Lord can accomplish.

The scriptures don't say this but the Lord shook loose something else that night—the guard's heart. God used an earthquake to bring salvation to this family that night. As far as I know, this is the second earthquake used by the Lord to save someone. The first earthquake, in which I believe souls were saved, happened when the Lord was crucified. You can read about this earthquake in Matthew 27:28–54. I believe since then, the Lord has used many earthquakes to change hearts and minds. If you find yourself in one of God's disasters, listen really closely for the Lord's voice; it just might be your time. If I ever get caught in an earthquake or bad storm, I believe that Lord Jesus will be the first thing that comes out of my mouth.

In Acts 19:11–12, you will find that the Lord worked special miracles through the hands of Paul. As you are about to find out, the Apostle Paul didn't have to come in physical contact with the sick or the demon-possessed. God used him to help people through a handkerchief or an apron. Now, the scriptures don't say what Paul actually did or spoke over these items, but whatever he did, it worked according to God's will. As you now know, Jesus can be a long-distance healer. I want to be really clear about all these healings. If the Apostle Paul were here, he would be the first to tell you that it is Jesus that heals.

The next healing can be found in Acts 20:7–12. I say that it's a healing, but it was much more than that. As you read these scriptures, you will learn that the Apostle Paul was a long-winded preacher. You should also learn not to go to sleep in church because you just might fall off the pew and find yourself in a similar situation. This young man was blessed to have the Apostle Paul preaching to them that night. But more blessed than that, this young man had found favor with Jesus, for Jesus was not through using him. Even though he died for a while, God's grace and mercy was still on his life. Again, the scriptures don't say this, but I believe after that night, this young man truly began serving the Lord. Wouldn't you? And I also believe that he never went to sleep in church again. Would you?

To hear how this next healing took place, you need to read Acts chapter 27. After the shipwreck, and when they all made it to land, the Apostle Paul was bitten by a snake. You can read about this in Acts 28:1–6. As you read about this, you will see that the snake was fastened on Paul's hand. The scriptures say that the snake hung on Paul's hand. You can see that the people of this island knew that this snake was poisonous, and it was pumping venom into Paul's hand. Verse 6 says, "Howbeit they looked when he should have swollen, or fallen down dead suddenly: but after they had looked a great while, and saw no harm come to him, they changed their minds, and said that he was a god."

Now, the snake bite was not the healing that I was referring to. The healing came after the people of this island saw no harm has come to Paul. In verse 7, the scriptures say that Publius was the chief man of the island.

Verse 7 also says that Publius gave them a place to stay for three days and did it courteously. In verse 8, you will find that Publius' father was sick of a fever and a bloody flux. I don't know for sure what a bloody flux would be, but I know that it doesn't matter, because Jesus is the GREAT PHYSICIAN.

At the end of verse 8, Paul went to where he was, prayed, and laid his hands on him and healed him. As I read these scriptures, I can see faith beginning to grow in these people. Verse 9 tells us that when they saw what was done to this sick man, the others from the island who had diseases came and were healed. And as one would imagine, when it was time for them to go on their way, Publius made sure they had everything they needed for their journey. Verse 11 says that after three months, they departed. Now, the scriptures don't speak of Paul preaching or salvation coming to anyone. But I believe if Apostle Paul stayed there for three months, there was preaching, and salvation came to these people. I don't believe that the Apostle Paul would even go one day without preaching and teaching the salvation message to whomever he came in contact with. That was just how he lived his Christian life.

Now that you have read about most of the healings that are in God's word, as you now know, the scriptures are really clear how to communicate with the Lord and how to be healed. Always remember that if we will obey what we learn from God's word, He will keep His word (promises). If we will pray and fast in faith, God will move every mountain that gets in our way.

Let your faith grow by reading Matthew 17:15–21. Also, read Matthew 6:5–8, Matthew 6:25–34, Matthew 7:7–11, and Matthew

18:18–20. Again, if you will do His word, He will keep His promises. In Matthew 12:50, Jesus says, "For whosoever shall do the will of my Father which is in heaven, the same is my brother, and sister, and mother." Believe me—if God had to, He would bankrupt heaven to meet His family's needs. Read Philippians 4:19.

Now, there are certain times wherein the Lord will not heal someone, even though they have faith. But in those rare cases, the Lord will have a specific reason for not doing so. I want you to read about Apostle Paul and his lack of ability to be healed. I hope you understand that very few of God's people will be as strong in the Lord as the Apostle Paul was while in our flesh. While you read these next scriptures, I want you to hear and understand what Paul learned from the Lord. Read 2 Corinthians 12:1–10.

As you read these scriptures, you will have a clearer understanding of why Paul wasn't healed. You will see that even the Apostle Paul knew why he wasn't healed. Paul knew where he stood in the Lord with the Lord. He also knew that he was a man of God and that he was still growing in the knowledge of God. Here in these scriptures, he wrote with his own hand that he would come to more visions and revelations. The simple fact is the Lord didn't heal him so he would stay humble. And Paul knew that and was glad to suffer in his flesh for the Lord's sake.

In 2 Corinthians 12:6, Paul says, "For though I would desire to glory [brag], I shall not be a fool; for I will say the TRUTH: but I forbear, lest [I fear that] any man should think of me above that which he seeth me, or he heareth of me." He continues in verse 7, "And lest [I fear that] I should be exalted above measure through the abundance of the revelations, there was given to me a thorn in the flesh, the messenger of Satan to buffet me, lest [I fear that] I should be exalted above measure." Verse 7 teaches me that the Lord with His foreseeable mind wanted to keep Apostle Paul humble.

And so the Lord allowed Satan to give Paul a thorn in his flesh so he would stay humble (not boast of what he has done) and preach the TRUTH. I have heard different preachers say that the thorn in his flesh was this or that, but no one would really know except when the Lord reveals it to them. Paul says in verse 8, "For this thing I besought the Lord thrice, that it might depart from me."

The Lord tells Paul in verse 9, "My grace is sufficient for thee: for my strength is made perfect in weakness." As soon as Paul heard these words from the Lord, Paul replies by saying, "Most gladly therefore will I rather glory in my infirmities, that the power of Christ may rest upon me. Therefore I take pleasure in infirmities, in reproaches, in necessities, in persecutions, in distresses for Christ's sake: for when I am weak, then am I strong" (verses 9– 10).

As I was proofreading this book, I could not stop crying as I read the last paragraph about how strong Apostle Paul was in the Lord, because he became humble before the Lord. He knew from where his strength came, and he allowed—yes, he allowed—Jesus to lead and guide him daily. I was crying, because I could see myself not having the mind of Jesus, as Apostle Paul had. Paul teaches us about having the mind of Jesus in Philippians 2:1–11. As I read these scriptures again, I saw something that I want to thank the Lord for. I'm so thankful to the Lord that He has given me enough sense to bow my knees and to confess with my tongue NOW that Jesus is Lord and not to be made to later as many will be.

I truly believe that I'm a part of the body of Christ. But as I read about Paul's humbleness and his position in the body, I feel as if I'm the little toenail. To know a little more about what I'm talking about, read 1 Corinthians 12:1–31. But this toenail continued reading 1 Corinthians chapter 13, and I'm learning to humble myself to our Lord and learning about the more excellent way to live. I truly thank the Lord for everything in my life. Jesus gave me my first breath, and He watched over me my whole life, and I plan to give Him my last breath. To tell you the TRUTH, I might be the little toenail, and that's okay with me. I am so blessed to be a part of the body, and this little toenail is going to work diligently for the rest of the body.

We must all seek for what Paul found in the Lord, and you can find what Paul teaches us in Romans, 1 Corinthians, 2 Corinthians, Galatians, Ephesians, Philippians, Colossians, 1 Thessalonians, 2 Thessalonians, 1 Timothy, 2 Timothy, Titus, and Philemon; and I also believe that the Apostle Paul wrote the book of Hebrews. In fact, the Apostle Paul wrote over half of the New Testament. Remember what he says in Romans 2:16.

Now that you have read the word of God that teaches us with the milk of the word, in the next four chapters, we are going to learn about some of the false teachings that are being taught every day. While we are leaning about the false teachings, we are also going to get into the meat of God's word. The milk is the TRUTH, while not only is the meat the TRUTH, but also it has always been tougher to chew and harder to swallow.

This is why we must grow in God so when it's time, we will be able to eat the meat (word) that the Lord has for us. We all must become mature in the Lord so that we can endure sound doctrine (teaching). Read Hebrews 5:11–14. Before we leave this chapter, here is something else that we all need to remember and never forget. Read again 1 Corinthians 6:18–20. The price has been paid (Jesus dying on the cross). If you will turn to the Lord and obey His word, He will answer your prayers.

Do you remember the woman who had the blood disease for twelve years in Matthew 9:20–22? She believed that if she could just touch the hem of Jesus' garment, it would make her whole. And she did touch the hem of His garment, and she was made whole. But Jesus told her "thy faith hath made thee whole".

The TRUTH is that she had done more than touch the hem of His garment. If you will read how Mark recorded this story in Mark 5:24–34, you will learn that this woman had drawn out virtue from Jesus. She had tapped into the fruit of the Spirit (Galatians 5:22–23) that day. Here, you will see that this woman was on her knees on the ground. When Jesus turned to see who it was that touched Him, He saw this woman at His feet. She humbled herself before the Lord and was healed because of her faith. I'm just saying. I hope you can hear what I just wrote.

If you can't hear, ask Jesus for spiritual ears, so you can hear. Notice that in Matthew 9:22, Jesus calls her His daughter. This tells me that He is the Father (Creator). As I have said earlier, the Creator created us, and He knows how to fix us. If we will do our part, Jesus will do His. I can't say it any plainer than that. Before I close this chapter, I want to give you a few scriptures that teach about being humble—Matthew 18:3–4, Matthew 23:12, James 4:6–10, and 1 Peter 5:5–6. Heaven is a kingdom, and God's words are the kingdom rules, and we had better obey His rules.

Chapter 2

THE MORMONS

In Jude verse 3, Jude says that there is a common salvation. As you now know, Apostles Peter and Paul knew what they were talking about, because both of these men had wisdom and understanding given to them by God. As you continue reading, you will find out why the religious groups and denominational churches all teach a different message. I don't like to throw around names, but we are looking for the TRUTH. I've got to mention some of these religious groups, because we can clearly see a false teaching that is not of God. This false teaching is what Peter was warning us about when he taught us about wresting the scriptures.

The first religious group I am going to write about are the Mormons. If you don't know, you will soon find out that you can't learn about the Mormons without hearing the names Joseph Smith and Brigham Young. In the new America, there were new religions sprouting up everywhere. It was such a religious fever in the land. These newfound religions brought around divisions in American society. These divisions were also in the Smith household. The history book teaches us that Joseph's father was a Universalist, and his mother was a Presbyterian, and their children didn't know which way they should go. This same confusion is still in the world today (2015) to everyone who do not know God's TRUTH.

It was in this time of confusion that young Joseph, then just fourteen years old, had the first of his visions. This is the story Joseph told and what devout Mormons believe happened. According to Smith, when he was fourteen years old, his visions started, and his first vision came to him in a small grove of trees. Smith tells how the power of God was so strong that he was afraid the trees were going to burst in flames. He says in this grove of trees, God the Father and Jesus Christ revealed themselves in human form to him.

A historian named K. Jensen, from the Church of Latter Day Saints, said that when God and Jesus came to Joseph, Joseph asked this question, which of the churches are true? This sounds so ridiculous for me to write, but I must write what I have learned. Jensen never said which one (God or Jesus) answered, but Jensen said that it was told to Joseph that none of the churches were true. And as you are about to find out in this book, the Mormon church is not true either.

If Joseph was fourteen years old, so that would be the year 1820. I have studied God's word for thirty-two years, and I know for sure that according to the scriptures, it was not God (Jesus) who gave this answer to Joseph. This vision, which Joseph had that day, could not have been God, because He (Jesus) had already begun establishing the true church 1,820 years before Joseph's fourteenth birthday. Someone has to be wrong about this, and I know it's not God, so that only leaves Joseph Smith. Joseph Smith will be held accountable for these false statements.

As I write this book, I know that I will be held accountable for any false statements I make.

About thirty minutes ago, before I started reading and writing, I anointed my head and heart with oil. I asked the Lord, in the name of Jesus, to help my brain for understanding and to touch my heart so I would obey His word. I truly believe that the Lord has inspired me to write this book and given me the words to write. I know this about myself before I started studying and writing about the Mormons, I knew nothing about them. I'm just writing about what I know in God, and it doesn't match up with what the Mormons teach. I have a delete button on my computer, and the Lord has not instructed me to delete, but as you can see, I'm still writing.

If you will continue reading this book, you will find out who has the TRUTH. I too want to make a bold statement. As you continue reading this book, you will hear my bold statement a few times, and it is the following: there is one true God and one true church. Here is another bold statement—I must say with full assurance from the Lord that I'm not falsely accusing anyone, but the Church of Latter Day Saints is not God's church.

The encyclopedias record that twenty-one-year-old Joseph Smith, in the year 1827, was guided to the top of a hill one night by an angel named Moroni. There, he found the golden plates that Moroni said that he and his father Mormon wrote. I have got to say at this time that I have never heard about an angel having a father or mother until now. I personally don't believe this, and I pray you don't either. I just had to throw in my two cents about that. For the next two and a half years, Joseph Smith translated the reformed Egyptian language that was written on the golden plates to what is now the Book of Mormons. According to the encyclopedia, he translated the writings from the golden plates with the aid of magic spectacles that he claimed to have found on a hill named Cumorah, near Palmyra, New York.

When Joseph Smith finished translating the writings, which were on these golden plates, he and five of his friends looked upon it as holding truths that should be added to those of the Bible. Remember what John wrote in Revelation 22:18–19 about what God will do to anyone who adds or takes away from His word. Joseph Smith didn't just take away from God's word, but he was used by Satan and added a whole book. Smith and his friends founded this church in April 1830, and throughout the years, they have numbered in the millions of members. Here is something else you should know about. The Mormons believe Joseph Smith to be a prophet equal to Mohammed, Isaiah, Jeremiah, and even Moses.

During the first few years, they had problems with the other religious groups in western New York, because they claimed to have found a new teaching from God. The Catholics and the Protestants thought they were the only religious groups that could change (add or take away) from God's word. I will explain a little later in chapters 4 and 5 how the Catholics and the Protestants have changed God's word.

The Mormons called their movement the New Church, and so it was to them. The Mormons had stirred up all of the other churches in western New York with this new teaching. These churches thought that the Mormons were wrong in their beliefs. They treated the Mormons so cruelly that they were forced to move westward. For several years, the Mormons found peace in Nauvoo, Illinois.

In the summer of 1843, in Joseph's office above the general store, Joseph says, that God visited him and commanded him, "My [God's] people to live in plural marriages." According to Smith, God told him that by doing so, they would progress to the highest level of heaven as gods. But the cruel and unjust treatment began again in 1844 when Joseph Smith and his brother Hyrum were murdered by a mob in the nearby town of Carthage.

The same year that Joseph was murdered, Brigham Young became the leader of their church. Young led the Mormons even farther west, to the Great Salt Lake in Utah. Satan used Young to teach what Smith began to teach that which is contrary to God's word, and the people fell for it. Some of the Mormons still practice this teaching today (2015). Young taught polygamy—that a man could marry more than one wife. I wonder why Young didn't teach that a woman could have five or six husbands. I believe when Young taught about a woman having five or six men, she was a whore. This is my belief, and you can have yours. I believe Brigham Young was a pervert, and it's no telling what else he taught that was false. God's word teaches that a man or a woman is to have only one spouse at a time.

Here is something else you should know while we are on this subject. There are two ways that is recorded in God's word that allow anyone to get a divorce. The first is for fornication, which means you found out that your spouse has been unfaithful and has had sex with another. Read Matthew 19:3–9. The other way is death. 1 Corinthians 7:39 tells us that after your spouse dies, you are at liberty to be married again. But there is only one catch—Paul says that only in the Lord. You can believe who you want to, Brigham Young or God! For your information, this church is known today as the Church of Jesus Christ of Latter Day Saints.

Here are two good questions I ask them, when they try to convert me. If the Book of Mormons is so important for our salvation, why did God wait one thousand eight hundred and twenty-seven years, after the New Testament church started, to send it? I would also like to know what will happen to all of the souls before this new teaching got to earth. God could have sent a tornado or an earthquake or any other method of destruction and snuffed out these six people who started this false church and stopped millions from following this false doctrine, but He didn't.

Jesus, which is God in the flesh, said in John 14:6, "I am the TRUTH." The devil, which is Satan, is the opposite of God. Satan is a liar, which is false. God has allowed Satan to have these false-doctrine religious groups throughout the whole world so all mankind would have a choice of whom they will serve.

I believe that all this really happened to Joseph Smith, but it is not God's TRUTH. God could have sent Joseph Smith a strong delusion so he and his followers would believe a lie and be dammed. You can read in God's word why God will send a strong delusion to someone. You can find this TRUTH in 2 Thessalonians 2:10–12. Verse 10 says, "They received not the love of the TRUTH." God will have them to believe a lie and be dammed. Again, I'm not going to leave Satan out of the equation; it could have been Satan's way of deceiving millions of people. Either way, it is false. Smith should not have listened to the angel Moroni; instead, he should have read what Paul wrote about listening to an angel in Galatians 1:6–9.

Remember that what Paul wrote—not we or an angel from heaven has the right to preach another gospel. I also want you to read 2 Corinthians 11:13–15. What I have learned about the history of the Mormons and how they got this religious group started, it sounds to me like the Santa Claus story, but billions have believed in Santa Claus for years also.

When Satan and the angels that followed him rebelled, they made war in heaven and lost. Satan and his angels were thrown out of heaven, down to earth. Paul called Satan the god of this world in 2 Corinthians 4:4. Do not be deceived; Satan has taken on the form of religions. He started a long time ago deceiving multitudes of people. Everyone can see Satan in the bars and in the dance halls, but most people are so spiritually blind that they can't see him in all of the false-doctrine churches. Don't just take my word for it; look up the Mormons in the encyclopedia or your computer and find out the history of this religious group for yourselves.

I thought that I was finished writing about the Mormons, but I have found something else that I believe is worth writing about. I believe that I found out something that most Mormons don't know. There was a TV show back in the 1960s called *Death Valley Days*. On the western channel, they have started running those old shows again. *Death Valley Days* was a show that told true stories about how in the 1800s, the pioneers made their way West to pursue happiness. As I watched one day, the show was about the Mormons and Salt Lake City, so I just had to watch.

The show was about a man who was prophesied to by Joseph Smith to be a defender of their church. His name was Orrin Porter Rockwell. I can only write the way I know how, so I am going to write about it scene by scene. The show starts with this man who just witnessed a gunfight. The man tells the gunslinger, "The man you killed had a wife and three kids." Then, he adds, "You're pretty fast with a gun."

The gunslinger replied, "You will never see faster."

The man tells him, "I've seen faster, but it was not here in California. It was up in Utah, in the land of Zion."

He said that he was passing through there once and saw this fellow take a gunslinger faster than an eye can blink. The Destroying Angel, they call him. He is Brigham Young's right hand. They say that he has killed over a hundred men, and everybody in Utah knows about him. Some call him a saint, and others call him a hard cold-blooded killer. The curious thing about him, the story goes, is that he can't be killed by a bullet—that he is invincible.

According to the man, when he passed through Salt Lake City, he witnessed one of Porter's gunfights. When Porter was shot, but the bullet did not even pass through his coat. In fact, the Destroying Angel simply shook his coat, and the bullet fell to the floor. Porter claimed that there was not a scratch on him.

The gunslinger says to the man, "You sure must have been liquored up."

The man tells him that he doesn't drink and never has. "I'm telling you just what I saw," said the man.

The man had just watched this gunslinger gun down a man, and he told the gunslinger. The man he just gunned down was just a plain old dirt farmer and not much with a gun. But the Avenging Angel, the man that could take him, would really have something to jaw (talk) about. The gunslinger tells him, "I've always wanted to see Utah."

Then, the man replied, "The one they call the Destroying Angel lives just outside of Salt Lake City."

The gunslinger asked him, "And he can't be killed by a bullet?"

The man replied, "So the story goes."

Then, the show jumped to Utah, where Porter Rockwell was having a gunfight with two men. After he kills them, he stood over them and said, "Lord have mercy on your black souls." Then, he went into the General Store and shook the bullet out of his coat and told the storekeeper, "Gunfighters keep coming to try me." Then, he asked the storekeeper, "Why do they seek me out?"

The storekeeper replied, "Porter's name is known throughout every State west of St. Louis. And you are a trophy to every gunslinger and a prize."

Porter told the storekeeper that he only did what had to be done. "Brigham Young, himself, weighed me with that obligation. Is this not true?" Porter asked the storekeeper.

The storekeeper replied, "Everyone in the land of Zion knows that, Brother Porter."

Then, Porter said, "But still they come."

The storekeeper replied, "One of those two men got off a shot at you. Are you sure you're all right?"

Porter told him, "Not a scratch. See for yourself."

When the storekeeper looked at him, he said, "I could have sworn."

As the story continues, the gunslinger from California arrives in Utah where Porter lives. The first place he stops is at the General Store. The storekeeper tells him that he is closing the store, because there is a funeral that afternoon and that folks around there pay respect for the dead. "We don't like to do business on a day of death," said the storekeeper.

The gunslinger tells him that he heard that Porter Rockwell killed these two men. And then he asked, "What happened?"

The storekeeper replied, "They defied Porter, and they would still be alive had they hightailed out of here. They made the grave mistake trying to take down Brother Rockwell."

Then, the gunslinger said, "Two against one ain't bad odds."

The storekeeper told him, "Maybe two ain't enough. Maybe three ain't enough against Brother Rockwell, or four, not with guns anyway."

The gunslinger said, "I've heard that story about him. He is supposed to be invincible. They say he can't be killed by bullets."

The storekeeper replied, "I have never seen him be touched by a bullet."

The gunslinger turned and walked away and said, "Hogwash."

The storekeeper told him, "For what it's worth mister, I've known Orrin Porter Rockwell ever since he came to Utah, and I've seen him in a dozen gunfights and never get a scratch. Just the way Joseph Smith prophesied."

The gunslinger asked, "Do you believe that?"

He replied, "So far, I ain't seen nothing to make me believe otherwise."

The gunslinger took twenty dollars from him and nailed it to his wall. Then, he bets the storekeeper the twenty dollars that he will put a bullet into their Destroying Angel, before he leaves the land of Zion. And then he told the storekeeper as he was walking out the door, "I will be back for that money tacked up there, after I have destroyed your Destroying Angel."

After the gunslinger left, the storekeeper goes to Porter's house and warns him of this gunslinger. He tells Porter, "This gunslinger looks meaner than the others and more determined."

Porter replied, "They are all mean and determined.

The storekeeper asked Porter, "What are you going to do?"

Porter said, "I'm going to pray, but I don't think my prayers will be heard. Somehow, it seems to be written in the book that I'm ordained to get rid of men like that."

Then, Porter went off looking for him. As Porter leaves, the storekeeper asked him, "Is there anything I can do?"

Porter replied, "There is nothing anyone can do."

When the storekeeper left, he stumbled across the gunslinger's camp first and tried to get him to leave and that he can have the twenty dollars. The storekeeper told him, "Any man's life is worth more than twenty dollars, even yours."

The gunslinger asked him, "Is Rockwell a friend of yours?"

The storekeeper told him, "Porter is a friend to everyone in this land, to the church."

The gunslinger said, "To the church, a man who is supposed to have killed over one hundred men."

The storekeeper replied, "I don't know how many he has had to kill. But I know he has blazed trails for the church to move here, to help Brigham Young to settle the land of Zion, and protected people with his own life."

Then, the gunslinger asked him, "And all those killings, what about them?"

The storekeeper answered, "Only God can judge such things."

As you can see by the gunslinger's question, he even knew that Porter was wrong for these killings.

As the gunslinger mounted his horse to leave, the storekeeper asked him his name. He told the storekeeper that his name is Emmet Cashman and added that he should remember it and that everybody from Missouri to California will know it one day soon. I don't believe so far that everybody knows that name (Emmet Cashman). Just maybe through this book, more will hear his name, but I don't believe it will make a whole lot of difference.

The storekeeper replied, "The reason I want to know your name is because I want to know what to write on your headstone, because you are already dead."

The gunslinger slapped him and rode off. As he rode away, the storekeeper said, "God have mercy on you."

Then, the show focused on Porter and his wife. As Porter started to leave to find the gunslinger, his wife said, "The Avenging Angel, they call you, yet the Lord said, 'Vengeance is mine.'"

Porter told her, "I protect my people that Brother Brigham Young put under my obligation."

His wife said to him, "You have changed. With each new killing, you become more of a stranger to me. I think even to yourself."

As he walked away, he stopped and said, "Has your female tongue had enough of its venomous exercise now?"

Then Porter rode away looking for the gunslinger. They crossed paths in a desert place, and the gunslinger must have been a little spooked, because he already had his gun in his hand, as he rode up behind Porter. Porter turned around and told him, "Go home stranger."

The gunslinger replied that he will leave, when he is finished.

Porter started telling him, "Those who live by the sword—"

But then the gunslinger stopped him midsentence, "Don't sob sing me. Besides, what about you? You're supposed to have killed a hundred men. I have only tallied nine, and you will make ten."

Porter asked, "Where do you get the gall to seek me out? Or even dare to dream that you can kill me?"

The gunslinger answered, "I don't buy all those stories about you, Rockwell. All that holy mumbo jumbo about prophecies. Don't ruffle my feathers one bit. Even God couldn't protect Himself against a .44 fired point blank into His gut."

Porter was angered at that statement and said, "You blaspheme. You defile His very name with your filthy tongue."

The gunslinger then told Porter, "I'm going to blow that prophecy and you full of holes—"

Holes was the last word the gunslinger said, just before Porter blew him out of his saddle. Porter just sat there looking at the gunslinger, as he died and never said a word. Then, Porter took the gunslinger's horse by the reins and rode away, leaving the gunslinger in the dirt.

The next scene shows a wagon with the gunslinger's casket and a headstone that reads

The next scene shows the storekeeper and Porter back at the store. He said to Porter, "I was there up on the hill, and I saw the whole thing. He could have shot you in the back and killed you."

Porter replied, "No, he wouldn't have killed me."

The storekeeper asked him, "Tell me, Brother Porter, do you believe in the prophecy of Joseph Smith, that you can't be killed by a bullet, that God protects you?"

He continued saying, "Yesterday when one of those two men shot you, and the bullet was lodged in your coat, has it happened before?"

Porter answered, "There are two layers of wool on the outside and a thick lining of sheep's skin on the inside. Maybe a bullet can't penetrate it.

The storekeeper then said, "Maybe, then you're not sure yourself how it happened."

Porter replied, "I don't know when it started, two, maybe three years ago. I felt something funny inside, something cold, but strong as steel. Then, suddenly I knew they couldn't kill me. None of them."

The storekeeper said, "Then you do believe in the prophecies."

Porter turned, walked across the store, and got his hat and said, "I know I'm alive."

The storekeeper asked him, "How else can you explain it?"

Porter replied, "How do we know what the Almighty has ordained for us? We can't question what will be—only what is and what has been." Then, he walked out of the store.

The show ends with the storekeeper looking at the bullet that fell from Porter's coat and him taking down his twenty-dollar bill off the wall.

At the end of each *Death Valley Days* show, they have the host explain the show that you have seen. I don't know the host's name, but a lot of the shows are hosted by Ronald Reagan. After this show was over, they showed the host sitting on a horse and saying, "A great controversy still surrounds the legend of the Avenging Angel. He is still revered by some and disclaimed and despised by others. Did divine providence really protect him from the bullets? Was Joseph Smith's prophecy true? Well, one fact is certain—Orrin Porter Rockwell, Mormon leader, pioneer, scout, and acute assassin, died of natural causes in Salt Lake City in 1878 at the age of sixty-five."

Please remember that I'm not trying to offend anyone. I'm trying to share the TRUTH so you will know the TRUTH. I can't help it if the TRUTH about the false teachings offends you, because that's not my intention, but this is the TRUTH to me. What most people don't understand is that the Old Testament is old and the New Testament is new. I still don't understand their thinking on that. We are not supposed to be living in, or living under, the Old Testament Laws. If you will read Hebrews 8:6–13, you will learn how the Old Covenant became old so the New Covenant could start. When you read Hebrews 8:6–13, just remember that when you read the word "Covenant," it is the same as agreement or testament.

Now, God has made a New Covenant or Testament so we must live according to those kingdom rules and not the Laws of the Old Covenant. Read Galatians 5:18 and then Hebrews 9:11–17, and you will see that the New Testament could not start until Jesus died on the cross.

Even though the Old Testament Laws (the Ten Commandments) were abolished, though we don't live under the Law, we can still learn from it. Read 1 Timothy 1:8–10 and 2 Timothy 3:16. They still apply to the New Testament Laws (the law of liberty). Remember about the law of liberty in James 1:21–25. Also read 2 Corinthians 3:17–18. Read Galatians 3:21–25 to learn that the Old Testament Laws were a schoolmaster for the Jewish nation, which are our ancestors, if you are born-again. When Jesus died for us on the cross, we (everyone on this planet) are supposed to be living under a New Agreement that God wanted with His people. If you don't want to serve God and man with His New Agreement, I can only say this—you will not be a part of His Bride. As you now know, after reading the scriptures in Hebrews chapter 8, God's Laws are no longer written on tables of stone (the Ten Commandments), but in the minds and hearts of His people. If you seek the Lord for the TRUTH, He will put His Laws into your mind and write them in your heart. Then, you will be living in the perfect law of liberty that Apostle James taught us.

I wrote all of that to explain how the Lord used avenging angels in the Old Testament, but in the New Testament, the Lord has reserved vengeance for Himself. Now in the Old Testament times, the Lord would send His angels to earth to take care of certain problems that were happening, and there were many times He did so.

Here is one of those times, and it's a great example. You can find this TRUTH in Isaiah chapter 37. To make a long story short, I'm just going to highlight the main points of this TRUTH. Hezekiah was the king of Judah, and the king of Assyria was trying to take control of Judah and some of the countries around them. Hezekiah went to the Lord in prayer and told Him how great He is and asked Him to take care of this problem. Read verses 33– 36 where you will learn how God can and will defend Jerusalem and His people. Verse 36 says, "The angel of the Lord went forth, and smote in the camp of the Assyrians." And then the scripture tells us that this angel killed 185,000 Assyrians that night. Now, that is what I call an Avenging Angel. Later, you will learn about God's angels that will release His wrath upon the earth, but that will not happen until the New Testament era is complete and the church has gone to heaven.

The Mormons' religion started in 1827, when the angel visited Joseph Smith on the hillside near Palmyra, New York. This means that the New Testament had already been established 1,827 years earlier. And as you now know, the Mormon teachings started off wrong. It happened when Joseph Smith listened to an angel, instead of obeying what Apostle Paul had written for us to do. Now, I know very little about the Book of Mormons. But what I do know about the Mormons is that I believe they are trying to live under the Old Testament rules, instead of the New Testament.

Remember back when Porter's wife said to him, "The Lord said, 'Vengeance is Mine.'" Read Romans 12:17–21. In these scriptures, Paul is teaching the opposite of what Porter Rockwell was doing. Now, Porter's wife was taught those words, which she quoted to him that day. She must have read these scriptures found in Romans. She knew that Porter was not doing the work of the Lord, because he killed. I have never heard of any time in the New Testament era, where the Lord has sent one of His angels to earth as an avenger. Again, the Lord has reserved vengeance for Himself, until He comes back for His Bride (the church). And then again, the Lord is going to display His vengeance one thousand years later when the last war (the Battle of Armageddon) takes place.

After I wrote this about Porter Rockwell, I Googled Orrin Porter Rockwell, and I learned more about him than the show had to teach. When I started writing about this man, I was ignorant and made a foolish statement. I said that I had found something that most Mormons didn't know about. I was wrong! This just goes to show that we must read and study before we can make a statement, about something being TRUTH. Now, I believe that not only do most Mormons know about Rockwell, but also they believe he was an

Avenging Angel. Google Orrin Porter Rockwell, and see for yourself what he was. If you want to watch this show, I'm sure you can find it on your computer. Just look for *Death Valley Days, Son of Thunder Series* and Episode 31 (1969). After reading this chapter, you now know what I believe about the Mormons' teachings. My prayer is that you come to the same conclusion about their false teaching, because we all need to find and obey God's TRUTH.

CHAPTER 3

THE MUSLIMS

The next religious group I'm going to write about are the Muslims. The Muslims are one of the largest religious groups in the world. As you read about the history of the Muslims in your encyclopedia or computer, you will see that they and the Mormons have a lot of similarities in terms of how both religious groups were started. The Muslim's religion is called Islam.

According to the encyclopedia, the Muslims believe that Jesus was just a prophet. They don't believe Jesus was God's son, nor do they believe that Jesus was and is the Lord from heaven. Being a servant of God and knowing what I know in the scriptures, I know what I just wrote about what the Muslims believe and don't believe will get them or anyone else in a lot of trouble with God.

Muslims said that God decided to send down a message whose meaning could not be twisted. The encyclopedia pointed out that this message would tell men what they needed to know in order to be happy in this world and in the next. I have to say something about these last two statements. I know for a fact that God didn't decide to send down another message.

I believe and study the King James Bible. I know for sure that our brother Paul wrote to us about six hundred years before this so-called new message came to earth. I'm going to mention this passage of scriptures a few times in this book, and I have to mention it now. You can find these scriptures in Galatians 1:6–9. Verse 8 tells us, "But though we [the apostles], or an angel from heaven, preach any other gospel unto you than that which we have preached unto you, let him be accursed." I believe that the interpretation of this verse is that every person in this world, since the day of Pentecost (first day of the church), needs to obey what Jesus told the apostles to preach and what they wrote and not to listen to any other doctrine, or they would find themselves separated from God.

I believe it is so important that we understand how Satan works. I will not hesitate to say that Satan is doing his job very well. If God has revealed the TRUTH to someone and they are born-again, called, and chosen of God, Satan will have a hard time convincing them of some other doctrine. Satan uses this false doctrine on the lost and unbelievers. In this book, you will read some of the same scriptures a few times, but that is what it takes sometimes to hear God's TRUTH. Paul wrote about this in 2 Corinthians 4:3–4: "But if our [the apostle's] gospel be hid, it is hid to them that are lost. In whom the god of this world hath blinded the minds of them which believe not, lest the light of this glorious gospel of Christ, who is the image of God, should shine unto them." In verse 4, Paul calls Satan the god of this world. Apostle Paul is so right about Satan being the god of this world. If you will go through your day, looking and listening, you will know that Satan is the god of this world.

Here in this paragraph, you will be able to see some similarities between the Mormons and the Muslims and how their religious groups were started. According to the encyclopedia, one night when Mohammed was forty years old, he was thinking about what he had learned about the God of the Jews and the Christians. He was sitting in a little cave on a hill outside of Mecca. Suddenly, he felt that he, himself, was called to be a prophet of God. Mohammed said that the angel Gabriel came and commanded him to recite the word of God to the Arabs in their own language.

When he asked the angel what words he should recite, the angel replied, "Recite, In the name of your God who has created, created man from a clot. Recite, And your Lord is most generous, who taught by the pen, taught man what he did not know." Mohammed also taught that polygamy was all right. He taught his followers that the Muslim men were allowed to have more than one wife at a time just as the men during the Old Testament dispensation (times).

As you study the word of God, in the New Testament, you will find that the scriptures are clear about having only one spouse at a time. I believe we have already read some scriptures, about God's sanctity of marriage between a man and a woman. At this time, I have to say something about same-sex marriages because in 2016, it is legal to marry the same sex in a big part of our world.

You had better hear God's word about this. As far as I know, God's word never said anything about same-sex marriages. But His word does say something about them going out on a date. Now, you who can hear, I'm not talking about two women or two men going to the movies or eating out. I'm talking about what happens afterward. To know the TRUTH about this, read Romans 1:21–32 and 1 Corinthians 6:9–10 for these scriptures will teach you what will happen to you if you do such wickedness.

Just in case you don't know, HELL is just as HOT for the homosexual as it is for the thief and murderer. Don't allow Satan to overcome you with this evil. The power that is in the name of Jesus can cure anything. Just remember that Jesus is the GREAT PHYSICIAN and Creator of all things. Read John1:1–14.

For you who don't know about Sodom and Gomorrah, read Genesis chapters 18 and 19. There is a whole lot more to learn in these two chapters, but I'm going to talk about the filthy deeds that were going on in Sodom and Gomorrah. In the beginning of chapter

18, you will learn about three men (angels) coming to Abraham. After these three angels finish telling Abraham and Sarah about their future, they went on their way to Sodom and Gomorrah.

In Genesis 18:17–19 the Lord decides to tell Abraham what He has planned to do to Sodom and Gomorrah for their wicked ways. In verses 22– 32, you will see that Abraham stood before the Lord and began dickering (bargaining) with the Lord. Abraham asked the Lord, "If there are fifty righteous people, will you spare the cities?" Abraham continued to dicker with the Lord and eventually got Him to say that if there were ten righteous people, He would not destroy the cities. As you are about to find out, there wasn't even ten righteous people in these cities.

In chapter 19:1, you will hear of a man named Lot, who was Abraham's nephew. Most of this story is about how God, Abraham, and the angels tried to save Lot's family out of Sodom before God destroyed the cities. In verses 2–3, you will see that the angels went home with Lot. In verses 4–5, you will see how the men of Sodom were homosexuals. Verse 5 says, the men tells Lot, "Bring them out unto us, that we may know [have sex with] them." Lot even tried to give those men his two virgin daughters in verse 8.

As you continue reading Genesis 19:15–16, you will see how the angels had to pull them out of the city. From these two cities, only four people were saved. In verse 17, the angel told Lot and his family not to look back. In verse 26, Lot's wife disobeyed the angels and looked back toward the city, and then, she turned into a pillar of salt.

There are many lessons to learn from these scriptures, but I'm trying to get you to see that same-sex couples will be in big trouble with our Creator on judgment day. If you can't hear God's opposition on same-sex couples in those scriptures, you may not ever hear. If you have a problem with this sinful act, I suggest you read those few scriptures again and again, until you really hear them. I believe that I have written enough about that subject. Now, I must get back writing about the Muslims and their leader.

At first, Mohammed was not certain he was receiving the revelations from God through the angel Gabriel. But his wife Khadijah and her cousin Waraqah encouraged him to believe in the revelations. And so he did. He claims that he received revelations in intervals for the rest of his life. The collection of all these revelations was put in book form, and it is called the Koran. This new teaching came to earth more than six hundred years after Jesus had already given the apostles God's plan of salvation. This religious group didn't change God's word by adding a few scriptures or taking a few out. They added a whole book, just like what the Mormons did, and the Muslims left out a whole book. The Muslims didn't acknowledge the New Testament as being God's word. This is one of those times I can truly say "the blind is leading the blind."

Just because Mohammed said that he received these new teachings from an angel named Gabriel, the Muslims believe the Koran is the direct word of God. They don't believe that Mohammed wrote it all. In fact, most of the Muslims believe that Mohammed could not read or write. They say he memorized the Koran as it was told to him by the angel Gabriel. Then, Mohammed recited it to his followers, who also memorized it. The Koran was put together in book form after Mohammed's death.

I also found out that Mohammed accepted Jesus as a prophet, but he denied that Jesus was God. He believed that the gospel was revealed to Jesus and recited by Him in the same way that the Koran was revealed and recited by him. As you can see in this last statement, Mohammed equaled himself equal with Jesus. What Mohammed didn't know was that Jesus was and is the living word. Here I go again. I don't think I know because of what the Holy Ghost has taught me, Mohammed is a false prophet. Throughout God's word, He warns us about false prophets. I know not to judge this man. But I believe when a servant of God learns about a wolf in sheep's clothing, they should scream it from the top of a mountain. Again, I will say it as clear as I can—Mohammed is a false prophet. Through all these false doctrines, which are in the world, the TRUTH will continue to stand. You should be able to see through the things I have written. Two thousand and fifteen years later, I Jessie Dunson is still standing for TRUTH (Jesus), because He is TRUTH.

Mohammed started this religious group Islam in the early years of the seventh century and now has deceived millions of followers. Don't be the next follower. Mohammed started this new doctrine about six hundred years after Apostle Paul wrote his letters to the church. I know I repeatedly mention these verses, but it is so important that we realize the importance in believing the apostle's teaching that they have conveyed to us. Remember and read again and again what Paul wrote in Galatians 1:6–9. If the teachings of God's word ever change from what the apostles have already written, it will be false.

When I hear such foolishness such as how Mohammed founded this new religious group, I have to put in my two cents, and it will probably be lengthy. This might have happened something like this, but I think it was Satan who deceived Mohammed and started this false teaching. In the previous chapter, I wrote about God sending a strong delusion to Joseph Smith, Brigham Young, and the Mormons. There is a good chance it was the Lord who sent Mohammed a strong delusion. I wrote a little earlier in this chapter how Mohammed was sitting in a little cave, thinking about what he had learned about the God of the Jews and the Christians. This tells me that at that time, Mohammed heard the apostle's teaching. When Mohammed heard this teaching and did not receive a love for this TRUTH, God could have sent him a strong delusion. I want you to read again 2 Thessalonians 2:10–12 and see what God will do to anyone that does not love His TRUTH. Like I said, it could have been God or Satan who gave Mohammed this false teaching. Either way, it is false.

The word of God that I know lets me know that Mohammed didn't know God's word. I personally don't believe Mohammed was a prophet of God. I believe he is a deceiver used by Satan. Therefore, I will never be a follower of his teachings. I also pray that you don't get caught up in this false teaching. Instead, I hope you will seek God for His TRUTH and that you will find in your heart a love for this TRUTH. Read this scripture and see how John says we are to express our love, after we know the TRUTH. 1 John 3:18 tells us that we are not to love in word, neither in tongue. Anyone can say I love you with their mouth, but in this scripture, John has a but—but we are to love in deed and in TRUTH. When we learn God's TRUTH and when we share this TRUTH with others, this is a clear demonstration of our love to our Lord Jesus and to our fellow man. Demonstrating our love is so much better than just using empty words.

Instead of Mohammed coming up with some other teaching, he should have asked God for the TRUTH, just as everyone must ask for the TRUTH, except for some who were raised in an apostolic family. This comes natural to some children who were brought up in the TRUTH. If Mohammed asked, the Lord would have sent someone to Mohammed with the apostolic teaching. He should have read what Paul wrote about listening to an angel or anyone else who changes God's word. I asked God for the TRUTH, and He revealed His word to me. If the Holy Ghost was not my teacher, I would not be able to RIGHTLY DIVIDE His word. It is not by chance that you are reading this book. If you will continue reading this book, compare it with God's word, and ask Jesus for the TRUTH, He will reveal Himself and His plan of salvation to you. It doesn't get any plainer than this. Read Matthew 7:7–11, and see what Jesus promises to anyone who will ask Him.

I also want you to read Ephesians 3:20 and pay close attention to what the scripture says. This will happen according to the power that works in you. If we will allow the Lord to lead and guide us into

His perfect will, He will do for His people exceeding abundantly above all that we ask or think. As I read this scripture and write about this, I realize that Jesus serves the church. I know we serve God and our fellow man, but truly, it is Jesus who serves us if we will do what we learn from His word. I hope you grasped what I just wrote; just in case you didn't, I will write it again—Jesus will do for His people, exceeding abundantly above all that we ask or think, if we do His word.

While you are asking, I also want you to ask Jesus for a fertile heart and a fertile mind. This is what everyone needs so God's word (seed) will have good ground to grow from. Read Matthew 13:1–23.

If you want a good crop, you have got to have good seed and fertile soil. Remember that the Lord wants to help us and to give us what we need, but He wants us to ask for it.

There is something else we need to help us grow. As you spend some time with the Lord in prayer, also ask Him to plant you near the river of Living Water. First, read from the book of Psalms chapter 1 and then Revelation 21:6. But, more importantly, I want you to hear what God's word says in Revelation 22:1: John says, "He shewed me a pure river of water of life, clear as crystal, proceeding [flowing] out of the Throne of God and of the Lamb."

The river of life is for everyone who lives for God, and only Jesus can give you Living Water. Read Revelation 22:17. I believe Mohammed heard what was written in the book of Revelation. Since he learned about the Jews and Christians, he should have asked the Lord to give him the Living Water.

Galatians 5:22–23 tells us about the crop that every Christian should try to grow. It is the fruit of the Spirit; and this fruit is love, joy, peace, long- suffering, gentleness, goodness, faith, meekness, and temperance. Verse 23 says that you can display all the fruits of the Spirit as much as is within you, and there is no law against it.

When Jesus told us to let our lights shine, I believe He was referring to the fruit of the Spirit. Read Ephesians 5:8–10. In John

15:16, Jesus says, "Ye have not chosen me, but I have chosen you, and ordained you, that ye should go and bring forth fruit, and your fruit should remain: that whatsoever ye shall ask of the Father in my name, he may give it you." In this scripture, I believe Jesus is telling us that there should not be a fall or winter season in our walk with God, because our fruit should remain until we pass from this life. We must stay hydrated with this Living Water to become a mature saint. Read James 1:1–8.

As we begin this race to be Christians, we are being watched by anyone and everyone. We are to have our lights on continually, twelve months a year—as someone once said and added to the English language, 24/7. I know it is hard to do sometimes, and we stumble, but it is as simple as this, "I am sorry, Lord. Help me to do better." As our faith grows in God, you will become stronger and stronger. Know this—we are all like snowflakes in that we all differ in the knowledge of God. I am not talking about TRUTH, because TRUTH is the TRUTH, and that is not going to change. We are all on different learning levels in God. I believe one of the main things we can learn that will make us stronger in this race that is set before us is to be able to say to the sinner, saint, or God, "I'm sorry. Please forgive me." I believe saying I'm sorry is literally music to God's ears.

I want you to read John 4:1–42 and see for yourself what Jesus did for someone even before their time. I am talking about the people (Samaritans) as a whole. One day, as Jesus was travelling, the Spirit revealed to Him that there was a woman in Samaria who needed the Living Water, which I spoke of earlier. This was truly her time to meet the Lord. As you continue reading, you will find out that through this woman's testimony, many more of the Samaritans believed in Jesus' words and knew for sure that He is Christ, the Savior of the world.

Here are two good examples of how Jesus will make a way for someone (you included) to come to the knowledge of who He is. If you know the word of God or after you learn it, you will know that Jesus came to the Jews first, but the Jews rejected Him. The time dispensation for the Gentiles and the Samaritans had not yet come. Read Matthew 10:5–6. This woman who Jesus was talking to in John chapter 4 was a Samaritan. Read John 4:9, and you will see the Samaritan woman knew how the Jews felt about them.

Here is the second example. In Matthew 15:21–28, Jesus was approached by another non-Jewish woman. Here, Jesus is about to say something that sounds awful and harsh, but He must have believed it, or He would not have said it. Jesus referred to this woman as if she were a DOG. Even though Jesus was God in the flesh, He was raised as a child in a time of persecution and in a sinful world. He knew how the Gentiles hated the Jews. I believe Jesus being a Jew and with His own mouth classified her as a DOG.

But Jesus stepped out and went around both of their time dispensations, and because of their faith, He showed compassion and met both of their needs. If you will have faith in God, you will get God's attention. Remember—exceeding abundantly above all that you ask or think. Truly, your faith can move mountains if you will study and get God's word in you and ask God to give you of His Living Water.

When you begin to grow in the Lord, then you will see God do exceeding abundantly above all that you ask or think.

Mohammed could not have known God's word, or he would not have denied that Jesus was God on earth. If Mohammed would have read the gospel of John 8:19–27, he would have known who Jesus was (is). In verse 19, Jesus was asked, "Where is your Father?" Jesus answered with a very clear statement in verse 24: "I said therefore unto you, that ye shall die in your sins, for if ye believe not that I AM, ye shall die in your sins."

In this scripture, Jesus said that if a person doesn't believe that He is God the Father, they will die a sinner. That means they will be waiting in the grave for the second resurrection to be judged as a sinner. Verse 27 says, "They understood not that He spake to them of the Father."

You have already read this once, but at this time, I think you should read again 2 Corinthians 11:13–15. God would not send another message six hundred years after He had already given the whole world His plan of salvation. We are going to study more about this a little later, but I have to mention something about this now. You will find the first day of the New Testament church in Acts chapter 2. Verse 5 says, "And there were dwelling at Jerusalem Jews, devout men, out of every nation under heaven." As you can see here, God had people from every nation under heaven there on the first day of the New Testament church.

When every person went back to their own nation, I believe they told their family and friends what they had experienced (saw and heard) on the day of Pentecost.

I know when my brother-in-law (Larry Taylor) experienced being born- again, he came and shared with me and my family what the Lord had shared with him and his family. If Larry ever reads this book, I want him to know that on August 11, 1983, it was Thursday 6:00 p.m., I remember this as if it was yesterday, but it has been thirty-two years now, and I am growing stronger. As you can see, Larry, God is helping me write a book to help populate heaven. When you shared this apostolic message with my family, the seed that you sowed that day fell on good ground. After all these years, the Lord is still blessing me every day through His word. Larry is a soul winner. He may not know, but I know; he is a repairer of the breach and a restorer of paths to dwell in, because he allowed God to use him. I know it was the Lord who called and saved me, but I will always have a special love for Larry, because he went the extra mile for my family.

The apostolic message is 2,015 years old now, and it has never changed, and this is the message that Jesus has given to the whole world that every human on this planet is to live by during the New

Testament times. If we obey this message, it will make us ready to meet Jesus, when He comes back for His Bride. In Matthew 24:14, Jesus says, "And this gospel of the kingdom shall be preached in all the world for a witness unto all nations; and then shall the end come."

There are a lot of different religious teachings in the world, but Jesus says here that this is the gospel for the whole world. I also want you to read what Paul wrote in Colossians 1:23. In Matthew 28:19, this is called the Great Commission. Here, Jesus tells His disciples to go and teach all nations. God would not have His disciples teaching different messages. They all taught the same thing. As I have said before, in Jude's letter to the church, in verse 3, Jude speaks of a common salvation. There are not two or three different ways to be saved. God's word still teaches that same plan of salvation for everyone today, as it was taught on the day of Pentecost.

While I am writing about every nation under heaven, I think back to 2006. As I was studying God's word one day, I was reading in Genesis chapter 11, about the Tower of Babel. When the people started building the city and Tower of Babel, all the people of the world still spoke the same language. God saw that the people were united in building this tower. They were building the tower so that it would reach unto heaven. God saw that the people were not going to stop building this tower until it was completed.

The Bible says that God came down and confounded their language. When they could not understand one another, they had to stop building.

This is why the city and tower are called Babel. This is also where God scattered the people all over the whole earth. As I was reading that day about Babel, God revealed to me that He had a reunion for the people from the Tower of Babel. Just as God was able to disperse the people from Babel, He was also able to bring every nation back together. This is not just a coincidence; God knew what He was doing. God had this reunion on the day of Pentecost. God wanted someone from every nation to be there on the first day of the New Testament church. God wanted them there so they could hear and see the beginning of the church. I was taught by God about this reunion. I don't know if scholars or doctors of theology know about the reunion, but I do. As I said, the Holy Ghost taught me about this reunion, and I will take this knowledge to the grave with me as the TRUTH.

The first two religious groups I wrote about were the Mormons and the Muslims. Both of these religious groups claimed that they received their teachings from an angel. This is just what Apostle Paul said not to do. You should know this by now, but just in case, I want you to read it again. In Galatians 1:6–9, Paul writes, "I marvel [am amazed] that ye are so soon removed from Him that called you into the grace of Christ unto another gospel: which is not another; but there be some that trouble you, and would pervert [change] the gospel of Christ. But though we [the apostles], or an angel from heaven, preach any other gospel unto you than that which we [the apostles] have preached unto you, let him be accursed."

Remember in Romans 2:16, Paul says that on judgment day, Jesus is going to judge the secrets of men, according to his (Paul's) gospel. Joseph Smith and Mohammed should have read and obeyed what Paul wrote for all of us to obey in Galatians 1:6–9.

I believe that Jesus is going to ask Mohammed this on judgment day, "Did you not read and understand what Apostle Paul wrote to the church in Galatia? Paul had already written my word, informing everyone how to stay saved, six hundred years before this so-called angel of Mine came to earth with this new teaching. Why did you listen to an angel and not to My apostles?" On judgment day, I what you to read what Jesus says to all sinners who will stand before Him that day in Matthew 7:21–23.

Now, for you Joseph Smith, "Did you not hear what I asked Mohammed, when he stood before me? What about you? Did you read what Apostle Paul wrote to the church in Galatia? Paul wrote

My TRUTHS, 1,827 years before this so-called angel of Mine came to you on earth with this new teaching. Why did you listen to an angel? I had already given my plan of salvation to the world through My apostles."

We all must study and seek Jesus for the TRUTH, and in doing so, we will learn to see and hear the false teachings of Satan. But at this time, I find myself with fewer words to write about the Muslims, so I think it is time to start a new chapter.

In the next chapter, I'm going to write about the GREAT WHORE that John wrote about in Revelation chapter 17. I have already written the next chapter with pen, so I know that it is filled with some very interesting and important facts that you will learn. Remember the Holy Ghost is our teacher. Jesus says in Revelation 2:7, "He that hath an ear, let him hear what the Spirit saith unto the Churches." Seek God (Jesus) day and night, and He will teach you His TRUTH. When you realize that Jesus has taught you something, no devil or any person can tell you any different as long as you keep your focus on Jesus.

Chapter 4

THE GREAT WHORE

The next religious group I am writing about was started by the Romans, when they allowed Satan to deceive them by changing (misinterpreting) God's word. This religious group that I am writing about is the largest religious group in the world. A little later in this chapter, I'm going to explain how the Lord revealed this TRUTH to me. But first, I have to set the scene. It will be lengthy, but educational.

According to the encyclopedia, Rome is believed to be founded by twin brothers named Remus and Romulus. Roman history teaches us that these two brothers were the sons of a pagan god, and they were abandoned when they were infants. It is also believed that these twin brothers were discovered in the marshes by a she-wolf, who nursed the infants. It is also believed that there was a conflict between the brothers, and it led to the slaying of Remus by Romulus. Images of the twins and the wolf adorn Roman emblems even today. I don't know about you, but it sounds to me that these two brothers are the sons of Satan.

Rome was founded in 753 BC. As Rome grew, it was under the rule of kings; and then from 510 BC, they were under a republic. The leaders used the Roman armies to steadily expand the city's territory. By the time the republic had become an empire in 27 BC, Rome ruled much of the known Western world.

At this time, let's go back in history and find out how the Roman Empire came to be. If you don't already know this, what you are about to learn is priceless. You are about to see a big part of God's master plan for humanity and how God raises and destroys kingdoms to bring this world to the end of time as we know it.

When I say look into the history, there is only one book that I know of that contains this TRUTH, the book of Daniel. Some scholars believe, the book of Daniel was written hundreds of years after his death around 165 BC. I believe this is FALSE! I believe Daniel wrote his book while he was alive. Read Daniel 12:4–5. Although I don't know the exact date, I know it was many years before Jesus came to earth. Daniel 7:1–7 records the Prophet Daniel having a dream and visions where he saw four beast (kingdoms) come out of the sea, (people) and they were all different one from the other.

The first beast Daniel saw was like a lion, referring to when Babylon ruled the world. Then, the second beast was like a bear, referring to when in 539 BC the Medes and Persians captured and killed Belshazzar, king of Babylon, and then ruled the world. The third beast was like a leopard, referring to Greece. In 331 BC, the Greek leader Alexander the Great defeated the Medes and Persians in the battle of Arbela. And then, Greece ruled the world.

Now, let's find out who the fourth beast is in Daniel's dream that was "dreadful and terrible, and exceedingly strong," that conquered Greece. The fourth kingdom—the Roman Empire—represents this terrible beast. The Romans went to war and conquered Greece in 168 BC and then ruled the world. In fact, they continually rule this world to the present day, with their leader the pope and their false doctrines. The Catholics will continue ruling this world, until the last kingdom comes and takes over, and that will be at the end of the tribulation period, when Jesus takes their kingdom from them and destroys it.

Some of the years mentioned above may vary a year or two, one way or the other, depending on your history book, but all of this is true. All these battles and kingdom takeovers took place in this order, just as Daniel said they would. God allowed Satan to think that this is his plan, but all this is in God's master plan.

I want you to understand this—if there was some other TRUTH, I would have written about that. But I want you to have a clear understanding of what I'm about to say. I have only written about the things that I have been taught. This is not my plan—it is God's plan to end the world. This part of Daniel's prophecy came true, but there is no way God will allow the Romans to have an everlasting kingdom. This kingdom will come to naught. In Daniel 7:13– 14 and 27, Daniel speaks of another kingdom that will take over. This last kingdom will be an everlasting kingdom, and this is the kingdom of God.

When the kingdom of heaven is brought down to our new earth, this is where our Lord Jesus and His Bride, His angels, and whomsoever or whatsoever else in the universe that serves Him will live forever. At that time, all false teachings will go away, and there will only be TRUTH.

You will learn about the Beast and his demise in Daniel 7:11. Before you finish reading this book, you are going to find out who the Beast is that takes over the world and where he comes from. You may not know who the Beast is yet, but you should know from what religious group he comes from in the things you have been reading. At the end-time, Satan is going to embody a person on this earth, and we need to know who it's going to be so we will not be deceived when he comes.

I know we keep going back and forth from the history, to the future, and back to the history; but that is what it takes to find the

TRUTH sometimes. You should now see the necessity of having the Holy Ghost teach us.

The Romans conquered Greece in 168 BC, and it took 140 years for the Romans to grow into their empire.

Hundreds of years before Jesus was born and hundreds of years after He died for us, the Romans conquered and took land and people to increase the size of their empire. By the time the Roman Empire fell, they had claimed and occupied all the land (now countries) that surrounds the Mediterranean Sea. Rome's maximum expansion was achieved under Emperor Trajan, who ruled from AD 98 to AD 117. During that time period, Rome governed not only the shores of the Mediterranean Sea but also much of what is now Austria, the Balkans, Hungary, Great Britain, Spain, Portugal, France, Switzerland, and parts of Asia Minor. This means Satan ruled over the most powerful kingdom on earth, and he had Judaea in his grasp, the country where Jesus was born. A little later, you are going to read in greater detail in chapter 8 of this book how Satan used Herod, a Roman appointed Jewish king, to try and kill Jesus when He was born. As you know, he couldn't. This is recorded in Matthew chapter 2 and in Revelation 12:4–5.

The persecution of the church was started by the Romans when Jesus was born, and the persecution got worse for the next 313 years. History books record that if you were a Christian, you were automatically a criminal. During the persecution, Romans would punish Christians. I'm sure at first the Romans would beat them with a whip or throw them into prison and then escalated to the point where Christians were stripped of their possessions and driven from their homes. You will later see that the persecution will worsen as the years go by. History books record that because Christians would not bow down and worship the emperor or their false gods, they were put to death. This time period is called the Age of the Martyrs. The worse part of the persecution came under the rule of Caesar Nero and later Emperor Diocletian.

When Nero ruled, the Christians were killed, and their executions were made into a game. They were covered with skins of wild animals and torn to pieces by dogs and lions. They were hung on crosses. They were beheaded. They were wrapped in flammable material and set on fire and used as human torches in arenas when gladiators would fight. Can you believe these people (the Catholics) claimed to be God's church?

The greatest persecution came under the rule of Emperor Diocletian. In AD 303, Diocletian began a war of extermination against the church. But the followers of Jesus spread throughout the region. At this time, the Romans were killing thousands of Christians, but for Satan, that was not good enough. Satan finally realized that every time he had a Christian killed, they went to heaven. Satan saw that he was defeating his own purpose. He knew that he had to change his tactics and come up with a better scheme to deceive more souls. What could the devil think of that would be better than killing Christians? He would let them live and continually deceive them! Satan would make things easy and infiltrate. Like a wise general, he would corrupt the world by wresting (changing) God's word and allowing people to live in false teachings.

At the end of Emperor Diocletian's reign, there was a civil war, and Constantine the Great, a new Roman emperor, emerged victorious from the war and succeeded as emperor following the resignation of Diocletian. Now, this is when Satan started his new work—deceiving multitudes of people with false doctrine. Under the reign of Constantine, the persecution became less and less. One day in AD 313, the Emperor Constantine claimed to be a Christian. When everyone in the empire heard this, they also heard that there will be no more persecution of the Christians.

Even though there were lesser persecution, it never completely stopped. I believe as we get closer to the end of this world, the persecution on the church will be as bad or even worse than when the church began. Revelation 13:2 says that Satan gives his power to the Beast. As you will see later in this book, the Catholic leader (the pope), I believe, is the Beast that Satan gives his power to. I also believe and teach that this pope will come back from the dead. I will explain later in Chapter 6, "Satan + Pope = Beast." Please don't stop reading now, I want you to continue reading so you will decide what is TRUTH and what is false.

Since Christian persecution under the reign of Constantine was becoming less and less, it seemed things were going great.

Satan was sitting back and watching. Little by little, when everyone was relaxing and not worrying about being persecuted and tormented to death, there was compromise—the Roman leaders started reading and changing God's word. The apostles had already written the New Testament, and Satan saw a new way of deceiving masses. I wrote about this in the first chapter of this book, and here, I need to mention it again. 2 Peter 3:15–16 teaches us that Apostle Paul wrote his epistles with the wisdom of God, and some of the things he wrote are going to be hard to understand—"And they that are unlearned, and unstable wrest [twist or change] God's word...unto their own destruction." Satan saw that if he could get the Romans to stop killing the Christians and wrest God's word, he could deceive billions of people in believing a false teaching.

Satan used the Catholics to change God's word in so many ways. Here are a few major—and I mean major—things that the Roman leaders changed in God's word. All scriptures are important, and none should be tampered with, but Satan went straight for the jugular vein when he started tampering with God's word. As you will see, Satan had them to change (misinterpret) some of the most important scriptures in God's word. This does not take a rocket scientist to understand. Satan will not teach anyone God's word completely, and he will always add or leave something out. Remember that his job is to deceive, not to teach. Satan used the Romans to misinterpret the scriptures, which teach a part of how to be born-again, which is water baptism.

First, I am going write what the Bible says to do, and then, I am going to write how the Catholics wrested (changed) God's word from its original meaning. The Roman leaders changed the true water baptism in a few different ways. You already know how to be baptized according to Peter when he gave the Jews Jesus' plan of salvation. Peter tells everyone there that day, which was the beginning of the church, that they are to be baptized in the name of Jesus. No matter who tries to change God's word, this TRUTH will stand far above all of the false teachings that are in the world. Water baptism is for the removal (washing away) of our sins. Read Acts 22:16. There are other major things that water baptism accomplishes, and I have written about them in chapter 9 of this book.

Here is one of the ways the Catholics misinterpreted God's plan of baptism. The Romans took Jesus' own words from Matthew 28:19 and used this verse out of context for their baptism. I will explain in just a little while when I write about the way they take the one God of the Jews and divide Him into three persons. The Catholics are just blind to the fact that Jesus is the Father of creation, the Son of redemption, and the Holy Ghost of regeneration. As I have said a couple of times in this book, I believe Matthew 28:19 is the most wrongfully used verse from God's word.

Billions have been baptized wrongly, when the preacher quotes this verse during baptism, just like Satan knew would happen. Jesus never told anyone to repeat what He said in Matthew 28:19, but He did tell us to be baptized in the name of the Father, and of the Son, and of the Holy Ghost, which is Jesus.

As God was preparing the church to be born, John the Baptist was preaching in the wilderness and baptizing people in lakes and rivers. When someone got into the water with John the Baptist, I believe they would be submerged. Read what Paul teaches in Romans 6:4–5. Verses 4–5 say, "We are buried with Him by baptism into death… For if we have been planted." God's word never said submerged, but I believe His word teaches total immersion. So every hair on your body should be washed and covered in the blood of Jesus.

After John the Baptist was murdered and the apostles started baptizing people, everyone in God's church was baptized and submerged in water, in the name of Jesus. As I have said before, don't just take my word for it; read the book of Acts and see (hear) for yourself.

Here is the second way the Catholics changed water baptism. Instead of them following the teachings of Jesus and the apostles, the Catholics would sprinkle a little bit of holy water on your forehead, for your baptism. I already knew this, but I wanted to know more about their teachings. As I was writing about this, I stopped writing for a few minutes so I could call a couple of Catholic churches to find out about their water baptism. I am so glad I did. The priest told me something that I have never heard before, and both priests told me the same thing. They said that before I could become a Catholic and before I could be baptized, I would have to take classes at a Catholic church for two years. Then, they told me that after the two years, I would have the opportunity of being sprinkled with holy water on my forehead or have holy water poured over my head. They said that sometimes, the Catholic church would accept you and your baptism from some other church, but only after two years of classes. This is not how the apostles taught to be born-again. Who gives them the right to change God's word? I know—SATAN DOES!

Here is another major change of God's word. It is found in Deuteronomy 6:4–7. God commanded Israel, saying, "There is only one God, and you are to love God with all of your heart, soul, and might. And these words, which I command thee this day, shall be in thine heart." In verse 7, notice the emphasis God put on how we are to teach our children about loving and knowing that there is one God. I'm going to paraphrase a little as I explain. This is how I interpret these verses. In verse 7, God says, "And you shall teach this TRUTH diligently to your children and shall talk of this TRUTH when you sit down in your house. I want you to share this TRUTH as you walk down the street and when you put your children to bed. I believe the bedtime story should be the Lord our God is one Lord. Love God with all of your heart, soul, and might. In the morning, when your children wake up, the first thing they should hear is, 'Son, daughter, there is one God. And I urge you to love God today with all your heart, soul, and might.'" Read these verses, and see if this is not the way you would interpret them.

Watch what Satan does here. He made the Catholics change the one God teaching that the Jews have had for thousands of years. He gives the Catholics a new revelation, and they start teaching that there is a Trinity. The Catholics have divided God into three separate persons. They will say that there is one God, but in three persons—God the Father, God the Son, and God the Holy Ghost. This terminology is not recorded in God's word anywhere. This is all made up by Satan so he can deceive billions of people. Read what the Bible says in Matthew 1:18–23. To those who believe in the Trinity, how would you explain verses 18 and 20? These two verses say that the third person in the Godhead, according to their teaching, the Holy Ghost is the Father of Jesus. Verse 23 says, "Behold, a virgin shall be with child, and shall bring forth a son, and they shall call his name Emmanuel." I want you to listen really closely to what this verse says about what Emmanuel means. Here it is—this baby Jesus is God with us. I believe that Holy Ghost simply means God's Spirit that can't be seen.

God's word is being fulfilled. Remember that God's will has two sides; pray and make sure that you are on God's side. God allowed Satan to use these false teachers to teach and gather his souls. At the same time, God is gathering His saints and preparing us daily for this warfare that we must face each and every day. I truly believe if you cannot feel and see yourself in this war fighting against Satan, it's time to look in the mirror. Read James 1:21– 25.

Even though the Roman Empire fell, their false teachings are still predominant today in the religious world as we know it. All this should be clearer to see, as you continue reading. You may have learned a lot from what you read a little earlier in Daniel chapter 7 about the four different kingdoms, but I wrote it to say this—when these kingdoms ruled the world, they all spoke of their gods, because they (all of them) had many gods. After learning these things, I am not surprised at all that the Romans, which was the fourth Beast that Daniel saw, would (try) to divide the one true God into three separate persons.

Just wait until you start reading chapter 6 of this book. You are going to find out how Satan used the head of the Catholic church (the pope). I believe Satan will use a pope to deceive every nation on earth. Continue seeking God for these answers, and remember that only God can teach you His TRUTH.

The Catholics have been taught to believe in the trinity for the past 1,700 years. Here is the reason Catholics baptize people by repeating Matthew 28:19. It is the only scripture in God's word that coincides with their teaching of the trinity. I believe it is ordained to them by Satan. When they baptize someone, the priest will sprinkle some holy water on their forehead and repeat what Jesus says to do in Matthew 28:19. Then, the priest says, "Now, I baptize you in the name of the Father and of the Son and of the Holy Ghost." Jesus never said to repeat this scripture. Jesus knew what He was talking about, and Peter did also in Acts 2:38 when he said that everyone is to be baptized in the name of Jesus. Peter knew God's name. I am so thankful that God revealed His name to me.

As I said in chapter 1, God's name was recorded only a dozen or so times in the entire Old Testament. What most people don't know, God's name (Jesus) was recorded 975 times in the New Testament. I'm not going to write it 975 times, but I do want you to know God's name.

JESUS! JESUS!

The name Jesus is recorded 975 times in the New Testament, and there will be no excuse for not knowing who God is on judgment day. Read Romans 1:20.

I know that I'm getting a little more off topic, but it's something I feel that I must share with you. I believe that there were two other names for God in the New Testament. I just wrote about one of them on the last page, and it was Emmanuel. And it was only mentioned one time to describe who Jesus is (God with us). The only other name that is given for God in the New Testament is controversial to most believers. But I believe that Melchisedec was God, and He walked this earth during the Old Testament times. Melchisedec was mentioned nine times in the book of Hebrews 5:6,10 and 6:20 and 7:1,10,11,15,17,21.

To hear what I'm about to say, you must have on your spiritual ears, because it is a conjecture, unless you know how to RIGHTLY DIVLDE the scriptures, which teach us this TRUTH. Now, this is just my educated theory by using the few scriptures about who Melchisedec was. First, you need to read Hebrews 7:1–4: Verse 1says,

> That Melchisedec was the king of Salem, priest of the most high God, who met Abraham returning from the slaughter of the kings, and blessed him.
>
> To whom also Abraham gave a tenth part of all; first being by interpretation King of righteousness, and after that also King of Salem, which is, King of peace. Without father, without mother, without descent, having neither beginning of days, nor end of life; but made like unto the Son of God; abideth a priest continually.

I believe that these scriptures are teaching us that Melchisedec was God. Genesis 14:14–20 teach us about Abraham giving a tenth of the spoils of the war to Melchisedec.

I want to bring something to your attention in Hebrews 7:2 that you might have missed. The writer described Melchisedec as "king of righteousness, and king of peace. As you now know from reading Isaiah 9:6, Isaiah described Jesus as "Wonderful, Counsellor, the Mighty God, the Everlasting Father, the Prince of Peace." I know that you know there is a difference in being a king and a prince. I'm in no way trying to put one over the other, because I believe they are the same God, but have different names and different human bodies.

Let me tell you how I came to believe this to be the TRUTH. I went to Phoenix, Arizona, back in the 1990s to remodel a house. When the first week passed, naturally it was time to wash clothes. I went down the street to the closest Laundromat to wash them. As I sat there waiting for my clothes to finish washing, a young couple came in to wash their clothes. As they sat there, they began talking about Jesus, and that was all I needed to hear. I could not help myself; I just had to chime into their conversation. You should now know that we talked about a little (a lot) of everything from God's word.

What I'm about to write was the first time I received this revelation, and let me tell you, it was one of those V8 moments. I began telling them about what Jesus taught the Jews in John chapter 8. In John 8:12–29, Jesus is teaching them that He is the Father. In verses 30–32, Jesus tells the people who believed in Him, "If ye continue in my word, are ye my disciples indeed; and ye shall know the TRUTH, and the TRUTH shall make you free." Now, I want you to read verses 33–55, and you will learn how Jesus schools them about their father Abraham.

You always need to have your spiritual ears on, but here is where you need to listen really closely to hear the TRUTH about Melchisedec. In verses 56–58, Jesus tells the Jews about something that took place a few thousand years earlier.

> Your father Abraham rejoiced to see my day: and he saw, and was glad. Then said the Jews unto Him, Thou art not yet fifty years old, and hast thou seen Abraham? Then Jesus said unto them, Verily, verily, I say unto you, before Abraham was, I AM.

When Jesus said, "I AM," it stirred the Jews so much that they tried to kill Him. Read verse 59. They knew that He was claiming to be I AM. When Moses went to God to free the Israelites/Jews from out of Egypt, Moses asked the Lord, "Who do I tell the children of Israel has sent me?" God tells Moses to say to the people, "I AM has sent me unto you." I believe when Jesus said to those Jews, "Your father Abraham rejoiced to see my day, and he saw, and was glad," He was speaking as God, when He was Melchisedec and met Abraham from the slaughter of the kings in Genesis chapter 14.

I have heard preachers teach that Jesus has been in heaven since the beginning, but that is a false teaching. They get this teaching from Genesis 1:26, because God said, "Let us make man in our image, after our likeness." Now, this is what I believe—through God's foreseeable knowledge, He made man in the image of Melchisedec and Jesus, because that is the image He saw in His future. The simple fact is Jesus' flesh had a beginning, and it was when He was born of Mary. I have written what you have read, and the Lord didn't stop me. Unless He changes my mind, I will take this to the grave as the TRUTH. To tell you the TRUTH, I have only scratched the surface concerning Melchisedec. I know that there is so much more to learn about him from God's word. We only have a few scriptures that teach about him, but God had the writer of Hebrews to write about Melchisedec so we could learn the TRUTH about him.

Even though the things I have written are true, it bothers me to keep writing about the Catholics, but we are looking for the TRUTH. So I must write. For the Catholics to believe in the Ten Commandments, the way they say they do, they do a lot of breaking and changing of these commandments. Another error on their part is that they made statues and images, such as Mary, the Lord's mother. My New Oxford American Dictionary says that this is an idol.

They also broke this commandment. The Catholics bow down and pray to Mary. They think just because she is Jesus' mother, she can tell Him what to do. I have a good question. What's up with that? If only they would read John 2:1–5. In verse 3, Mary comes to Jesus and says, "They have no wine." In verses 4–5, Jesus says to His mother, "Woman, what have I to do with thee? Mine hour is not yet come. His mother saith unto the servants, Whatsoever he [Jesus] saith unto you, do." In plain Mississippi language, "Y'all have got to listen to Jesus. I can't make Him do nothing."

When Apostle Paul writes to the church at Ephesus, he says in Ephesians 5:23, "Jesus is the head of the church." Let's look at another big mistake that the Catholics have made. According to my dictionary, the Roman Catholic church acknowledges the pope as the head of the church. I want you to look in your dictionary under Roman Catholic church and see if your dictionary doesn't say the same thing. If by some chance you can't find it there, look under pope. The definition of pope clearly says it.

I believe what Apostle Paul wrote is true. Jesus is the head of His church. I also believe that the pope is the head of the Catholics. I'm personally going to stay with Jesus as my head (leader). I don't know anyone smarter than our Lord Jesus. I would hate to be caught up in that false doctrine, having the pope as my leader. I'm so thankful that I have the Holy Ghost (Jesus) as my head (leader). Here is something else that the Catholics believe—they call the pope the most Holy Father. Read for yourself what Jesus says about this in Matthew 23:9.

I believe Revelation chapter 17 teaches God's people about the Catholic church and how the Catholics were used by Satan to spread false doctrines. Chapter 17 also speaks of the popes of the Catholic church and of the Beast, which you will learn about in chapter 6 of this book. Notice that in Revelation 18:1, John writes, "And after these things." This tells me that John continued writing that day, and his writing in chapter 18 was still talking about the GREAT WHORE (Catholics). In verses 1–3, John says,

> I saw another angel come down from heaven, having great power; and the earth was lightened with his glory. And he cried mightily with a strong voice, saying, Babylon the great [Rome] is fallen, is fallen, and is become the habitation of devils, and the hold of every foul spirit, and a cage of every unclean and hateful bird. For all nations have drunk of the wine of the wrath of her fornication,

and the kings of the earth have committed fornication with her, and the merchants of the earth are waxed rich through the abundance of her delicacies.

Now, let's read Revelation 18:4. Jesus is going to tell John something that is clear as any crystal made on this earth. John says in verse 4, "And I heard another voice from heaven, saying, Come out of her, my people, that ye be not partakers of her sins, and that ye receive not of her plagues." You can stay in that false doctrine if you want to, but for me and my house, we don't want any part of it. I know that Jesus called my name one day, and I was believing in the false doctrine when He called me. I believe all the scriptures in God's word, but what John says in Revelation 18:4 happened to me, and I have lived it. I came out of that false doctrine, and I will never return.

I'm so thankful to God, because He called me out, and that is why I write so I can help you learn to hear God's voice. And not to be entangled with Satan's deceiving teachings. Don't think that I am crazy when I say to you that you can hear God's voice. As a matter of fact, it would be terrible (for the lack of a better word) if we couldn't hear Him. In Hebrews 13:16, Paul says, "But to do good and to communicate forget not: for with such sacrifices God is well pleased." I know if you will talk with the Lord, He will communicate with you in His own way. Read John chapter 10 for a better understanding.

Here is another commandment the Catholics have changed. They have changed the Jew's Sabbath (Saturday) to Sunday for the day of rest and worship. You can find what God said to Moses as He was giving him the Ten Commandments in Exodus 20:8–11:

Remember the Sabbath day, to keep it Holy. Six days shalt thou labour, and do all thy work. But the seventh day the Sabbath of the Lord thy God: thou shalt not do any work, thou, nor thy son, nor thy daughter, thy manservant, nor thy maidservant, nor thy cattle, nor thy stranger that within thy gates. For six days, the Lord made heaven and earth, the sea, and all that in them, and rested the seventh day: wherefore the Lord blessed the Sabbath day, and hallowed it [made it Holy].

In Mark 2:27, Jesus says, "The Sabbath was made for man, and not man for the Sabbath."

You will find out how long this commandment of keeping the Sabbath day is in effect in Exodus 31:12–18. I must bring out this point—if you are born-again, you are of the children of Israel (of Judas), and verse 13 is speaking of you. Read Matthew 1:1–2 again. Verse 16 says that keeping the Sabbath is a perpetual covenant. I believe your dictionary gives the same definition of perpetual. According to my dictionary, it means "never ending or never changing." Verse 17 says that keeping the Sabbath it a sign between God and the children of Israel, FOREVER. Some of you may think that God was only speaking to the Jewish nation. I believe God was speaking to the Jews at that time, but I also believe that God was looking into the future and speaking to everyone who is born-again.

The Bible says that Jesus came unto His own (the Jews) and His own received Him not. Read John 1:11 and also read Romans chapter 11, and see what Paul writes about the Jews being rejected in part. In Romans 11:20, Paul says, "Because of unbelief they [the Jews] were broken off." This has allowed a place for the non-Jews to be grafted into the olive tree and the root (Jesus). God's word teaches us when a person is born-again, the Lord grafts them into the Jewish nation, and they become Jews. Read what Paul writes to the Gentiles in Romans 2:25–29.

You will find what Paul wrote about how the Gentiles became the children of Abraham in Galatians chapter 3. Verse 7 says, "Know ye therefore that they which are of faith, the same are the children of Abraham." "That the blessing of Abraham might come on the Gentiles [all non-Jewish] through Jesus Christ; that we might receive the promise of the Spirit through faith" (verse 14). "And if ye Christ's, then are ye Abraham's seed, and heirs according to the promise" (verse 29). Again, I will say that when you are born-again, you become Jewish.

Now, let's read other scriptures in God's word and see what it says about the Sabbath. Luke chapter 23 tells us about the death of Jesus and when He was in His grave. Verses 55–56 say that the followers of Jesus rested the Sabbath day according to the commandment. Jesus had been with these people for the last few years of His life teaching them. I believe Jesus kept the Sabbath day each week. I can see by reading these scriptures that Jesus taught His followers to keep the Sabbath holy, even in the New Testament times.

You will learn that Jesus speaks of keeping the Sabbath at the end of the church era on this earth in Matthew chapter 24. In verse 15, Jesus says, "When ye therefore shall see the abomination of desolation, spoken of by Daniel the prophet, stand in the holy place." You can read about this in Daniel chapters 11 and 12. When Daniel spoke of the abomination of desolation, he is referring to the Beast setting up his kingdom on earth, making ALL non-Christians and even some Christians receive the mark of the Beast, or the name of the Beast, or the number of his name (666).

Going back to Matthew 24:15–20.

> When ye therefore shall see the abomination of desolation, spoken of by Daniel the prophet, stand in the holy place… Then let them which be in Judaea flee into the mountains. Let him which is on the housetop not come down to take any thing out of his house. Neither let him which is in the field return back to take his clothes. And woe unto them that are with child and to them that give

suck in those days! But pray ye that your flight be not in the winter, neither on the Sabbath day.

Notice that when I wrote what Jesus said in verse 15, I didn't write "Whoso readeth, let him understand," because Jesus didn't say it. I believe that Matthew was just putting in his two cents about the importance of having an understanding of what Jesus and Daniel were teaching us. These scriptures are so important for us to know, and we will study them a few times in this book. We all must know about the Beast, because he is going to be Satan in human form, and God's word teaches us that he is coming to deceive everyone he can.

Jesus says, "Pray that your flight be not on the Sabbath day." I have heard over the years that the Jews were not allowed to travel on the Sabbath, but a certain distance. I have searched the scriptures for this, but I have never found how far they could travel on a Sabbath day. I did find this verse in Acts 1:12, "Then returned they unto Jerusalem from the mount called Olivet, which is from Jerusalem a Sabbath day's journey." I believe Jesus said, "Pray that your flight be not on the Sabbath day," because they could not go far enough to get away from their adversaries (the Beast). This tells me that the Sabbath is still God's holy day, even until the end of the church era, here on this earth.

A few decades after Jesus had died for us and was resurrected, John wrote in Revelation 1:10: "I [John] was in the Spirit on the Lord's Day [the Sabbath]." Even though John was exiled on the island of Patmos, as you can see as you read this verse, John was still spiritual and kept the Sabbath holy. As you can see in Revelation chapter 1, Jesus revealed Himself to John, which is the word. Just imagine what the Lord will show you, and do for you, if you will be spiritual and keep the Sabbath holy.

I have said it before, and I will say it again. Exodus 31:16–17 tells us, "Wherefore the children of Israel shall keep the Sabbath, to observe the Sabbath throughout their generations, a perpetual covenant. It a sign between me [God] and the children of Israel for ever." I believe that everyone who has been born-again and who has been grafted into the olive tree should keep the Sabbath holy to the best of their ability.

I have been taught God's TRUTH for thirty-two years, and I have never been taught about keeping the Sabbath day holy by any preacher. I believe our ONE GOD, APOSTOLIC, TONGUE-TALKING, HOLY ROLLER, BORN-AGAIN, HEAVEN-BOUND BELIEVING pastors, preachers, teachers, and evangelists should teach God's people to keep the Sabbath holy. In Isaiah chapter 58, you will find God's promises to those who will obey His word, do His will, and keep the Sabbath holy. The Lord has been teaching me about the Sabbath, and if you will read Isaiah chapter 58 until you hear him, the Lord will teach you also. I truly believe that I'm doing Isaiah 58:1, as I write this book and warn you to obey God's word.

Everyone who reads this book will not understand what I'm about to say, but to those who know me personally, you will see what God is doing for me and my family, because I keep the Sabbath holy. I just want to say one word that is in Isaiah 58:14—heritage. For those who know me, I want you to look up and find the meaning of heritage. I believe, my friends and family will know what I'm talking about. I truly believe God's word. I am speaking by faith, because what I am writing about is in the future. To those who can understand, I am not boasting about myself, but I am boasting about God and how He has given me faith and allowed me to work for the kingdom by writing this book. Truly, this is my faith and my works, working hand in hand, just as James said it should in James 2:14–26.

Most of this chapter that I have already written, I learned from history books. I wrote at the beginning of this chapter that I was going to explain how God revealed to me the largest religious group in the world. Just as God revealed this TRUTH to me, I believe

God is about to teach you this TRUTH also. This one will shock most of you. All I can say is—screw down tight in the saddle, and hold on. Speaking as a carpenter, this one is going to cut across the grain, if you know what I mean. But if you will keep an open mind and ask Him, God will teach you His TRUTH.

In 1991, I (Jessie Dunson) was doing fixturing work on the inside of the pyramid in downtown Memphis, Tennessee. I went to work on a Monday morning; and there, I met a man named Bill. As we sat on the tailgate of my truck, I began to witness to Bill about God and His goodness. I also talked about Satan and his ability to deceive. We talked for about an hour, and the Holy Ghost was really moving or, in other words, anointing. Normally, when I witness to someone, God feeds them with the milk of the word, one teaspoon at a time. This Monday morning was different. The anointing of God's Spirit was so strong that it seemed as if God was feeding Bill with a snow scoop. The more we talked, the closer Bill got to my face. I could clearly see the hunger and a desire in Bill's face to know more about God.

God has been revealing Himself to me through His word for the past thirty-two years. But like I said earlier, this Monday morning was different. God has spoken to me in an audible voice six times in those thirty-two years, and this Monday morning was one of those times. What I am about to say is what brought me to this great revelation of the largest religious group in the world. I said to Bill, "Revelation 17:5 says, 'MYSTERY, BABYLON THE GREAT, THE MOTHER OF HARLOTS.'" Before I finished quoting the whole verse, as soon as I said, "THE MOTHER OF HARLOTS," God asked me, "Did you understand what you just said?" Now, Bill has gotten even closer to my face, listening to every word that I was saying, and I responded by saying out loud, "THE MOTHER OF HARLOTS, THE MOTHER OF HARLOTS, THE MOTHER OF HARLOTS." When I said, "THE MOTHER OF HARLOTS" for the third time, God spoke immediately again and said, "If she is a mother, she has children." God hesitated for a split-second; then, He told me, "Go and find the children."

I immediately got up and told Bill that I had to go. When I got home, I started studying and reading encyclopedias, comparing the so-called Christian history in the encyclopedias to God's word, trying to find these children that God told me to find. I already knew where the Bible spoke of the MOTHER, so I started studying Revelation chapter 17 about the MOTHER OF HARLOTS. As I studied, God began opening up the eyes of my understanding and revealed to me who the MOTHER was. It took about an hour of studying God's word, and when I found out who the GREAT WHORE was, I knew who the children were; it all became very clear. In Revelation 17, John writes that the children would be HARLOTS, which means false teachers or deceivers. Notice that the Bible says the children are HARLOTS, which are females. This tells me that these HARLOTS have the ability to reproduce and spread false doctrines across this whole world, and they have.

Truly, this is some of the meat of God's word—and I mean porterhouse! To those who understands or seeking to understand God's word, this is good stuff. There is nothing else like a porterhouse steak. This meat is going to be tough to chew for some of you who read this book. The only way anyone can understand these scriptures is if they seek God for the correct interpretation, and God will teach them. Jesus will teach anyone who seeks for the TRUTH and will obey Him, as they learn.

I have been stopped at this point from writing for days. I have prayed and thought, and I have thought and prayed, trying to find the best way to reveal to you who the MOTHER OF HARLOTS and her children are. I have come to this conclusion; I have to just say it. THE MOTHER OF HARLOTS is the Catholic church; and the HARLOTS, her children, are the Protestant churches.

Please don't stop reading now. Besides learning the TRUTH about being born-again. I believe learning about the MOTHER OF

HARLOTS and her children (the Protestant churches) is one of the best parts of this book. If we realized how Satan has been deceiving billions of people in these false- doctrine churches, it should strike a hunger deep in our souls to find God's TRUTH, and we are as soon as I finish writing about the Catholics, the Protestants, the popes, and Satan. If the Lord is willing, I will end this book by revealing God's plan of salvation for everyone since the day Jesus died on the cross.

I said at the beginning of this chapter that I was going to write about the largest religious group in the world. When you put the GREAT WHORE (Catholics) and her offspring the HARLOTS (Protestants) together, you will have the largest religious group in the world. I don't see how you can separate them, because the Protestants came out of her, so they are a part of her.

We are going to learn more about the Protestants in the next chapter, but first, we need to learn about this GREAT WHORE— that is, the MOTHER of most of the false teachings in the world. I have said it before, and I will probably say it a few more times in this book. If the message you are hearing is not what the apostles taught in its proper context, it is a false doctrine. I believe you are going to learn this before you finish reading this book.

As you continue reading and God reveals the apostolic message to you, you will be able to see for yourself that the Catholics and Protestants do not know how the Bible teaches someone to be born-again. Matthew 23:24 Jesus calls them "blind guides, which strain at a gnat, and swallow a camel." This verse only applies in certain situations, and the Catholics and the Protestants is one of those situations. Also, this tells me that they have missed the true interpretation of God's word. You can see what Jesus says about the blind leading the blind in Matthew 15:14. Jesus says that both the teacher and the follower are going to "fall into a ditch," and I say, that ditch is HELL.

Now, let us find out what the Bible says about the MOTHER. You can read about her in Revelation chapter 17. You need to read your Bible along with this book so you can RIGHTLY DIVIDE the scriptures and learn the TRUTH about the MOTHER and her children. Chapter 17 is written in such a way that we are going to have to skip around to RIGHTLY DIVIDE the scriptures so we can find the TRUTH. As we skip around in the verses, you will see what I'm talking about.

In verse 1, the angel tells John that she is the GREAT WHORE and she sits upon many waters. Now, read verse 15, because it explains verse 1— "The waters which thou sawest, where the WHORE sitteth, are peoples, and multitudes, and nations, and tongues." These scriptures teach us that the GREAT WHORE is over a large number of people.

As I said before, Revelation chapter 17 is talking about the Catholic church and how Satan is using it to accomplish his work here on earth. As you continue reading, you will see all the dots connected, and it will be a clear picture. This is called RIGHTLY DIVIDING THE WORD OF TRUTH. I also believe that you will understand, as you read and study Revelation chapter 17, that the MOTHER OF HARLOTS is the Catholic church. And that one of the popes is going to come back from the dead and become the Beast that makes everyone who is not born-again receive his mark, or the name of the Beast, or the Beast's number, which is 666. I will explain a little later in chapter 6.

You are about to hear about a scarlet-colored Beast (Satan). Read Revelation 17:2–7. Verse 3 teaches us that the GREAT WHORE is allowing a scarlet-colored Beast to carry (rule over) her and that this scarlet-colored Beast has seven heads and ten horns. First, let us find out who the scarlet- colored Beast is according to the scriptures. Revelation 12:3 says that he is a great red dragon, and verse 9 says that this great dragon is called the devil and Satan, and he deceives the whole world! How does Satan deceive the whole world? I believe through all the false teaching that I have been writing about and his ability to make sinning seem to be fun and long-lasting. I will not lie. I have had a lot of fun while I was living in sin. But beware—this fun is only for a season (short time). The second death (HELL) will be the price you will pay for your sins, if you don't change your life, when Jesus calls your name. I was just smart enough to choose the Lord back when He chose and called me.

Revelation 17:7 says, "And the angel said unto me [John], Wherefore didst thou marvel? I will tell thee the mystery of the woman." John records the mystery in this chapter, so we (the church) would know this "mystery of the woman, and of the Beast that carrieth her." In verse 9, the angel reveals to John what the seven heads are. I am going to paraphrase a little. Verse 9 says, "If you have a spiritual mind, you can comprehend what this scripture is saying. The seven heads are seven mountains on which the woman sits." Verse 18 tells us what the woman is and that she is that great city. I don't know about you, but when I read this, I had to find out what city was built on seven mountains. I knew that if I could find the city that was built on seven mountains, I would have found a big piece of the puzzle. To my knowledge, there is only one city that is built on seven mountains. If you will look in your encyclopedia or search online, you will find that the city of Rome is built on seven mountains. Revelation chapter 17 is not just a coincidence, but it is the TRUTH if you RIGHTLY DIVIDE these scriptures.

The ten horns mentioned in verse 3 are partly revealed in verse 12: "The ten horns…are ten kings." During the end-time when the Beast takes over, these ten kings will be united with the Beast for a short period, which God's word says is one hour. Verse 16 says that these ten horns (kings)—for some reason, the Lord has not revealed this to me—begin to hate the WHORE. There will be no more peace between these ten kingdoms and the GREAT WHORE. These ten kingdoms go into war with the GREAT WHORE and destroy her. Verse 17 says that God has put this in their hearts so His will, will be fulfilled. As I have said before, it's God's plan. You can read about the city of Rome being destroyed in Revelation chapter 18.

I personally don't want to be on that side of God's will. One thing is for sure—God's will is going to be fulfilled no matter what. I am so thankful to God that He chose me to be on His side, the good side, the loving side, the side of God's will where I can find life. I know that the second death (HELL) has no power over me in the future.

Through God, I have chosen blessing, and I have chosen life. I pray that you will also choose Jesus when He chooses you, because Jesus is life. Read John 15:16 and also Matthew 20:16. Read carefully Deuteronomy 30:19.

I mentioned earlier in this book that finding out the TRUTH about the Catholics and Protestants was going to cut across the grain. However, I want everyone who reads this book to know that I didn't write this book to offend anyone, but I know it will offend some; and to them, I am sorry, but they will just have to get over it. I am sharing the TRUTH that God has revealed to me. I am trying to help you, if you will listen, so you will not be entangled in all of these false teachings and so you can learn God's TRUTH and obey it.

I'm not against the Catholic people, the Protestants, or any other religious group. I'm against Satan and their false teachings. I will never be against the people, because God has some of His people still in these false churches. I don't believe God put them in these false teachings. I believe they got in these false teachings themselves or with the help of Satan. But either way, God is calling His people out of the GREAT WHORE and out of all of the other false doctrines in the world. Remember Revelation 18:4, "Come out of her, My people."

I will do whatever God wants me to do, but my desire is to win souls for our kingdom. One day, as I was reading John 4:34–38, these verses came alive. God began speaking to me through His word. In these verses, Jesus was speaking about the harvest of souls. Knowing all the things that I know about God and Satan, I had to get busy doing something to win souls. I started seeking the Lord for what I should do. I don't remember the day or the hour when God inspired me to write this book, but He did. So I wrote, and now you're reading.

It has been twenty-three years since that day Bill and I were sitting on my tailgate, talking and learning about the MOTHER OF HARLOTS. I never saw Bill again, but when I do, I will share with him what the Lord has shared with me these past twenty-three years. I said earlier in this chapter that it seemed as if God was feeding Bill that day with a snow scoop. But after all this time, as I began writing this book, I realized it was me that God was feeding that day with a snow scoop. The Lord was preparing me for the day I would write this book.

Here is something else you need to know. Don't be deceived by the false teachings that are being taught by these false churches. They teach that the church will be taken to heaven before the tribulation period and the reign of the Beast. Again, don't be deceived! These teachings are false. Let's go and find in the scriptures what Jesus says is going to happen. In Matthew chapter 24, Jesus is teaching us about the end-time and about the great tribulation. You need to read the whole chapter, but I want you to pay close attention to verses 29–31. In verse 29, Jesus says, "IMMEDIATELY AFTER the tribulation of those days." In verse 30, Jesus starts off by saying, "And THEN shall appear the sign of the Son of man in heaven."

In verse 31, something will happen, and it is what the Christians call the rapture. Now, the word rapture is not recorded in God's word. But Apostle Paul teaches us in 1 Thessalonians 4:13–17 about the church being caught up together with them in the clouds. Verse 14 teaches us that all the people, who have died as Christians, have been in heaven with the Lord. In verse 16, Paul writes, "And the dead in Christ shall rise first." At that time, the Lord is going to reunite all of the souls that are with Him with their new spiritual bodies. Verse 17 tells us how the living Christians are going to meet the Lord and the Christians who have been in the grave.

Apostle Paul confirms the rapture in 1 Corinthians 15:42–58. When you read these scriptures, you will see that the Lord is going to give all Christians a new spiritual body. In my dictionary, the second definition of rapture is the transporting of believers to heaven at the second coming of Christ. And that is good, but I like the first definition, and it is a feeling of intense pleasure or joy. I try not to ride airplanes anymore, but I do believe it's going to be an intense feeling when we take a plain air ride. No matter what you want to call it, it's not going to happen until "IMMEDIATELY AFTER the tribulation," according to Jesus. This is discussed in greater detail in chapter 6.

When you begin living for the Lord, you will find out that it will be hard at times, because we are fighting a war against Satan. If anyone tells you any different, they will be lying to you. The more you do for the Lord, the harder Satan will try to stop you. But as you study His word and the more you pray and kneel at Jesus' feet, you will grow in the Lord. As the Lord teaches you His word, you will come to know that you don't have to live in sin, because Jesus gave Himself on the cross for the whole world. And if you will hear His voice when He calls you and obey His word as you learn, you will get to live in heaven with Him throughout eternity. When you die in Jesus, you will immediately come alive as never before. I have not physically died yet, but I have died spiritually. And I know God's word teaches us that if you die in Jesus, you will truly come alive.

I know there are so many other things recorded in the Bible and in our history books that I have not written about. I have only written about some of the things that God has taught me. There is no limit to the knowledge that the Lord will share with you if you will apply yourself to studying for the TRUTH. If you have read this book up to this point, I believe you are seeking for the TRUTH. Please continue reading! No matter who you are and what you think you know in God's word, there is always room to gain more knowledge. If I had to name the Bible, my first choice would be The Book of Knowledge.

Before I start writing another chapter, there are two questions I would like to ask that may stir up your curiosity enough for you to seek God for the answers. Why does the Catholic priest think he has the authority to forgive sins? There is no person that has walked this earth since Jesus that can forgive sins. Only Jesus (God) can forgive sins. The second question is, Who do they think they are?

Here is something else that I want to share with you about the pope. On May 13, 2017, Pope Francis celebrated Canonization Mass at the Shrine for the Virgin Mary in Fatima, Portugal. The Vatican says that a half a million people came to the Canonization Mass. At this mass, the pope made two shepherd children saints. This ceremony occurred a hundred years after they said the Virgin Mary appeared to them. If you are Catholic, most likely you have heard about these two shepherd children's vision. But if you have not heard about them, simply search and read about them online. I have just got one more question, and this time, it is for the pope— who do you think you are that you can make someone a saint? The Lord doesn't even make anyone a saint. A person who is born-again grows in God from an infant to a saint. You will learn more about our growth in the Lord in chapter 7.

Chapter 5

THE HARLOTS

Now, it is time to find out about the children of the GREAT WHORE, the HARLOTS, which are the Protestants. To be able to find the TRUTH, we all need to know the answer to this question—how did the Protestants come to be? When you find out what the word Protestant means, then you will begin to know where they came from. If you will look in your dictionary at the word just above Protestant, you will find the true meaning of Protestant. Here is another way to find the true meaning. If you will look at the word Protestant and take off the ant from the end of Protestant, you will find the true meaning. Yes, Protestant means to protest.

We are about to find out when and where the Protestants came from and who started this false teaching according to our history books. Protestantism is the general term for the religious faith and practice within the Christian church that resulted from the Reformation in Europe in the sixteenth century. Protestants protested against the Catholic church, because of some of their newfound beliefs. This answers the when and where question about the Protestants.

According to the encyclopedia, during the early Middle Ages, Christianity in Europe was united by a common way of thinking and by a strong system of church government. But in the later part of the Middle Ages, this unity was broken by new kinds of political, social, and religious ideas. You should be able to see what Satan has corrupted now is going to get even worse. The true word of God that Satan wrested into a lie at the beginning is now starting to break apart, as it seems.

As I was writing about this, I thought about what Jesus said in Matthew 12:25, so I had to read it again. Jesus said, "Every Kingdom divided against itself is brought to desolation; and every city or house divided against itself shall not stand."

As we realize how deceiving Satan is, we must understand that Satan was not dividing his kingdom—he was strengthening it. When the Protestants protested against the Catholic teachings, this is when the HARLOTS (Protestants) came out of the GREAT WHORE (Catholics). This rebellion has allowed Satan to now spread even more false teachings. This is why the world has so many different kinds of religious teachings, just in case you have ever wondered.

I'm sure that the Protestants have a few doctrines in common with their fellow Protestants, but here is one doctrine that they all have in common— they all teach the Trinity doctrine. I have heard in thirty-two years of some (maybe two) individual churches within the Protestant movement that have received God's TRUTH and came out of that false teaching just as the Lord Jesus told them to do in Revelation 18:4.

On December 30, 2015, while flipping through the channels, I heard Pastor Wayne Webb from Macon Road Baptist church, in Arlington, Tennessee, teach how Jesus was and is God. What I heard him teach that day was as clear word as I have ever heard any apostolic preacher teach. Some people in these false-doctrine churches are hearing God's TRUTH and coming out of her (the GREAT WHORE), just as the Lord told them to.

It's like this. If you have ever tried this, you will know what I'm writing is true. If you take a room full of people and let everyone pass a message by whispering it in the next person's ear, by the time this message reaches the last person, 99.9% of the time, it has been changed. Now, imagine sending a message through a room full of people, but this time, Satan will be the manipulative lying force behind the message. Here is what you would get—a lie! This is true. Satan has used the Catholics and the Protestants to change God's word into a lie by taking the word out of context.

Now, we are about to find out who started the Reformation, and by doing so, we are going to find out a little more about how the Protestants came to be. The people who felt so strongly that something ought to be done about bringing the church up to date were called Protestants or sometimes simply Reformers. Both names describe two different but related features of Protestantism. First, there was a protest against many of the beliefs and practices of the Roman Catholic church, as the Reformation developed during the Middle Ages by a man named Martin Luther. History teaches us that in Martin Luther, there was a deep desire to reform the principles, worship, and government of the Catholic church so that they would be nearer to the New Testament teachings. Meanwhile the encyclopedia notes that in its earliest forms and often in later years, Protestantism showed itself as both a negative (protesting) and a positive (reforming) religious movement.

The birth date of the Protestant Reformation is usually given as 1517. This is the year that Martin Luther, a German monk, first spoke out officially against the Roman Catholic church and some of its beliefs. The encyclopedia also points out that Luther didn't want to leave the Catholic church or start a new church. Even though Luther didn't want to start a new church, his protest was so strong that in a few years, he became the recognized leader of the whole of Protestantism.

As Martin Luther continued going to the Catholic church, he simply believed that they were missing the point of what God's word was trying to teach. As Martin was reading God's word one day, he found Romans 1:16–17. These scriptures teach the TRUTH about a powerful individual relationship that each person could have with the Lord. He had found a revolutionary idea that changed his way of thinking. Now, Martin knew that salvation comes not from the man-made rituals of the Catholic church, but by faith in the gospel of Christ because each individual person has the ability to learn about Jesus and how they are to live. This means that neither the Pope, the Vatican, nor even a priest is necessary to ensure a person's entrance into the kingdom of heaven. This new revelation that Luther had found began to set him free from the Catholic's teachings. The words that he found in Romans 1:16–17 started (gave birth) the Protestants separation from the GREAT WHORE.

For Luther, this was a great personal revelation. But he had no way of knowing that the debate he was going to have with the Catholics was going to turn the Vatican upside down and launch wars and revolutions. He did know that after finding and reading Romans 1:16–17, he had to get into God's word and find out more about the personal relationship each person could have with the Lord. History books teach us that after Luther had completed his studies of God's word, he came up with ninety-five different things from God's word that he didn't think the Catholics were teaching correctly. What Luther had learned in Romans 1:16–17 was at the top of the list of complaints. Luther wanted to address the limits of power that the pope and the priest had on the people.

Luther started his debate with the Catholics with a set of ideas about what he thinks is wrong with the Catholic church. It's easy to imagine how that goes over with the Catholic church. His thesis, which he had written was ninety-five oppositions in all, and the next thing on his list to debate was the selling of indulgences (insurance policies). When Luther saw and heard of the stupid practices the

Catholic church was participating in, he had to say stop. The Catholics had gotten so far out in left field that they started selling their people an insurance policy. During the Middle Ages, a person could buy an insurance policy for themselves, family, friend, or even someone who had already died. Through the Catholic church, a person could purchase an official church document. This document had blank spaces where you would fill in the name of the person who it was bought for and another blank space where they could write in the date it was purchased. I'm not making this stuff up. You can find out about this in your dictionary or in a history book. The Catholic leaders started selling their people an afterlife insurance policy, and it guaranteed that whoever had one of these policies would go to heaven no matter what they had done in their life.

As the years went by, Martin Luther was not alone. He was followed by other leaders in other places in Europe. Some of the main leaders were John Calvin from Geneva, John Knox of Scotland, and later in the eighteenth century John Wesley from England. Now, I know them better as John, John, and John. I truly believe that if Martin Luther's name would have been John Luther, I believe the people would have discovered this conspiracy a long time ago. I know that I'm not the first to write about these men and the false teachings that they have started. But at this very moment, I feel honored to be allowed by God to know and write about the GREATEST CONSPIRACY that has taken place in this world. I'm so glad that the Lord is allowing and helping me to shine some (a lot) light on these false teachings. It's not over yet; there will be more splits and debates from the original Protestant Reformation. The Protestant Reformation is still alive and will continue until the Lord comes back and puts an end to the false teachings of this world.

Here's a good idea—let's turn up the light so we can see even clearer. Protestants believe that Roman Catholics didn't make the Bible central enough in their teachings. So Protestants began a fresh study of the Old and New Testaments. One of Luther's first tasks was to translate the Bible from Greek and Hebrew to German, which was the common language of his people. This placed the basic document of Christianity (the Bible) into the hands of the people. Now, they were no longer completely dependent on priests for the interpretation of God's word, but could be encouraged to interpret the scriptures for themselves. Protestants also objected to the supreme authority and power of the pope.

At first, Protestants defined their doctrines and beliefs in terms of their opposition to Roman Catholicism. Protestants believe in salvation "by faith" in Jesus Christ, rather than "by works" (of righteous living); they also believed in the authority of the Bible, rather than the authority of the pope. Additionally, they believe in the divinity of Jesus Christ, but with less emphasis on devotion to the Virgin Mary and a "priesthood of believers" (private interpretation of the scriptures) rather than several different ranks of priests (hierarchy); the church as the community of believers, rather than the divine institution of the clergy as stated by Rome; and the two essential sacraments of water baptism and communion (the Lord's Supper) rather than the seven sacraments of the Roman Catholic church. The Catholic's seven sacraments are baptism, confirmation, Holy Communion, penance, sacrament of the sick, holy orders, and marriage. Simply put, it was just time for these false churches (HARLOTS) to be born.

There are three major types of Protestantism that emerged from the sixteenth-century European Reformation. First, it was the Lutheran and Calvinistic churches, sometimes called Reformed or Presbyterian churches. These churches spread throughout Germany, the Netherlands, the Scandinavian countries, Britain, and later North America. There were differences between Lutherans and Calvinists, mostly on the interpretation about what the sacraments meant and how the church should be governed. The Lutherans and the Calvinists formed the main movement of Protestantism in Europe and America.

As the names suggest, the various branches of the Lutheran church, adopted the doctrinal views of Martin Luther.

Calvinists (Reformed and Presbyterians) looked to John Calvin as their spiritual ancestor. They stress the primary authority of the Bible in matters of belief and worship.

The second major type of Protestantism began in England, under Henry VIII. This Protestant Reformation resulted in a church tradition often called Anglican or Protestant Episcopal. Through the years, some groups have dropped the word Protestant from their title. The English Reformation was not as critical of Roman Catholic doctrine or forms of worship, as the Lutheran and Calvinistic churches. The Church of England is sometimes called a bridge church because it combines and brings together elements from both Catholic and Protestant traditions.

The encyclopedia points that there was a third group of churches mostly in Switzerland, Germany, and the Netherlands. They tried to carry the reform of the church much further than either Luther or Calvin had. These smaller, and usually unorganized, churches became known as the Radical Reformation, or "left-wing" Protestantism. They were highly independent in terms of church governance, interpretation of the scriptures, and doctrinal beliefs. These radical reforming movements had a great influence on the development of such churches as the Baptist. This type of Protestantism was never strong in Europe or England. But in America, it grew rapidly into many different kinds of independent churches. I did not and could not make this stuff up. If you will read your encyclopedias and history books, you will find these same words that I have written.

Let's turn the light up a little bit more so we can see even more clearly. Baptists believe that people from the age of accountability through adulthood (not infants) should receive the sacrament of baptism by total immersion in water rather than by mere sprinkling. I have said this before somewhere in this book, and it looks like it's time to say it again. In my teenage years, I considered myself to be a Baptist. I don't know everything about everyone, but I do know this about the Baptist. Satan revealed a little bit of TRUTH to this religious group through his deceiving ways. He allowed them to see that being baptized by being sprinkled with holy water was wrong and that a person should be totally immersed in the water. But Satan would not and could not reveal to them that they should be baptized in the name of Jesus. It is what they say when they baptize someone that makes it wrong.

The only reason that I am naming names is because we are looking for the TRUTH. I believe if the Lord and I can get you to see how Satan used these false teachings (churches), then just maybe you will be inspired to seek the Lord for His TRUTH. But no matter what, I must continue writing about what I have learned, and it is up to you what you do with what you learn.

Even though the Baptist started baptizing in water through total immersion, they held on to the Trinitarian baptismal doctrine that the Catholics used in their baptism. You should be able to tell by their teaching that they came out of the GREAT WHORE. The Catholics and the Protestants repeat what Jesus said to do in Matthew 28:19. Please read Matthew 28:19, and see for yourself what Jesus said to do. After you read this book and see (hear) the TRUTH, it will be up to you if you obey or reject it.

Remember what Jesus said in John 12:48.

I want you to take a pen and paper and write what Jesus tells us to do in Matthew 28:19. Now, I want you to write what Peter says in Acts 2:38 and then read these two scriptures side by side, and you will be able to see (hear) that Acts 2:38 is the fulfillment of what Jesus said in Matthew 28:19. I am challenging you to ask your preacher, your mother's preacher, or just the preacher down the street about water baptism. They are going to give you all kinds of excuses why they don't baptize in Jesus' name. But if you have studied these scriptures as I have, there will be no way they can convince you of any other way to be baptized than in the name of Jesus.

The next scripture is how I learned who Jesus is. Read Isaiah 9:6. Now that you just heard who Jesus is, this is what I believe Isaiah is teaching us in verse 6. Jesus is synonymous (same as) with WONDERFUL, COUNSELLOR, THE MIGHTY GOD, THE EVERLASTING FATHER,

AND THE PRINCE OF PEACE. Now, it is clear to me who Jesus is. All so- called Christians will agree that Jesus is WONDERFUL, that He is a COUNSELLOR, and that He is the PRINCE OF PEACE. But most of them don't and will not admit that Jesus is the MIGHTY GOD and the EVERLASTING FATHER. I'm so thankful to know God's TRUTH.

By the time a preacher would call themselves a preacher, they would have already read and known what is said in Acts 2:38–39. But the Catholics and the Protestants will not obey these scriptures. I didn't make up this plan of salvation. The words in Acts 2:38–39 are God's plan of salvation. When you read Acts 2:38–39 and then close your Bible, and when you open your Bible the next day, the next year, or even ten thousand years from now, these scriptures are going to say the same thing as they did the last time you read them.

Peter says that everyone has to be baptized in the name of Jesus, and that includes you. Peter knew what he was saying. I am going to write about this later in greater details, but at this time, I want you to read Matthew 16:13–19. In these scriptures, Jesus gives Apostle Peter the keys to the kingdom of heaven. Jesus did not give Peter a literal door key, but Jesus gave Peter the words of salvation to speak to the world (everyone in the New Testament times). I will show you in chapter 9, in the scriptures, where Apostle Peter opened three doors to God's people with this TRUTH (keys). Again, Peter knew what he was saying in Acts 2:38–39. He knew that he was speaking the fulfillment of what Jesus said to do in Matthew 28:19.

The Delivery of the Keys, by Pietro Perugino, shows the first pope, Saint Peter, receiving the keys of the kingdom of heaven from Jesus Christ.

The picture I placed here shows Jesus giving Apostle Peter a literal door key. I found this picture in my encyclopedia at the beginning of the article about the Roman Catholic church. This is not what Jesus gave to Peter in Matthew 16:13–19. Jesus gave Peter the one, and only, true plan of salvation, to teach and preach to the whole world. I believe that Pietro Perugino was using his carnal mind when he painted this picture, and the Catholics were using more of a carnal mind (if there is such a thing) to use this picture to head the history of their church.

There is something else that is written under this picture that is false. They have stated falsely that Apostle Peter was the first pope. When Jesus gave Peter the keys to heaven, there was no such thing as a pope. Look in your encyclopedia for the Roman Catholic church and begin reading. You'll discover that it starts off with a lie. It says that the Roman Catholic church began in an upper room in Jerusalem almost 2,000 years ago. The Catholic church did not start on the Day of Pentecost. That is the day that God's church started.

They claimed that their church started on the Day of Pentecost, and I know that is not true. So I believe no one really knows when their church started. From the things that the Holy Ghost has taught me, let me tell you what the fact is—God's church was persecuted for the first three hundred years or so by the Romans. I have already written about some of this in chapter 4. I believe the Catholic church didn't start until after Constantine the Great, a Roman emperor, claimed to be a Christian. At that time, Constantine stopped the persecution of the church. This tells me that Apostle Peter could not have been the first pope because Peter had been in his grave for almost two hundred years before the Catholic church started.

The main reason why the Catholics and the Protestants repeat what Jesus said to do in Matthew 28:19 is because Satan has blinded them. They do not understand that Jesus is the Father, the Son, and the Holy Ghost. Another reason they repeat Matthew 28:19 as their method of baptism is that it is the only scripture in God's word that coincides (fits) with their Trinitarian doctrine. So they continue teaching, listening, and obeying this false doctrine. For the past 1,700 years, Catholics have been used by Satan to spread this false doctrine. The Protestants also have been used by Satan to spread their false teaching, for more than four hundred years in America. Do you remember what Jesus said in Matthew 15:14? Jesus says, "If the blind lead the blind, both shall fall into the ditch." Listen to what this scripture said. I believe this ditch that Jesus spoke of is HELL.

I want to be clear of this TRUTH. I have said it before, and I will say it again as I witness to my fellow man. Matthew 28:19 is the most wrongfully used scripture from God's word. When I found out that I had not been baptized correctly, I knew that I had to get back into the water and be baptized the right way. If you find yourself in this same predicament, don't be ashamed or embarrassed because you need to be baptized again; instead, be thankful to God that He has taught you His TRUTH.

When you are baptized in the name of Jesus, God's word promises us that He washes away all the bad things (sin) we have ever done. From that time, God will only remember the good things we have done in our past and the good that we will do in our future. I believe that there is one other thing the Lord will remember and keep a record of after you are born-again, and that is every bad thing we do that we don't ask Him to forgive us of. I believe that is why it's called being born-again, because we get a brand new start in life.

How good is that? Through the years, I have heard many people say, "I wish I could have another chance to do it all over again." I'm here to tell you—you have your chance now, if you will take it.

I want you to read Acts 19:1–7, and see what Apostle Paul says and does when he finds about twelve men who have not been baptized correctly. In verse 2, when Paul found out that they were believers, Paul started questioning them. As you can see, Paul did not beat around the bush; the first thing he asked them, "Have ye received the Holy Ghost, since ye believed?" They replied, "We have not so much as heard whether there be any Holy Ghost." In verse 3, Paul asked, "Unto what then were ye baptized?" They answered, "Unto John's baptism."

In verses 4–5, Paul tells them, "John verily [truly] baptized with the baptism of repentance, saying unto the people, that they should believe on Him which should come after him, that is, on Christ Jesus. When they heard, they were baptized in the name of the Lord Jesus." As Paul baptized these twelve men, he did not repeat Matthew 28:19, but he did baptize them in the name of the Father and the Son, and of the Holy Ghost, when he baptized them in the name of Jesus. Verse 6 says, "When Paul had laid hands upon them, the Holy Ghost came on them; and they spake with tongues, and prophesied." These twelve men were born-again according to God's word. If you were not born-again in the same manner, you had better go and do it right. Read Acts 4:12. Just remember this—the apostles taught God's TRUTH, and Satan is going to wrest (twist or change) that TRUTH into a lie, if you will allow him to.

These twelve men had just obeyed Matthew 28:19 and what Jesus told His apostles to teach all nations. Here, you can see Paul teaching God's plan of salvation, and it was the same plan of salvation that Peter taught. These twelve men had been born-again by hearing a preacher and then obeying what he told them to do. Acts 2:38–39 has been fulfilled in their lives. Here in these scriptures is proof that if someone has not been baptized in the name of Jesus, they must get back into the water and be baptized correctly. This is why we (apostolic) call ourselves apostolic, because we still after all these years believe and obey what the apostles wrote for us to do.

Now, for the conclusion of chapter 5, let's continue learning about the Protestants. Now, we need to find out when and why the Protestant movement came to America. First, we need to find out why they left the place where they lived. To find out about this, we must seek the TRUTH about England. To find the TRUTH about this time dispensation in England, we must find out about the leader and this would be King Henry VIII.

For you who don't know, here is how it happened. In order to divorce the first of his six famous wives, Henry VIII broke away from the Catholic church and made himself head of the Protestant church of England. One reason for this separation from the Catholic church was the refusal of Pope Clement VII to annul Henry's marriage to Catherine of Aragon.

Henry knew how important it was to have a male heir. However, he had only one daughter by Catherine. She was his elder brother's widow, and it was not customary for Catholics to marry relatives. Henry decided to ask Pope Clement VII to annul (undo) the marriage from Catherine so he could marry Anne Boleyn, a lady of the court. But the Pope refused. The encyclopedia notes that Henry loved Anne and hoped she would give him a son.

When the pope refused, Henry persuaded Parliament to pass a series of acts between 1529 and 1536 to take away the pope's authority in England. Then, Henry dissolved the monasteries, seized their property, and declared that the king of England (himself) was head of both church and state. I remember in Ephesians 5:23, Apostle Paul said, "Christ [Jesus] is the head of the church." Henry evidently wasn't reading and studying his Bible.

In 1533, the marriage to Catherine was annulled by Archbishop of Canterbury, Thomas Cranmer, and Henry married Anne. But Henry still had no male heir, for Anne's child was a girl, who became Queen Elizabeth I. Suspecting that Anne was interested in men other than himself, Henry had Anne beheaded.

Finally, his next wife Jane Seymour had a son, Edward VI. Unfortunately, Jane died during childbirth.

After that, Henry VIII had three more wives. His fourth wife was also named Anne, a German princess. But Henry did not like this Anne and soon divorced her. Here goes my two cents. At least, Henry didn't have this Anne beheaded. His fifth wife's name was Catherine Howard, and she too was beheaded for being unfaithful. Henry was married for the sixth and last time to Catherine Parr, and this wife outlived him. I was going to put in my two cents again, but I had better not say that she poisoned him so she would not be beheaded. I cannot falsely accuse, so I had better leave it at that.

Henry's quarrel with the pope was not the only reason for the separation with Rome. The people and even many of the clergy disliked the way that the pope interfered with the Church of England and how he collected money from it. Some of the clergy and monks in England did not lead good lives, and so they had lost the respect of ordinary people. The people hoped that if the king were head of the church, he would reform it. However, because there was no pope to tell the people what they must believe, they disagreed as to the kind of church they wanted.

After Henry VIII died in 1547, the religious disagreements became much worse. Some people wanted services very much like the old Roman Catholic ones; others hoped for a simpler or, as they said, purer service. For this reason, these people later became known as the Puritans. In just a few paragraphs, I am going to write a little more about the Puritans.

Catholicism returned briefly under Mary I. In 1553, England returned to the Roman Catholic church. This started when Mary Tudor became the queen of England. At first, Mary was popular, because many people had disliked the new Protestant prayer book. But some of the people came to hate her when she married Philip II of Spain. Then, she persuaded Parliament to restore the pope's authority and began to have men and women, including Archbishop Cranmer, burned at the stake for continuing to be a Protestant. For this, the people gave her the nickname of Bloody Mary.

As you can see, the leaders of England could not make up their minds as to which teachings to follow.

As time went on, this uncertainty of which teaching the people of England should believe, they did something that in Mississippi is called to bust a move, and they did. Sixty-five or so years after Mary Tudor returned to the Catholic teachings, some of the people decided that they have had enough.

Now, most of you have heard about the story how this land (America) was founded, but if not, here it is. Also, you must remember that this story (how America was founded) is a conjecture, because we don't have all of the facts. This is how I know the story, and this story fits with God's TRUTH about the false churches. Now, these religious seekers (the Pilgrims) as they were called got into a ship called the Mayflower and sailed West across the Atlantic from England.

They dropped anchor in 1620 at Plymouth Harbor, in what is now Massachusetts. They wanted to separate themselves from the Church of England, so they could worship God in their own way.

The Pilgrims have had enough. They were tired of being tossed to and fro and carried about with every wind of doctrine. Paul wrote about this in Ephesians 4:14. They felt the church had too many traces of Catholic ritual and too little emphasis on sermons and Bible readings.

When the Pilgrims landed at Plymouth Harbor in 1620, not only did they bring our ancestors, but also they brought across the Atlantic these false doctrines. These false teachings that were in Europe and England have now come to Canada, Mexico, North, Central, and South America.

Ten years after the landing of the Mayflower, another group of English settlers established Massachusetts Bay Colony. They settled first at Salem and then at Boston. These people were called Puritans and shared many of the Pilgrim's religious beliefs. But the Puritans, however, wished to remain members of the Church of England in order to "purify" it, instead of leaving the church as the Pilgrims had. Because the Puritans had more wealth than the Pilgrims, they came in greater numbers and possessed more intellectual leaders. So they quickly dominated New England.

The Pilgrims started this false teaching movement across America and then came the Puritans.

There was no way to stop it; this false teaching spread like wildfire. The chief forms of early Protestantism spread quickly as explorers discovered this new land and as the German, Dutch, English, Swedish, and other colonies in North America settled. Before the Revolutionary War, Anglicans and Episcopalians had settled in New England and in the South. Reformed (Calvinistic) churches were established by the Dutch in New York and New Jersey. Puritans came from England, Presbyterians from Scotland, and Lutherans from Germany and Scandinavia. The Mennonites and Moravians were two more religious groups that came from Germany. Methodist looked to John Wesley as their spiritual father. The Baptist remembered the courage and independence of Roger

Williams. As you read and found out in chapter 2, in 1830, Joseph Smith founded what is known today as the Church of Jesus Christ of Latter Day Saints.

By the first half of the twentieth century, there were more than two hundred different Protestant church bodies in America. Today, there are even more. Most of these came from the Lutheran, Calvinistic, Anglican, and "radical" traditions. These HARLOTS (Protestants) have spread this false teaching from one side of this nation to the other. To top it off, the GREAT WHORE (Catholics) followed right behind the Protestants and came to America. This false teaching has been moving across the United States for almost four hundred years, and it is growing with leaps and bounds, just as Satan knew it would.

I don't know when the apostolic doctrine came to America, but it did. It is the reason I'm writing this book. I'm so thankful that the Lord wanted to share His word with me and my family, and I want to share with you what God has taught me. You have already read about some of the apostolic teachings in this book. But in chapter 9, we will learn in greater details how to be born-again according to God's word. You are not going to hear about false teaching in chapter 9. You will only hear the TRUTH and nothing but the TRUTH so help me God. If you will ask God to teach you, the scriptures will be really clear and easy to understand. As far as the Protestants, I think that I have written enough to reveal some of their false teachings. I know that there is a lot more to learn about these false teachers, so it is up to you to seek God for the TRUTH, and you will be able to see the FALSE.

My brother Tommy told me this story one day. He told me about a man who he heard about, and his job was looking for counterfeit money. The man was asked, "I bet you look at a lot of counterfeit money." His response was, "I hardly ever look at counterfeit. I mostly look at the real thing, and when the counterfeit shows up, I can immediately see the counterfeit."

This is the same way with God's word. When God reveals the apostolic doctrine to you, you will be able to see all the false teachings in the world. As I have said before, I want you to know that I am not against the people. I am against Satan and his false teachings.

CHAPTER 6

SATAN + POPE = BEAST

You have learned about the GREAT WHORE (Catholics) in chapter 4 and her children, the HARLOTS (Protestants), in chapter 5. Now, in chapter 6, you are going to learn some things about the leader of the GREAT WHORE—the pope. What I have learned in my studies is the Catholic people call the pope the head of the church. I have written about this before, but it's got to be said again. The pope is the head of the Catholic church, but in Ephesians 5:23, Apostle Paul says, "Jesus is the head of His church." I personally am going to listen and believe what Paul says, so should you. As you will learn from this book, they are two different churches. Before you finish reading this chapter, you will see how the pope is going to be used by Satan at the end of the church era on earth.

I have never been a book reader until now, and I will not call myself a book reader even now. But I had to read different books in my studies to find the TRUTH about these false teachings. In the beginning, when I first started learning the things that I have been writing about, it was on a Fall Monday morning back in 1991, when God revealed to me who the GREAT WHORE is and who her children are.

It was seventeen years later when God inspired me to write this book. So I started studying in the book of Revelation chapter 17 again. During those seventeen years, I would read and study the scriptures in Revelation chapter 17, because the Lord had revealed something to me that most people don't know. This is a real treasure that God has given me. I don't know why it took so long for me to start writing, but I did start; and if it's the Lord's will, I will finish writing this book. I hope it's the Lord's will for this book to be completed and given to millions of people. I wrote this book so the whole human race can hear and then see what Satan is doing and trying to do to us all.

While writing this book, I have come to know that we are shining the Great Light (Jesus) on Satan. I believe the Lord and I are revealing the GREATEST CONSPIRACY known to man. I have not made up my mind yet, but I have been contemplating if I should contact Jesse "the Body" Ventura about doing a show about this conspiracy on his show called *The Conspiracy Theory*. I believe it would be his best show ever.

Before I started writing this book, I would read and study Revelation chapter 17 every day for months. I have read and studied these scriptures dozens and dozens of times. Only the Lord knows how many times I have read and studied them. I know the Lord saw my determination and showed me favor, as I was seeking for more TRUTH from His word. I knew God gave us Revelation chapter 17 so we (the church) could know the TRUTH about the GREAT WHORE and her children, the HARLOTS. I don't know why; but for some reason, in those seventeen years, I never tried to find out about the leader of the GREAT WHORE. Now, that's what I call a slow learner.

One day as I was reading Revelation chapter 17, I saw and understood that verses 10 and 11 were talking about the popes. What a day it was. I had found a great big piece of the puzzle. I really hate to admit that it took me dozens and dozens of times reading the same scriptures to finally get the message. I can only believe and say that it was mostly my ignorance and stupidity, and as I have said before, it's all in God's time. I'm so thankful the day came that I became hungry for more TRUTH about the false teachings that are in the world. When I became hungry, the Lord opened up the eyes of my understanding and allowed me to see and hear His word (TRUTH).

I have written about the milk of the word, and now, it's time to eat some more meat. I'm here to tell you, as you continue reading and learning these TRUTHS, that you are truly stepping into the meat house of God's word. If you are a meat eater, this is a place that you can get as full as you desire, but it is according to the power that works in you. I know it was worth every hour that I spent reading and studying to find this TRUTH so I could share it with you. I can see and feel myself growing in the Lord. I'm so thankful to my Lord Jesus, because I know He loves me and had patience with me and my peabrain. Jesus opened up my peabrain and revealed this wonderful TRUTH to me that is found in Revelation chapter 17. Now, the Lord has allowed me to share this TRUTH with you. If you will bite off a piece of this knowledge and chew on it a while, you will see and feel yourself growing in the Lord also.

It's like this. If you want to know about the creation of the world, you have got to go and read the first chapter of Genesis. The creation of the world is not recorded anywhere else in God's word. If you want to find out about salvation, you have got to go and read the book of Acts. This is the only book in God's word that records God's people being born-again by obeying the apostles' doctrine. If you want to find out about the GREAT WHORE and learn how Satan, the pope, and the Beast are going to be one in the same, you have got to read and study Revelation chapter 17, because this is the chapter to find these answers.

Before I write and reveal the TRUTH that I have learned about how Satan, the pope, and the Beast are going to become the same being, I want you to read Revelation 11:1–12. The reason I want you to read this chapter is that you need your faith and your knowledge of Jesus to grow. You need to know that God can do anything. In Revelation chapter 11, you will find the scriptures that teach us how and when the Lord turns back to the Jewish nation. Chapter 11 teaches us how God is going to send His two prophets from heaven to preach the gospel to the Jews during the tribulation period. Believe me, they are going to preach the same salvation (TRUTH) that I have written in this book.

Let's look into God's word, because I want to share with you who I believe these two prophets will be. I believe that they are John who wrote the book of Revelation and the Prophet Elijah. As far as I know, neither of these men's death was ever recorded. God's word says in Hebrews 9:27, "It is appointed unto men once to die, but after this the judgment."

First, let's look in the word and see what it says about Elijah. 2 Kings chapter 2 tells us how Elijah and Elisha went on their journey from Gilgal to beyond the Jordan River. Verse 11 says, "A chariot of fire, and horses of fire, and parted them both asunder [separated them], and Elijah went up by a whirlwind into heaven." Notice that there was no mention of his death. On the last page of the Old Testament, you will find the book of Malachi chapter 4. Verse 5 says, "I [God] will send you Elijah the prophet before the coming of the great and dreadful day of the Lord."

Now, let's find out about John. History teaches us that John was exiled from his homeland to the Greek island of Patmos for preaching the gospel. And that may be true to a certain point, but I believe that this all happened so the Lord could give His church the book of Revelation. Some history books teach that before the Romans put John on the island of Patmos, they blinded him. I don't know if that is true, because the writer of that history book might not have had all the facts. But the one thing I do believe—on Patmos, John received revelations from the Lord. As you will read and study the book of Revelation, you will see that most of the time, the Lord would send an angel to John with His message; but sometimes, the Lord would speak directly to John.

What I have read and heard about John is that he was put on the island in AD 95. According to that date, that would make John well over a hundred years old. I have never read or heard of his death. To make my point, let's look at Revelation 10:11, where you will see and hear a revelation given to John by an angel. The angel tells John in verse 11, "Thou must prophesy [preach] again before many peoples, and nations, and tongues, and kings." The angel told John that he is going to prophesy again, which tells me that John is going to preach sometime in the future to a large number of people. As soon as the angel gave John this message from God, the angel begins explaining John's mission to him in Revelation 11:1–12. I truly believe that Elijah and John will be God's preachers for the Jewish nation during the tribulation period.

It really doesn't matter to me who the Lord sends to preach His TRUTH to the Jews. I'm just letting you know who I believe they are. One thing is for sure—the Lord is sending two preachers to preach to the Jewish people during the tribulation period.

Let's look at Revelation 11:1–12 again, and this time, let's look at the scriptures a little closer. Verse 2 teaches us about the 3 ½ years, the Beast is going to be in power. Verse 3 lets us know how long the two preachers will preach God's word to the Jews and that they will preach a "thousand two hundred and threescore [3x20] days," which would equal to 1,260 days. By using the Jewish calendar, if you will multiply forty-two months with thirty days, you should come up with 1,260 days, which is 3 ½ years. These scriptures in Revelation chapter 11 teach us that these two prophets are going to be preaching during the reign of the Beast to the Jewish nation.

Verse 7 says, "And when they [these two preachers] have finished their testimony [in other words, preached to the last Jew], the Beast that ascendeth out of the bottomless pit [HELL] shall make war against them, and shall overcome them, and kill them.

Verse 8 says that their dead bodies are going to stay out in the street. As you can see, God is even being fair with Satan. He allowed Satan time to do what he is able to do. The word says that for three and a half days, these two prophets will lie in the streets where our Lord was crucified (Jerusalem).

Verse 9 says, "And they of the people and kindreds and tongues and nations shall see their dead bodies for three days and a half, and shall not suffer [allow] their dead bodies to be put in graves." In verse 10, you should be able to see the evilness that is in the world. The people all over this world are going to have a party over their death—"And they that dwell upon the earth shall rejoice over them and make merry, and shall send gifts one to another; because these two prophets tormented them that dwelt on the earth."

Here comes the good part—"And after three days and a half, the Spirit of life from God entered into them, and they stood upon their feet; and great fear fell upon them which saw them" (verse 11). At that time, God calls both of them home to heaven. Mark my words with God's word. "The people and kindreds and tongues and nations shall see their dead bodies in the streets of Jerusalem," through the lens of Fox News Channel and CNN or one of the other news channels. Later in this chapter, you are going to read about one of the popes coming back from the dead. I just want you to remember that God is God, and He can do anything.

Now, let's learn about the 144,000 Jews that these two prophets are going to preach God's plan of salvation to. I'm sure that they preach to more than 144,000 Jews, but that is all that will hear and obey them. First, I want to say this about Jesus—in Revelation 1:8, He says, "I AM Alpha and Omega, the beginning and the ending." Then, John finishes that scripture by declaring who Jesus is, "Which is, and which was, and which is to come, the Almighty." Before you finish reading this book, you too will know who Jesus is. I know Him as the Almighty God. In the New Testament, from which we live, Jesus is the only God mentioned. And that is the reason I serve Him. If His name was still Jehovah, then I would be a Jehovah's Witness, but that's not the case. This is one of the greatest stumbling stones in the religious world, ever. The TRUTH is He just changed His name, when He came to earth as a human to save His people/church/Bride. Just as the apostles and prophets taught us about Jesus, these two prophets will teach and preach Jesus to the Jews during the tribulation period.

I had to write all of that so I could share with you the TRUTH about the 144,000 Jews that the Lord is going to save just before His angels pour out His wrath upon this earth. If you will flip your Bible to Exodus 1:1–6, you will find the names of Jacob's (Israel's) twelve sons. Today, these twelve sons of Israel are better known by the Jews and most Christians as the fathers of the twelve tribes of Israel.

As you can see, you have been reading from the front (Alpha=the beginning) of God's word.

Now, to find the TRUTH about the 144,000 Jews that will be saved during the tribulation period, you must flip your Bible to the back (Omega=the ending) of God's word. When you realize that Jesus is the beginning and the ending, then you will know that Jesus is the all-seeing and all-knowing God. Later in this chapter, I'm going to bring out other scriptures and tie all these events in order as they are predestined to happen. At that time, you will see more clearly and know this is the TRUTH.

Read Revelation 7:1–8 where you will find in these scriptures the number of Jews that are going to have the gospel preached to them during the tribulation period. In verses 1–3, you will learn that the Lord is not going to allow His angels to start His wrath until they have sealed the servants of God in their foreheads.

In verse 4, John tells us that there are 144,000 Jews that the Lord is going to redeem during the tribulation period. There are twelve tribes of Israel, and the Lord has chosen 12,000 from each tribe. And as you should know, 12,000 x 12 = 144,000. These 144,000 Jews will go through the tribulation period as they hear and obey the two preachers that the Lord sends from heaven. As you can see from these scriptures, the Lord is not going to start His wrath until the 144,000 Jews are sealed with the name Jesus in their foreheads. Read Revelation 22:1–4. I must say again, that is the TRUTH.

Now, read Revelation 14:1–5, where you will learn a little more about these 144,000 Jews that will be save. In these scriptures, you will find that God already knew about all of them. Verses 4–5 tell us, "These are they [these men] which were not defiled with women; for they are virgins… And in their mouth was found no guile: for they are without fault before the throne of God."

While I was writing about this, again I proved to myself my ignorance and looked up the word guile. Just in case you don't know the meaning, I want to share with you what I learned today. Guile means "sly or cunning intelligence."

But guile is not what the scripture said; it said no guile. So while I was in my dictionary, I looked at the word under guile, and I found guileless. Now, that is what I was looking for. Guileless means "free from guile, innocent and without deception."

One of the reasons I wanted you to read those scriptures is that I wanted you to see the Lord already knows about all those 144,000 Jews, including us. I know that these are bold statements, but God even knows their parents and their siblings. I have already said the word predestination a couple of times in this book, and I will say it again—predestination.

I have written in chapter 9 how the scriptures teach us to be born-again, and I have written about two other important subjects that we all need to know. These two topics that I am going to share with you from God's word teach about predestination and the Book of Life, because there are a lot of false teachings and misconceptions about both of these topics. For a while, I could not figure out where in this book to write about the Book of Life and predestination. But the more I thought about it, they both fit like a glove with God's plan of salvation. And I will explain in chapter 9.

All I ask is that you start praying now and put on your spiritual ears and hear what the Spirit is saying to the church. Jesus says eight times in the four gospels, "He that hath ears to hear, let him hear." Then, Jesus says seven times in Revelation chapters 2 and 3, "He that hath an ear, let him hear what the Spirit saith unto the churches." Therefore, you will need your spiritual ears on to hear the TRUTH about the Book of Life and predestination. I have already written about them, so I truly believe after you have read and studied the scriptures, this TRUTH will be clear to you.

Before we leave Revelation chapter 14, I want to make a comment about verse 6: "And I saw another angel fly in the midst of heaven, having the everlasting gospel to preach unto them that dwell on the earth." As you have read and will read again, there is only one true gospel for all humanity. For the most part, the Jews rejected Jesus and His teaching. But before they (the Jews) can be saved (born-again), they must hear and obey Jesus' gospel. Notice that this scripture says, "The everlasting gospel." Man has changed the everlasting gospel to fit their lives, but Jesus will never change it. It is as simple as this—we must change our lives to fit God's word. The same apostolic gospel must be preached and received by these 144,000 Jews, or they cannot be saved. I realize that is another bold statement, but it is the TRUTH, and that is what we are looking for.

I have written quite a few times in this book how the word teaches us that God's people (the church) are going to go through the tribulation period. The question in your mind must be, If the church is going to be here on earth during the tribulation period, how will the church survive? The TRUTH is it is going to take faith in Jesus and the power that is in His name to make it through these troubled times. I believe you can find how God's people are going to make it through the tribulation in Revelation chapter 12. Read verses 6 and 14. Verse 14 says, "And to the woman [the church] were given two wings of a great eagle, that she might fly into the wilderness, into her place, where she is nourished for a time, and times, and half a time [3 ½ years, forty-two months, or 1,260 days], from the face of the serpent [the Devil]." Both of these scriptures give us the time period when the Beast is going to be in control of this world (the people).

Remember that Jesus teaches us about the end of this world and the great tribulation period in Matthew chapter 24. Read verses 15–22 again and never forget. Jesus teaches us in verse 16 to flee when they see the Beast that Daniel the prophet has spoken about in verse 15. I know, from reading and studying the scriptures, God will take care of His people IF they will only believe and obey Him.

You have to realize that there is a SUPER POWER (Satan) fighting for our souls, through deception. Satan is trying to deceive you and me. There is another SUPER POWER (God) that is competing for and desiring our souls. But God has left it upon us if we want to serve Him and our fellow man. God is not going to make us serve Him. From the beginning, God and Satan have been displaying supernatural powers in heaven and on earth. As we get closer to the end of this world, we are going to see more of these supernatural powers in action, from both God and Satan.

Here are some things you need to learn and remember. Satan is doing everything he can to deceive us and to keep God's TRUTH from getting to us. Just because we get into God's word doesn't mean that Satan is going to stop trying to deceive us. As a matter of fact, Satan is going to come against us even stronger than ever. He is going to come with both barrels, blazing! Satan can show up anytime he wants, and he will show up in your life. And unless you are spiritually discerning, you will not even know it's him.

Know and remember this—God's word was written by the inspiration of God, and the word is spiritually discerned. The only way anyone can understand, even the milk of God's word, is if they allow the Holy Ghost to teach them. I don't want to choke anyone with God's word. I believe these scriptures in Revelation chapter 17 are some of the hardest TRUTHS to swallow from God's word, especially for those who believe in the Catholic and Protestant teachings. But no matter what, I can't stop writing what the Lord has taught me. And before you finish studying your King James Version Bible with my book, you will realize Jesus has been personally tutoring you, and you must obey what you learn to go to Heaven. Jesus will be your teacher, if you will simply ask Him to teach you His TRUTH from His word.

As I sit here writing on a Sabbath day, I was praying and asking the Lord to show me what I must be doing, because I felt as if I'm not doing enough. My mind immediately flashed back to 1991, when He told me to go and find the children of the GREAT WHORE. At that moment, I felt a great peace come over me, and I began back writing, because I know what Jesus told me to do that day.

I hate to admit this, but the last time I heard Jesus speak to me was twenty-five years ago, and the last words Jesus spoke to me out loud in English was this. "'If she is a mother, she has children.' Then, the Lord hesitated for a split-second and then said, 'Go find the children.'" It has taken me about two hours to write these couple of paragraphs, because of the shame I'm feeling for having such dull hearing. But it's hard for me to write when I can't see and with my head hanging low. I was telling my grandson (Braxton) the other night about how I have heard the Lord speak to me and that it has been many years since I heard Him speak and that I long to hear His voice.

But I cannot continue to wallow in this shame, because the last four words Jesus said to me was, "Go find the children." I don't believe the Lord told me to go find the children just for my own benefit. The Lord inspired me to write this book, or I would not have written it. The Lord has not spoken to me in an audible voice for many years, but He teaches me His word daily. And I believe if I don't share with others these things that Jesus has taught me, there will be eternal ramifications on my soul. If I see this danger (how Satan is deceiving) and I don't warn you, I will be held accountable. By the grace of God, and if He is willing, His TRUTH that I have written will enter your heart through your eyes and ears by His Spirit.

Read Ezekiel 33:1–20. I believe that I have been made a watchman, so I must warn you. My witness is that you are still reading this book and you have been warned. I want you to remember the things you have read so far, and I want you to pay close attention to the rest of the things you are about to read in this book. You will always hear me say that you are to compare the things written in this book with God's word and seek God, Jesus, the Lord, or the Holy Ghost—they are all the same God—for the TRUTH. I must say again that you have been warned. It's up to you to seek the Lord for the TRUTH.

My prayer is that these scriptures that I'm writing about in Daniel and in Revelation will not choke you, but instead make you stronger in the faith and knowledge of our Lord Jesus. I also pray that you can see how hard Satan is working for souls. As you continue reading, I hope you will be able to see how Satan is using his supernatural powers to get our fellow man to follow him into HELL. As you will know from reading God's word, you cannot have a carnal mind and understand His word. As I have said, the word of the Lord is spiritually discerned. In John 6:63, Jesus says, "My words are Spirit." I don't believe I can express this too much. Without God's Spirit teaching us, we will never understand His word.

I have not written anything in this book that I, myself, have not experienced or seeking to experience. I'm in this same race, with all of the other Christians. I'm not going to tell you something to do that I wouldn't do. As you can tell by reading this book, I have eaten steak a few times in my walk with the Lord. But thirty-two years later, I find myself going back to the milk jug, all the time, strengthening my faith.

No matter how many times I read how, when, and where Jesus was born and the miracles that He did, there is always something else I can learn from His word. I believe that is called growing in God.

God's word never says that we are to have broccoli or peas in our diet; it is always milk or meat, when talking about learning from the scriptures. Let me give you a few scriptures that talk about the milk and meat of God's word. Remember that milk or meat, we all need to have the Holy Ghost to teach us. Read 1 Peter 2:1–2, 1 Corinthians 2:9–16 and 1 Corinthians 3:1–2 because they go together, and then Hebrews 5:11–14.

These scriptures teaches us that there is a difference between God's word (milk or meat,) and in Revelation chapter 17, you will eat from a filet mignon. If we are not careful, the word of God can and has choked some people in the past and will do so in the future. The reason some things in God's word are hard to understand is because we try to figure the scriptures out for ourselves. I hate to keep repeating myself, but it is worth repeating. Read John 14:26. Without the Holy Ghost teaching us, none of us can learn anything from God's word.

My advice to everyone (myself included)—we all need to spend some time on our knees communicating with the Lord. Listen what God's word says in Hebrews 13:16: "But to do good and to communicate forget not: for with such sacrifices God is well pleased." Notice that the words are about communicating with the Lord. If we do all the talking during our prayer time, and we never listen for God's voice, what will we have accomplished? If we don't hear the Lord speak to us and if we find ourselves growing in God, it will be at a snail's pace.

At this time, I feel that I must explain something that I wrote a couple of pages ago. I said that I have not heard the Lord speak to me in the past twenty-five years. Since then, I have not heard the Lord speak to me in English and given me a specific order. You should be able to see from the words written in this book that the Lord has spoken and taught me through the years. All I can say is that it's hard to explain how the Lord teaches (talks) me, but He does. Sometimes, the Lord speaks so soft that you can't hear Him with your natural ears. That is why we must have spiritual ears.

The Lord speaks to us in many ways. For example, the Lord speaks to us through earthquakes and storms and other disasters if you can hear Him. Read Nahum 1:3. Notice that there are very few sunny days; most of the time, it is cloudy. This scripture tells me that the Lord is not happy with this world (people). There are some people who believe that Satan causes and makes the storms, but now you know that it is Jesus who is in control.

There are trillions of ways, but here are two more examples how the Lord has spoken to man. The first way is hard to believe, if you don't know the Lord. You can find out how the Lord used a donkey in Numbers 22:21–34. Here, the Lord used an angel and a donkey to get Balaam's attention. All I know is that we never know how He is going to speak to us. This is why we must be born-again and have God's Spirit to teach us.

Now, I want to tell you how I have come to believe that John was going to be one of the prophets who will preach to the 144,000 Jews during the great tribulation. The angel tells John in Revelation 10:11, "Thou must prophesy again before many peoples, and nations, and tongues, and kings." One day, a few years ago, Anthony and I were talking about the Lord, and he brought this scripture to my mind. As soon as I heard him say what he believed, I believed it also. I believe that day, the Lord used Anthony to reveal this TRUTH to me. Again, I will say this—you never know how the Lord is going to talk to you, but if you will listen, you will hear Him.

Listen to what Jesus says in John 10:1–5:

> Verily, verily, I say unto you, He that entereth not by the door into the sheepfold, but climbeth up some other way, the same is a thief and a robber. But he that entereth in by the door is the Shepherd of the sheep. To him the porter openeth; and the sheep hear his voice: and He calleth His own sheep by name, and leadeth them out. And when He putteth forth His own sheep, He goeth before them, and the sheep follow Him: for they know His voice. And a stranger will they not follow, but will flee from him: for they know not the voice of strangers.

In John 10:27, Jesus says, "My sheep [the church] hear my voice, and I know them, and they follow me."

Again, you must understand the things that I am writing about are spiritual, and to a carnal-minded person, they will think that I have flipped my lid. Even to some of God's chosen, they will think that I am way out in left field, and some will think that I have completely left the ball field. But to you who read this book, all I want you to do is seek the Lord for the TRUTH.

The things that I've been writing about pertaining to the end-time could start at any moment. We all need to spend some time seeking the Lord about the end-time, because we are definitely living in the last days. The book of Revelation was given to us so we (the church) would know what is going to happen in our future. You need to know what is going to happen before it happens so you will be strong in faith and ready and able to withstand what Satan has to offer—666 = HELL! As you can see, I like simple arithmetic.

I believe most of you have heard about antichrist. The word antichrist is mentioned only five times in the entire Bible and is recorded in 1 John and in 2 John and is not recorded anywhere else in God's word. Most of the so- called Christian world has been taught that the antichrist and the Beast are the same. This is a false teaching. An antichrist is simply someone who does not believe that God came to earth and became flesh.

Believe me, Satan knows who Jesus is. In Matthew 8:28–29, you will see that the devil knows who Jesus is. You may not, but the devil knows His name and that Jesus is the Father of creation, the Son of redemption, and the Holy Ghost of the regeneration.

In these scriptures, the devil asked Jesus this question, "Art thou come hither to torment us, before the time?" Satan knows that he has but a short time, and that is why he is working so hard for our souls. The Beast (Satan) knows that God came to earth in the flesh. Remember Satan served the Lord, when he was Lucifer, and he knows who the Lord is.

The only way I see a connection between the antichrist and the Beast is that both do not follow the teachings of Jesus. An antichrist is a person who doesn't believe Jesus is the Christ, and the Beast wants to take His place as the Lord. You can find this out by studying the scriptures. Apostle Paul writes and warns us about the Beast in 2 Thessalonians 2:1–9. Paul lets us know in verse 1 about Jesus coming back for His church. In verse 2, Paul tells us to keep a sound mind and not let anything trouble us—in other words, don't lose focus because the day that Jesus is coming back for His Bride is close at hand. In verse 3, Paul says, "Let no man deceive you by any means."

Here, Paul is prophesying (telling the future) and warning us about the Beast that is to come. Apostle Paul also tells us in this scripture how we will be able to see and know the true believers, because he says, "There will be a falling away first." If you are here during this time, I want you to remember what you have been reading. The church (God's people) will stand for Jesus all the way to the end. No matter who they are, if they are not following Jesus, they are not of God, and they will fall.

This means a lot of churchgoers and some Christians are going to lose the faith. If you will read these scriptures in their proper context, you will see that Paul was writing to the Christians in Thessalonica; he was not writing to sinners. I have to say at this time—this blows a giant hole in the false teaching of "once saved, always saved." The teaching of "once saved, always saved" is man's teaching, and it is not found in God's word. A matter of fact, God's word teaches the opposite of "once saved, always saved." Here is one of the best examples found in God's word, that I know about. In James 5:19, he starts off by calling his example (brethren). This lets me know, that he is speaking to a born-again person. Then James lets any born-again person know "if any of you do err (leave or fall away) from the TRUTH, and one (another Christian) convert (or bring him or her back to God's TRUTH)". Verse 20 says, let him know, that he which converteth the sinner (which used to be a Christian) from the error of his ways, shall save a soul (a future entity) from death (HELL), and shall hide a multitude of sin. Remember what Jesus says in Matthew 24:13. "Once saved, always saved" is not TRUTH. There is one book in God's word that shows us how to be born-again, and that is the book of Acts. Then, Paul writes over half of the New Testament, teaching us how to stay saved. Read what Paul says in 1 Corinthians 15:1–2. When you read these scriptures, you are going to find that BIG word IF again.

At the end of verse 3 in 2 Thessalonians chapter 2, Paul says, "That man of sin be revealed, the son of perdition." If you don't know, soon you are going to find out that the son of perdition is the Beast. In verse 4, Paul tells us what the son of perdition (the Beast) is trying to achieve (he wants to take God's place) before the end of the world. When the Beast comes on the scene, he is going to oppose and exalt himself above all that is called God or that is worshipped so that he as God sits in the temple of God, showing himself that he is God. Very soon, you will find out the name of the person who I believe will be the Beast. In verses 5–6, Paul says,

"I have warned you. And now you know how to recognize the son of perdition, when he comes." He is going to be easy to spot. As Paul said, the Beast will be the one who sits in the temple of God in Jerusalem, claiming to be God.

Jesus also warns us about false Christ and false prophets. In Matthew 24:23–27, Jesus says,

> Then if any man shall say unto you, Lo, here Christ, or there; believe not. For there shall arise false Christ, and false prophets, and shall shew great signs and wonders; insomuch that, if possible, they shall deceive the very elect [God's people]. Behold, I have told you before. Wherefore if they shall say unto you, Behold, he is in the desert; go not forth: Behold, in the secret chambers; believe not. For as the lightning cometh out of the east, and shineth even unto the west; so shall also the coming of the Son of man be.
>
> And then shall appear the sign of the Son of man in heaven: and then shall all the tribes of the earth mourn, and they shall see the Son of man coming in the clouds of heaven with power and great glory. (Verse 30)

Jesus says in these scriptures that you don't have to look for Him in the desert or in any secret chambers. "When I return for My Bride, everyone will see me coming in the clouds of heaven." Notice what these scriptures don't say. When Jesus comes this time, He will not come as a baby. He will come with power and great glory. But Jesus will come and visit you before that great day wherever you may be whenever you speak to Him from a pure heart.

You need to remember what you just read in God's word about the Beast and Jesus coming back for His church. If you are here during the tribulation period, the Beast will be ever so easy to recognize. And if you make it through the tribulation period, you with everyone else will see Jesus "coming in the clouds" to gather His church. As you can see, God's word is clear about both of these events.

We have already studied these scriptures before, but they need to be read again, again, and again. The reason we need to study these scriptures over and over is because in them are many TRUTHS to learn. We are about to read a few scriptures from Acts chapter 1. And I believe that there are a couple of angels mentioned in these verses that confirms what Jesus said in Matthew 24:30, about Him "coming in the clouds."

The time period that Luke is writing about would be just before the church was born, which would be about 10 days. Read Acts 1:3. Luke recorded that Jesus has been seen by His apostles for forty days after His resurrection. So this tells us that this was sometime between the 40th and 49th day, after Jesus was resurrected, because the church began on the 50th day after Jesus rose from the dead. This is the day of Pentecost, which is recorded in Acts chapter 2, the day the church began. We must study these chapters so we will know how the church was born and that we can do what they did to be saved. If you claim to be born-again (saved), and you didn't accomplish it in the same manner as they did in Acts chapter 2, you are born again. Again, I will let you fill in the blank.

In Acts 1:8–11, Jesus had just promised His disciples power, and that same promise is for you and me also.

> But ye shall receive power, after that the Holy Ghost is come upon you: and ye shall be witnesses unto me both in Jerusalem, and in all Judaea, and in Samaria, and unto the uttermost part of the earth. And when He had spoken these things, while they beheld, He was taken up; and a cloud received Him out of their sight. And while they looked steadfastly toward heaven as He went up, behold, two men stood by them in white

apparel; which also said, Ye men of Galilee, why stand ye gazing up into heaven? This same Jesus, which is taken up from you into heaven, shall so come in like manner [on a cloud] as ye have seen Him go into heaven.

No matter what anyone tries to tell you, if you don't see Jesus coming back on a cloud, it will not be Jesus. You have been warned by Jesus, two of His angels, and me. Remember that Satan is deceiving anyone in any way he can. Don't let him deceive you.

I know that a lot of you will say that the book of Revelation is so hard to understand, with all the different kinds of terminology—like good angels; bad angels; Alpha and Omega; the four beast that has six wings and full of eyes; elders; the great red dragon that has seven heads and ten horns; man child; time, times, and half a time; the Beast that rises up out of the sea that has seven heads and ten horns; the mark of the Beast; the supper of the Great God; I promise you, you don't want to be there; the books were opened; the Book of Life; lake of fire; new heaven and a new earth; the Holy City; new Jerusalem; all liars; second death; the Lamb's Wife; I Jesus have sent mine angel; I am the root and the offspring of David; the bright and morning star; and the Spirit and the Bride say, come, take the water of Life freely, blot.

I believe everyone should find out the meaning of the word blot.

If you will read Revelation 1:1–3, you will see that Jesus gave us (the church) the book of Revelation so we (the church) would know the future of the human race. Jesus allowed us to know the good and bad things that are going to be in everyone's future. As I have said before, the word of God is Spirit, and the word of God is spiritually discerned. The Lord would not give us the book of Revelation if it could not be understood. So let's look into the book of Revelation and see what else we can learn.

The best way that I can describe the Beast is that the Beast is Satan in human form. The Beast, referring to Satan's end-time human body, is mentioned in Daniel chapter 7. This is the same Beast Apostle Paul wrote about in 2 Thessalonians 2:1–9 and is the same Beast that John warned us about in Revelation chapters 11, 13, 14, 15, 16, 17, 19, and 20. Now, you are going to learn about the great persecution that I wrote about earlier in this book. Like I said, this persecution is going to be as bad if not worse than when the persecution started about 2,050 years ago when Jesus was born.

This Beast that Satan will use will come against not only the church but also every person on earth with a great persecution, just before the church goes to heaven. You should read Revelation 13:7–8. Verse 15 says that if you don't worship this Beast, you will be killed. Paraphrasing verses 16–17, this Beast will make everyone who does not have their name written in the Book or Life receive the mark of the Beast, or the name of the Beast, or the number of his name (666), in their right hand or in their forehead. If you don't take one of these marks of the Beast, you cannot buy or sell anything, such as FOOD, GAS FOR OUR CAR, ELECTRICITY, YOU WILL NOT BE ABLE TO PAY YOUR MORTGAGE, YOUR RENT, AND NOT EVEN YOUR TAXES ON YOUR PROPERTY.

When it gets to the point that they take away your home and land, where will you go? You will not be able to hide for long. If you don't have faith in Jesus to take care of you, you will take one of those marks, or they will kill you. Here is some good advice. Don't be deceived. Do not let Satan, or anyone, especially deceive yourself in thinking that you want take one of these marks. If your name is not written in the Book of Life, you will take a mark. It is as simple as this—if you will not live for the Lord, you will not die for Him. It is going to take faith in Jesus and His name to make it through these tough times. The Apostle Paul writes in Romans 10:17 that we get faith by hearing the word of God. It is truly going to be a bad time on earth.

If you don't have a strong faith, I suggest you get into God's word and spend the rest of your life seeking Him and His will for your life. Read what Jesus says in Matthew 7:21–27. Here, Jesus is teaching and talking about judgment day and what will happen if we do not do (live) God's word. If we do not do His will, look at verse 23 and see what Jesus is going to say to those who do not obey His word. "And then will I profess unto them, I never knew you: depart from me, ye that work iniquity [you sinner]." I believe we should ask Jesus for more faith every day just like what the apostles did in Luke 17:5.

Most people think astronauts, rocket scientist, and even Harvard professors are smart. Don't get me wrong, they are very smart, but let me tell you who the smart people living on earth really are. They are the ones who seek, hear, and live God's TRUTH. Now, since you have learned what the Beast (Satan) is going to do to the whole human race, if you are one of the smart people who wants to know who the Beast is and how to escape his supernatural powers, it is time to go to work, seeking God every moment of the day and night.

I said that soon, I was going to tell you who the Beast is going to be, but you have to wait a little longer. Let me explain. I have been stopped at this point from writing this chapter for the past three to four months. For some reason, the Lord had me write the next chapter, which is chapter 7. I had other plans for chapter 7. It was supposed to be about Satan, but the Lord had me write about something else. As you are about to find out, I wrote chapter 7 with an empty red pen that the Lord has truly blessed. In chapter 7, I will tell you how I am going to come back and write in this chapter with my empty red pen. The same empty red pen is writing the words that you are reading now. All I can say is that it's not my doing—it is the Lord, because I and everyone else in the world knows that an empty red pen cannot write. The only empty red pen that can continue to write that I have ever seen or heard about is this one, and I am so blessed to have it. I will explain in greater details about the empty red pen in chapter 7. Lord willing, I will show y'all my red pen when we get to that story.

This is not the only thing like this the Lord has done for me in the past thirty-two years. If I told you some of the things He has done for me, you would think I'm crazy. All I can say is that I know what the Lord has put in my right hand, and while this empty red pen is still writing, let's continue looking into God's word and find out what it says about the leader of the Catholic Church. As we look into God's word, we are about to find out the TRUTH about the head of the GREAT WHORE.

The Beast is going to come in the last days and persecute not only the church but also the whole human race until they obey him. He is going to come out of the fourth kingdom, which was seen by Daniel in his dream. As you have learned already in chapter 4 of this book, the fourth kingdom in Daniel's dream was the Roman Empire. You can learn more about the fourth kingdom in Daniel chapter 7 and in your encyclopedias.

Remember that they (most Catholics and Protestants) call the Beast the antichrist, but he is not an antichrist—he is the Beast. From the time the book of Revelation was written, people have been trying to figure out who the Beast will be. People have accused leaders from different countries of being the Beast for hundreds of years, from Nero to Napoleon, Mussolini to Hitler, some popes, and even some American presidents.

Now, as I sit here writing on June 19, 2010, I find myself about to accuse someone of being the Beast. As I sat in front of my computer, I began to think, *Who do you think you are? How can you make an accusation such as this?* As my mind began to wonder, I thought about having only an eighth- grade education and how I was born a son of a Mississippi farmer, from the cotton fields of Tunica County, Mississippi. As I sat there thinking, suddenly it dawned on me. I have been looking forward to writing about this for over a year. So I rebuked Satan and told him to leave me alone in the name of Jesus.

When I rebuked Satan, I told him, "I may have only an eighth-grade education, but the Lord has been teaching me His word for thirty-two years. I was inspired by the Lord to write this book, and no devil is going to stop me." I learned at church last Sunday, as Brother Jackson preached—it is not over, until the Lord says it's over. I truly believe I will know when to stop writing, but until then, I will keep writing what I have learned from God's word so I can help my fellow man find the TRUTH.

I have always believed if you are going to do something, the best way to get it done is to start. So without any further delay, let's find out who the Beast will be. I am not scared to say it. I believe Satan's end-time body (the Beast) is going to be Pope John Paul II. Please bear with me, and I will explain. But before I tell you how I came to this conclusion, let's do a brief summary of what we have already learned so we will have a fresh understanding of God's TRUTH.

In Daniel chapter 7, Daniel tells us where the Beast comes from. Daniel's writings teach that the Beast comes from the fourth kingdom (the Roman Empire). In Revelation 13:5, the Lord reveals to us how long the Beast is going to be in power. Verse 5 says, "And power was given unto him to continue forty-two months." As you will find out a little later, this forty- two-month time period is referred to as time, and times, and the dividing of time. The Beast will be in power the 3 ½ years during the tribulation period. After the 3 ½ years of tribulation, the church goes to heaven, and then, God pours out His wrath on earth and the people.

All these scriptures are good and helpful, but none of these scriptures let us know who the Beast is. As I have said before, when you are looking for the TRUTH, you have got to find the book, chapter, and verse that teach about that subject. And in this case, the book is Revelation, and the chapter is 17. There is no other chapter in God's word that teaches about this in these details. Now, we have already read and studied this chapter when we found out about the GREAT WHORE in chapter 4.

I have said it before, and here, I need to say it again. The Lord is teaching us in Revelation chapter 17 about the fourth kingdom that Daniel wrote about in his book. The fourth kingdom is the Roman Empire. Sure, the world is not under the rule of the Roman Empire today, but most of this world (people) are indoctrinated with this false teaching. The Roman Catholic's teaching will continue to dominate the world, until the fifth kingdom takes over. You can read about the takeover of the fifth and last kingdom in Daniel 7:9–27.

As I was writing about this one night, I went outside, and when I looked up into the heavens, there was a bright full moon, and the stars were out. I thought, there is only one KING that deserves a kingdom like this, and His name is Jesus. Jesus is going to rule the fifth and final kingdom. There will be no sixth kingdom. God's word says that His kingdom is an everlasting one.

We are going to have to skip around (RIGHTLY DIVIDE) these scriptures so we can find the TRUTH that we are looking for. I want you to know that I didn't just call the Catholic church the GREAT WHORE out of ignorance or spite. God's angel calls her the GREAT WHORE in Revelation 17:1: Also in verse 1, the angel tells John, "I will shew unto thee the judgment of the GREAT WHORE that sitteth upon many waters." If you will read verse 15, it will reveal to you what the many waters represent.

Verse 3 says that the angel carried John away in the Spirit into the wilderness. For this TRUTH to be revealed to him, and now, we can find this same TRUTH in John's writings. In the wilderness, John saw a woman, and she was sitting upon a scarlet-colored Beast (Satan), full of names of blasphemy, having seven heads and ten horns. In verse 18, the angel reveals to John the woman that he saw, "And the woman which thou sawest is that great city." If you will read these scriptures in their proper context, you will learn that these scriptures are talking about the city of Rome. In verse 7, the angel asked John, "Wherefore didst thou marvel? I will tell thee the mystery of the woman, and of the Beast that carrieth her, which hath the seven heads and ten horns." Here, the angel tells John that he is going to reveal the TRUTH about the woman, the Beast, the seven heads, and the ten horns.

Next, we need to read verse 9, because it reveals to us what the seven heads are, "And here the mind which hath wisdom [understanding]." I believe this means that anyone who reads verse 9 and can understand that the seven heads are seven mountains on which the woman sits, and if you put this scripture with verse 18 ("The woman that you saw is that great city") and verse 3 and understand that this woman (Rome) has allowed Satan to rule over her, then you will understand what the Lord is teaching His church.

Read your encyclopedia or search online to confirm what you have just found in God's word. Look up the Roman Catholic church to find this TRUTH. If you will read this whole article, you will learn a lot about their false teaching, because this article confirms most of the things you have read about them in this book. As you read this article and come to where it tells about the city of Rome, you will find that Rome was built on seven mountains. This is just as the angel told John it would be. As far as I know, Rome is the only city in the world that is built on seven mountains. If you can understand these scriptures, which are the meat of God's word, then you too will be RIGHTLY DIVIDING God's TRUTH.

Now, let's find out a little about the ten horns that Daniel wrote about in the seventh chapter of his book. Daniel 7:23–25 teaches us about the Beast and the fourth kingdom (the Roman Empire). Daniel says,

> And the ten horns out of this kingdom ten kings shall arise [from the fourth kingdom]: and another [the Beast] shall rise after them; and he shall be diverse [different] from the first, and he shall subdue three kings.
>
> And he [the Beast] shall speak words against the most High [God], and shall wear out the saints of the most High, and think to change times and laws: and

they [the saints] shall be given into his [the Beast] hand, until a time and times and the dividing of time [or in other words, 3 ½ years]. (Verses 24–25)

This scripture is referring to the Beast that is going to rule the world during the great tribulation.

Pay close attention to what you just read in God's word. Read it again, and you will see that the church will be on this earth during the tribulation period. Don't be deceived in believing the false teachings, which are in the world. Some preachers teach that the church will go to heaven pre-tribulation, some teach mid-tribulation, and some teach post-tribulation. It's not just that; I believe I know God's word teaches us that the church will go home to heaven post-tribulation, just before the wrath of God is poured out on earth. I will explain in greater details a little later.

John also wrote about these same ten horns in Revelation chapters 12, 13, and 17. In chapter 17, the ten horns mentioned in verse 3 are partly revealed in verse 12, and the ten horns are ten kings. During the tribulation period, these ten kings will be united with the Beast for a short period. In verse 12, God's word says that these ten kings will be united with the Beast for one hour. Verse 16 says that these ten kings—for some reason, the Lord has not revealed this to me—will begin to hate the GREAT WHORE. There will be no more peace between these ten kings and the GREAT WHORE. These ten kings make war with the GREAT WHORE and destroy her. Verse 17 says that God has put this in their hearts so His will be fulfilled. As I have said so many times before, this is God's master plan for the human race. You can read about the city of Rome being destroyed in Revelation chapter 18.

I realize that I have been using a lot of the same scriptures in chapters 4, 5, and 6 of this book; but I hope you realize that these three chapters all go together. I could have written all three chapters as one. But this is what it takes to RIGHTLY DIVIDE God's word.

Now, let's go to Revelation chapter 13, where you will find John's prophecy about this same Beast. You need to read and study this chapter over and over again. You need to study it, until God reveals this TRUTH to you. In verse 1, you will hear John's recollection of the fourth kingdom (the Roman Empire).

At the end of verse 2, John writes, "And the dragon [Satan] gave him [the Beast] his power, and his seat, and great authority." Verse 5 gives the same time period that Daniel gave in his book, letting us know how long the Beast is going to be in power. Verse 7 says, "And it was given unto him [the Beast] to make war with the Saints, and to overcome them: and power was given him over all kindred, and tongues, and nations." Here comes that same question again, How can the Beast make war with the saints, unless the saints are here on earth during the tribulation period? No matter what anyone tries to teach you from God's word, always seek Jesus for the TRUTH.

I know I am committing heresy, as I write this book. I never knew I was a heretic until I got to this part of my book and had to look up the word heresy. To tell you the TRUTH, I am proud to be a heretic. Before I compromise with anyone pertaining to God's word with what is generally accepted by the false churches, I pray the Lord would end my life here on this earth. I know the Lord has taught me His word. The things I have been writing about, I was not taught by any man. Most people of the false church world might say that I have been taught this by Satan, because the contents of this book go against what they have been taught and brought up to believe. They will say that I am committing heresy, but that's okay, because I am.

Just because someone is taught something from God's word doesn't mean that it is the TRUTH. God's word has been taken out of its proper context from the beginning, because man has interpreted it and has not allowed God to teach them. Remember the word wrest. Read 2 Peter 3:15–17 again.

Believe this—Satan will not teach anyone God's word; it's against his nature. Satan would not teach anyone God's word, because it would be defeating his purpose. Satan doesn't want me to help anyone hear God's TRUTH. Satan had nothing to do with the writing of this book, except that he gave me the material for me to write the TRUTH about his false teachings, which are in the world. I learned the things I have been writing about on my knees in prayer and by studying God's word and asking the Lord for His TRUTH. For thirty-two years, I have been studying God's word and seeking Him for the TRUTH. I know that I have written this book with an eighth- grade reading level, but that is all I have. I have never written anything before in my life, but as you can see, by the TRUTHS written in this book, my seeking God in His word paid off. The Lord has truly blessed me with His TRUTH.

Let's look a little further in God's word and find out what the Lord has taught me that He wants me to share with you. Revelation 11:7 says, "The Beast that ascendeth out of the bottomless pit." This scripture says that the Beast comes out of HELL. Now, don't start pointing your finger and thinking all kinds of bad things about me, because of what I'm about to say. One of the first scriptures that I learned in God's word was Matthew 7:1. I know that no one is supposed to judge another person, but I am going to say what God's word says.

God's word teaches us that if you die in Jesus, you will immediately go to heaven and be there until Jesus returns to earth for His church. The scriptures teach us that when Jesus comes back for His church, it is the first resurrection. God's word also teaches us that when any person not living for the Lord dies, they are put in the ground and will not be released from their grave, until 1,000 years after the first resurrection. After the thousand years has passed, and the sinners are resurrected, then God's righteous judgment will be given to each one of them.

I believe the scriptures teach us that there is only one person in HELL at this time. The scriptures also teach us in Jude 6 and 2 Peter 2:4 that God cast the angels who rebelled with Satan in heaven to HELL. Again, I can only say what the scriptures say, and they say that the Beast comes out of the bottomless pit, which is HELL. We will never know all that God has done or will do, but we do know according to the scriptures that the Beast is in HELL at this time. I want to say one other thing about this. I don't know how or why God has already passed judgment on the Beast, but He has. All I know—this is the Lord's plan to end this earth and the human race. As you continue reading and studying, my prayer is that the scriptures will be clear for you to understand.

Now, we need to find out through the scriptures by comparing them with the Catholic's history who the Beast is before he dies and comes back to life to take control of this world for 3 ½ years. Let me tell you how I came to believe that the pope is going to be the Beast during the tribulation period. I know without a doubt that in Revelation chapter 17, the Lord is teaching us (the church) about the false church (the Catholic church). God is not going to give us names in every case. The Lord wants us to study and seek for the TRUTH.

On that Monday morning back in 1991, when the Lord spoke to me and told me to go find the children of the GREAT WHORE, I did. As I continued studying chapter 17 about the MOTHER OF HARLOTS, it dawned on me the answer of verses 10–11. Verse 10 says, "And there are seven Kings." For some reason, that scripture did not register in my mind. Now, if verse 10 would have said, "And there are seven popes," that would have been too easy.

These scriptures in Revelation chapter 17 are speaking of seven heads and ten horns; it also speaks of the GREAT WHORE and a scarlet-colored beast (Satan). In verse 8, the angel tells John about the man who is going to be the Beast, dying and coming back to life. Verse 10 speaks of seven kings. When it dawned on me that this scripture was speaking about the head of the Catholic church (the pope), I went immediately to my encyclopedia. Here's what I found. My encyclopedia matched perfectly with verses 10–11.

I want you to look in your encyclopedia for the Roman Catholic church and then find the popes of the church. You can find the popes in the Pontifical Yearbook. Since I knew these scriptures were talking about the popes and that Revelation chapter 17 was talking about the end of the church world here on earth, it must be talking about the last eight popes. I made a list of the last eight popes, and then, I RIGHTLY DIVIDED verses 10–11 by using the last eight popes. Just look how this fits together, making TRUTH:

1.	1903	St. Pius X	
2.	1914	St. Benedict XV	
3.	1922	Pius XI	These five kings have fallen—in other words, died.
4.	1939	Pius XII	
5.	1958	John XXIII	
6.	1963	Paul VI	This is the one who is in office (One is).
7.	1978	John Paul I	This is the one who has not come yet. The scripture says that when he comes, he must conTinue a short space. When John Paul I became the pope in 1978, he was in office for thirty-three days, and he died. A month later, Cardinal Wojtyla of Poland was elected pope and took the name John Paul II. You can read about this in the encyclopedia or online.

8.   1978   John Paul II   John Paul II is the eighth king
                                 (pope), and God's word says that
                                 he goes into perdition (HELL). I
                                 believe that Pope John Paul II is the
                                 Beast that comes out of HELL. Read
                                 Revelation 17:8 again.

Let's recap what we have been reading. Verses 10–11 say, "There are seven kings, five are fallen, and one is, and the other is not yet come; and when he cometh, he must continue a short space. And the Beast that was, and is not, even he is the eighth, and is of the seven, and he goeth into perdition." This scripture said that the Beast that was, which means he was alive. This scripture also said that the Beast is not, which means that he died. If you take these two scriptures and compare them with these eight popes, which I have listed, I believe you will find the TRUTH about the Beast.

Now, what I have written in this book is my interpretation of these scriptures. As I have told you before, after you have read and studied God's word for yourself, there is no telling what the Lord will teach you from these same scriptures. But for me, I don't see how it can get any clearer after you RIGHTLY DIVIDE these scriptures. It only makes sense to me that the leader (most Holy Father) of the GREAT WHORE would be the Beast during the tribulation period.

If the Beast was alive at one time and he died and if the Beast is going to be here on this earth during the tribulation period, he has to come back from the dead. As I have stated a few times in this book, I believe Pope John Paul II is going to be the Beast that persecutes the world (people) during the tribulation period. Almost everyone on earth knows Pope John Paul II died a few years ago, back in 2005. Maybe I should have said this earlier in this book, but before you think I'm crazy, I want you to remember this one thing—God can do anything!

Now, let's read Revelation chapter 13 and look at some scriptures that we have not read. Now we know that verses 1–2 John is writing about the fourth kingdom (Roman Empire) that Daniel wrote about. Verse 3 says, "And I saw one of his heads [the pope] as it were wounded to death; and his deadly wound was healed: and all the world wondered after the Beast." Now, read verses 11–12: "And I [John] beheld another Beast coming up out of the earth; and he had two horns like a lamb, and he spake as a dragon" (verse 11). I believe these scriptures are talking about another pope who is soon to come. I know the second Beast is coming soon, because it is written. Verse 12 says that this second Beast will exercise "all the power of the first Beast before him and causeth the earth, and them which dwell therein to worship the first Beast, whose deadly wound was healed."

While we are learning about the other Beast that came up out of the earth, if you will continue reading Revelation 13:13–14, you will see this second Beast works miracles before the first Beast and the whole human race. The reason I brought this up is because the next time you hear about this second Beast, he will be referred to as the false prophet. There are many false prophets in the world, but these scriptures are referring to the end-time false prophet that works hand in hand with the Beast. As you can clearly see, they (the Beast and the false prophet) are two different people.

There are only a few scriptures in God's word that teach us about the end-time false prophet. You can read about the false prophet in Revelation 19:11–21. These scriptures teach us about what will happen to the Beast and the false prophet when the Lord comes for His church. Verse 20 says, "And the Beast was taken, and with him the false prophet that wrought miracles before him, with which he deceived them that had received the mark of the Beast, and them that worshipped his image. These both were cast alive into a lake of fire burning with brimstone." A little later in this chapter, you will learn that the Beast and the false prophet will be loosed out of

HELL with Satan to gather their army to fight against God in their last battle (the Battle of Armageddon). After that battle, all three will be put back in HELL, and that is where they will spend eternity. Finally, there will be no more evil. In heaven, which will be on our new earth will be only the fruits of the Spirit.

You have already read 2 Thessalonians 2:1–6 a few times. I want you to read it again, but this time, also read verses 7 and 8. If you RIGHTLY DIVIDE these scriptures, you will see that verse 8 tells us that when Jesus comes after His Bride, He is going to destroy the Beast at His coming. As you seek the Lord for this TRUTH, and He reveals it to you, you will know what John wrote in Revelation 19:11–21 is the same event that Paul wrote about in 2 Thessalonians 2:1–8. Revelation 19:20 teaches us that the Lord is also going to get rid of the false prophet when He takes care of the Beast.

If you will RIGHTLY DIVIDE these scriptures that I have shared with you concerning the Beast, you will see Satan + Pope = Beast. I know that all of this sounds over the top; it even sounds that way to me, but I must write what I have learned and what I believe the Lord has shared with me.

Now, for one more important piece of the puzzle. I know it takes the whole TRUTH to make something true. It's hard to determine what part of this TRUTH would be more important to learn. After I learned all the things that you have been reading about, I got to the last piece of the puzzle. To me, the last piece of the puzzle was the most important, because I didn't know the answer. Again, I'm about to show my ignorance. It took me years to find this answer.

Revelation 13:16–18 teach us things concerning the last piece of the puzzle. I want to bring your attention to verse 18 that says, "Here is wisdom [insight in the TRUTH]. Let him that hath understanding count the number of the Beast: for it is the number of a man; and his number is Six hundred threescore [60] six [which equals 666]."

Again, I will say that no man has taught me about this GREAT CONSPIRACY. The Holy Ghost is my teacher, because I believe what Jesus told us in John 14:26. Now, don't get me wrong, but I believe in what some Christians call the fivefold ministry. The fivefold ministry is made up of apostles, prophets, evangelists, pastors, and teachers.

You can find this teaching by Apostle Paul in Ephesians 4:11–13. I was going to ask you to read it for yourself, but instead I've written it below so you will have to read it.

> And He [God] gave some, apostles; and some, prophets; and some, evangelists; and some, pastors and teachers. For the perfecting of the Saints, for the work of the ministry, for the edifying of the body of Christ. Till we all come in the unity of the faith, and of the knowledge of the Son of God, unto a perfect man, unto the measure of the stature of the fullness of Christ.

I believe the scriptures, and I must share this TRUTH with you. Please don't quit reading this book, because of what I'm about to say. I have said this TRUTH to many people over the past thirty-two plus years, but they tell me every time that it is impossible. Before I go any further, I want you to know I am not there yet—no, not even close—but I do believe in perfection. Read again Ephesians 4:11–13, and see if you don't see it for yourself.

There are other scriptures in God's word, but I want you to read this one and see what Jesus has to say about it. Matthew 5:48 is the scripture, and Jesus could not say it any clearer. Just in case you don't know, Jesus was teaching us in Matthew chapters 5, 6, and 7. No one spoke in these chapters, but the Lord. He taught everyone who will listen in these chapters how to pray and how not to pray, how to give and how not to give, how to fast and how not to fast, where to have your bank account and where not to have your bank account, who to serve and who not to serve, how to build our foundation and how not to build our foundation. Basically, Jesus was teaching us in these scriptures how to live a Christian life and how to become a saint in Him. You need to read Matthew chapters 5, 6, and 7 and see what the Lord has to say about becoming a saint (perfection).

In the middle of His teaching in these three chapters, Jesus commands everyone to be perfect. Jesus didn't make any mistakes, as He taught that day. Here is my question to you, the reader—how would you believe what Jesus taught in all of these other scriptures and not believe what He teaches in Matthew 5:48? Jesus says, "Be ye therefore perfect, even as your Father which in Heaven is perfect." Believe me, He meant what He said. He was simply saying, "If you will obey these teachings, you will grow into a mature saint." Jesus would not have said it if it were impossible. If I placed my phone number here _ _ _ _ _ _ _ _ _ _, it would not stop ringing with people saying, "No one can be perfect." Jesus says, and I say, "Yes, you can IF you obey [live] His word." Read James 1:1–4. I know you have already read Hebrews 5:12–14, but this time, I want you to also read Hebrews 6:1–3, because these scriptures go together. That is all I have to say about that, at this time, but later in chapter 7, I share some other scriptures that teach us how to become perfect in Jesus.

Before we get back to learning more about the Beast, I feel like I should explain something I just mentioned, a couple of paragraphs ago. And it is how to give to Jesus, and our fellow man. Most preachers teach people, that we are supposed to pay tithes (10% of our increase,) but the Lord didn't bring that rule, into the New Testament era. We now live under the Law of Liberty. Read James 1:25 and the Church will be judged by the Law of Liberty. James 2:12.

There are no scriptures in the New Testament, that teach us to tithe. Tithes were a part of the Mosaic Law of the Old Testament, and ended when Jesus died on the cross. Tithes ended, when the New Testament began. Jesus chose a different method for giving for His Church. Read 2 Corinthians 9:6-8. "Every man according as he purposeth in his heart, not grudgingly, or of necessity: for God loveth a cheerful giver." Apostle Paul never said to get your tithes ready, he said "Every man according as he purposeth in his heart…" The Lord has left it up to us, how much money and time we sow. Read Matthew 19:21 and Luke 6:38. Again, don't listen to these preacher's lies about tithing a tenth of your money received. And what the preachers don't know is, if they would just teach their congregation to freely give, they would collect more money. What I just wrote, most preachers want agree with. But I speak God's TRUTH in love. There is nothing wrong with giving 10%, but it is not required. Jesus left it up to us what we give. But beware, read Acts 5:1-11.

Now, we need to finish finding out how the number of the Beast (666) and John Paul II are connected. I found most of this TRUTH about all of this false teaching from God's word and our history books. I knew that I had found favor with the Lord, as He taught me His TRUTH and allowed me to write this book. So that means I have an understanding of God's word. Revelation 13:18 teaches us that if the Lord has given me (any one) wisdom and an understanding of this hidden TRUTH, we would be able to count the number of the Beast.

Let me tell you how I found the last piece of the puzzle. My sister-in-law Sandra gave me her old computer a few years back, which allowed me to start writing this book. Before that, I have never turned on a computer, nor did I know how to type. I don't remember ever writing more than a couple of pages in a book report in my life, until I wrote this book. I am amazed as I look down on my new computer and see I have already written over 13,000 words in this chapter alone.

On that old computer, I learned how to send an e-mail and receive one. I very seldom browsed the Internet, because of the old computer and because I only had dial-up. It was so bad I could literally turn on my computer and go take a shower, and by the time I'm done showering, it was ready to use. As I have said, I finally had to buy a new computer.

As you know, I believe John Paul II is going to be the Beast during the tribulation and the last days of the church here on earth. My theory of the Beast would not be possible if I was not able to connect John Paul II with the number 666. I had asked the Lord many times for this TRUTH. One day while in prayer, I asked the Lord to show me this TRUTH however He wanted to. I asked Him to show me in a storm or in a whisper, because I had to know the TRUTH.

No storm came, and I heard not a whisper from the Lord. During the first week that I had my new computer, the Lord led me to the last piece of the puzzle. I simply asked Google. I asked, "How is the number 666 and John Paul II connected?" The answer to my prayer had been in my old computer all that time. I know that this sounds so stupid, but I had to ask Google. Evidently, the Lord wanted me to ask Google, because someone had posted the answer on their website that I had been searching for. I'm so thankful for the people who had sought the Lord for this TRUTH before me. They helped me find the TRUTH, just as I'm helping you find the TRUTH. Let me explain.

I knew that I should be seeking the culture of the Roman Empire. So I figured I should use their numeric system to count the number of the Beast. Not only are their letters used as alphabet, but also they are used as their numeral system. To this day, the Roman numeral system is called Roman numerals. You should be able to remember the Roman numerals you learned in grade school. If you can't remember them, I'm about to jog your memory. The seven basic Roman numerals are listed below. All other numerals are represented by the combinations of these seven numerals.

I=	1
U and V=	5
X=	10
L=	50
C=	100
D=	500
M=	1,000

I had tried counting all the names of Pope John Paul II, and no matter how I tried, I could not connect his name with the number 666. If my theory was true, there had to be another name for John Paul II. Again, I hate to admit it, but my problem is I have a peabrain. I never thought about trying to count his name in a different language, but the person who posted it on their website did. Here is what I found in my studies. To this day, the majority of the population of Rome speaks Italian and English. Their original language is Latin. Even in this day and time, priests still read and teach each week from their Latin Bibles. When one of these priests speaks of John Paul II, they call him Ioanes Pavlvs Secvndo. I hope you can pronounce his name, because I sure can't. Take a look at the name John Paul II in the ancient Roman language (Latin) and add up the letters by using Roman numerals.

IOANES PAVLVS SECVNDO (John Paul II)

I=	1
O=	0
A=	0
N=	0
E=	0
S=	0
P=	0
A=	0
V=	5
L=	50
V=	5
S=	0
S=	0
E=	0
C=	100
V=	5
N=	0
D=	500
O=	+ 0
	666

I want to bring your attention to a couple of scriptures I have mentioned a few times already in this book. In Revelation 22:18–19, John lets us all know what will happen to anyone who changes God's word. In prior chapters of this book, I have pointed my finger and blamed the Mormons, the Muslims, the Catholics, and the Protestants for adding and taking away from God's word. I am not scared to say it again. I know for a fact (because I know the TRUTH) that they all have changed God's word, and they all will again, because it is not in them to speak the TRUTH. I am speaking as a whole, not as individual people.

I believe all false teachers are of Satan, and these people will stay in these false teachings, until the Lord calls them out into His TRUTH.

In the last few days, Satan has been telling me that I too have been adding to God's word. I rebuked Satan in the name of Jesus, and I informed him that I am writing about the TRUTH. I realize what Revelation 22:18–19 says about adding and taking from God's word, and I know the consequences of my actions. But I also know this—if the Lord made me His watchman, I must write what I have learned and what I believe so I can warn my fellow man of what is to come. I'm not trying to mislead anyone. I would not try to make God's word say something that it doesn't say.

In God's word, He never gives the name of the Beast. The Lord does tells us in Revelation 13:18 that if you have an understanding of His word, count the number of the Beast, and I believe that is just what I have done. You know how I came to my conclusion. I believe that I RIGHTLY DIVIDED the scriptures found in Revelation chapter 17, about the eight kings (popes), and I believe John Paul II is going to be the Beast during the tribulation period. The only thing I did is fill in the blanks and told you who I believe the Beast is going to be. It is truly up to you (the reader) to seek Jesus for the TRUTH.

Even though I believe that John Paul II is going to be the Beast during the tribulation period, I am not 100% sure that it is a fact. By me saying this, I am not in no way trying to crawfish (go back on what I believe). These are my strong beliefs, and I have pretty good evidence to prove it, according to my interpretation of the scriptures (Revelation chapter 17). And as of today, if I died, I will carry this knowledge I have learned to the grave with me as the TRUTH.

I know that when I get to heaven, the Lord will set me straight if I'm wrong. But if I'm right, the Lord will say to me, "Enter into our kingdom, thy good and faithful servant." As you read this book and the Bible together, you should be able to see that I'm only trying to help you find God's TRUTH. But you had better believe this—all the things that you have read in this book have happened, or is going to happen, because it is written.

As I have said earlier in this book, the Lord has spoken to me seven times in English in the past thirty-two years. But the Lord has not ever spoken and told me that Pope John Paul II was the end-time Beast. I can also say that the Lord has not told me that Pope John Paul II wasn't the Beast. I believe the Lord has taught me His TRUTH and given me an understanding of His word. That coupled with my peabrain is how I came to my conclusion concerning the Beast. Satan I rebuke, and in Jesus, I put my trust. I can only believe what I have been taught to believe, because Jesus is my teacher, and I say, "Yes, sir," to Him. I believe that I have RIGHTLY DIVIDED the scriptures, coupled with the history of man, and found God's TRUTH. If there are any discrepancies in my calculations concerning the Beast, it will be my fault.

Here is how much I believe in what I have written in this book. My family (wife, son, daughter, grandsons, and son-in-law) were the first to receive this book. If I didn't believe that this is God's TRUTH, I would not give them or you this book. My prayer for all of you is that you will seek the Lord for His TRUTH and not allow Satan to deceive you with his false teachings, which are in the world. Also, if you are alive when the Beast comes on the scene and the tribulation period begins, you will know how to recognize the Beast. He will be the one who sits in the new temple in Jerusalem, claiming to be God. My advice to everyone is to continue serving the Lord until death. If you serve the Lord, death is but a moment; then, life is everlasting.

Remember that Satan is going to give his power and authority to the Beast. The Beast will be a powerful human. While reading, don't just think of the people of this country; think of the people of the whole world. Everyone who doesn't have their name written in the Book of Life, to those people during the tribulation period, the Beast will have supernatural intelligence and powers. They will see him as a leader. To them, the Beast will be charismatic, persuasive, and well liked. He will seem spiritual and insightful and will encourage them with a false hope. They will not know the Beast is Satan. The Beast will deceive everyone who doesn't have their name written in the Book of Life. As I witness, I hear all the time people saying, "I will never take the mark." I have never heard anyone say that they are going to take the mark of the Beast.

I want to be really clear about this. If you will not live for God, you will not die for Him. As you read Revelation chapter 13, you will see how the Beast is going to persecute everyone who is not in the church. I'm not saying the church is not going to be persecuted. I'm saying that we (the church) will not fall for Satan's deceiving ways. If you are one of the people who will be deceived by the Beast and take the mark of the Beast, here is what is going to happen to you. Read Revelation 14:9–11.

Before I finish writing this chapter, I want to bring some other things to your attention that you should know, because we are getting close to the end. Matthew chapter 24 is a chapter in God's word you should study over and over, until you understand what those scriptures teach. In Matthew chapter 24, Jesus is teaching us (anyone) who will read and pay attention to what is going on in the world how we will know when the tribulation period will start and when He will return to earth to take us (the church) home.

Matthew 24:3 says, "And as he [Jesus] sat upon the Mount of Olives, the disciples came unto Him privately, saying, Tell us, when shall these things be? and what the sign of thy coming, and of the end of the world?" In this chapter, Jesus answers all three of these questions. When Jesus started teaching His disciples, the first thing He tells them in verse 4 is to "take heed that no man deceive you." This is one of the main reasons why I wrote this book. I am trying to help equip you (the reader) with TRUTHS in and out of God's word so you will not be deceived by Satan or man.

Read verse 5 where you will see how Jesus says that they will deceive the people—"For many shall come in my name, saying, I am Christ; and shall deceive many." Many people who are in church and those who are not in church will read this scripture and think that Jesus said, "Many will claim to be Him [Jesus]"; but that is not what Jesus meant. When Jesus said, "Many shall come in my name, saying, I am Christ," what Jesus meant was just what He said; but most people don't know that the word Christ is derived from the Greek word Christos, which means anointed. Jesus says here that when someone says they are Christ (anointed), take heed not to be deceived. You have to be careful of who you listen to, because Jesus says that many shall come claiming to be anointed (Christ). Just remember to always seek the Lord for the TRUTH, and after you learn the TRUTH, the false teachers will be easy to recognize.

Jesus says in verses 6–8, "And ye shall hear of wars and rumours of wars: see that ye be not troubled: for all must come to pass, but the end is not yet. For nation shall rise against nation, and kingdom against kingdom: and there shall be famines, and pestilences, and earthquakes, in divers places. All these the beginning of sorrows."

If you watch the evening news, you will see all these things happening now (every day). I don't have to explain the statement that Jesus just made about the wars and rumors of wars. In 2015, war is just a part of our lives, while famines are something else that has spread worldwide. There are people dying from starvation every minute of every day.

For those who don't know, the word pestilences means fatal epidemic diseases. I could write a long list of fatal diseases that have come upon the people of this world, but I believe you know what I'm talking about. There are new fatal diseases that pop up every other year worldwide. I also believe that some of the fatal epidemic diseases from our past will come back as we get closer to the end of the church era on earth. This has not happened yet, but there will be someone, most likely from the radical Satan-filled Muslims, to spread a chemical or a biological toxin across the world in our near future. Believe me, with all of the world travels going on today, these diseases will spread like wildfire. I will only mention one (Covid-19).

Now, I come to the one that we hear about almost every day, and that is earthquakes. If you watch the news, you will see God in action. The U.S. Geological surveyors reported that throughout the world, we had 440 earthquakes in the month of February. That equals to about fifteen earthquakes per day. According to the U.S. Geological survey, the earth now has over 4,000 earthquakes each year. They say that the earth experiences an annual average of eighteen earthquakes with a 7.0 magnitude or greater.

As I watch the news, I can see all these things that Jesus warned us about on a daily basis. It may not be to you, but it is really clear to me. Jesus is going to return for His church real soon. Jesus is teaching us in Matthew 24:27–31 about what we (the church) call the rapture. To the church, the word rapture means Jesus is coming back to earth and taking His Bride home. As I have written earlier, there are different teachings in the world about when the rapture will take place. Some people have been taught to believe in the pre-tribulation rapture, while some in the mid-tribulation rapture, and others have been taught that Jesus is coming back post-tribulation. Only one of these time periods can be correct.

Now, you have already read in this book about when the rapture will take place, but it needs to be studied again in greater detail so we won't be deceived by these false teachings. You must read Matthew 24:29–31 to know the TRUTH about when the rapture will take place. Jesus plainly tells us when He is coming back for His Bride. In verse 29, Jesus says, "IMMEDIATELY AFTER THE TRIBULATION of those days shall the sun be darkened, and the moon shall not give her light, and the stars shall fall from heaven, and the powers of the heavens shall be shaken." Paraphrasing verses 30–31, Jesus continues, "AND THEN you will see me coming in the clouds to gather my church and to take them home." Read these three scriptures and see if you can hear God's TRUTH.

Most people, during the past 2,000 plus years, have been taught that there will be seven years of trials and tribulations at the end of the church era on earth. I simply don't see in God's word the teaching of the seven-year tribulation period. As you will find out, from reading the next chapter of this book, in many cases, God uses the number seven (7), for His completion. I do believe there is going to be an end-time tribulation period, but not seven years. Let me explain.

I just wrote about three time periods, which are being taught, that could determine when the Lord would return to earth for His Bride. Here is the simple TRUTH. The three time periods are pre-tribulation, mid-tribulation, and post-tribulation. The Lord is not coming in the pre-tribulation time period or mid-tribulation. According to what Jesus said, He is coming IMMEDIATELY AFTER THE TRIBULATION, and He knows what He's talking about. IMMEDIATELY AFTER THE TRIBULATION means post- tribulation.

I don't understand why that is so hard to understand. But people have been taught by man and Satan so many different things over the years. I'm going to give you an example of what I'm talking about. I listen to gospel music, and as I was listening today, a song came up that told me that they (the singers) didn't know the TRUTH about the rapture of the church. Their course in the song was, "He could be on the next cloud passing by." Now, that would have been the perfect song if the 3 ½-year tribulation period had just ended. I can only write what I know to be true, and the TRUTH is Jesus is coming back on a cloud, but He is not coming back on the next cloud. That is a very bold statement, but I know there are some things that must happen before Jesus comes back.

I know the Lord doesn't teach anything but the TRUTH, and He teaches us in Matthew 24:29–31 that He's coming back to earth

IMMEDIATELY AFTER THE TRIBULATION. So now you know the TRUTH about when the Lord is coming back for His Bride. After you have learned God's TRUTH, I challenge you to ask your preacher or the preacher down the street and just see for yourself what they know about God's TRUTH.

I know what the problem is with their thinking. They have been taught to believe in the seven years of trials and tribulations. Most just don't understand that the Lord separated the tribulation period from His wrath. My prayer for you is that you will be able to see and understand how God divided the tribulation period from His wrath. The first 3 ½ years (time, times, and a half) will be when the Beast is in control of everyone who doesn't have their name written in the Book of Life. This will also be when the Christian's faith will be tried. Truly, without faith, it will be impossible to stand in those days.

No matter what you have been taught in the past, the Christians in that day will be here on earth and their faith will be tried. You can read about the Beast and the persecution in Daniel 11:31–45. In verses 32–35, Daniel prophesied about the church being on earth during the tribulation period a few thousand years before the tribulation period happens. Verse 45 says, "And he [the Beast] shall plant the tabernacles of his palace between the seas in the glorious Holy Mountain; yet he shall come to his end, and none shall help him."

You have just read about the 3 ½ years of the tribulation period recorded by Daniel. If you continue reading Daniel 12:1, you will be able to see and hear the TRUTH about the rapture. Verse 1 says, "And at that time [after 3 ½ years and when the Beast comes to his end] shall Michael stand up, the great Prince which standeth for the children of Thy people: and there shall be a time of trouble, such as never was since there was a nation to that same time: and at that time [just before God pours out His wrath] thy people shall be delivered, every one that shall be found written in the book [Book of Life]," which will be IMMEDIATELY AFTER THE TRIBULATION and just before the Lord unleashes His angels with the wrath of Almighty God.

The wrath of God will take on a completely different meaning than trials and tribulations (troubled times). I don't believe what man has taught me about the seven years of tribulations, as you can see in my writings. The preachers in the past thirty-two years that I have heard have tried to teach about this. And the scriptures that they have shared have never convinced me of how long it will take God to finish pouring out His wrath.

I do know this to be the TRUTH—the Beast is going to be on this earth for 3 ½ years, and the Lord does use the number 7 for His completion in many cases. It just might be 3 ½ years of God's wrath, but it's not 7 years of trials and tribulations as they have been teaching. To tell you the TRUTH, I don't care how long it takes the angels to complete this mission (pouring out God's wrath), because I believe I'm going to be in heaven with my heavenly family; and if you will listen and obey God's word, you will be there too.

At this time, I want to thank God for the rapture and God's timing. God loves His church, and He is not going to let His Bride go through His wrath that He will pour out upon this world and people. You can read about God's wrath in Revelation 8:2–13, 9:1–21, 10:1–11, 15:1–8, and 16:1–21. Here is something else I believe. Have you ever heard of the old saying "this is like HELL on earth"? When the angels pour out the wrath of God upon this earth, that old saying will come close to being true. During that time, it will be like HELL on earth.

In Matthew 24:32–33, Jesus says, "Now learn a parable of the fig tree; When his branch is yet tender, and putteth forth leaves, ye know that summer nigh: So likewise ye, when ye shall see all these things, know that it is near, at the doors." What is near at the door? In this chapter, Jesus is teaching us when you hear (turn on your television or computer or read your newspaper) about "wars and rumors of wars, nations shall rise against nations, and kingdoms against kingdoms: and there shall be famines, and pestilences, and earthquakes in divers places…that my return is near." Jesus will be coming soon!

Jesus says in verse 34, "Verily [truly] I say unto you, this generation shall not pass till all these things be fulfilled." I have seen and heard preachers, scholars, and doctors of theology say that Jesus did not get this prophecy right, because He said, "This generation shall not pass, till all these things be fulfilled." Here is the TRUTH about this—Jesus was not talking about the people (generation) that He was talking to that day. Those preacher, scholars, and doctors of theology were the wrong ones.

Jesus knew what He was talking about, and I am here to tell you He did get it right. As you know by reading Matthew chapter 24, Jesus was teaching us about the end times and about His return to earth for His Bride. What Jesus was talking about is that the generation that is able to see and hear all of these things would be the generation that would see Him return to earth for His Bride. Let me explain. I believe we are the generation that Jesus was prophesying about, because we see all these things in abundance, because we have televisions and computers. Just a short time ago (about a hundred years), the television had not been invented, and the world could not see all these things happening, as we see them today. Just watch the news, and you will see what I have been writing about. I know that when I watch the news, I can clearly see the fig tree blooming, and the message that I get is the return of Jesus will be soon.

In 2 Peter 3:3–4, Peter writes, "Knowing this first, that there shall come in the last days scoffers, walking after their own lusts, and saying, Where is the promise of His coming? For since the fathers fell asleep [died], all things continue as from the beginning of the creation." First, let me say that I am not a scoffer. I know that Jesus is coming back, and it won't be very long. Most people who read this will think that I'm a scoffer, because of the statement that I am about to make. I believe it will be at least more than 3 ½ years from the day that I wrote this paragraph, which is October 6, 2010. The reason I said that there is at least more than 3 ½ years is because the tribulation period is 3 ½ years, and it has not begun yet.

Here is something else that I want to be really clear about. God is the only one who knows the time of His return. I'm not trying to make a prediction, but I am speaking the TRUTH as I know it. I'm not telling you all this so you will have a license to sin and for you not to serve God. You need to start serving the Lord now. You may live to see the Beast and go through the tribulation period, but the Lord could let you take your last breath, before you get to the end of this sentence. It looks like you got another breath!

When I said it would be at least 3 ½ years plus, until the Lord comes back, this is what the plus means. There are some things that must happen before Jesus returns. Here are a couple of things that must happen before He comes for His Bride. One is the rebuilding of the Jewish temple in Jerusalem. The Jewish temple was destroyed in AD 70 by the Romans, and it needs to be rebuilt for the third time. Remember what you read in 2 Thessalonians 2:1–4 about how the Beast is going to sit in the temple claiming to be God. Before Jesus comes for His church, the Jewish temple must be rebuilt so the Beast can do his thing and so God can do His. I want you to understand this. I'm not writing just what I want to write in this book. I'm writing about God's plan for humanity and the evil that came to earth with Satan. Believe me, if there was something else to write about, I would write it.

We need to do another recap of what we learned a little earlier about the four Beasts (kingdoms) that Daniel wrote about in his book. Again, I find myself going the long way around, but it will be worth reading, because I bring out other TRUTHS you should know.

Solomon built the first Jewish temple in Jerusalem. He built this temple in the tenth century BC for the Lord. As the years passed, there grew giant armies that surrounded Judah, which is now the country of Israel. They were on all sides and were strong and greedy.

In 586 BC, Jerusalem fell to the conquering Babylonians. At that time, the temple that Solomon built for the Lord was destroyed, and the Judean survivors were exiled.

The Babylonians kept Jerusalem under their thumb for almost fifty years. Then, the Medes and Persians captured and killed Belshazzar, king of Babylon, in 539 BC. Cyrus, king of Persia, permitted the exiles (Jews) to return to their homes and allowed them to rebuild the temple for the second time. A remnant of Judeans that were strong and healthy and full of energy joyously accepted the challenge, and so they rebuilt a new temple.

For the next 208 years, the Medes and the Persians ruled the world, until the Greek leader Alexander the Great defeated them in 331 BC in the battle of Arbela. During the reign of Alexander the Great, the Jewish temple was left alone and was not destroyed. The Greek Empire lasted for 163 years and was overthrown by the Roman Empire in 168 BC. Three years after the Roman Empire conquered Greece, a revolt flared up by a man named Judah Maccabee and his brothers. Again, a Jewish victory came in 165 BC, and the Jewish state was independent once again. This victory evolved into a Jewish festival that lasted for eight days in December. When the Jews celebrate Hanukkah, they are commemorating the rededication of the temple in 165 BC by the Maccabees, after its desecration by the Syrians.

In the second century BC, the Jewish state came under the power of the Roman Empire. When the Romans started exercising their power in a cruel and arbitrary (heavy-handed) way, a Jewish revolt began in Jerusalem in AD 66. After a long and fierce Jewish resistance, the Roman legions conquered Jerusalem in AD 70. They executed the Jewish leaders and exiled the whole people. In AD 70, the Romans destroyed the ancient temple, and they left only the western wall standing. This became known as the Wailing Wall and has remained the holiest place of prayer for Jews to this day.

For the past 1,940 years (give or take a year or two), the Jews have been going to the Wailing Wall to pray. There has been talk about the rebuilding of the new Jewish temple for some years now. But lately, the talks are becoming a little more serious. If you will do a little research and look up Rockefeller Banking and the rebuilding of the new Jewish temple, you will find that there is a lot of talk these days about the rebuilding of the new temple. This is a fact! The Jewish temple will be built for the third and last time here on earth. The rebuilding of the temple is a major piece of the puzzle to complete God's plan for ending this world and starting His new kingdom with His saints, angels, whomsoever, and whatsoever He choses.

Without the new temple, the Beast can't come and make his stand.

Here is another piece of the puzzle that is in God's plan that must begin—the Jews have been planning to reinstitute the sacrificing of the Passover lambs. Truly, this should be exciting news to all true believers, who are seriously studying the prophecies of the end times. Reinstating the slaughter of animals is a clear indication that the end of this present-time dispensation is close. Let me explain.

The Jews stopped sacrificing animals 1,940 years ago, for the most part. I don't believe that anyone can say for sure the day they stopped, but they did. If I had to guess, I would say the Jews stopped sacrificing animals in AD 70 when the Romans destroyed the ancient temple. I'm sure some Jews continued to sacrifice animals to God, but nothing like they did in the temple just before it was destroyed. We are going to learn more about the temple of the Lord, but first, there is more that we need to learn about the sacrificing of the animals. As you are about to learn, the stopping of the sacrificing of animals will be one of the first things the Beast does as he makes his stand in the new temple.

We will find out a little more about this later, but first, let's read and find out about the animals that Solomon sacrificed when he was bringing up the Ark of the Covenant and the rest of the holy vessels from Zion, as he was furnishing the first temple. Just in case you don't know, the Ark of the Covenant is what Harrison Ford was looking for in the movie *Raiders of the Lost Ark*. The Bible doesn't say that they sacrificed any animals in Zion, as they gathered the furniture from the old Tabernacle. God's word does tell us what they did when the Ark of the Covenant arrived at the first temple in Jerusalem. You can find these scriptures, which teach us about this, in 1 Kings 8:1–5. These scriptures say that King Solomon and the elders of Israel gathered together in the seventh month for their feast.

Verse 5 says, "And King Solomon, and all the congregation of Israel, that were assembled unto him, with him before the Ark, sacrificing sheep and oxen, that could not be told nor numbered for multitude."

Just imagine how bloody it was, as they sacrificed so many animals. People who are not in church and have never been taught about the blood don't know the significance of the blood. If you don't know the significance of the blood, you will when you read chapter 9 about being born-again.

You may be thinking—as I did—that it's hard to imagine there were so many animals sacrificed that day, that they didn't know the number. In 1 Kings chapter 8 does give a number of animals sacrificed, as they showed their dedication to the new temple and to the Lord. These numbers will help us understand the magnitude of animals that could not be told nor numbered for multitude, when they were sacrificed before the Ark. Verse 63 says that King Solomon and the children of Israel dedicated the new temple to the Lord and that "Solomon offered a sacrifice of peace offerings, which he offered unto the Lord, two and twenty thousand [22,000] oxen, and an hundred and twenty thousand [120,000] sheep." Again, I will ask you to imagine the blood that flowed that day from 142,000 animals, and the day that they were assembled together before the

Ark and there were so many animals sacrificed, that day "...that they could not be numbered for multitude." God loves blood, because life is in the blood I guess. You will learn later, more about how our Creator, uses blood from Genesis through Revelation. He must love it!

According to the scriptures, the Beast is going to make the Jews stop sacrificing animals. For the Beast to stop sacrificing animals, they must at some point start sacrificing them again. Read Daniel 9:27, where you will find the scriptures that teach us about the Beast making the Jews stop sacrificing and the oblation (offering). As you have just learned from God's word, the Beast is going to stop the sacrificing during his reign. Do you remember me telling you, that I got to edit my book, I got to add in this TRUTH also, and here is the beginning of the prophesy, that the Beast will make the Jews stop sacrificing animals. For the Beast to make them stop sacrificing animals, they MUST, start sacrificing animals again in the near future. And just look what I get to add to this TRUTH. September 20, 2022 THE JERUSALEM POST proclaimed "From Texas to Israel: Red heifers needed for Temple arrive." I learned about the five perfect red heifers, that the Jews are going to start with, after my book was published, but I got a chance to warn you. Google Jerusalem and the five red heifers and it will pop up. The Beast is coming very soon! While we are reading and studying the book of Daniel, let's learn some other important lessons from Daniel. Now, you are about to learn that God allowed Daniel to write and let the church know some very important timelines in our (the church's) future, such as when the rapture should take place. If you have studied your Bible with my book guiding you to God's word, you must believe by now, that Jesus has been teaching me His TRUTH, and Jesus is trying to teach you also. When I make a statement as bold as "when the rapture should take place." I believe, that I should give you book, chapter, and verses, so you can learn according to God's word. Here are some scriptures that will help you see and hear, how the Holy Ghost can teach you things about our future. My God, it is God teaching you, ask Jesus to give you Spiritual eyes and ears, so you can see and hear His TRUTH. Read Matthew 13:11-17 before you read these scriptures 1Corinthians 2:10, John 16:13, Ephesians 1:17-18, and Daniel 2:21-22.

That should be enough scriptures to teach you, that Jesus knows how to teach about Himself and our future. This timeline about when Jesus is coming back for His church is really simple, if Jesus teaches you. I know, that Jesus said in Matthew 24:36 "…that day and hour only God knows…"

You have already learned about the tribulation period, and how many years the Beast will be in control of his people, but in Daniel chapter 12, Daniel adds 30 more days to complete the Beast's mission than John wrote about, in the book of Revelation. In Daniel 7:25 he describes how "…the saints shall be given into his (the Beast) hand until a time, and times, and the dividing of time," which is 31/2 years. John uses the terminology in Revelation 11:2-3 as forty-two months, and in verse 3 teaches us about the two witnesses, will preach a thousand two hundred threescore (60) days or 1,260. In Revelation 12:14 John says "…a time, and times, and half a time" like Daniel taught us in Daniel 7:25.

Let's read Daniel chapter 12, and learn from the person, that gives us the closest time line, of when Jesus WILL return for His Church. But first let's find out what Daniel, experienced as he finished writing his writings. If you read Daniel 11:45 you will learn, that the Beast "…yet he shall come to his end…" Now you will learn, that Daniel had to get persistent with the Lord, to warn us about when Jesus will return.

Let's RIGHTLY DIVIDE Daniel chapter 12 starting at verse1. The Beast just died and you need to hear the first four words in verse 1. Do you remember, how the Lord was there in the fire, waiting on Shadrach, Meshach, and Abednego? Simultaneously the Lord had to command the regular fire, not to harm His three men that completely trusted in Him, and at the very same time He destroyed the soldiers, that threw them into the furnace. Always remember that "For our God a consuming fire." Hebrews 12:29.

What Jesus is going to do in Daniel 12:1, will not happen in that type of time period, but will be simultaneously, because Daniel starts with "And at that time..." Which is speaking of the death of the Beast, and Michael the archangel stands up to defend Jesus' Church from Satan's evilness. And Jesus will gather His people "... at that time..." "For the Lord Himself shall descend from Heaven with a shout, with the voice of the archangel, and with the trump of God, and the dead in Christ shall rise first: Then we which are alive remain shall be caught up together with them in the clouds, to meet the Lord in the air..." (1 Thessalonians 4:16-17)

After Jesus gathers His Church, He will command Michael to throw the Beast, the false prophet, and Satan in HELL for a thousand years. And during this thousand years (or Saturday) (or the Sabbath) we (the Church) will be in Heaven with our Creator. The Lord tells Daniel in verse 4 to "...shut up the words, and seal the book..." But as you can see, Daniel continued to write. And in verse 9, the Lord has to tell Daniel again, "...go thy way, Daniel for the words closed up and sealed till the time of the end."

And again Daniel doesn't listen, because he must warn the Church Jesus' return timeline. And he writes 4 more scriptures, while risking what the Lord would do, to make him stop writing. If Daniel wouldn't have persisted, we would not have this accurate timeline to follow. Thank you Lord, for allowing Daniel to continue writing this important message to us. And in verse 13 Daniel finally listens to the Lord, and stops writing. I just want to put in my two cents about this. I don't believe, that you can get this kind of teaching from Harvard, or Yale. Just my belief! I sorta did something like Daniel, when I wrote My Personal Warning to the people, on the last page of this book, about their future during the thousand years that we are in Heaven.

You can read and learn about this timeline in Daniel 12:11-12. Verse 11 says, "And from the time the daily shall be taken away, and the abomination that maketh desolate set up [the mark of the Beast], a thousand two hundred and ninety days [1,290 days]." Paraphrasing verse 12, Daniel writes that if you can make it through these trouble times, just forty-five more days, you will be blessed. After these forty-five days, Jesus should come back for His Bride. Notice that I have used the word "should" when I spoke of when Jesus would return for His Bride.

In Daniel 12:11–12, Daniel gives us a precise timeline to follow, if you are a serious studier of end-time prophecies. I believe the reason you are reading this book is that you are looking for the TRUTH. Here is the TRUTH, and here is the reason I used the word "should" when I wrote about when the rapture would take place. Even though Daniel was writing under the inspiration of God's Spirit, and he wrote what the Lord instructed him to write, neither Daniel nor anyone else knows when Jesus will return for His Bride. In Matthew chapter 24, Jesus teaches us about the end-time and His return to earth. Paraphrasing Matthew 24:36, Jesus says that only the Father knows when He is coming for His Bride.

Also in Matthew chapter 24, Jesus teaches us about the Beast that Daniel warned us about that would take over the new temple in Jerusalem. In Matthew 24:15–21, Jesus says,

> When ye therefore shall see the abomination of desolation, spoken of by Daniel the prophet, stand in the Holy Place, (whoso readeth, let him understand). Then let them which be in Judaea flee into the mountains: Let him which is on the housetop not come down to take any thing out of his house: Neither let him which is in the field return back to take his clothes. And woe unto them that are with child, and to them that give suck in those days! But pray ye that your flight be not in the

winter, neither on the Sabbath day. For then shall be
Great Tribulation, such as was not since the beginning
of the world to this time, no, nor ever shall be.

I wanted you to read this to make this one point from Matthew
24:22. Jesus say, "And except those days [when the mark of the Beast
is enforced] should be shortened, there should no flesh be saved: but
for the elect's [God's people's] sake those days shall be shortened."
Again, I must say don't be deceived by the false teachings that are
in the world. You have read God's word for yourself, and you are so
blessed to know God's TRUTH about the rapture of the church.

In Revelation 13:5, John tells us that the Beast will reign for
forty-two months (3 ½ years). In Daniel 7:25, Daniel tells us that
the Beast will reign for time and times and the dividing of time (3
½ years). Neither Daniel nor John knows the day or the hour of
Jesus' return, but they both give us the TRUTH about the reign of
the Beast and a timeline to follow. Remember what you have read in
Daniel 12:11–12. Daniel is the only prophet that gives us a specific
timeline to follow as far as I know.

If you are here when the Beast comes on the scene, and you hear
about the Beast stopping the daily sacrifice in Jerusalem and starts
making people take his mark, pay close attention to the timeline
given in Daniel 12:11–12. Daniel's prophecy will be really close to
the time of the rapture. You had better remember what you just
read and teach it to friends and family so they won't be deceived.

I'm a carpenter by trade, and when I build a building, the
first and most important thing I do is to build a strong and firm
foundation. As you are about to find out, by reading God's word,
our walk with the Lord must be built on a strong foundation also.

I want you to read these two scriptures in Ephesians 2:19–20
and see where we get our material to build our foundation so we
can be strong in the Lord. As you read these two scriptures you can
see that we are to obey what the apostles and prophets tell us to do

and how Jesus is the chief corner of our foundation. Now, that's a strong foundation to build on!

Let's read a few more scriptures and see how and when the apostles, prophets, and Jesus tell us the rapture will take place. These scriptures, which you are about to read, will reveal to you a few signs that are easily discerned in their time; and also, these signs will help us (the church) know that the Lord is on His way to take us home. Remember what you have learned from God's word and how we are to hear and obey what the apostles and prophets tell us to do.

These scriptures tell us the TRUTH about how and when the rapture will take place. The Prophet Joel prophesied about these events. In Joel 2:28–31, he writes,

> And it shall come to pass afterward, I will pour out My Spirit upon all flesh; and your sons and your daughters shall prophesy, your old men shall dream dreams, your young men shall see visions. And also upon the servants, and upon the handmaids in those days will I pour out My Spirit. [You are about to read about the signs (events) that I mentioned that would let us (the church) know that the Lord is on His way to take us home.] And I will shew wonders in the heavens and in the earth, blood, and fire, and pillars of smoke. The sun shall be turned into darkness, and the moon into blood BEFORE the great and the terrible day of the Lord come [the rapture].

Now, let's read what Luke recorded in the book of Acts concerning the church and the last days. Always remember this—the first and second chapters of the book of Acts are the only TRUTHS where you will find facts about how, when, and where the New Testament church began. You need to read and study these two chapters, until you can explain them to your friends and family.

Read Acts 2:14 where you will see that Peter was preaching that historical day. Peter had to preach that day because he was given the keys to heaven to open the door (Jesus), for the Jewish nation. In verse 16, Peter lets us know that the beginning and the end of the church are what Joel prophesied about in Joel 2:28–31. Peter says in Acts 2:16, "But this is that [the beginning of the church] which was spoken by the Prophet Joel." In the next couple of scriptures (17–18), Peter quotes what Joel prophesied would happen in the last days of the church era on earth. But I want to bring your attention to verses 19–20 where you will see that these end-time signs (events) are mentioned again. Paraphrasing verse 20, these signs will happen before the Lord comes for His Bride. As you read these scriptures, you should be able to see that Peter was a witness to a big part of the fulfillment of Joel's prophecy.

John writes in Revelation 6:1 about how he saw the Lamb (Jesus) open a seal. When Jesus opens one of these seven seals will trigger the events that will take place that you have been reading about, just before Jesus returns. In chapter 7 of this book, I will explain the TRUTH about that seal being opened, and tie all of these events together.

I know that I have been a little off the main subject (Satan + Pope = Beast). But most of the things I have been writing about in this chapter are about the end of the world and coincide with Satan + Pope = Beast. Before I finish writing this chapter, I want to end it by sharing with you what the Lord has taught me about the last two wars between Satan and God on earth and about judgment day for the saints and sinners.

As you now know, God's word also teaches us that the Beast comes out of HELL and that the Beast is cast back into HELL, when Jesus comes back for His Bride. Read Revelation 19:20. As you will see, this time, the false prophet will join him in HELL. As you are about to learn, they (the Beast, the false prophet, and Satan) will be locked up in HELL for a thousand years. After this one thousand years has expired, the last war (Armageddon) will take place. Most Christians have been taught to believe that these two wars are the same, but I'm here to inform you they are not the same.

In chapter 8 of this book, I have written about Satan and included the scriptures that show where he came from and, what I believe, the reason he was thrown into HELL. But at this time, I am getting ahead of myself with this story (facts) and showing you how Satan finally loses the war.

Now, I want to RIGHTLY DIVIDE the scriptures and show you the TRUTH about these last two wars against evil here on earth. Do you remember in chapter 2 of this book when I wrote how the Lord reserved vengeance for Himself'? You are about to read where the Lord uses that vengeance against our enemies.

To those who do not know, the soul of every Christian that has died is in heaven, waiting for the first resurrection. You can find this TRUTH in Revelation 6:9–11: John says,

> And when He [Jesus] had opened the fifth seal, I saw under the altar the souls of them that were slain for the word of God, and for the testimony which they held. And they cried with a loud voice, saying, How long, O Lord, Holy and True, dost thou not judge and avenge our blood on them that dwell on the earth?
>
> And white robes were given unto every one of them; and it was said unto them, that they should rest yet for a little season [a short time], until their fellow servants also and their brethren that should be killed as they, should be fulfilled.

In other words, "You are going to have to wait a little more time until the tribulation period is completed. And then, we will saddle up our white horses and go to earth and gather the saints that have died for me and those that made it through the great tribulation. And then, I will avenge your blood and theirs." Now, that is TRUTH!

Here are some more scriptures that will help you to understand what you have read about when Jesus opens the fifth seal. Apostle Paul teaches us about the rapture in 1 Thessalonians 4:13–17. In verse 14, Paul says, "For if we believe that Jesus died and rose again, even so them also which sleep [die] in Jesus will God bring with Him."

I believe that this is another priceless revelation. Revelation 17:12–14 and Revelation 19:11–21 teach us about Satan's army fighting against the Lord when He returns for His church. Revelation 16:12–16 and Revelation 20:7–10 teach us about the last war (Armageddon). If you take all of these scriptures and RIGHTLY DIVIDE them, you will see that these last two wars are a thousand years apart. Since you know where to find the TRUTH about the last two end-time wars, you need to study these scriptures.

God's word never says that we (the church) do anything, but ride our white horses and follow Jesus. Revelation 19:15 says that out of His mouth goeth a sharp sword. This sharp sword means whatever Jesus speaks will happen. The sharp sword is His tongue. Jesus is simply going to conquer Satan's army with His tongue. Good is going to triumph over evil that day, but it is going to take the second (last) war to overcome evil forever. As you now know, this world is going to stand a thousand years after the rapture of the church.

I want to confirm something I have said before in this book. I am not ashamed to say that I have a peabrain. I'm neither a scholar nor a doctor of theology—no, not even close. But to my friends and family, I over the years have jokingly said that I was this close (with my finger and thumb held close together) to being a genius. But I would always say that if I'm this close to being a genius, I'm this close to being a dumbass. Believe me, I know what I am. I said all that to say this. Let's look a little deeper into God's word and see what the Lord can teach a person who has a peabrain.

When the Lord comes back for His Bride, He is going to accomplish three major things, and they are: the rapture of the church; conquering the Beast, the false prophet, and their army; and finally, taking away temptation from everyone who is left on this earth when He binds Satan and puts him in HELL for a thousand years.

1 Thessalonians 4:16–17 says that the Lord is going to open the graves of all the saints first. After the Lord has reunited the souls that came with Him with their new (glorified) bodies, He is going to change us (those who are alive on earth) into our new (glorified) bodies. At that time, He is going to command gravity to turn loose of His Bride. That is when we (the Bride) will take that plain air ride. I believe when Jesus gets His church together, He will utterly destroy the Beast, the false prophet, and their armies with His tongue. Always remember to ask the Lord to teach you the TRUTH. You can learn about our new (glorified) bodies in 1 Corinthians 15:35–58.

Now for the last thing the Lord will do when He comes back for His church. You can find this TRUTH in Revelation 20:1–3.

> And I [John] saw an angel come down from heaven, having the key of the bottomless pit [HELL] and a great chain in his hand.
>
> And he laid hold on the dragon, that old serpent, which is the Devil, and Satan, and bound him a thousand years. And cast him into the bottom less pit [HELL], and shut him up, and set a seal upon him, that he should deceive the nations no more, till the thousand years should be fulfilled: and after that, he must be loosed a little season [a while].

Before we study some facts about the last war (Armageddon), here is something else most so-called Christians don't know—when and by whom the saints will be judged. Let's look up the scriptures that teach us when and by whom the saints will be judged. This is another misconception. Most Christians and non-Christians alike have been taught that Jesus will judge everyone on judgment day. That is not TRUTH.

You have just read Revelation 20:1–3, how the angel binds and cast Satan into HELL for a thousand years. Now, I have quoted verse 4 so you can hear the TRUTH about how the saints will be judged, "And I [John] saw thrones, and they sat upon them, and judgment was given unto them: and the souls of them that were beheaded for the witness of Jesus, and for the word of God, and which had not worshipped the Beast, neither his image, neither had received mark upon their foreheads, or in their hands; and they [the saints] lived, and reigned with Christ a thousand years." Now that tells us when and where (after the church gets to heaven).

As far as I know, the answer to the judgment of the saints is only found in three passages of scriptures, and you just read one of them. But that scripture didn't teach us who was on the thrones judging the church. Another set of the scriptures where we can find this TRUTH is in Matthew 19:27–28. As Jesus makes a statement in the previous scriptures, Peter says unto Him, "Behold, we have forsaken all, and followed thee. What shall we have therefore?" And Jesus said unto them, "Verily [truly] I say unto you, that ye which have followed me, in the regeneration when the Son of man shall sit in the throne of his glory, ye also shall sit upon twelve thrones, judging the twelve tribes of Israel." The TRUTH is if you are born-again, you have become a child of God and the seed of Abraham. If you make it to heaven, you are a part of the twelve tribes of Israel, because you have been grafted in when you were born-again.

This next scripture also confirms who will judge the saints in heaven. In Luke 22:30, Jesus says, "That ye may eat and drink at my table in my kingdom, and sit on thrones, judging the twelve tribes of Israel." Jesus' prophesy in Matthew 19:27–28 and Luke 22:30 comes to pass in Revelation 20:4. As you can now see, the apostles are going to judge the church, just as Jesus said they would. You also can see in Revelation 20:4 that the apostles will judge the twelve tribes of Israel that went through the tribulation period.

We are going to skip Revelation 20:5 for now and come back to it a little later, when we find the TRUTH about the judgment day for the sinner. Verse 6 says, "Blessed and holy he that hath part in the first resurrection: on such the second death hath no power, but they [saints] shall be priests of God, and of Christ, and shall reign with Him a thousand years."

This is the TRUTH (order) in which the world will end. IMMEDIATELY AFTER THE TRIBULATION, the Lord comes back for His church and takes care of the Beast and the false prophet. Then, the Lord is going to give His angel authority and strength to bind Satan and cast him into HELL for a thousand years. Then, after the church gets to heaven, the Lord is going to allow the twelve apostles to judge the church. I believe that the original twelve apostles will be those judges. I realize that I have not mentioned Apostle Paul, because I know he was the fourteenth apostle. But I believe we don't have to worry about him. If I had to guess what Apostle Paul would be doing in heaven, I believe he will be sitting on the left or right seat next to Jesus. That is just what I believe.

Only God knows what the church will be doing during those thousand years. During the thousand years that Satan is in HELL, man will live on this earth without temptation from Satan. God's word never speaks of anyone being saved during that time period. As far as I know, only God knows. But, just as the Lord begins and ends many time dispensations, those thousand years will expire.

Now, we are going to find the TRUTH about the last war on this earth. To most Christians, this last battle is commonly called the Battle of Armageddon. Revelation 16:12–16 gives us a brief description of how this last war will come to be. As you can see from these scriptures, Satan, the Beast, and the false prophet will be loosed from HELL so they can deceive all the nations once again. Satan and all his demons, are going to be loosed from HELL. The Lord will allow them time to gather their army to fight their last battle.

John lets us know in Revelation chapter 20, when the last war will begin and end. John writes in Revelation 20:7–8, "And when the thousand years are expired, Satan shall be loosed out of his prison. And shall go out to deceive the nations which are in the four quarters of the earth, Gog, and Magog, to gather them together to battle: the number of whom as the sand of the sea."

I want to tell you what I know about Gog and Magog, and that is very little. I should clarify something, which I should have said at the beginning of this book—I don't know everything. Gog and Magog are only mentioned in a few places in God's word. You can read about Gog and Magog in Revelation 20:8 and in Ezekiel chapters 38 and 39.

In Genesis chapter 10, you can find the TRUTH about who Magog is and where he comes from. In Genesis 10:1–3, you will find out that Magog is the son of Japheth, which would make him Noah's grandson. So when the Bible speaks of Magog, it means they are the decedents of Magog. And Gog is the land in which Magog lived. Ezekiel 38:5 says that Persia (modern-day Iran), Ethiopia, and Libya will fight alongside Magog's descendants in the last battle against God.

It won't take Satan very much to get Iran to fight, because they (for the most part) are evil and ready to destroy that which is good. If you know anything about Persia (Iran), you should know that they want to wipe Israel and the United States off the face of the earth. God informs us some of the names of Magog's family in Ezekiel 38:6. God's word says that Gomer, one of Japheth's sons, and his son Togarmah's descendants will also be at the Battle of Armageddon fighting alongside Satan against God.

I have read and studied these two chapters in Ezekiel a few times. But I have not studied them as well as I should. I planned on reading and studying these two chapters in Ezekiel in the near future. I'm going to leave it up to you to study these two chapters for yourselves. If you will seek the TRUTH, you will not believe what the Lord will teach you from the scriptures found in Ezekiel. I am going to say it again.

You need to ask the Lord to show you this TRUTH, which is found in Ezekiel, because He is the only one who can teach you about the past, which will eventually be in the future.

Revelation 20:9 shows us how this war will end—"And they [Satan's army] went up on the breath of the earth, and compassed the camp of the saints about, and the beloved city: and fire came down from God out of heaven, and devoured them." You can clearly see that there are two different end-time wars, and they are a thousand years apart.

After the Battle of Armageddon comes judgment day. While you are still alive, here are a few things you must learn. There is one true God, one true gospel, and one true Judge for all nations, and His name is Jesus. In Matthew 25:31–34, Jesus says that when He sits on His throne to judge, every nation will stand before Him.

God's word teaches that both saint and sinner are already being judged on earth. According to the scriptures, our own words are going to save us or condemn us. Most people don't realize how powerful our words are, but you are about to find out. Let's read Matthew 12:34–37. If any of us want to be on God's side of His will, we must study and obey His word. If we seek God's TRUTH, He will write His word in our minds and in our hearts, and only then can we obey Him. What goes into our minds and our hearts will eventually come out of our mouth. Revelation 12:11 says, "And they [the saints] overcame him [Satan] by the blood of the Lamb, and by the word of their testimony." If you will learn about Jesus, you will talk about Jesus. So I must say at this time, watch your mouth!

As soon as the Battle of Armageddon is finished, Jesus is going to have a second resurrection with all the people left on, and in the earth. Do you remember when we skipped Revelation 20:5? Now, it is time to read it. Verse 5 says, "But the rest of the dead [sinners] lived not again until the thousand years were finished." After the second resurrection takes place, it will be time for the Great White Throne Judgment. Revelation 20:11–15 teaches us about the Great White Throne Judgment day. Verse 12 says, "And I [John] saw the dead [sinners], small and great, stand before God, and the books were opened." This scripture says the dead were judged out of those things which were written in the books. These books, which are opened on judgment day, are the 66 books of the Bible.

Jesus says in John 12:48 that His word is going to judge the sinner on judgment day. Now, let's go to Romans 2:16 and see what Paul says about this. Here, Paul says, that Jesus is going to judge according to Paul's gospel. You can believe this. No one will be judged from the Book of Mormons or the Koran. Revelation 20:12 also says, "Another book was opened, which is of Life." You need to read verse 15 again.

On judgment day, I believe Jesus will ask some questions they should know, if they have been studying His word. Jesus could ask such questions as "I gave the keys to heaven to a man on earth. Who did I give them to?" If you don't know the answer to that question, it is a good chance you want know the answer to the next question. "This man, whom I gave the keys to, opened three doors with these keys." Where in the scriptures did he open the doors? In John 8:32, "Did I say you shall know the TRUTH and the TRUTH shall set you free, or did I say make you free? What does Acts 2:38–39 say? I said in Matthew 5:16 to let your light shine before men. What did I mean by that? As my servants witnessed to you of my love for you, why did you not believe? I gave my life for you so that you could live. I purchased you with my own blood, but you chose death."

From the beginning of time, when Satan and man's path crossed until judgment day, man will have all kinds of excuses why they didn't serve the Lord. When the sinners stand before Jesus, some might even try to use the excuse that the comedian Flip Wilson used back in the 1970s—"the devil made me do it." I know that excuse is not going to be good enough, but I believe it will be used.

You can find the last few words that a sinner will hear on judgment day and very possibly throughout eternity in Matthew 7:23. I believe they will not make it through the whole statement, just only until the fifth word—depart. Read Luke 10:17–19. I have to say this again. In John 12:48, Jesus says that the sinner will be judged by God's word. If you don't know the answers to the questions that Jesus could ask you on judgment day, I suggest you seek God (Jesus) for these answers and learn them today.

Satan finally loses the war against good. Read Revelation 20:10 and see what happens to him and his followers. Verse 10 says that the devil was cast into the lake of fire with the beast and the false prophet. This scripture also says that they will be there being tormented day and night forever. As judgment day continues, the souls of everyone who did not obey (live) the word of God will follow their leader into HELL. If you don't want to go to HELL, you must keep your name written in the Book of Life by serving the Lord and your fellow man. You have a choice to make, but you're on your own. No one can make this choice for you. Read Deuteronomy 30:19–20.

I only covered a very small part of God's word in this book. So it is up to you to find more TRUTH. If you will raise your voice to heaven and ask the teacher (Jesus) for the TRUTH, He will teach you things that you didn't believe you could learn. I didn't learn a whole lot during the years I went to school, but I did learned how to read and write. I am so glad I accomplished that much. Although I said I know how to write, but I am amazed when I look down on my computer and see that I have now written 23,818 words in this chapter up to this point. I am in no way boasting, and I'm not just seeing how many words I can write. All I can say is that it is what it is.

I have not accomplished a whole lot in my life, but let me tell you about my greatest accomplishment. I took what I learned in those eight years in school and allowed the Holy Ghost to teach me the TRUTH. I have not only read but also I studied God's word for the past thirty-three years. During those thirty-three years, I might have missed a couple of dozen days reading and studying God's word. As you can see by the things written in this book, the Lord has truly blessed me and shared His word with me.

Just imagine how much more the Lord will teach you from these same scriptures if you will study His word and seek the TRUTH. I'm sure I could have written a little more about the Beast. But I believe I have written enough for you to see and hear God's TRUTH and just maybe enough to peak your curiosity so you will seek the Lord for more TRUTH than you now know.

I thought I was finished writing this chapter, but as I looked across the page of my Bible, I saw something else that I needed to mention. Some people don't know that this heaven and earth are going to be destroyed. This world was first destroyed by water during the days of Noah. But the Lord didn't completely destroy the world; He simply got rid of all the evil of that time. However, as we all know, the evil returned when Satan deceived Noah's decedents. And as you now know, that evil that began with Noah's decedents will be the same evil that will come against the Lord at the Battle of Armageddon.

In 2 Peter 3:10–13, God's word teaches us that the next time this world will be destroyed by FIRE, it will not exist anymore. I believe that is why it is called the end of the world. Read what John wrote in Revelation 21:1–2 about Apostle Peter's prophesy coming to pass.

> I saw a new heaven and a new earth: for the first heaven
> and the first earth were passed away; and there was no
> more sea.

> And I John saw the holy city, new Jerusalem, coming down from God out of heaven, prepared as a Bride adorned for her husband.

At that time, that old saying "heaven on earth" will be true. I believe this is where the church will spend eternity with our Lord Jesus.

Here is something else that came to my ears that I need to share with you. Again, I thought that I was finished writing this chapter, but I must warn you of this important news, which I just heard. There has been talk for years now that some of the people in Europe have been experimenting with a microchip implanted in their bodies to purchase goods so there would be a cashless society. In May 2017, the news reported that some people of Sweden had started implanting microchips trying this new method of a cashless society.

I have always believed that the technology of the microchips for the cashless society would start in Europe. But listen really close to what is taking place in America. Fox News reported that on July 24, 2017, in Wisconsin, fifty employees volunteered to have these microchips implants, between their thumb and forefinger. A Wisconsin company, Three Square Market, introduced a new way of purchasing items from company break rooms.

Three Square Market is replacing the vending machines in company break rooms with MicroMarkets (mini convenient stores). When making a purchase, simply take the item to the self-checkout kiosk and then wave your hand over the screen, and the items that you have chosen will be yours. So far, this company already has about 20,000 MicroMarkets spread across the world. This company is the first in the United States that I know of to offer its employees microchip implants, which are the size of a grain of rice. After you receive the microchip, you will no longer need a credit card or a mobile device such as an iPhone to purchase anything from the MicroMarket; you just scan your hand.

A Three Square Market spokesman said that the program is not mandatory. "I say not yet." The company said that the microchip can gain access to the building and log in into the company computers. Then, the reporter ended his segment by saying that according to the experts, it won't be long until microchips will be used in passports, driver's license, and even paying for things like public transportation. The chips used by Three Square Market were developed by a company in Sweden. I want to be really clear about this. This is the beginning of the mark of the Beast in the United States. Mark my words, this technology is in its infant stage, and the microchip will start off really slow, but it will catch on like a wildfire. You have been warned—don't take a microchip implant for your purchasing method. When the mark of the Beast comes like a wildfire, you had better learned how to pray to the Lord, because Jesus is the only help you will have. I believe that even your family and friends will turn on you, during the tribulation period.

You have already learned about the mark of the Beast, but I believe that this new technology that has come to America gives us cause to read about it again. I must warn you again. Don't take the microchip implant for any reason! Revelation 13:15–18 teaches us about the Beast and his mark. I want to bring your attention to what verse 16 says, wherein John records that the mark will be placed in peoples' right hand or in their forehead.

From now own, every time you go to the supermarket or your local hardware store, you will remember what you have learned about a cashless society, as you checkout at the checkout counter. The barcode system started in 1932 when a group of students at the Harvard University Graduate School of Business Administration undertook a project that would make shopping by catalog easier for customers. All the customer had to do was remove a card from the catalog corresponding to the item they wanted to purchase and then hand that card to the clerk, who would place the card into a mechanical reader. The reader contained the information of the product and its location in the storeroom, and the product would be immediately delivered to the checkout counter, where the customer would pay for it. The information on the card also updated the store's inventory information so that when the time came to reorder that product, the store owner or manager would know how many had to be reordered.

The first modern scanning system was installed by RCA at a Kroger's grocery store in 1972. And as you now know, this system is in almost every store. Next time, when you checkout, I want you to pay attention to the scanners. The stores are already set up for the microchip technology (mark of the Beast). The barcode system is placed inside the microchip. After (IF) you take the microchip, when you come to the checkout counter, you will simply swipe your right hand across the screen that is mounted on the counter; or if you chose to place the microchip in your forehead, you will simply swipe your forehead with the handheld device that you see the casher using at your local store. I just don't see people scanning their foreheads across the counter, but you never know about people.

Now, this is what the Lord taught me about the transformation from virtually no cash being spent in America to a cashless society. If you don't know, you are about to learn that there are five steps, which are clear to see, that bring the world to the mark of the Beast. I believe that it's not the mark of the Beast coming to us, but we (the world) are going to the mark of the Beast. I hope you heard that; if not, read it again. It has been the same throughout the world, but I'm going to explain what happened in America, because I know it is the TRUTH. I believe you will be able to see and understand the steps we have taken to get to where a thief could not steal from us. But as you are about to find out, the thief will always take from us until the Lord destroys him (Satan).

First step. When the Pilgrims arrived on the shores of New England, at first, they didn't have stores to go and purchase their food or clothing. At the time, they would trap for furs, raise animals and grow food, and trade with others the things they needed to survive. But the thieves would come and steal chickens, corn, or pigs from their neighbors and would take what they could, even if they had to kill to get away with it.

Second step. As time passed, they started having markets and building stores where they could shop, and they began using money much more often. Now, this is just what the thieves had been waiting for. When they were able to steal your money, they didn't have to steal food or livestock, even though that continued to happen. Now, they could buy anything they wanted with your money.

Third step. As the thieves grew in number and became bolder, people were just tired of being robbed of their possessions. This inspired someone to come up with a bright idea to build a bank to hold people's money so they would simply write checks. At first, the thieves were not worried about stealing from their personal bank account; they would just simply blow up the bank and take everyone's money. There are a few people who still rob banks, but the clever thief these days simply steal from people's personal account. It didn't take long for the thieves to learn how to steal from people's checking account.

Fourth step. Then, someone came up with another brilliant idea of credit cards. Not only are the credit card companies taking from you, but you know how easy it is, for the thief to steal your credit cards.

The fifth and final step to arrive to a cashless society.
People are still tired of thieves stealing from them, so there are certain groups in our world introducing new technologies such as the use of microchip.

My prayer is that you will see and hear this TRUTH. Truly, this is Satan's way of preparing the naive people of this world and make it easier for the Beast when he comes on the scene. For now, they are just implanting the microchip in your hand. But when the Beast comes out of the bottomless pit (HELL) and takes over the world, he will make everyone whose name is not written in the Book of Life have microchip implants in their right hand or forehead. The beginning of the mark of the Beast is now in America and will be coming to you real soon. Don't be naive and take it! After what you have learned from God's word, you should know that Satan is behind this from the beginning. Satan is the one who makes the thief steal. BELIEVE THIS! From the beginning, this has been Satan's plan to deceive us, if we allow him to. I, Jessie Dunson, will not let anyone implant a microchip anywhere in my body. And you had better not either. The mark of the Beast will soon be a reality, and then, the end will come.

Now, let's go to the next chapter and learn some more TRUTH from God's word.

Chapter 7

GOD'S COMPLETION NUMBER [7]

had no intention of writing this chapter, about God's number of completion, but I did. I am so glad the Lord gave me this chapter to write. I believe the Lord inspired me to write this whole book, but this chapter is special. At this time, I want to share with you how the Lord blessed me while writing this chapter. Most authors will never say to the reader that they can skip ahead to the middle of the chapter, but in this case, I believe it will be inspiring if you can believe. So feel free to skip and read ahead, and read pages where I have put the five asterisks (page 268.)

My intention was to write this chapter about Satan, but God's number of completion fits together with the previous chapter. So the Lord had me write about how He used the number seven (7) many times for His completion. I am going to use a lot of the same verses I used in the previous chapters because Satan, the pope, and the Beast are going to be used by the Lord to complete the end-time dispensation for this earth. There is no way to write about the end of this world without writing about Satan and the Beast.

As we find out about one small part of God's timetable, we are going to keep running into the number 7 in God's word. For some reason, the Lord likes the number 7, and He uses it often to fulfill His will. As you read God's word, you can find the number 7 being used by the Lord throughout His word. God uses the number 7 in Genesis, which is at the beginning of His word, and throughout the book of Revelation, which is at the end of His word.

As a teenager, I would sometimes visit the little Baptist church down the road from our house. At that time, I considered myself to be a Baptist. The Lord had not shown me the TRUTH at that time, so I tried to believe what they taught me. I believe most of the people who has heard about the Lord and His word has also heard about the seven years of trials and tribulations, which are supposed to come, at the end-time.

I first heard about the seven years of trials and tribulations from a Baptist preacher, and he taught about what he believed to be the TRUTH. Later, as I got into God's word for myself and learned what I know now, I realized he (the Baptist preacher) didn't know how to fill in the blanks. I'm so thankful that the Lord helped me fill in the blanks and for all the things that He has taught me so far. Now, you already know what I believe about the tribulation period. If you want to study about the great tribulation period, you can go back and study chapter 6 of this book.

I want to explain somewhat how the Lord reveals His TRUTH to me. If you know God's TRUTH, you will understand what I'm talking about. It is as simple as this—the reason I read and study God's word is because I'm always looking for a new revelation from the Lord. Here is something else that I want to share with you, and that is, I'm an inventor. I now have well over a hundred inventions that the Lord has blessed me with. I have always said and believed that when an invention comes to me, it's like when the Lord reveals something to me. I'm not comparing them as equal, but an invention and a revelation from the Lord come to me the same way. God's

TRUTH only comes by revelation from Him. That is why we must seek Him for the TRUTH.

As inventions keep coming to me, I will continue writing them down, which I now have plenty of inventions. My desire is to have more revelations from the Lord concerning His will for my life and that I will have this knowledge to help whomever the Lord desires. I never know when the next revelation will come. I started to say that I was always ready, but that's not true. However, the moment the Lord reveals something to me, I start paying attention. I start seeking the Lord in prayer and in His word for the TRUTH. I guess the best way to explain how an invention and a revelation come to me is it's like a V8 moment. I just slap myself on my forehead and say WOW! And for over thirty-three years, I have slapped my forehead quite a few times.

It started in that little Baptist church, and for years, I heard that the number 7 is the number that God uses as His number of completion. After you finish reading this chapter, I believe you too will know that the number 7 is the number the Lord uses for the completion on many of His projects, if I can call them projects, for a lack of a better word. The number 7 is not used in every case, but many times, the Lord uses the number 7.

Man's first recording of God using the number 7 is found in the first book of the Old Testament—Genesis. God's word teaches us that He created the heavens and the earth and all that is on and in them in six days, and on the seventh day, God rested. And doing so, God created what we go by in our everyday lives, and that is a week. And as you know, the Lord used seven twenty-four hour days for his completion of a week. You can learn about the creation of this world in Genesis chapters 1 and 2. The Lord has used the number 7 throughout His word, but let's find out how the Lord used the number 7 in the book of Revelation, because we are looking for the TRUTH, about the end-time.

Just remember that when you read the book of Revelation, there are a lot of symbolic messages and only the Holy Ghost (Jesus) can teach you these. For the most part, I understand the book of Revelation, but there are some things that I may never know. I truly believe that no one knows everything in God's word. If someone knew everything, we would know about them, because they would be walking "ten feet off of Beale," just as the song goes. Even the Prophet Daniel was told by God in Daniel 12:4 to "shut up the words, and seal the book, to the time of the end." In other words, God said, "You have told them enough, Daniel." Only God can teach you what Daniel didn't write. So let's read and study the book of Revelation and see what we can learn, or not learn.

You will find the number 7 being used by the Lord in Revelation chapter 1. In Revelation 1:4, John writes about the seven churches that are in Asia and about the seven Spirits that are before God's throne. Now, that last statement was a little confusing to me, but I will try to explain it below. Jesus tells John in verse 11 the locations of the seven churches, which are in Asia. In verse 12, John says that he saw seven golden candle sticks. In verse 20, Jesus tells us what the candle sticks represent. Jesus says, the seven candle sticks are the seven churches. In verse 16, John saw seven stars in Jesus' right hand. Also, in verse 20, Jesus tells us what the seven stars represent. Jesus says, they are the angels of the seven churches.

In Revelation chapter 3, Jesus mentions the seven Spirits of God again. Now, you may understand these verses, but I do not completely understand, but I am trying. I will explain it as best I can. I can only write what the word says, and besides, I will not know any more about it, except what the Lord reveals to me. In Revelation 3:1, Jesus says, "These things saith he that hath the seven Spirits of God." Reading this part is a little confusing to me, because I know Apostle Paul was inspired by God when he wrote his letters to the church. Paul teaches us in 1 Corinthians 12:1–13 that there is only one Spirit.

Also, in Ephesians 4:4–6, Paul wrote, "One body, and one Spirit, even as ye are called in one hope of your calling; One Lord, one faith, one baptism, one God and Father of all, who above all, and through all, and in you all." As I have said before, the Holy Ghost that lives inside of us (the church) is the same Spirit, because there is only one Spirit of God. This is what I believe to be the TRUTH. But I must also believe what Jesus said about the seven Spirits of God, because if it were not so, Jesus would not have said it.

As I continued reading, I came to the fourth chapter of Revelation, and I found the answer about the seven Spirits of God in verse 5: "And out of the throne proceeded lightnings and thunderings and voices, and seven lamps of fire burning before the throne, which are the seven Spirits of God." This helps me understand a little better, but not completely. I do admit that the seven Spirits of God is conjecture to me.

As I continued reading God's word, I came to the fifth chapter of Revelation, and in verse 6, I found something else that made me ask the Lord for understanding. John said, "And I beheld, and lo, in the midst of the throne and of the four beasts, and in the midst of the elders, stood a Lamb as it had been slain, having seven horns and seven eyes, which are the seven Spirits of God sent forth into all the earth." I know I have said somewhere in this book that I don't know everything. I can only tell you what the Lord has taught me.

You should know by now that if I know about it, I will write about it. But this is just not completely clear to me. One thing I want you to know— unequivocally, there is one true God, and He is one Spirit, and His name is Jesus. I do know that God may divide Himself, but He is still the same Spirit.

Next, we are going to find out how God uses the number 7 when He opens seven seals. In Revelation chapter 5, John writes about a book that he saw the Lord holding in His right hand. The Lamb of God, which is Jesus, is the only one in heaven worthy of opening the book by loosening the seven seals. In Revelation 6:1–8, John writes about Jesus opening the first four seals. These four horsemen mentioned here are commonly known by the church as the four horsemen of the Apocalypse.

I have heard a few preachers teach about the four horsemen, and they all have had different messages. These four horsemen are conjecture (opinions based on incomplete evidence) found in the book of Revelation. I have my own opinion, but it is still conjecture on my part, because these verses don't give us facts about these events. If you will remember that in the movie *Pale Rider,* Clint Eastwood was the rider of the pale horse from verse 8. You also need to study these verses and see what you can learn from them. The TRUTH is you must seek the Holy Ghost (Jesus) for these answers, because He is the teacher who knows the TRUTH about the four horsemen.

But when Jesus opens the fifth, sixth, and seventh seals, John gives us more facts in these verses. When the fifth and sixth seals were opened, they are not conjecture, because we have other verses we can refer to in order to find the TRUTH confirming them. We have already read about the fifth seal being opened in chapter 6 of this book. But this time, I am going to share with you some more TRUTH from these scriptures.

Revelation 6:9–11 teaches us about the saints that have already passed from this life when the Lamb opens the fifth seal. I don't want to get to far off the main subject, but verses 9–11 need to be read and looked at very closely, because so many people don't have a clue what these verses teach when one of God's chosen passes from this life. This is what I know to be true. I will give you a couple of passages that will help you understand what I'm talking about. Let's read the first set of scriptures.

> And when Jesus opened the fifth seal, I [John] saw under the altar the souls of them that were slain for the word of God, and for the testimony, which they held: And they cried with a loud voice, saying, how long, O Lord,

holy and true, dost thou not judge and avenge our blood on them that dwell on the earth? And white robes were given unto every one of them; and it was said unto them, that they should rest yet for a little season, until their fellow servants also and their brethren that should be killed as they, should be fulfilled. (Revelation 6:9–11)

These scriptures tell me that when we (the church) pass from this life, we go and rest in the Lord in heaven. Read what Jesus says to the church in Matthew 11:28–30.

Now, let's read what Apostle Paul has to say about this. In 1 Thessalonians 4:13, Paul writes, "But I would not have you to be ignorant, brethren, concerning them which are asleep [dead] that ye sorrow not, even as others which have no hope." In verses 13–17, Apostle Paul wrote about the rapture (when the Lord comes for His Bride). I want you to pay close attention to verse 14: "For if we believe that Jesus died and rose again, even so them also which sleep in Jesus will God bring with Him."

I don't know what you have been taught to believe, but these scriptures that you have just read in Revelation chapter 6 and 1 Thessalonians chapter 4 teach us the TRUTH about where the dead in Christ are. The dead in Christ are in heaven, awaiting the rapture. Do you remember what Jesus said to the thief on the cross? In Luke 23:43, Jesus says, "TODAY shalt thou be with me in paradise."

In chapter 6, I told you that I was going to explain about one of these seals being opened. When this seal is opened, it will trigger the onetime events that lets the church know that Jesus is on His way to take us home (to heaven). Let's look into God's word and find out when the sixth seal will be opened and what will be the last four signs just before Jesus comes back for His Bride. Read Revelation 6:12–13, because these scriptures tell us what the four signs will be. John writes, "And I beheld [saw] when He had opened the sixth seal, and, lo, there was a great earthquake; and the sun became black as sackcloth of hair, and the moon became as blood. And the stars of heaven fell unto the earth." But to RIGHTLY DIVIDE these scriptures, you must read and study other scriptures that confirm this TRUTH.

You can find the confirmation of Revelation 6:12–13 in three other places in God's word that I know of. Now we have already read these three sets of scriptures before, but this time we are going to connect them with Revelation 6:12–13. You can find these scriptures in Joel chapter 2, Acts chapter 2, and in Matthew chapter 24. First, let's read Matthew 24:29–31 and then Joel 2:28–32. Here, Joel is prophesying of the mighty move of God's Spirit during the end-time church and the events that take place when the sixth seal is opened. Read Acts 2:19–20. Luke also writes about a part of Joel's prophecy coming to pass in Acts chapter 2, which is the outpouring of God's Spirit. As you also now know, not only will you find the beginning of the New Testament church in Acts chapter 2, but also you will see and hear how God's Spirit is being poured out upon the Jewish people first.

Peter tells them, and us, that what has been happening in Acts 2:1–11 is God's plan of salvation coming to pass (the beginning of the church). In verse 16, Peter says, "But this is that which was spoken by the Prophet Joel," and that is when the church started about 2,000 years ago, it started in the last days. I believe they were all speaking of the last part of the fourth, fifth, and sixth days of the church. These days are the two thousand plus years of the church era on this earth, according to God's timeline.

Do you remember what Apostle Peter wrote in 2 Peter 3:1–10? Just in case you don't, I will refresh your memory. Peter starts off by telling us that he wants to stir up our pure minds by way of remembrance. And that is exactly what I'm trying to do. We want you to remember with your pure mind what you have learned from the apostles and prophets. In these scriptures, Peter is trying to teach us the TRUTH by giving us God's timeline for this world. In verse

8, Peter warns us not to be "ignorant of this one thing, that one day with the Lord as a thousand years, and a thousand years as one day." Jesus came to earth at the end of the Old Testament, which was around four thousand years or four days (Sunday, Monday, Tuesday, and most of Wednesday) and the church started sometimes at the end of Wednesday, Thursday, and Friday. This is why God's word says in Acts 2:17 "And it shall come to pass in the last days." Because the church was here on earth, during the end of Wednesday, Thursday, and Friday, and as soon as Friday ends, Jesus will return for His Bride, because Saturday (the Sabbath) will begin, and this will be the thousand year millennium (or one day), that the church will be in Heaven. Remember, we must RIGHTLY DIVIDE God's word, and this is a great example, of how to RIGHTLY DIVIDE God's word to find TRUTH. Praise Jesus for His TRUTH! What you just learned is priceless.

Scientist say that this earth has been here for millions, or even billions, of years. I just don't believe that. I saw a bone in the woods yesterday, and I could not tell if it had been there for a year or five years. And I don't believe the scientists can either. It is a fact that dinosaurs walked this earth at one time, but it was not millions of years ago. I believe that the dinosaurs walked this earth six thousand years ago, when Adam and Eve were alive. If you looked at a bone that is six thousand years old, it would most likely look a million years old. I know that most scientists are smarter than me in many ways. But in this case, I believe I've beaten them because I believe God's word and His timeline for this earth. I have been taught over the past thirty- three years that man's history only goes back around six thousand years, and that is all we have to go by, and only God can teach us what happened before that.

Read these scriptures in 2 Peter 3:1–10, and you can learn the TRUTH from the Lord as Apostle Peter stirs up your pure mind. I truly believe that we are living in the sixth day (six thousand years), and when this day ends, Jesus must come back for His Bride, because on the seventh day, the Lord and His Bride will rest for a thousand years (the seventh day, or the Sabbath) in Heaven. This is when Satan is bound and thrown into HELL for a thousand years. If all this is becoming clear to you, then you are truly being blessed from the Lord with the TRUTH.

Now, it is time for Jesus to open the seventh seal, which you can read in Revelation 8:1: "When he [Jesus] opened the seventh seal, there was silence in heaven, about the space of half an hour." As you now know, the Lord comes back for His church, after He opens the sixth seal. So I believe the Lord is going to open the seventh seal after the church gets to heaven. I know that you have heard of being so quiet that you could hear a pin drop. But I believe when the Lord says that there is going to be silence, it will be so quiet that you can't hear the pin drop. When the seventh seal is opened, it indicates the completion of the tribulation period and the rapture of the church. I believe that when the half an hour has passed, God is going to give the command to His angels to pour out His wrath upon this world and its ungodly people.

You have just read Revelation 8:1, about the seventh seal being opened. If you will read the rest of Revelation chapters 8 and 9, you will find where God is going to unleash seven angels with His wrath. I'm not going to write about each individual angel, because you will see for yourself the destruction caused by each angel as they obey the voice of the Lord when you read the word of God. But I will write about the seventh angel, because we are looking for the completion of this phase of the wrath of God when He uses the seventh angel. What I'm about to say may sound harsh to the reader of this book, but this wrath is one of God's righteous work. The scriptures will explain that statement a little later. Revelation 11:15 details when the seventh angel sounds his trumpet, indicating the completion of the kingdoms of this world and the beginning of the Lord's Kingdom.

Revelation chapter 10 is something that I don't have an answer for, and as far as I know, God and John are the only ones who know the answer.

> And I [John] saw another mighty angel come down from heaven, clothed with a cloud: and a rainbow upon his head, and his face as it were the sun, and his feet as pillars of fire: And he had in his hand a little book open: and he set his right foot upon the sea, and left on the earth.
>
> And cried with a loud voice, as a lion roareth: and when he had cried, seven thunders uttered their voices. And when the seven thunders had uttered their voices, I was about to write: and I heard a voice from heaven saying unto me, Seal up those things which the seven thunders uttered, and write them not. (Verses 1–4)

God has done many things that we don't know about, and we may not ever know what the thunders uttered. Only the Lord can teach us what He didn't teach us from these scriptures.

Now, let's read about seven more angels that God is going to unleash with His wrath.

Revelation 15:1 says that there are seven angels that have the seven last plagues. Verse 7 says, "And one of the four beasts gave unto the seven angels seven golden vials [bowls], full of the wrath of God." Revelation 16:1 teaches us how God commanded the angels to pour out the vials of His wrath upon the earth.

> And the first [angel] went, and poured out his vial upon the earth: and there fell a noisome and grievous sore upon the men which had the mark of the Beast, and them which worshipped his image. And the second angel poured out his vial upon the sea; and it became as the blood of a dead: and every living soul died in the sea.

And the third angel poured out his vial upon the rivers and fountains of waters, and they became blood.

And I [John] heard the angel of the waters say, Thou art righteous, O Lord, which art, and wast, and shalt be, because thou hast judged thus.

For they have shed the blood of saints and prophets, and thou hast given them blood to drink; for they are worthy.

And I [John] heard another out of the altar say, Even so, Lord God Almighty, true and righteous thy judgments. (Verses 2–7)

Can you hear how the angels are praising God for being righteous in His judgments?

"And I [John] saw heaven opened, and behold a white horse; and he that sat upon him called Faithful and True, and in righteousness he doth judge and make war" (Revelation 19:11). This passage talks about Jesus passing the judgement on the ungodly. Again, I will say that it sounds harsh, but God has given them all a chance to serve Him, yet they chose to serve Satan and the Beast.

You can read about the fourth, fifth, and sixth angels in Revelation 16:8–16. Notice that the angels did what God commanded them, and God's master plan was coming to pass. Now, it is time for the seventh angel to empty his vial. Verse 17 teaches us about the seventh angel—"And the seventh angel poured out his vial into the air; and there came a great voice out of the temple of heaven, from the throne, saying, It is done." Again, we see the number 7 being used as the completion of God's judgment.

* * * * *

I'm about to get off the main subject for a little bit, but I believe it will be inspiring if you would believe. I know that most of you reading this book will think that I have gone crazy, but I have been writing this chapter with an empty red pen. This pen ran out of ink a few days ago. When the red pen ran out of ink, I naturally threw it into the garbage can. In writing this book, I have emptied a few pens, so I knew that it was out of ink. As I was praying and seeking for the TRUTH to write, I asked the Lord to let me know if what I was writing is correct and true. I don't know why, but I told the Lord that I would continue to write with this empty red pen if it would write. Immediately, I found myself digging around in the garbage can for that empty red pen. And as you would know, it was on the bottom. But I continued writing using that empty red pen.

I have five witnesses of this empty red pen, and they are God, Satan, my wife, my sister-in-law (Gracie), and myself. I have spoken of supernatural powers before in this book, and I believe God is demonstrating His supernatural powers in this empty red pen. The words that you have been reading in this chapter were written from an empty red pen. I believe that I will keep this empty red pen for the rest of my life here on this earth, and I will tell this story to anyone who wants to hear it.

Oh, by the way, I am still writing with my empty red pen. It is March 28, 2010. I just had to indicate the date, as I sit here quivering and with tears flowing from my eyes, because I realized that I'm holding a miracle empty red pen in my right hand. I almost said that this empty red pen is like the Energizer Bunny, but it is so much more than that. I am going to go back and finish writing the previous chapter, and if the Lord is willing and this empty red pen continues to write, I will mention this empty red pen at that time. I have now written 5,791 words in this chapter with my empty red pen. I just showed Tiffany today that my empty red pen stills writes four years later. It is now January 4, 2014. I now have another witness. I just want to say again—I am BLESSED beyond measure.

A year later, I started thinking about my empty red pen, so I got it out of the drawer to see if it would still write. Not only would it still write, but also something else happened that I thought was pretty amazing. I wrote Jesus with my empty red pen, and I wrote down the date.

Then, I began wondering about the date that I was writing in chapter 7 with it. So I went back and looked in chapter 7 to see when it was, and just look what I discovered. The date was March 28, 2015; and when I looked back at the date that I was writing with my empty red pen, it was March 28, 2010—exactly five years to the day. And if the TRUTH was known, it is the same hour. I'm not trying to prove anything, but I took a picture of my empty red pen and the dates with Jesus' name so you could see what the Lord has blessed me with. Remember I got to edit our book and on 10/19/25 and it still writes. Now go back to the beginning of chapter 7 and continue reading it.

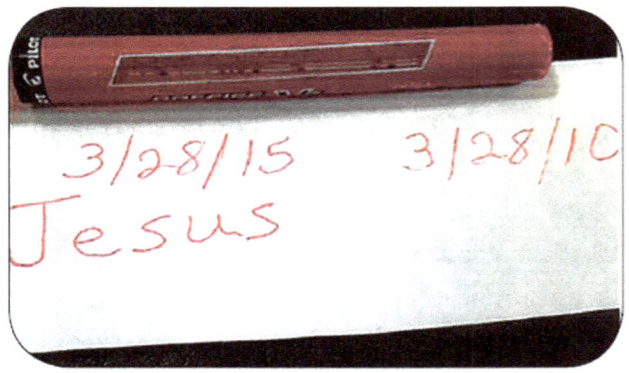

Here is something else that I have come to believe. In 2016, I heard on the news channel that there are now seven billion people in the world. Now, I know that I'm about to begin speculating, but I believe there could be something to this. As you now know, the Lord works through using the number 7 in many cases. No one knows exactly how many people there are in the world, but God does. As people are being born, there are as many or more dying. If the Lord uses the number 7 in our population to end this world, I believe seven billion will be the number.

Now, we know that it wasn't seven hundred or seven thousand or even seven million people that the Lord was going to use to end this world. The scriptures teach us that we are living in the last days. Remember that the church started in the last days, and that was over 2,000 years ago. I just don't see the Lord waiting for our population to reach seven trillion. I don't believe that this earth could support seven trillion people. You had better think about this, because if the Lord does use the seven billion, it will be in our near future.

The Lord is not going to keep looking over the corruption of this world, or He will have to apologize to Sodom and Gomorrah. I don't believe the Lord will have to ever apologize for anything. These two cities were destroyed by God, because of the people's sinful acts. You can read and learn about the destruction of Sodom and Gomorrah in Genesis chapters 18 and 19. Start reading 18:16–33 and chapter 19. Notice in Genesis 18:22–33 how Abraham was bargaining with God, trying to get the Lord not to destroy these cities. You will never convince me that the Lord doesn't talk to His people. Abraham bargained with the Lord from fifth righteous people to ten righteous, but God found less than ten. And they were Lot and his wife and two daughters. You can read about this in Genesis 19:15–16.

Sodom and Gomorrah were destroyed by fire for the same thing that is going on in the world today. The Lord knows and remembers what He had to do to Sodom and Gomorrah. Jesus used Sodom and Gomorrah a few times in His word as examples to the ungodly of what could happen to them if they didn't change. In these scriptures, Jesus warns us not to live ungodly lives. Read Matthew 10:11–15, Matthew 11:23–24, 2 Peter 2:6, and Jude verses 5–7.

Let me tell you how bad it is here in America. Just this week (May 2016), President Obama sent letters to all the public school districts in the United States, issuing them an order that they must allow transgender bathrooms in their schools or lose their federal funding. Just imagine your daughter in the restroom and any boy could walk in, claiming he's a female. But by the time you read this book, you won't have to imagine. I believe this (Obama's stupidity) is going to increase homeschooling and private schools. Now, you can imagine what will become of the children that are left in these public schools. I already knew this, but this tells me that the world is going to HELL.

Here is something else I learned in my studies that I believe is interesting. During our life here on earth, as we seek the Lord to become His Bride, we go through different stages in our walk with Jesus. Romans 3:23 says, "For all have sinned, and come short of the glory of God." The word teaches us that from the time Adam and Eve sinned, every person born on this earth except Jesus was born in sin. This is why the Lord came to earth and gave Himself for a blood sacrifice to deliver us from our sins. Only God's blood could redeem His creation (man) back unto Himself. Read Hebrews 9:6–12.

Most people have heard the term born-again. I'm about to share a part of this TRUTH with you. You will learn the whole TRUTH about being born- again in chapter 9. In John chapter 3, Jesus warns us of the consequences if we are not born-again. Read John 3:1–8 where you will hear Jesus say, "Except a man be born again, he cannot see the kingdom of God." And then Jesus answered, "Verily, verily I say unto thee, Except a man be born of water and the Spirit, he cannot enter into the kingdom of God" (verse 3, 5).

According to God's word, you must be born-again, so that means you will become a baby once again. Just as you taught your child what he or she learned, now the Lord gets His turn to teach each person who is born-again. Apostle Peter speaks of the born-again experience as being babies and teaches us about being born-again in 1 Peter 1:23. He continues this teaching in 1 Peter 2:2, saying, "As newborn babes, desire the sincere milk of the word, that ye may grow thereby." You know from reading the first chapter of this book the importance of drinking the milk of God's word. If you didn't feed your baby with milk when it was born and just gave it water to drink, it would not survive very long.

Now, you know that I'm a meat eater by the things you have read in this book. But when I get thirsty, I will gladly go and drink from God's milk jug. I believe we must grow into adults so we can be able to eat and digest the meat of God's word. I also believe we must drink all the milk from God's word as much as we can. There is an old saying, "milk does a body good," and this is especially true with God's word.

You know from experience that from milk, babies transition to eating solid foods as you grow up. It is the same way when you read and study the scriptures; you will grow in the Lord.

> At the same time came the disciples unto Jesus, saying, Who is the greatest in the kingdom of heaven? And Jesus called a little child unto Him, and set him in the midst of them, and said, Verily I say unto you, Except ye be converted, and become as little children, ye shall not enter into the kingdom of heaven. (Matthew 18:1–3)

In this passage, I can see the growth from an infant (converted) to a child. As we leave our infant stage and grow in the Lord, we become a child of God. Now, when we grow into a child of God, we begin to get confidence in the Lord, because of what we see Him doing in our lives, and as we learn His word, we start running. And it is good to run in this race, but it is also dangerous. If you are not careful, you will fall. If you ever fall, simply ask the Lord to forgive you and ask Him for His help. He will help you, if you ask Him for help.

Believe me, the Lord can fix any situation that you get yourself into. I have seen other people fall in this race, and I have fallen hard a few times in the past thirty-three years. I can't speak for everyone else, but the Lord has always been there to help me get back up on my feet. I started running this race on August 11, 1983; and it is now June 2, 2016; and by God's Grace, I'm still running. Soon, we are going to read some scriptures from 2 Peter, which teach us how to run and never fall.

During our childhood in the Lord, we will grow into another stage as we walk with the Lord; we will grow into a servant of God. As we read and study these scriptures, we learn certain things (kingdom rules) that the Lord expects of us. As you begin doing the word, you will become a servant of God and your fellow man. Read Hebrews 9:14.

I am so thankful the Lord has allowed me to be a servant. As I write about being a servant, I began thinking of the past. In the early 1980s, I began praying one day that I could be a soul winner. I have always wanted to be a soul winner. I believe the Lord is allowing me to achieve my greatest desire. He has truly blessed me in allowing me to write this book. In writing this book, I hope to help my fellow man find God's TRUTH, and that will help populate heaven. I have witnessed through the years, and I have seen some hear the TRUTH and turn to the Lord. But I believe with this book, by comparing it with the Bible, many souls will be won to the Lord.

I have tried to explain before how illiterate I am. To tell you the TRUTH, I had to look up illiterate to see how to spell it. It has taken me ten years to write this book, and Lord willing, I will finish it in the next few weeks. Since I started writing this book, I have had to start wearing reading glasses and have stayed up late, a lots of nights; and only God knows how much I have talked to Him. Only in God I am boasting, but I would spend the next ten years doing the same thing, if only one soul would receive God's TRUTH, while comparing this book to His word. Thank you, Lord.

All the stages that we live in are good places to be in the Lord, but our next stage of growth is a special stage. After we have served the Lord for a certain time period, and we learn to obey His word,

Jesus becomes friends with us. In John 15:13–15, Jesus teaches us about His friendship with the church.

> Greater love hath no man than this, that a man lay down his life for his friends. Ye are my friends, IF ye do whatsoever I command you. Henceforth [now and forever] I call you not servants; for the servant knoweth not what his Lord doeth: but I have called you friends; for all things that I have heard of my Father I have made known unto you. I can't think of anything on this earth that would be greater than, having Jesus as a friend.

The Lord showed His love to us when He died on the cross for us. This is what I believe that Jesus was telling us in John 15:14: "Ye are my friends, IF ye do whatsoever I command you." And here, notice the BIG word IF again. I believe James says it in James 1:22–25 better than anyone else. He starts off by saying, "But be ye doers of the word, and not hearers only, deceiving your own selves." Here is my interpretation of verses 23–24. For when you hear the word and don't do it, you will be like someone that looks into a mirror, and you see that you need to wash your face, and your hair needs to be brushed. But you turn and walk away, not doing what you know that you need to do, to be presentable. Believe me, everyone that you come in contact with will be able to see you as you are. The only thing in verse 25 that I want to explain is the perfect law of liberty, which is the word of God. Everything else in that scripture is self-explanatory.

In Matthew 16:24–25, Jesus says, "If any will come after me, let him deny himself, and take up his cross, and follow me. For whosoever will save his life shall lose it: and whosoever will lose his life for my sake shall find it." It's not just that I believe, but I know we must give our lives to God and our fellow man IF we want to become friends with Jesus. We may never have to lay down our lives literally for the Lord and our fellow man. But I do believe when we learn to love as the Lord teaches, we will begin to truly deny our own lives and begin being more concern for the welfare of others. Read Philippians 2:4.

IF you continue to grow in the Lord, you will mature into an adult. I want to explain why I wrote IF you continue to grow in the Lord. I have written about this before, but I believe that this is a good place to mention it again. The Bible teaches us that you can quit (give up) living for the Lord anytime you want to. The false teaching "once saved, always saved" is not God's TRUTH.

I'm going to give you a couple of different scriptures that teach the TRUTH about quitting the race to heaven. Apostle Paul writes in 1 Corinthians 15:1–2 the TRUTH about quitting the race. He says, "Moreover, brethren, I declare unto you the gospel [God's TRUTH] which I preached unto you, which also ye have received, and wherein ye stand; By which also ye are saved, IF ye keep in memory what I have preached unto you." IF you are able to read this book, you should know that IF is the key word in these scriptures. To answer the question that many want to know—is "once saved, always saved" true? This is as simple as I can say it. IF you don't remember what Apostle Paul taught us and you erase the gospel (God's TRUTH) from your mind, you would be the opposite of saved, and that is lost.

Remember that reading and studying God's word is not rocket science. It says what it says, and it means what it means. The next scripture can't get any clearer, and you are about to find out what Jesus has to say about you quitting the race to heaven. You can find Jesus teaching us about the end- time of the church on earth in Matthew chapter 24. And in Matthew 24:13, you can also find the TRUTH about "once save, always saved." Jesus says, "But he that shall endure unto the end, the same shall be saved."

Also, read 1 Timothy 4:1–2. Paraphrasing verse 1, Apostle Paul says that the Spirit of God speaks about this expressly (clearly). As this world gets closer to the end, some will depart from the faith, by allowing Satan to deceive them. In verse 2, it sounds like to me, Satan deceived them with a disease called dementia. Paul says in this scripture that Satan has seared their conscience (brain) with a hot iron, making them forget God's TRUTH and begin speaking lies. If you don't hear what the Lord is teaching us in those scriptures, you may never hear Him.

I have been watching Bill O' Reilly on The O' Reilly Factor, which comes on Fox News, because his show is known to be the NO SPIN ZONE. THE NO SPIN ZONE concept has kept him number one in the cable news channels for 180 months (fifteen straight years) and counting. I can only think of one other person that has a better record, and that would be Jesus. Jesus' words for the New Testament believers have been a NO SPIN ZONE for His people for more than 2,000 years. Even though man has wrested (twisted or changed) His word, they can't factually change what the Lord has ordained to be TRUTH. I will say this again, because it is the TRUTH— God's word says what it says, and it means what it means.

Again, we must look for the key words in these scripture. I am going to write these words again, because it can't get any clearer. Jesus says, "But he that shall endure unto the end, the same shall be saved." This scripture is what I call the NO SPIN ZONE. No one can wrest this scripture and make it say something that it doesn't say. This also teaches me that anyone living for the Lord must live for Him, until they draw their last breath. Imagine if the Lord would have quoted this scripture like this: if you don't endure till you die, you will be lost. Now, I know that this is the opposite of what the Lord said, but it will be the same outcome if you don't do what He said.

Let me try this again. IF you continue to grow in the Lord, you will mature into an adult. If we grow in the Lord, we must read and study His word. As you now know, this is where we get our nourishment (milk and meat) from. Hebrews 5:13–14 says, "For every one that useth milk unskillful in the word of righteousness: for he is a babe. But strong meat (revelations in TRUTH) belongeth to them that are of full age, those who by reason of use have their senses exercised to discern both good and evil." In this passage, Apostle Paul is speaking of adults being able to consume the meat of God's word. Also, this scripture teaches us how they became adults. It says, "Those who by reason of use [as they live for God] have their senses exercised to discern both good and evil [make right choices]."

Do I even dare to say that you can become a saint of God here on earth? Do you remember when I wrote about being perfect? Jesus says in Matthew 5:48, "Be ye therefore perfect, even as your Father which is in heaven is perfect." I am not yet, but ever since I started reading and studying God's word, I have always believed this scripture about becoming perfect, just as Jesus said we should. To tell you the TRUTH, I will always believe in perfection (becoming a saint) because Jesus told us to.

Hebrews 6:1 says, "Therefore leaving the principles of the doctrine of Christ, let us go on unto perfection." This scripture teaches me that there is another stage of growth after we become an adult in the Lord. If you will read Hebrews 6:1–2, you will see that there is more to God's TRUTH than repentance from "dead works, and of faith toward God, of the doctrine of baptisms, and laying on of hands, and of resurrection of the dead, and of eternal judgment." Read James 1:1-5. And do you remember the PERFECT Law of Liberty that we are to live in, in James 1:25?

I learned many years ago, what Apostle Paul shared with us in Ephesians 4:11 about what most call the fivefold ministry, which are made up of apostles, prophets, evangelist, pastors, and teachers. And if you will continue reading the next three scriptures (12-14), you should learn that the fivefold ministry God chose is "For the perfecting of the saints, for the work of the ministry, for the edifying of the body of Christ: Till we all come in the unity of the faith, and of the knowledge of the Son of God, unto a perfect man, unto the measure of the stature of the fullness of Christ." And every time, that I get a chance to inform you who it is turning up the Light of your understanding. Read Ephesian 1:17-18, and allow Jesus to write it in your mind and heart.

And there are plenty of scriptures that teach us to become PERFECT in Jesus, so I will give you a few more. Luke 6:40, John 17:23, 1 Corinthians 2:4-7, and Philippians 3:15. And here is another good one. 2 Timothy 3:16-17. Just use the word PERFECT to people, and 9 times out of 10, you will hear them respond: "no one is PERFECT except Jesus." But they don't know what God's word teaches, but you now do. With just using your carnal mind, you should have heard that, but just in case you didn't hear, here are some more scriptures for you to read and learn. It is sorta ironic, how I am giving you scriptures, trying to convince you to grow up in Jesus, because we are going to live with a PERFECT God throughout eternity.

Read 2 Peter 1:1–11, and I believe you will find the TRUTH about how to become a saint. Just look at the Lord's promises for us in these scriptures. The TRUTH that you are going to read can help you grow from an adult into a saint of God. I believe these scriptures are some of that perfection that Jesus spoke of in Matthew 5:48. IF we will just do what these scriptures teach us to do, the Lord will do His part. I want to say again—the Lord will not and cannot lie.

While reading 2 Peter 1:4, you will not see the word perfection. But I can see perfection, but it is not spelled with these letters (perfection). This is how I see perfection from this passage. Apostle Peter is going to give us a list of things we must do in verses 5–7. But before he tells us what we must do, he says in verse 4, "that by these you might be partakers of the divine nature."

I looked up divine in my dictionary, and this is what I learned. The word divine has a few different meanings, and I'm going to list them. They go in this order, "of, from, or like God and excellent."

To me, all these meanings mean perfection. This is really simple to me; IF you grow from a baby into a saint and become like God, then that would be excellent. When a person becomes a partaker of God's divine nature, they will have become perfect in God. At the end of verse 4, the Lord gives us another exceedingly great and precious promise. This scripture says that IF we are "partakers of the divine nature, having escaped the corruption that is in the world through lust." My interpretation is that IF you become a partaker of the divine nature, you will have escaped all of the bad things that would have come into your life, which are caused by lust.

Verse 8 says, "For IF these things be in you, and abound, they make neither barren nor unfruitful in the knowledge of our Lord Jesus Christ." The two key words in this scripture that I want you to see are IF and abound. You should know what IF means. Abound means "to have in large numbers or amounts, to be overflowing, or be abundant." IF you give "all diligence, and add to your faith virtue; and to virtue knowledge; and to knowledge temperance; and to temperance patience; and to patience Godliness; and to Godliness brotherly kindness; and to brotherly kindness charity" (verses 5–7). IF you have these attributes (features) of God in your life, and they overflow and abound, there is no other word that I can think of except perfection. I'm far from it, but I believe in perfection because it is written.

Verse 9 says, "But he that lacketh these things is blind, and cannot see afar off, and hath forgotten that he was purged from his old sins." It sounds like that their minds have been seared with a hot iron. "Wherefore the rather [so then], brethren, give diligence to make your calling and election sure: for IF ye do these things, ye shall never fall" (verse 10). In verse 11, the Lord gives us one of His exceedingly great and precious promises. Peter is teaching us in verse 11 that IF we change as these scriptures teach us to change, an entrance shall be ministered unto us abundantly into the everlasting kingdom of our Lord and Savior Jesus Christ.

The last thing Apostle Peter tells us in verse 7 is for us to have charity (love) in our lives. We are supposed to love God and our fellow man. In 1 John 4:19–21, John writes, "We love Him, because He first loved us. If a man say, I love God, and hateth his brother, he is a liar: for he that loveth not his brother whom he hath seen, how can he love God whom he hath not seen? And this commandment [kingdom rule] have we from Him, That he who loveth God love his brother also."

When we add love to our lives, we will be truly a partaker of God's divine nature.

"God is love" (1 John 4:8). "There is no fear in love; but perfect love casteth out fear, because fear hath torment. He that feareth is not made perfect in love" (1 John 4:18). Read 1 Corinthians 12:27–31. In verse 31, Apostle Paul says, "But covet earnestly the best gifts: and yet shew I unto you a more excellent way." Paul teaches us a more excellent way to live in 1 Corinthians chapter 13. Read the entire chapter of 1 Corinthians 13 and you will learn what Apostle Paul was referring to, when he said "yet shew I unto you a more excellent way."

Here is something that I have written about a few times in this book, and here, you should be able to see that it is the TRUTH. Jesus says in John 8:32, "And ye shall know the TRUTH, and the TRUTH shall make you free." When I quote this scripture when I'm witnessing, I will always say, "And you shall know the TRUTH, and the TRUTH shall." When I get to "make you free," I pause, and nine times out of ten, they eagerly try to finish the scripture by saying, "Set you free." The TRUTH is they have never been taught what Jesus said in John 8:32. Most people are just going along with what the world teaches. But now that you know the TRUTH about being made free, let's teach the world the TRUTH from now on.

I wrote in chapter 1 that to set you free is an immediate action, but to make you free is a process. As you mature in the Lord, the TRUTH WILL MAKE YOU FREE! IT IS DEFINITELY A

PROCESS. No one has ever become a saint immediately. When a person is born-again, it is the beginning of a lifelong journey. We must grow in the Lord, because it is one of the kingdom rules.

I made a list of the different stages of our walk with the Lord. Notice that there are six stages to grow into here on earth. When you are born-again, the Lord begins teaching you what He wants you to know. I truly believe that it is up to us IF we continue to grow in the Lord, because IF we seek God's TRUTH, He will teach us. It is as simple as this. Reading, studying, and obeying God's word—this is how we grow in the Lord. On the bottom of the list, you will see that there is another stage to grow into, but it will not happen until the church gets to heaven. Again, we see the Lord using the number 7 for His completion of the church.

1. Baby
2. Child
3. Servant
4. Friend
5. Adult
6. Saint
7. Bride

I believe when we get to heaven, the Lord and His church are going to have the biggest and best wedding ever. You can only find a few scriptures in God's word that teach us about the church and the Lord being married. Read Revelation 19:7–9 and also Revelation 21:9 and 27, which teaches us who the Bride is.

What you are about to read is not going to cost you anything, unless you oppose these scriptures.

But while I'm writing about marriage, I want to tell you according to the scriptures how the Lord feels about it. Read 1 Corinthians 7:1–11. Now, I want you to read Ephesians 5:21–33, and you should be able to see the importance the Lord puts on marriage. I also want you to see from these scriptures that Apostle Paul taught that marriage is between a man and a woman (period).

Since the people of this world are the way they are, I believe if I make a statement like that, I must also give scriptures to show you what will happen to anyone who believes differently (does their own thing). For you who believe in being with the same sex, you need to read Romans 1:21–32. I'm not trying to offend anyone, but we are RIGHTLY DIVIDING God's TRUTH, and I must write what I know to be TRUTH. And I know what I'm writing is the TRUTH. When God made man and woman, He named them Adam and Eve, not Adam and Steve. I just heard the other day (November 2017) that 80% of young people believe that being born with a penis or a vagina doesn't determine what sex a baby is. I just want you to think about this, because these young people will be running our country, in the very near future.

Satan has deceived some, and they don't know God made male and female so they would be able to multiply and to populate the earth. As far as I know, up to this point in time, there is no way two men can have a baby, neither can two women. I don't believe that they will ever be able to, because God is the only one who gives life. Here is another fact—if you have allowed Satan to entangle you in this sinful act, you had better change because God is not going to change His word just for you. You will be held accountable for your sin. That is all I'm going to say about this, at this time.

There are other times the Lord used the number 7 for His completion. But I just wrote about the times I knew about, concerning the beginning and end of this world. I remember back in 1983, when I first went to an apostolic church. I was so amazed at the preacher's knowledge of God's word. For a few years, I often wondered if I would ever learn as much as they knew about God's word.

After thirty-three years of studying God's word, I can see certain things from God's word that they didn't teach. I'm not trying to say that I know more than they did. What I'm saying is that I have been blessed by God with His word. He opened up the eyes of my understanding so I would be able to know His TRUTH. I believe everyone is on a different learning level in God's word. I'm not talking about knowing who He is or knowing His plan of salvation; I'm just saying in general knowledge. You had better believe this—every member of the church knows that Jesus is the Lord from heaven, and they know how to be born-again.

I believe the main lesson that you can learn from this book is that as you study God's word, you are to obey what you learn from the Lord, or die trying. I believe if you die trying to do God's word, you will be blessed on the other side of the grave. God looks upon the heart, and the Lord knows the desires of your heart. He will be a righteous judge. And as you read and study God's word, there is no telling what the Lord will reveal to you concerning the number 7, among many other things.

Just remember that God's word is our road map to heaven. If you don't study the road map (the Bible), you will not make it to heaven. You will be sidetracked by Satan. Just look at what Jesus says in Matthew 7:13–14. He tells us "enter ye in at the strait gate, for wide the gate, and broad the way, that leadeth to destruction, and many there be which go in thereat. Because strait the gate and narrow the way, which leadeth unto life, and few there be that find it."

Now let's go to a new chapter and find out more about Satan, and his deceiving ways.

CHAPTER 8

SATAN: THE GREATEST CONSPIRATOR

Satan is where I got a part of the title of this book, because he is the GREATEST CONSPIRATOR. Now, let's find out about Satan and where he came from. We need to read all of Revelation chapter 12 to find out a little about Satan. As you read, you will see that there was a conflict in heaven. This is where Lucifer, which is now Satan, started a war in heaven. Lucifer was one of God's angels. Lucifer is mentioned only one time in the entire word of God, and you can find it in Isaiah 14:12. Read verses 12–14, and you will see that Lucifer, from somewhere, found the sin that is now called envy or jealousy. After jealousy entered into him, rebellion took over.

I know that God invented (created) jealousy, and some way, Lucifer found it. Look what happened when jealousy got into Lucifer's heart. In verse 13, Lucifer says, "I will ascend into heaven." Now as jealousy filled his heart, Lucifer sees God's throne and wants his own throne. He says, "I will exalt my throne above the stars of God." He wanted his throne above God's throne and that "will ascend above the heights of the clouds. I will be like the most High (God)." Here, you can see that Lucifer wants to take God's place. It is very clear that Lucifer wanted a different position than what he already had in heaven. I want you to remember what you read in chapter 6 of this book about the Beast. Lucifer is that same Satan that is going to enter into the Beast, stroll into God's temple in Jerusalem, and try to take God's place again.

Lucifer being translated is day star or morning star. I believe Lucifer was one of, if not, God's favorite angel, but he was not satisfied with being the day star. He chose to be rebellious, and now, he is called Satan or the devil. Now, Satan is the opposite of God. It is the same with humans; we can choose who we serve. We can be like Satan, or we can be like God—it is up to us. Read Revelation 22:16.

It is a good possibility that this saying started when the Lord looked at Michael and said, "Lucifer wants to have his cake and eat it too. Throw him and his followers out of heaven." This is my theory; almost everyone has one. I believe what started the jealousy in Lucifer's heart is recorded in Genesis chapter 1. Verse 1 says "In the beginning God created the heaven and the earth." I believe Lucifer was watching God create the heaven and the earth, all the animals, the fish, and the birds through the fifth day. He could have even been bragging about God to the other angels for an excellent work. The only thing in the scriptures that I can find that would be so devastating that would make Lucifer be jealous would be about what happened on the sixth day of creation. Genesis 1:26 records what happened on the sixth day of creation. "And God said, Let us make man in our image, after our likeness: and let them have dominion over the fish of the sea, and over the fowl of the air, and over the cattle, and over all the earth, and over every creeping thing that creepeth upon the earth."

I don't believe jealousy got into Lucifer by seeing the creation of the heaven and the earth and of the birds, the fish, and the cattle. I believe Lucifer was jealous when he saw God create man in His own image. I believe Lucifer could see the relationship that man would have with God. Like I said, this is my theory. As I was praying and seeking the Lord for the TRUTH and how to put this book in the right order, what you are reading is what the Lord gave me to write. I am writing this on April 12, 2008, which is a Saturday. Before this day, I have never—out of the twenty-seven years that I have been reading and studying God's word—thought of these things that I have been writing about. I know that I have an eraser, but I have not been told to erase anything. I believe this is what I'm supposed to write. When I started writing about Lucifer and his fall, out of all the scriptures in the Old and New Testaments, God impressed upon me to read and study His creation.

Now, let's go back and review what we read in Revelation chapter 12. In verse 3, Satan was described as a great red dragon. This is the same Satan, but described a little differently in Revelation 17:3 as a scarlet-colored beast. Revelation 12:4 says that Satan got a third of God's angels to follow him in his rebellious act against God. Revelation 12:7–9 teaches us about the war in heaven and how Satan and his new army fought and lost that battle. At that time, Satan and his angels were cast out of heaven, down to the earth, to play their roll in God's master plan.

As I have said before in this book, in this world, there are two SUPER POWERS—God and Satan. As you read God's word, you should be able to see that Satan is not going to give up so easily. This is a fact—Satan lost the war in heaven against God's angels, which are celestial beings. But if you will look around and do a little fruit inspecting, you can clearly see Satan is winning the battle against human beings. Satan is not going to win the war; ultimately, he is going to lose, but he is winning now, according to numbers.

John wrote in the book of Revelation about our past, present, and future. A big part of the book of Revelation has not been fulfilled yet. The book of Revelation briefly teaches us about our past and present, but mostly about our future. Seeking the TRUTH from God's prophet's writings about our present and our future can sometimes be hard to RIGHTLY DIVIDE. This is why we all need the Holy Ghost to teach us. Without the Lord's Spirit teaching us, we will wrest the scriptures unto our own destruction just as Apostle Peter said we would (2 Peter 3:15–16). Our past is a little different; in many cases, we have our history books to refer to, but it still takes God's Spirit to help us know the TRUTH about our past. To RIGHTLY DIVIDE God's word and learn about our present and our future without the Lord would be imposable. There is no way that I could have even written this book about our past without God's help.

Now, let's look into God's word and learn some things about Jesus' past. You're about to find out how Satan used the Romans to try to destroy Jesus, when He was born. You can read about this in Revelation chapter 12 and in Matthew chapter 2. I know that we have already read some of these scriptures, but we must read them again to RIGHTLY DIVIDE God's word and put these scriptures in their proper context. You may read about something in Revelation and find the answer in Genesis. The Lord had the apostles and prophets write His word this way so everyone would have to study to RIGHTLY DIVIDE His word. So let's continue RIGHTLY DIVIDING God's word.

In Revelation 12:1–4, I can see that the great red dragon (Satan) is going to use the Romans to try to kill Jesus as soon as He was born. To RIGHTLY DIVIDE these scriptures, we must remember and read again Revelation 17:9,18. Verse 9 says, "The seven heads are seven mountains, on which the woman sitteth." Verse 18 says, "And the woman which thou [John] sawest is that great city, which reigneth over the kings of the earth." The city of Rome is the only city that I know of that is built on seven mountains. All this is really clear to me, but I have had the Lord teaching me His word for twenty-seven years. I hope you realize how blessed you are to have this book, because with it and your Bible, you can learn about this TRUTH in the matter of days.

Rome was founded 753 years before Jesus was born. During that time, the Romans began expanding their boundaries. Within a thousand or so years, the Romans occupied and controlled all the land (now countries) that surrounds the Mediterranean Sea. Rome's maximum expansion was achieved under the Emperor Trajan, who ruled from AD 98 to AD 117. During that time period, Rome governed not only the shores of the Mediterranean Sea but also much of what is now Austria, the Balkans, Hungary, Great Britain, Spain, Portugal, France, Switzerland, and part of Asia Minor.

Now, Satan was ruling the most powerful kingdom on this earth, and he had Judaea in his grasp, the country where Jesus was born. Like I have said a few times in this book, most of the things that I'm writing about are in our history books. Please read and study this for yourself, and then, you will know that it is the TRUTH. Read Matthew chapters 1 and 2 to learn about Jesus' birth and how Satan used fear tactics on Joseph and Mary. When you read Matthew chapter 1, the first fifteen verses most likely would not make a lot of sense to you. I know that they didn't make any sense to me when I first read them twenty-seven years ago. But when I write the TRUTH about being born-again in chapter 9 of this book, I'm going to explain a part of the TRUTH found in these fifteen verses. The reason I say that I will explain a part is because there is more TRUTH in these scriptures than a person can learn in their lifetime.

I can't, and you might not be able to pronounce every name in these scriptures, but that doesn't matter as much as the TRUTH that you will find from them. You will be doing good when you learn the TRUTH about the church's forefathers (Abraham and his son Isaac and his son Jacob) and their descendants forty-two generations later, which include Jesus and His earthly parents (Joseph and Mary).

Revelation 12:4 says, "The dragon [Satan] stood before the woman which was ready to be delivered, for to devour [kill] her child [Jesus], as soon as it was born." As you read Matthew chapter 2, you should have a clearer understanding how King Herod was used by Satan to try and kill Jesus (the word) from reaching man's ears and heart. Remember what you learned about how Satan rebelled against God and was thrown out of heaven. And as I have said, I believe it was because of jealousy. Here, Satan saw another opportunity to stop the relationship between God and man. Satan failed that day, but he has been sowing the sin seed in every heart he can, since that day. And I'm here to inform you Satan is doing a good job of it.

The scriptures in Matthew chapter 2 are really clear about how Satan used King Herod to try and stop the word of God from reaching man. I am here to tell you there is no way Satan could stop God from coming to earth and finding Himself a Bride. What Satan didn't know was that he was being used by God to complete His plan for humanity. In other word he is being played. Matthew 2:1 says, "Now when Jesus was born in Bethlehem of Judaea in the days of Herod the king, behold, there came wise men from the east to Jerusalem."

Matthew records in verse 2 that the wise men that came from the east to Jerusalem began asking questions about Jesus, the new king of the Jews. Just imagine Herod, the Roman appointed Jewish king, hearing that there is another king in town. Verse 3 says that this news troubled Herod and all Jerusalem. Now, Satan had lost the battle in heaven, but like I said earlier, he is not going to give up so easily. In verses 7–8, you can hear the deception coming forth from Herod. In verse 8, Herod tells the wise men, "When you find Jesus, come and tell me, so I can come and worship him also." As you continue reading Matthew chapter 2, you will see that worshiping the new king was the furthest thing on Herod's mind.

As I read Matthew chapter 2, I can clearly see it is not Herod that wants to kill Jesus—it is the devil that lived inside of him. Satan could not overthrow God in heaven, so he came after Him as soon as He was born on earth. Believe me, Satan knew that Jesus was the Lord from heaven. He knew that Jesus was God manifested (revealed) in the flesh. If you will read 1 Timothy 3:16, you too will know that Jesus is God. When you read Matthew 2:12–13, you also can see how the Spirit of God was protecting His earthly body from Satan.

You will see in verse 16 that Herod was full of Satan. This scripture says, "When he saw that he was mocked of the wise men, was exceeding wroth [angry], and sent forth, and slew all the children that were in Bethlehem, and in all the coasts thereof, from two years old and under, according to the time, which he had diligently inquired of the wise men." Just imagine how much fear you would have if your firstborn baby arrives and the president of the United States sends the army to kill him. That is the kind of fear that Joseph and Mary felt, when Jesus was born. After reading these scriptures, if you can't see Satan controlling Herod, something is wrong with your thinking.

We are about to see in Luke chapter 2 how Satan went after Jesus' parents again with fear. Fear is one of Satan's most effective weapons in his warfare against Christians and non-Christians alike. If you have ever misplaced (lost) your child for a few minutes, you have experienced fear. But if you lost your child for three days, as Joseph and Mary did, you would have experienced the fear, which Satan dishes out.

Read 1 John 4:8 and then read verse 18. Satan has been trying to use fear tactic on me for years now, because we (the Lord and me) are revealing him and his false teachings in this book. But Lord willing, I am going to keep resisting (rebuking) him in the name of Jesus and keep pressing on and writing God's TRUTH. I will not lie—it gets really hard sometimes when Satan comes against me, but I will not stop writing God's TRUTH, until we finish this book. We have come too far to let that devil stop this work. I too must be about my Father's business. Even as I write these words, Satan keeps coming, but at the same time, I know Jesus is with me. I believe Satan trembles at the name of Jesus. As you continue learning about the Lord, you will learn that there is POWER in the name of Jesus—WONDERFUL WORKING POWER!

The next time Jesus was mentioned in the scriptures was when He was twelve years old. In these scriptures, is where Joseph and Mary lost their son for three days. Read Luke 2:40–52. Verse 40 says, "And the child [Jesus] grew and waxed strong in Spirit, filled with wisdom: and the grace of God was upon Him." Notice how Jesus was full of wisdom at twelve years old. Verse 52 says, "And Jesus increased in wisdom and stature, and in favour with God and man." Just as when you were growing up and experiencing Satan's temptations, I believe that Satan also tempted Jesus when He was young.

But Jesus being tempted when He was a boy is not recorded in the scriptures. We also need to grow in wisdom, and I believe we grow in wisdom as we learn and obey (live) God's word.

As Joseph and Mary were leaving Jerusalem after the feast of the Passover had ended, they thought that Jesus was with some of the family members. I believe when they didn't find their son on the first day, they began to be nervous for their son's well-being. So they turned around and began backtracking their steps to Jerusalem to find their son. Verses 46–47 say, "After three days they found Him in the temple, sitting in the midst of the doctors, both hearing them, and asking them questions. And all that heard Him were astonished at His understanding and answers."

Verse 48 says, "And when they [His parents] saw Him, they were amazed: and His mother said unto Him, Son, why hast thou thus dealt with us? Behold, thy father and I have sought thee sorrowing." This is how this would have been said in Mississippi, "Son, what do you think you are doing? You have scared me and your father half to death." I am going to write verse 49 the way it is said in Mississippi also. Jesus says to His parents, "Why were you looking for me? Didn't you know that I must be doing my Father's business?"

Verses 50–52 say that they understood not the saying which He spake unto them. "And He went down with them, and came to Nazareth, and was subject unto them." In other words, Jesus obeyed His parents and went with them. The scriptures say, "But His mother kept all these sayings in her heart. And Jesus increased in wisdom and stature, and in favour with God and man." Sometimes, it's hard for us to understand God's plan in our lives. I believe that is why we must continue reading and studying His word for the TRUTH. Now, Jesus' parents couldn't understand their son when He was just twelve years old, because He had grew in wisdom that He received from God.

I want you to look at a couple more scriptures in Luke chapter 2. I want to bring out this TRUTH from Luke 2:34–35: "And Simeon blessed them, and said unto Mary His mother, Behold, this is set for the fall and rising again of many in Israel; and for a sign which shall be spoken against; (Yea, a sword shall pierce through thy own soul also,) that the thoughts of many hearts may be revealed." In these scriptures, Simeon prophesied (foretold their future) to Mary about her and her son.

These two verses teach me that Simeon prophesied to Mary about the Jews rejecting Jesus and then Jesus counters the Jews' rejection with a rejection. Truly, if the Lord rejects you, as He did with the Jews, you will fall. And then Simeon tells Mary that later during the tribulation period, many Israelites will rise (turn) to her son Jesus as their Messiah.

Then, in verse 35, Simeon tells Mary about something that is going to happen to her and Jesus, more than twenty years later. Simeon told Mary about seeing her son being crucified for all humanity. No one really knows the sorrow and pain that Mary felt the day her son gave His life for us. But Simeon tells her that her pain and sorrow are going to feel like a sword piercing through her soul. Then, he tells Mary that this must come to pass so Jesus could reveal what is in the hearts of man through His death. Paraphrasing. Now, that is what these two verses teach me.

Jesus is the word. Here are a couple of scriptures that will reveal to you who Jesus is. John 1:1 says, "In the beginning was the word, and the word was with God, and the word was God." If you jump to verse 14, you will know that God came to earth to dwell among His creation (man).

Now, read Hebrews 4:12, and see how the word (Jesus) can see what is in our hearts and minds. He truly is an all-knowing God. If you are a Christian and know God's word, it will direct your mind to hear and your heart to obey it. This word is alive.

Everyone needs to read and study Luke chapter 1 about how Mary got pregnant with her firstborn child. In verse 30, the angel Gabriel tells Mary not to fear and that she has found favor with God. As Gabriel begins revealing to her about her firstborn baby, Mary has questions. In verse 34, Mary asks Gabriel, "How shall this be, seeing I know not a man?" Gabriel explains this mystery to Mary in verse 37, "For with God nothing shall be impossible." I believe we have already established that fact. Mary tells Gabriel in verse 38, "Behold the handmaid of the Lord. Be it unto me according to thy word." Now, Mary had accepted her part in bringing the word to earth so He could save His people from their sinful lives.

Mary could not comprehend some of Jesus' words when He was only twelve years old, such as when He tells her, "I must be about my Father's business." I truly believe that when Mary got Jesus back home that day, she asked Him a lot of questions.

As Jesus grew into a man, He would teach in the temple on the Sabbath. Mary probably sat on the front pew, being amazed, hearing the wisdom spoken by her son. I'm sure Mary heard Jesus teach about His death, which was in His future. And if He taught about His death, Jesus also had to teach about His resurrection on the third day. I can only imagine the questions His mother asked Him after the services.

Here is something else that we can only imagine. What would it be like living with ALMIGHTY GOD in the next bedroom under our roof? I believe when Jesus would come home from a long day's work or from speaking to the people, He would talk to His parents. Jesus most likely told His parents what He was going to go through to be able to redeem man from their sin, and He probably blew their minds revealing His future to them. Then, He tells them that they must be born-again, "Mother, just as you delivered me as a baby, there is coming a day that I will deliver you in your new birth."

I believe Mary was no different from any other Christian. As you now know, Satan came after her with fear for a big part of her life. There's no telling how many times Mary had to rebuke Satan in her life, especially after the angel Gabriel greets Mary for the first time and tells her about Jesus' birth. When Gabriel tells her not to fear, you can believe Satan heard him tell her not to fear. Satan comes after us when he hears about our weak points, so watch what you say. You can find the TRUTH about Gabriel meeting Mary in Luke 1:26–38.

Mary had to be at the lowest point of her life, as she watched her son be beaten and then crucified. There's no telling how many times Mary rebuked Satan that day alone. I believe Satan kept coming after Mary with fear, until she saw her son after His death. I don't believe that there was no more fear found in Mary, when she saw that her son was alive and walked this earth again. I believe Jesus gave His mother the peace that passes all understanding. Read Philippians 4:6–7.

I want to bring a couple of things to your attention from Luke chapter 4.

> And the devil, taking him [Jesus] up into an high mountain, shewed unto him all the kingdoms of the world in a moment of time. And the devil said unto Him, All this power will I give thee, and the glory of

them: for that is delivered unto me; and to whomsoever I will give it. If thou therefore wilt worship me, all shall be thine.

And Jesus answered and said unto him, Get thee behind me, Satan: for it is written, Thou shalt worship the Lord thy God, and him only shalt thou serve. (Verses 5–8)

In verse 8, you can see (hear) the sharp sword that came out of Jesus' mouth. Remember that Satan is the second SUPER POWER known to man, and he will give unto you also because he wants you to spend eternity in HELL with him. The TRUTH is if you don't live for God, you serve Satan daily by your actions. We too must know God's word, because Satan will come after us (the church), and we must know how to defend ourselves against Satan. The only way to fight Satan and be victorious is if we know and obey God's word.

As you continue to read and learn God's word, you will see that Satan has tried to deceive and has used some of God's greatest men. There are others, but I want to tell you about how God allowed Satan to take everything from Job, but his life. You will find this TRUTH in Job chapter 1. As you start reading verse 1, you will see how Job lived his life for the Lord. In verse 2 tells us how Job was blessed with ten children. Verse 3 lets us know how wealthy he was. Verses 4–5 teach us that Job's children were not as close to God as Job. These scriptures also teach us that Job did sacrifice to the Lord, with burnt offerings for his children's sin. In verse 5, you will learn that Job didn't just offer one animal for his burnt offering, Job offered animals for each of his children, and he did it continually.

Revelation 12:7–10 teaches us about Satan being thrown out of heaven. Verses 9–10 say,

And the great dragon was cast out, that old serpent, called the devil, and Satan, which deceiveth the whole world: he was cast out into the earth, and his angels were cast out with him.

And I heard a loud voice saying in heaven, Now is come salvation, and strength, and the kingdom of our God, and the power of His Christ: for the accuser of our brethren is cast down, which accused them before our God day and night.

Pay close attention to what verse 10 says. This scripture tells me that before Lucifer was cast out of heaven, he was always in God's ear, falsely accusing His people. As I have said before, I believe that after Lucifer saw God create man in His own image, jealousy got into Lucifer's heart. After Lucifer got jealous of the relationship between God and man, he stayed in the Lord's ear, accusing man every time he got a chance. Remember when Lucifer was cast out of heaven, he was no longer called Lucifer—he is called Satan. In this rebellious act, Lucifer lost his position in heaven, and the Lord took away his heavenly name. Last year, there was a television show that started, and it was called *Lucifer*. The TRUTH is they didn't know who they were trying to portray.

You are about to learn from this next TRUTH that Satan still has access to the Father's ear and is trying to deceive as many souls as he can. Now, let's go back to Job chapter 1 and find out how Satan comes after Job and his family. In the next few scriptures, you will learn how Satan comes to the Lord and challenges Him by coming against Job's integrity. Verse 6 says that a day when the sons of God came to present themselves before the Lord, and Satan came also among them. You had better believe this; Satan will come to church and try to interfere with your mind and keep you from receiving God's blessings.

As you can see in verse 7, the Lord and Satan are having a conversation. Remember that Lucifer (Satan) has been thrown out of heaven, but he still keeps coming to the Lord, trying to steal our souls from Him. And as you are about to find out, the Lord allows Satan to try. The Lord asked Satan, Where did you come from? Then, Satan answered the Lord, "From going to and fro in the earth, and from walking up and down in it."

1 Peter 5:8 says that your "adversary the devil, as a roaring lion, walketh about, seeking whom he may devour." Notice that this scripture doesn't say that Satan is a roaring lion—it says, "As a roaring lion." Now, God knew what Satan meant when he said that he was "going to and fro in the earth, and from walking up and down in it." God knew Satan was looking for someone to devour (deceive and destroy).

As you are about to find out, Satan was just looking for a soul to steal. Job might not have even been on Satan's list, but God knew that His servant Job would be able to stand against Satan's powers. Listen to what the Lord asked Satan in Job 1:8, "Hast thou considered my servant Job? That none like him in the earth. A perfect and an upright man—one that feareth God and escheweth (avoids) evil." After hearing the Lord describe Job to Satan, he should have known if Job was God's first choice, he was going to have a hard time deceiving him.

After you have read verse 10, you will be able to see how the Lord can take care of your family. As you read verses 9–11, you will learn that Satan convinces the Lord to quite protecting Job, and he would get Job to curse God to His face. Paraphrasing verse 12, the Lord says to Satan, "Behold, all that he has in your power; but you can't put your hands on him." At the end of verse 12, Satan went forth from the presence of the Lord. Although I know that the word doesn't say this, I believe when Satan left the Lord, he began to strategize how he would make Job curse God to His face.

After you hear what Satan does to Job's children, then you will know that Satan starts his strategy in verse 13 by getting Job's sons and his daughters to have a party at their eldest brother's house. As you are about to learn, Satan takes all of Job's possessions, but the

Lord tells Satan that he can't hurt Job physically. I believe this is the only person on earth who has experienced this much bad news, sorrow, and pain from Satan in such a short time period. You can read about this in verses 14–19.

I'm going to include these verses so I can comment on them as I write. Verses 14–15 say, "And there came a messenger unto Job, and said, The oxen were plowing, and the asses feeding beside them: and the Sabeans fell [or came], and took them away; yea, they have slain the servants with the edge of the sword; and I only am escaped alone to tell thee."

Pay close attention as to how verse 16 starts. I'm going to paraphrase the beginning of verse 16 just a little so you can see how Satan is bombarding Job with bad news. Verse 16 says, "While that servant was still speaking, "there also come another, and said, The fire of God is fallen from heaven, and hath burned up the sheep, and the servants, and consumed them; and I only am escaped alone to tell thee."

Again, I'm going to paraphrase the beginning of the next verse, just a little. Verse 17 says, while that servant was still speaking, "there come also another, and said, The Chaldeans made out three bands, and fell upon the camels, and have carried them away, yea, and slain the servants with the edge of the sword; and I only am escaped alone to tell thee.

Paraphrasing the beginning of verses 18–19, while that servant was still speaking, "there came also another, and said, Thy sons and thy daughters eating and drinking wine in their eldest brother's house: And, behold, there came a great wind from the wilderness, and smote the four corners of the house, and it fell upon the young men, and they are dead; and I only am escaped alone to tell thee."

Before I tell you what Job did, after getting all these bad news, I want to ask you a question. What would you do, if within one hour, all was taken from you? Or better yet, I should ask myself that same question. You have already learned in this book that the day would come when all will be taken from us, if we don't take the mark of the Beast. Again, what would you do? Do you remember what the Lord said about Job when Satan first came to Him?

In verse 8, the Lord asked Satan, "Hast thou considered my servant Job? That none like him in the earth. A perfect and an upright man, one that feareth God, and escheweth evil."

When Satan comes to the Lord desiring your soul, what do you think God will say to Satan about you?

Just listen how Job handled these attacks from Satan. When Job heard what the last messenger told him about his children, Job began to reveal his integrity that he had toward God. You can find out what he did and said in verses 20–22. Job starts off by humbling himself before the Lord. Now, the scriptures don't say if Job was sitting or lying flat on his back after hearing this terrible news. But the word says, "Job arose, and rent his mantle [tore his robe], and shaved his head, and fell down upon the ground, and worshipped." Just listen to what Job says to the Lord. Job says, "Naked came I out of my mother's womb, and naked shall I return thither: the Lord gave, and the Lord hath taken away; blessed be the name of the Lord." If those words don't get to you, I don't know what will.

Verse 22 says, "In all this Job sinned not, nor charged God foolishly." Now, Job had held on to his integrity, through this test. But what he didn't know was there were other tests coming in his near future. As you are about to find out, Satan was not through with Job. It didn't impress Satan one bit to see that Job tore his robe or shave his head or even fall down on the ground and worship God. Satan was trying to steal Job's soul. You had better learn from this TRUTH Satan doesn't give up so easily.

In Job chapter 2, Satan comes back after Job's health. Here, you will see Satan does about the same thing he did in chapter 1. He follows God's people to church, looking for souls to steal. And the Lord asked Satan again, "Hast thou considered my servant Job?" But this time, the Lord adds something to His description that He couldn't say the first time. God says at the end of verse 3 that Job still holds fast his integrity, "although you move me against him, to destroy him without cause." Satan tells the Lord in verses 4–5, "Skin for skin, yea, all that a man hath will he give for his life. But put forth thine hand now, and touch his bone and his flesh, and he will curse thee to thy face." In verse 6, the Lord tells Satan, "Behold, he in thine hand; but save his life." This was all Satan needed to hear.

Verse 7 tells us that Satan left "the presence of the Lord, and smote Job with sore boils from the sole of his foot unto his crown." There is no way to know how much pain Job experienced. If you have ever had a boil, you still wouldn't know the pain that Job was in. He was covered from head to toe with sore boils. I do know this—Job was a lot tougher than I am. Verse 8 says, "He took him a potsherd [a piece of broken pottery] to scrape himself withal [his sores]; and he sat down among the ashes." Even though Job was in pain, he was still holding on to his integrity before God and man.

But as you can see in verse 9, Job's wife was losing it. She asked Job, "Are you still going to keep your integrity?" Then at the end of verse 9, she does lose it. She tells Job to go ahead and curse God and die. In verse 10, you can hear what a real man of God would say when he is faced with such a test. Job tells his wife that she is talking like a foolish woman. Then, Job asked her a question, "Shall we receive good at the hand of God, and shall we not receive evil?" At the end of verse 10, the scripture says, "In all this did not Job sin with his lips."

Verse 11 tells us about Job's three friends who heard about the problems that he was going through. These three friends came to mourn with him and to comfort him. In verse 12, you will see that when they saw him, they didn't even know him. He must have had boils covering his face, because his friends were not able to recognize him. As soon as they knew that it was him, they began to cry out and weep. Then, they began to tear their robes and sprinkle dust upon their heads toward heaven. Verse 13 says, "So they sat down with him upon the ground seven days and seven nights, and none spake a word unto him: for they saw, that grief was very great." After the seven days and nights had past, Job opened his mouth and began to curse the day that he was born.

As you read Job chapter 3, you will see that Job had finally had enough of what he was going through and began to wish he had never been born. In verse 25, Job says, "For the thing which I greatly feared is come upon me." As you can see, Satan is not just attacking Job's body; he is also attacking Job's mind with fear. And as you read the book of Job, it seems as if Satan has gotten to him. I have read through chapter 15, but so far, I haven't found where Satan forced Job to curse the Lord.

Remember at first, Job's three friends came to comfort and encourage him. But after seven days and seven nights without speaking and after hearing Job complain about his situation, his friends had to say something. In Job 4:1–5, his friends began to talk. Eliphaz speaks first and says, "We assay to commune with thee, will thou be grieved?" Now with my lack of education, I hear words in this question that I don't understand. So I have to depend on my New Oxford American Dictionary to find out what Eliphaz asked Job. The first word that I'm going to look at is assay, and it means "to test or examine." The next word is commune. According to the dictionary, it means "to share one's intimate thoughts, or feelings with someone especially, when the exchange is on a spiritual level." This is how, I believe, Eliphaz asked Job in Mississippi language, "We want to examine you and see if you are still serving God, because with what you are going through, it looks like you have backslid. Is this going to bother you, because we have got to find out your problem?"

Then, in verse 12, Eliphaz began to hear God's voice, and he says that he received a little of what he heard. In chapters 4 and 5, you will see that Job's friend tells him what he heard from the visions he had received. In Job 5:25, Eliphaz informs Job that he will have more children and that his offspring will be as the grass of the earth and that he will live to be of full age. In verse 27, Eliphaz tells Job that what he is going through is for his own good. Job must have been in so much pain that he could not hear his friend.

In Job 6:1, Job begins speaking again, and in verse 4, he accuses the Lord for the pain that he is experiencing. In Job 6:8–9, he wants God to grant him a request for he has had enough and wants the Lord to allow him to die and get him out of his misery. In the first few verses of chapter 7, you will feel some of what Job was going through. In Job 7:20, he tells God that he has sinned and he acknowledges God as a preserver of men. And in verse 21, Job asked the Lord two questions that I believe is what will help get him out of this test he is going through. Job asked the Lord, "Why dost thou not pardon my transgression, and take away my iniquity?" In other words, "Why have you not forgiven my sin and removed it from my life?"

As you read the book of Job, you will hear that Satan has put so much pressure on his mind and body that he is beginning to lose his desire to live. If you ever find yourself in that place, my best advice would be begin calling on Jesus and don't stop until you hear from Him. Now, I don't see if Job ever cursed the Lord, but he does accuse God for the things he is going through.

In chapter 8, another one of Job's friends begins to speak, and his name is Bildad. Now, Bildad is going to tell Job what he believes about God. Job tells Bildad in chapter 9:2, I know what you are saying is true. Then, Job starts to tell his friends what he knows about God. As you read the book of Job, you will see how Job's three friends took turns trying to school him in the ways of righteousness.

After Job's three friends finished lecturing him, Job began to speak in chapter 26 and he continued through chapters 27, 28, 29, 30, and 31. As Job ended his words in chapter 31, the word says, "So these three men ceased to answer Job, because they believed, that Job was righteous in his own eyes" (Job 32:1). Job 32:2 records another one of Job's friends, and his name was Elihu. The scriptures say that he was angry with Job because Job justified himself rather than God. And Elihu was also angry with Job's other three friends, because they didn't find an answer for Job and had condemned him.

Elihu waited until Job and his friends had spoken, because they were elders and he was much younger than them. Elihu says that he was afraid and didn't want to give his opinion, but he does. Elihu truly says a mouthful. He begins lecturing them in chapters 32 and finishes in chapter 37. In Job 37:14, Elihu tells Job to listen to him and "to stand still, and consider the wondrous works of God." "Then, the Lord answered Job out of a whirlwind" (Job 38:1). In chapter 38, you will see that the Lord started asking Job questions. In chapters 38, 39, 40, and 41, the Lord asked Job eighty-five questions. In these four chapters, you will learn the nature of these eighty-five questions. What I get from these questions are that the Lord is letting Job (us) know that He is God, and Job (we) is not.

Now, for the conclusion of Job's story (life). After the Lord had explained to Job that He is God, read chapter 42 to find out how Job is blessed for holding on to his integrity with God. Paraphrasing verse 3, Job says, "I have said some things that I shouldn't have, because I didn't know what I was talking about." You're about to see that what Job has gone through is about to pay off. What happens in verse 5 is going to be a life- changing experience for Job. He is about to experience something very few people get to do. In verse 5, Job says, "I have heard of thee by the hearing of the ear, but now mine eye seeth thee." I don't know how Job could see the Holy Ghost (God's Spirit), but God allowed him to see.

Job is about to do something that everyone must do to be in good standing with the Lord. In verse 6, Job repents. The only thing that I can find in the book of Job that he would have to repent of is found in Job 6:4. As you and I now know, it was not God, but it was Satan that was coming against Job. But I believe when Job saw the Lord, his mind began to flashback on his life. And when I say flashback, I mean he looked back over his life in seconds. I know I haven't stolen anything, lied, or been unfaithful to my wife; but I did accuse the Lord of what I'm going through. As soon as Job remembered what he had done, he repented.

If Jesus stood in my bedroom right now and revealed Himself to me, I believe I would get as low as I could to the floor even trying to get under the carpet. I would not have to flashback through my life. I would immediately ask Him to forgive me. I have said before in this book, and I will say it again. We all must come to God and repent our sins. When you repent with a pure heart by saying, "I'm sorry. Forgive me," God will turn His ear and begin listening to you. Read 1 Peter 3:12.

In Job chapter 42, you will see how the Lord begins blessing him and his family. In verse 7, you will find that the Lord was angry with Job's three friends, because they didn't speak right about Him as Job did. In verse 8, the Lord tells Eliphaz "to take unto you now seven bullocks and seven rams, and go to my servant Job, and offer up for yourselves a burnt offering; and my servant Job shall pray for you: for him will I accept." In verse 9, Job's three friends went and did what the Lord has commanded. At the end of verse 9, the Lord also accepted Job.

The Lord is about to bless Job for the rest of his life. It started when Job repented, and now, Job needs to do one more thing to start the blessings. Verse 10 says, "And the Lord turned the captivity of Job." In other words, the Lord forgave him and healed his body. When did the Lord free Job? In the middle of verse 10, you will find the answer to that question. And it was "WHEN he [Job] prayed for his friends." There is a big lesson to be learned from that last statement. If we will learn to pray for others, God will bless our families also. And here comes more blessings in Job's life. Verse 10 also says, "The Lord gave Job twice as much as he had before." In verse 11, "Then came there unto him all his brethren, and all his sisters, and all they that had been of his acquaintance before, and did eat bread with him in his house. And they bemoaned him, and comforted him over all the evil that the Lord had brought upon him. And every man also gave him a piece of money, and every one an earring of gold."

In verse 12, "The Lord blessed the latter end of Job more than his beginning." The Lord blessed Job because of his steadfastness in the faith. The Lord blessed Job with "fourteen thousand sheep, and six thousand camels, and a thousand yoke of oxen, and a thousand she asses. The Lord also blessed Job with seven new sons and three new daughters. The word also says that there were no women in all that land as fair as his three daughters.

After Job went through his ordeal with Satan and God, he lived one hundred and forty years, and he saw his sons and his son's sons through four generations. Then, the Bible tells us Job died old and full of days. I wanted to share this part of Job's life with you because there are so many lessons to be learned by looking at his life during his ordeal. Everyone will learn different lessons when reading and studying God's word. I learned about a dozen different things from the book of Job that I should or should not do if I find myself in a similar situation. After you have learned what Job had to go through, I should not have to tell you this, but you should be praising Jesus right now and thanking Him for your life.

In Luke 4:13, something is recorded that Matthew didn't mention when Satan was tempting Jesus. After Satan had finished tempting Jesus, he departed for a season (a while). This tells me that Satan was not giving up so easily and that he would return at a later time to try to deceive Jesus again in the near future. If Satan will attack the Lord of heaven, he will come after anyone who he doesn't already have. We too must be able to say, "It is written," and use the word (sword) to stick that devil to make him leave us alone. If you have never rebuked Satan in the name of Jesus and quoted scriptures to him, you are not fighting him with your full potential, and most of the time, you will lose that battle.

You will have to rebuke Satan when you start living for the Lord. The better you know God's word, the more ammunition you will have to fight Satan with. When Jesus rebuked Satan, He simply said, "It is written," because He is the word. I always rebuke Satan by saying, "I rebuke you Satan in the name of Jesus," and then tell him the reason that I'm rebuking him. Apostle Paul said in Colossians 3:17, "Whatsoever you do in word or deed, all in the name of the Lord Jesus, giving thanks to God and the Father by Him." If you don't use the name of Jesus, when you rebuke Satan, you will lose.

About 99 % of the time, I rebuke Satan by calling him a liar, because he is always coming to me in his deceiving ways. Jesus teaches us that Satan is not only a liar but also the father of lies. Read John 8:44. As I have said, the more of God's word you know, the better off you will be in your walk with the Lord. Just remember that Satan is going to come after you, and when he does, rebuke him in the name of Jesus. James 4:7–8 says, "If you will submit yourself to God, resist the devil, and he will flee from you. Draw nigh to God, and He will draw nigh to you."

Satan comes at us ever so often, with his bag of tricks (deceiving ways). If he can't deceive us one way, he will just try something else. When he finds out just what you will fall for, he will use it often. If you keep falling for that same trick, he will begin to add others until he gets you so bound that it will seem that there is no way to get from under his grasp. And if his tricks don't work, as you now know by hearing Job's story, he will use drastic measures to destroy whomever he can.

But now you know from reading your Bible and this book that there is hope. Read 1 Corinthians 10:13. Here is a scripture that you should learn, because it teaches us that Satan continues to use the same temptations on each of us. Notice that at the end of that verse, Apostle Paul says, the Lord "will not suffer [allow] you to be tempted above that ye are able; but will with the temptation also make a way to escape, that ye may be able to bear [whatever] it is" that Satan is tempting you with.

Always remember that the Lord loves us and He wants us to turn from our evil ways and serve Him.

In 1 Corinthians 10:13, Apostle Paul tells us that the Lord will make a way to escape the temptation that you are going through. This is what I believe is happening. Most people don't know the Lord or His word, and they don't seek that way of escape, which the Lord has provided for them, because they are blind. When Satan sees that they don't know which way out of the temptation, he entangles them with sin and sickness.

You just remember that when you find yourself being tempted by Satan, look around and ask the Lord to show you the way to escape. If you will seek Jesus, He is ready to help you escape Satan's temptations. Read 1 Corinthians 10:13 again, and you will see that it says, "God is faithful, who will not suffer you to be tempted above you are able." You better believe Jesus knows who you are, and He knows how much you can go through.

Now, this is the TRUTH. Satan could not defeat the Lord in heaven. The Romans (Satan-filled Herod) could not kill Jesus when He was a baby, because it was not in God's master plan. And Satan could not deceive Jesus, when He was fasting for forty days and forty nights in the wilderness. What most people don't know is that Jesus gave Himself for us. Read John 10:15–18. Jesus could have fought back and won, but He willingly gave Himself. Read Matthew 26:36–57. These scriptures record some of what happened the night Jesus was betrayed. These scriptures teach us that Jesus took Peter, James, and John with Him that night to the garden called Gethsemane to pray. Jesus knew what was about to happen; He knew that He had to die for humanity.

This is the night that Judas Iscariot betrayed the Lord with a kiss. Read Luke 22:3, and you will see that Satan used Judas Iscariot and tried one more time to destroy Jesus before He goes to heaven.

And as you now know, Satan had a very small part (deceiving Judas) in Jesus' death. It is a fact that the man Jesus died that day on the cross, but it was far from being over. On the third day, Jesus came out of His grave and is alive forevermore. Sure, the flesh died that day, but the God in that body could not die.

John 18:10 says that it was Peter who was angered enough that he took out his sword and smote the high priest's servant named Malchus. I truly believe Peter was trying to split his skull, but the Lord redirected the sword and cut off Malchus' right ear. In Matthew chapter 26, you can hear what Jesus tells Peter about defending Himself. In Matthew 26:52, Jesus tells Peter to put up again thy sword. Then, Jesus tells him in verse 53, "Thinkest thou that I cannot now pray to my Father, and He shall presently give me more than twelve legions [more than 72,000] of angels. In verse 56, Jesus said, "But all this was done, that the scriptures of the prophets might be fulfilled."

From the time Jesus was born, His destiny on earth was to come to this day and the next few days that followed. Mary was about to feel the sword piercing her soul. The word is clear about this. Jesus could have fought back, but He wanted to bring man back from the sin that Satan had entangled us in.

Jesus died, and His blood was shed so we could live this life above Satan and his deceiving ways. When Jesus finished His work here on earth, God allowed the Satan-filled Romans to fulfill His will by hanging Jesus on the cross. Jesus was hung on the cross, and His blood was shed for the redemption of mankind. I don't want to just point a finger at the Romans, because Satan also used the Jews of that time as much or maybe even more than he used the Romans. Read Matthew 20:17–19, and you will find out how Satan used the Jewish leaders to deliver Jesus to the Romans so He could be crucified.

Before I finish writing this chapter, I want to share with you what I believe the reason why the Jews have had so many problems up to this point in time. This is what the word teaches us about the Jewish people—they are God's chosen people. From the beginning, the Jewish people had the writings of the prophets foretelling the coming of the Messiah.

The Jews had prayed for hundreds of years for the Lord to come and deliver them out of their bondage. They knew the Lord as a Spirit. But they could not believe that God would come to earth as a baby (human). This is the TRUTH about the Jewish people. They have been blinded from the TRUTH, "until the fullness of the Gentiles be come in." Read Romans 11:25. The day came that the Prince of Peace (Jesus) came to help His people, but they rejected Him.

Now, this is what the Lord taught me why Israel and the Jewish people have so many problems. I know that the Jews already had problems, but they added more problems to themselves in the New Testament era—the day Jesus was put on trial. You can read about His trial in Matthew chapter 27, and please read all of it. But I want to bring your attention to verse 25. Verse 25 says, "Then answered all the people [Jews], and said, His blood on us, and on our children." When they said, "His blood on us, and on our children," that meant until the Gentile's dispensation of time was fulfilled or, in other words, until the last Gentile be saved/born-again.

The Jews who were at the trial cursed their whole nation that day. But don't get me wrong. If a Jew under the conviction of the Lord repents of their sin and is baptized in the name of Jesus, they will be saved. There is that big word IF again—if they continue to obey the New Testament kingdom rules.

Here are a few scriptures that teach us about the blindness of the Jews. Read 2 Corinthians 3:13–16, and you can find some TRUTH about their blindness. These scriptures teach us how the Jews were blinded and still live in accordance with the Old Testament. Verse 16 teaches us the TRUTH that I've been writing about some Jews who will be saved/born-again, during the Gentiles dispensation.

Verse 16 says, "Nevertheless when it [the Jews] shall turn to the Lord, the veil shall be taken away."

I started this chapter writing about Satan, and I believe that I should finish it writing about him. As I have said, Satan is winning this battle, but God will eventually win the war. Satan is winning more souls than ever and will have more followers than the Lord. I will say again—Satan is working very hard for souls, and he has always known that he only has a short time to do so. Read Revelation 12:12. You are about to find out in the next set of scriptures that Satan knows his days are numbered.

Read Matthew 8:23–29. As you read this story, you will see that Jesus' disciples were afraid when a storm came up when they crossed the sea. They awoke Jesus and said, "Save us. We are going to perish." As you now know, they didn't perish, because the Lord "rebuked the winds and the sea; and there was a great calm." Then, His disciples said, "What manner of man is this, that even the winds and sea obey Him!" What His disciples didn't know yet was that Jesus was and is the Creator of the winds and sea, so they (the winds and sea) had to obey Him.

This story happened over two thousand years ago, and in verse 29, you will see that Satan knew then that he didn't have long to gather his followers (souls). As Jesus walked up on the land, two men "possessed with devils" came to Jesus and asked Him two questions. First, they asked Him, "What have we to do with thee [Jesus]?" And then they acknowledged Him as the Son of God. The second question was, "Art thou come hither to torment us before the time?" This last question tells me that Satan knows his days are numbered.

You should know by now Jesus can and will calm the storms in your life. Deuteronomy 30:19 says that the Lord calls "heaven and earth to record this day against you, I have set before you life and death, blessing and cursing. Therefore choose life that both thou and thy seed [family] may live." This scripture is clear—if you will choose the Lord when He chooses you, He will give you and your family life. And also remember that if you live for God, the Lord has given you power over Satan. When Satan comes against you, always seek the Lord for the way to escape whatever it is you're going through. If you choose life and blessings, Jesus will be there for you when you need Him.

I could have written so many other things about Satan, but I believe you get the picture from what I have written. I have told you where he came from, and I have warned you of where he and his followers are going. My prayer is that you don't allow him to deceive you. At this time, I began looking through the scriptures, trying to find the right words (scriptures) to give you so you could stand strong for the Lord.

There are plenty of scriptures to choose from, when you are looking for help. But I believe that there is only one set of scriptures that gives us this magnitude of TRUTH all in one place in God's word. I want you to pay close attention to the words that you are about to read, because in them, you will find how to protect yourself from Satan.

In Ephesians 6:10–17, Apostle Paul teaches us the church to be "strong in the Lord and in the power of His might." If you become strong in the Lord, Satan is going to have big problems with you. In the next scripture, Paul is going to teach us how to be strong in the Lord. In verse 11, Paul tells us, "Put on the whole armour of God, that ye may be able to stand against the wiles of the devil." Notice that Paul tells us to put on the whole armor. He didn't tell us that we could put on the parts of the armor we wanted.

In verse 12, Paul says, "We wrestle not against flesh and blood, but against principalities, against powers, against the rulers of the darkness of this world, against spiritual wickedness in high." Apostle Paul just described Satan as the SUPER POWER that he is, and without the whole armor of God, Satan will get his fingernail in you and he will devour you.

Paul repeats himself in verse 13: "Take unto you the whole armour of God, that ye may be able to withstand in the evil day, and having done all, to stand." Here, Paul warns us of the importance of putting and keeping on the whole armor of God, because he knows how powerful Satan is at this time. In this last verse, notice what it didn't say. Verse 13 didn't tell us to run, but it did say for us to stand. We must face Satan when he comes after us. Jesus has already given us a way to escape Satan's deceit, but we must be spiritual- minded so we can find the right path from Satan.

The first piece of armor that Paul tells us to put on is TRUTH. Starting in verse 14, Paul teaches us to "stand therefore, having your loins girt about with TRUTH," which is what I've been trying to convey to you throughout this entire book. I have written TRUTH 640 times in this book. And you have seen the word TRUTH written in capital letters because I wanted to emphasize the importance of God's TRUTH. It is the main reason I wrote this book. I wanted to share the TRUTH, which the Lord has shared with me, with anyone who will listen. The TRUTH is what separates the church from the world (other people). As Jesus was praying in John 17:17, He says, "Sanctify them through thy TRUTH: thy word is TRUTH." Knowing the TRUTH about the Lord should be the second most important thing for us to do, while we are here on earth. The first and most important thing is for us to obey His TRUTH, as we learn it.

At the end of verse 14 Paul tells us to put on the breastplate of righteousness, which I believe simply means for us to live right. In verses 15– 17, he tells us to shod our feet with the preparation of the gospel of peace and, above all, for us to take the shield of faith, "wherewith ye shall be able to quench all the fiery darts of the wicked [Satan]. And take the helmet of salvation, and the sword of the Spirit, which is the word of God." The word of God is an offensive and defensive weapon in this warfare, as we serve God and our fellow man.

Read Matthew 4:1–11, and you will see, every time, that Satan came to Jesus to tempt Him, the sword (word) comes out of Jesus' mouth, and He says, "It is written." Jesus quotes scriptures every time Satan tempts Him. Jesus stuck Satan three times with the word, and verse 11 says, "Then the devil leaveth Him." Satan had been stuck with God's word, and he knew firsthand the power of God's word.

Satan knew he could not take on Jesus face to face. Now, when Satan saw that he could not deceive Jesus, he goes after the church. Satan gets inside of Judas Iscariot, and he betrays the Lord.

If we will put on and wear the whole armor that the Lord has provided us, Satan will not be able to get to us. We will be victorious over Satan, as we walk with the Lord. I know that the whole armor is necessary and needs to be worn and used, but I want to talk about the shield of faith. I wrote about the shield of faith in chapter 1, but I want to explain again how important it is to have a large shield of faith in our walk with Jesus. I hope you can remember what I wrote about the large shield of faith, because I thought it was great.

Just by memory, I will attempt to make it as good as it was before, or maybe even better. I'm going to refer to how Matthew recorded Jesus' words, just because I like Matthew's book and how he wrote the TRUTH. Jesus teaches us a parable of the kingdom of heaven, being like a mustard seed, in Matthew 13:31–32.

Jesus says that the mustard seed is the least of all seeds, but when it is grown, it is the greatest among herbs and becomes a tree so that the birds of the air come and lodge in the branches thereof. We are about to hear Jesus compare our faith to a mustard seed.

Matthew 17:14–16 tells about how this man came to Jesus, because His disciples could not help his son. Jesus says to His disciples in verse 17, "O faithless and perverse generation, how long shall I be with you? How long shall I suffer you? Bring him hither to me." And as you should know, Jesus rebuked and cast out the devil from this man's son. After this, Jesus' disciples came to Him and asked.

"Why could not we cast him out?" In verses 20–21, Jesus answers their question, "Because of your unbelief; for verily I say unto you, if ye have faith as a grain of mustard seed, ye shall say unto this mountain, remove hence to yonder place: and it shall remove; and nothing shall be impossible unto you."

Then, Jesus tells them how to achieve such great faith. In verse 21, Jesus tells His disciples, "Howbeit this kind goeth not out but by prayer and fasting." In other words, if you are going to try to rebuke and cast out Satan, you had better get yourself prepared by fasting and seeking the Lord and allowing your faith to grow.

When I first wrote about the shield of faith, I believe that I started off last time and asked you to hold up a pencil as your shield of faith in front of you and let a friend throw something at you. I will tell you that it is going to be hard for you to block the thrown object with a pencil. Now, get a book and try the same thing. You just might have a better chance at blocking it this time. But if you will go outside and get the garbage can lid, you will be able to block almost anything they throw at you.

Romans 10:17 says that we get faith by hearing the word of God. Now that you know how to grow your faith; it is up to you to study God's word and grow your faith into the perfect size that fits your own life. Remember that Apostle Paul said, "ABOVE ALL, take the shield of faith, wherewith ye shall be able to quench all the fiery darts of the wicked."

I'm about to say something that could be controversial to some Christians, but I believe what I'm about to say. In Ephesians chapter 6, most people stop at the end of verse 17 when dressing themselves with the armor of God. I believe what Apostle Paul says in verse 18 is how the Christians grow in the strength of God, which is another pathway for the Lord to bless us and our families.

Paul tells us in verse 18 to pray always with all prayer and supplication in the Spirit and watching thereunto with all perseverance and supplication for all saints. Now, I have to admit I'm preaching to myself with this last scripture. I often find myself seeking the Lord about myself and my family when I should be praying for others because I truly believe that is the way to be blessed by God.

I want you to remember Job and how he was blessed. In Job chapter 42, Job repented and was forgiven for his sins, and they were removed from his life. But the blessings from God didn't start until Job prayed for his friends. Job 42:10 says that the Lord turned the captivity of Job WHEN he prayed for his friends. Then, verse 10 says that the Lord gave Job twice as much as he had before. I believe if we all will read, study, learn, and obey what Apostle Paul teaches us in Ephesians 6:10–18, we will be able to run the race before us with less problems.

May God bless you and teach you how to tread upon the serpent called Satan. Luke 10:18–19 Jesus said, "I beheld Satan as lightning fall from heaven. Behold, I give unto you power to tread on serpents and scorpions [Satan and his demons], and over all the power of the enemy, and nothing shall by any means hurt you." Again, I will say that if we will do our part, the Lord will do His. His promises are throughout His word, and He cannot and will not lie. But you had better be on your toes (knees), because Satan will lie to you. He wants you and me to spend eternity with him in HELL. I want you to read verse 18 again, but this time, I want you to hear what it says. When Satan was cast out of heaven, it was about four thousand years before Jesus was born. In this scripture, the TRUTH is Jesus was referring to when He was the Creator.

To tell you the TRUTH, Satan has been coming after me in the past seven months, more than he has ever came after me before. And I realized why; as you can see, I'm trying to finish writing this book, and he doesn't like it. But that's okay; I'm going to keep rebuking him in the name of Jesus, and as you can see, I'm still writing. If you are not in this warfare against Satan, you don't have a clue what we must endure, to get to heaven. If you want to go to heaven, I suggest you start praying and asking Jesus to teach you His TRUTH, and that will get Satan's attention, and he will come after you. Just remember that when Satan comes after you, he is a loser and begin calling on Jesus, because He is Satan's Creator too. Just as the winds and waves had to obey Him, Satan does too. Satan is the one who doesn't have Jesus on his side—you do.

If you will stand for Jesus, Jesus will stand with you, and no devil can harm you. It may seem sometimes as if you will not make it, but you must hang on to Jesus and keep your focus on Him. Do you remember in the scriptures when we learned about Apostle Peter walking on the water? As long as Peter kept his eyes on the Lord, he was buoyant, but when he began looking at the winds and waves, he began to sink. Now, this maybe just a story to you, but it is the TRUTH to me. There is no doubt in my mind—I believe every word of it. My prayer is to be stronger in the Lord, because for years, I have been wading around in ankle-deep water, thinking I'm doing something for the Lord. But the TRUTH is, I know, that there are oceans to swim in the Lord and waves that I could walk on.

Satan is in my ears and mind, night and day. The reason that I'm writing this is when I woke up this morning, all of this was on my mind, so let me tell you a little more about what is on my mind. I fight sickness daily. I'm not going through what Job did, but I believe I'm in the same boat with him. But by the grace of God, and only by the grace of God, I will continue to stand for my Lord and the church. I do know this—the Lord will not forget my labor of love toward Him and His church.

Just remember this—if you are not living for the Lord, you are serving Satan, and you are following the loser into HELL. In the future, Satan is going to have two more chances to destroy Jesus. Thank God you have already learned this TRUTH. He will have a chance at the rapture and at the battle of Armageddon. But you already know that he loses both times. The Lord has defeated Satan every time that he came against Him, and as you now know, Jesus and His followers are the winners. I'm a winner, because I'm not quitting this race. I'm going all the way to heaven and beyond.

The Lord has shared so much (and I mean on the high end of so much) of Himself with me. I can't quit. In Luke 12:48, Jesus says, "For unto whomsoever much is given of him shall be much required." As you read the next chapter, you will learn how to be the winner that you were born to be. And always remember this—it is only by the grace of God that you are alive and studying God's word. My prayer is that you get enough time to read and study chapter 9, "God's Plan of Salvation," and obey it.

There is one more thing that I want to share with you before I finish this chapter. Here is something else that was added to God's word. When I started reading the Bible, I always wondered why there were words written in italics. But like many of you, I continued to read them without asking.

Why are these words in God's word?

As I was witnessing to a lady one day, she asked me about the words written in italics, and I could not give her an answer. When I left there, I asked the Lord why they were in His word. I didn't get an immediate answer, but I did finally get the answer. As time passed and I continued reading God's word, it would bother me every time I would come across a word written in italics. One day, as I was starting to read, instead of me looking into the scriptures, I opened up my Bible to the front of it; and on the third page was the answer that I had been looking for. It was right under my nose all this time.

The answer was literally at my fingertips every time I picked up my Bible. For twenty-five years, I had been reading God's word, and when I found this TRUTH, I felt stupid and blessed at the same time. It is weird to feel stupid and blessed, but finally, the blessing of knowing the TRUTH overshadowed the feeling of being stupid.

The third page of my old Bible says that one characteristic of the King James Version is its use of italics. They are used to indicate words "supplied by the editors" to help clarify the meaning and better relate the original language into English. Now, you know as well as I do the Holy Ghost (Jesus) is the teacher of His word. It's too late for Satan or any person to try and tell me that Jesus needs an editor to edit the living word. The editor even added from to God's word in Revelation 22:18–19. In these scriptures is where the Lord teaches us not to add or take away from His word. Evidently, the editor couldn't understand the words that he or she was reading.

For the past eight years, I have been reading and skipping over the words written in italics, because I don't believe that they are supposed to be in God's word. If you will try reading and skipping over those words, the Lord will give you the correct interpretation of His word. I believe that is enough about Satan and all of his deceiving ways and his false teachings. It's time to find God's plan of salvation, so you can begin your walk with the Lord. As you read and study chapter 9, and comparing it with your Bible, you will find the TRUTH of God's salvation.

CHAPTER 9

GOD'S PLAN OF SALVATION

I just can't help it. I am going to go the long way around to getting to God's plan of salvation, but you will hear God's TRUTH. I believe that this is the last chapter of this book, so I must say everything in this book, even though some of this book is about the false, is 99.9% TRUTH according to our history books, especially our most valuable history book (the Bible). I have studied the Bible for thirty-four years now, and I just realized I have been studying God's word for over half of my life. The years that I have been studying God's word has surpassed the years when I knew nothing at all. I'm not bragging, but I am boasting about all the TRUTH the Lord has taught me. He has truly blessed me with a right mind, a good heart, and a mouth full of His word (TRUTH).

When I first started writing this book, I started off by calling it a tract. I wanted to be able to give whomever I was witnessing to some TRUTH to carry home with them. As time passed, my writings grew into a letter. As I kept writing, I began calling it a pamphlet, but as you can see, it is neither. What I embarked on ten years ago turned into a book. It is my first book, but I can't say that it is the last, because no one really knows what the Lord has in store for us to do for our kingdom.

If you can remember in chapter 6, I said that I was going to explain the TRUTH about God's plan of salvation in chapter 9. I also said that I was going to share with you what the Lord has taught me about the Book of Life and predestination. As you now know, it's hard for me to stay on a certain subject because there is so much to write about concerning God's word. I'm trying to tell you that I'm about to get a little bit off those three subjects, but I will get back to God's plan of salvation soon.

I have learned some very important lessons in the past thirty-four years, and here are a couple of them. The Lord has allowed me to see that my ignorance of His word will not be tolerated. I cannot speak of your ignorance. If we seek Him for His TRUTH, He will teach anyone who will apply themselves to learning. I guess I can speak of your ignorance. If you don't learn God's word, it will be your own fault.

Through these years, I have seen that I have tripped and fallen hard a few times in my walk with the Lord because of my own stupidity and my lack of faith. But God has always been there to pick me up, but only when I have asked Him these six simple words, Forgive me, Lord. I am sorry. I believe that everything is in God's time. But I have to say that if it were not for my stupidity and lack of faith, the Lord would move on my behalf so much faster in every situation. I can truly say with shame that I have hindered God from time to time in my race. Therefore, if God is sometimes delayed, it will be our own fault, and if it is our own fault, we make it in God's time.

You should know by now that Jesus is King of Kings and that heaven is a kingdom. If you expect to get into heaven when you pass away from this world, you must obey the kingdom rules. The kingdom rules have been put in book form, and it is called the Bible. Read Hebrews 10:16. As you read and study God's word, you need to ask the Lord to put His laws in your heart and mind. Then, you will be able to know His word and obey it from your heart. Read Romans 6:16–18. The Old Testament is good to read and study, because the prophets help lead us to the New Testament era. Now, don't get me wrong—you can learn a whole lot from the Old Testament, but it is old, and we must live the New Testament. Even though the New Testament has been wrested, God's true plan of salvation is still written on the pages of the Bible.

We know from our history books that the Jewish nation has always been under the oppression of many countries for their belief in one God. We know from reading and studying the book of Daniel that for many years, Israel was kept under the thumb of dictators. This is what brought the Jewish people to their knees, and they began calling on the Lord for a deliverer. As the Jews cried out unto the Lord this time, He decided to come Himself. The God of Glory made Himself a body and came to live on earth so He would know what humans go through in their daily lives. The Lord was going to fix the sin problem once and for all, which started with Adam and Eve.

Jesus came to earth for one main reason—and that was to redeem His people from Satan's grasp. Every person born on this earth are sinners from the day Adam and Eve disobeyed the Lord, except Jesus. Jesus was the only baby that came into this world who was not born in sin. The Lord was not going to be denied the relationship He started with man. God's master plan is going to come to pass, and nothing can stop it.

To find out the Lord's pathway to earth as a human, you need to read and study Matthew chapters 1 and 2. In Matthew chapter 1, start reading at verse 16, because most likely verses 1–15 will not make a lot of sense to you. Now, don't get me wrong—verses 1–15 are really important for the church to know. Most people who read Matthew 1:1–15 don't have a clue of the importance of these forty-two generations of people. When you read verse 16, you will learn that God's Bride comes from this lineage. After the Holy Ghost (Jesus) has taught you His TRUTH, you will be able to understand the importance of these sixteen scriptures.

Do you remember what Jesus told us to do in the book of Revelation? Hear what the Spirit is saying to the church. To hear (understand) what I'm about to say, you must put on and open up your spiritual ears. If you are naturally born anything other than a Jew, you are not of the lineage that is recorded in Matthew 1:1–16. When you read verse 16, you should begin to know how to get into this lineage. To all non-Jewish people, read and study Romans chapter 11 and find out how the Lord chose to bring us into His lineage. Jesus is a Jew, and we must become Jewish to be in the lineage of Jesus. When a person is born-again, they become Jewish. Adoption and being grafted into the Jewish nation is how the Lord chose to redeem us (non- Jewish people) unto Himself. Read Ephesians 2:1 1–16.

Apostle Paul teaches us in Galatians chapter 3 that we (Gentiles) become sons of Abraham through faith. In Galatians 3:14, Apostle Paul teaches us, "We [Gentiles] might receive the promise of the Spirit through faith. In Galatians chapter 3, Apostle Paul teaches us that to become a child of Abraham, you must be born-again. If you will just look at the opposite of being born-again, it can only be not born-again, and that means you are not grafted into the lineage of our Lord. Jesus says in John 3:5, "Verily, verily I say unto thee, Except a man be born of water and the Spirit, he cannot enter into the kingdom of God." When you RIGHTLY DIVIDE these scriptures and read them in their proper context, you will learn that if you are not born- again, you cannot go to heaven.

Being born-again is one of those kingdom rules that I wrote about that you must do.

As you know, everyone claims to have God's TRUTH. From Judaism, Buddhism, Muslim, Mormons, Catholics, Protestant, and especially the apostolic believers—all these different religions can't be right. I am an apostolic believer myself, because of what Jesus says in John 17:1–20 and all the other scriptures that teach us that we are to obey what the apostles taught. Remember the sinner will be judged from the apostles' writings. You had better become an apostolic believer and obey their teachings. Read 2 Thessalonians 1:7–10. The end of verse 10 says, "Because our testimony among you was believed in that day."

Remember in the first chapter, you learned about these three words, we, our, and us, that refer to the apostles. John says in 1 John 4:6, "We are of God: he that knoweth God heareth us; he that is not of God heareth not us. Hereby know we the Spirit of TRUTH, and the spirit of error." To tell you the TRUTH, what the apostles wrote in the scriptures are just as important as if it was the Lord Himself speaking to us. No matter who claims to have the TRUTH, if what they teach is not what the apostles taught, it is not the TRUTH. It is as simple as that.

Let's look at the scriptures and find God's plan of salvation just as the Lord revealed it to His apostles. Now, you have already learned about some of God's TRUTH, but this time, I am going to give you other scriptures that will help you understand more clearly. You first need to read Matthew 16:13–19. In these scriptures, you will find that the Lord gave Apostle Peter the keys to heaven. In verse 13, Jesus asked His disciples, "Whom do men say that I the Son of man am?" They began saying, "Some John the Baptist: some, Elias; and others, Jeremias, or one of the prophets."

Then, in verse 15, Jesus wants to know who they think He is and He asked them, "But whom say ye that I am?" In verse 16, Apostle Peter answers Jesus, saying, "Thou art the Christ, the Son of the living God." Then, in verse 17, Jesus looks at Peter and says, "Blessed art thou, Simon Barjona: for flesh and blood [no man] hath revealed unto thee, but my Father which is in heaven." Jesus continues speaking to Peter in verses 18–19 and says, "And I say also unto thee, That thou art Peter, and upon this rock I will build my church; and the gates of HELL shall not prevail against it. And I will give unto thee the keys of the kingdom of heaven. And whatsoever thou shalt bind on earth shall be bound in heaven. And whatsoever thou shalt loose on earth shall be loosed in heaven."

When reading these scriptures, you can see that at first, Jesus was talking to all of His Apostles, but then He turned His focus to Apostle Peter. There is a lot you can learn from these scriptures, but I want you to focus on Jesus giving Apostle Peter the keys to heaven. Soon, you will find out from God's word that Jesus was giving Peter His plan of salvation to start His church. When we get into the book of Acts, where God's plan of salvation is taught, you will learn how Apostle Peter opens three doors with the keys that Jesus gave him. But first, I want to set the scene so you can see where and how Jesus instructed His Apostles to start His church.

First, let's read again what I believe to be the most wrongfully used scripture in God's word. I know that we have read this scripture before, but if it is the most wrongfully used scripture in God's word, we must study it until we find God's TRUTH. These scriptures teach us what most Christians call the Great Commission. Jesus had just resurrected from His grave, and He commissioned His apostles to go and start His work on earth—in other words, start the church. These scriptures are found in Matthew 28:18–20. Jesus starts off by telling them, "All power is given unto me in heaven and in earth. Go ye therefore, and teach all nations, baptizing them in the name of the Father, and of the Son, and of the Holy Ghost. Teaching them to observe all things whatsoever I have command you: and, lo, I am with you alway unto the end of the world. Amen."

Here, Jesus didn't tell them where to go to start His church. You already know the importance of having the Holy Ghost/Comforter/ Jesus living inside of you to teach and guide you on your journey to heaven. Read John 14:26 again. As we RIGHTLY DIVIDE how and where the church started, you will hear God's TRUTH.

Now, let's read in the scriptures and learn what Mark wanted to share with us about that same day just before Jesus was taken up into heaven.

> And He [Jesus] said unto them, Go ye into all the world, and preach the gospel to every creature. He that believeth and is baptized shall be saved; but he that believeth not shall be damned. And these signs shall follow them that believe; In my name shall they cast out devils; they shall speak with new tongues; they shall take up serpents; and if they drink any deadly thing, it shall not hurt them; they shall lay hands on the sick, and they shall recover. (Mark 16:15–18)

Now, here, Mark added a little more to what Matthew recorded in his gospel. But neither Matthew nor Mark tell us where Jesus wanted them to go to start the church.

In the gospel of Luke, he gives us even more insight about the beginning of the church than any other person in the Bible. Read Luke 24:44–53. In verse 44, Jesus explained to His apostles the things that must be fulfilled in His life to bring salvation to the world. Jesus was making sure that His apostles knew who He is and that He was about to bring salvation to the world according to His word. I don't want to get too far off the main subject, but notice that in verse 45, Luke begins to speak, saying, "Then opened He their understanding, that they might understand the scriptures."

The New Testament was written by the apostles, and three of Jesus' disciples, which were Mark that wrote the gospel of Mark, and Jude Jesus' brother that wrote Jude. Luke was the third disciple, and he was chosen by Jesus to write the gospel of Luke and the book of Acts. Even though we are supposed to obey the apostles' teachings, we also must believe and obey what Luke recorded, just as if it were one of the apostles or Jesus, Himself, speaking to us. In verse 45, when Luke says, "Then opened He their understanding, that they might understand the scriptures," he was referring to the eleven apostles.

Then, Jesus begins to speak again in verses 46–48, saying, "Thus it is written, and thus it behooved Christ to suffer, and to rise from the dead the third day. And that repentance and remission of sins should be preached in His name among all nations, beginning at Jerusalem. And ye are witnesses of these things." In these verses, Jesus informed them and us about His death, burial, and resurrection; and He also teaches us that salvation is going to come to all nations through the name of Jesus. At the end of verse 47, Jesus teaches them and us that the church will begin at Jerusalem.

In verse 49, Jesus tells them, "And, behold, I send the promise of my Father upon you: but tarry ye in the city of Jerusalem, until ye be endued with power from on high." Here, Jesus tells His apostles that when they get to Jerusalem, they should not leave, because He is going to send the promise of my Father which is the Holy Ghost so they will have power to live victorious lives.

To find God's TRUTH that He wants to share with everyone who will learn and obey Him, we will have to go and read what Luke recorded in Acts chapters 1 and 2. But before we read God's TRUTH about the beginning of the church, I want to bring back your attention to Apostle Peter. The reason I want you to read these scriptures is because if you will remember, Jesus gave Peter the keys to heaven. Read John 21:15–17, and you will see that Jesus asked Peter three questions.

> So when they had dined, Jesus saith to Simon Peter, Simon, of Jonas, lovest thou me more than these? He saith unto Him, Yea Lord; thou knowest that I love thee. He [Jesus] saith unto him, Feed my lambs.
>
> He [Jesus] saith to him [Peter] the second time, Simon, of Jonas, lovest thou me? He [Peter] saith unto

Him, Yea, Lord; thou knowest that I love thee. He [Jesus] saith to him [Peter], Feed my sheep.

He [Jesus] saith to him [Peter] the third time, Simon, of Jonas, lovest thou me? Peter was grieved because Jesus said unto him the third time, Lovest thou me? And he said unto Him, Lord, thou knowest all things; thou knowest that I love thee. Jesus saith unto him, Feed my sheep. (Verses 15–17)

Now, I don't know the significance why Jesus asks Peter three times to feed His sheep, but He does.

We are about to read in the book of Acts and see where Apostle Peter opens the three doors to all three different types of people, who lives on earth.

First, let's read Luke 1:1–4. Now, as you read Acts 1:1, you will see that Luke also wrote the book of Acts because he was referring back to when he wrote the gospel of Luke. I want you to see the timeline from when Jesus was resurrected until the church began. From the beginning, there has been misconceptions of the timeline of Jesus' death, burial, and resurrection. Now, this is the TRUTH of the timeline when Jesus died and the beginning of the church. You should know this by now, but just in case you have forgotten, Saturday is the Sabbath.

You should read the whole chapter 19 of John, but at this time, I want you to read 19:31 and 42. You will learn that Jesus was crucified on Friday (preparation day) and buried that afternoon. There has been teachings that Jesus was in the grave for three days and nights, but that is false. Jesus says in Luke 24:7, "The Son of man must be delivered into the hands of sinful men, and be crucified, and the third day rise again." John 20:1 teaches us, "The first of the week cometh Mary Magdalene early, when it was yet dark, unto the sepulcher [grave], and seeth the stone taken away from the sepulcher.

These scriptures tell me that Jesus was in His grave Friday afternoon, Friday night, Saturday, and Saturday night. Then, He comes out of His grave early Sunday morning, which would be the third day, just as He said He would.

In John 20:17, Jesus tells Mary, "Touch me not; for I am not yet ascended to my Father." I believe that after Mary left Him, He ascended to heaven. In John 20:19, you will see that Jesus comes right back to earth to visit with His apostles. Now, I want you to read Acts 1:3, because Luke teaches us that after Jesus was resurrected, He came back to earth and was seen by His apostles forty days. He taught them things pertaining to the kingdom of God. In Acts 1:4–5, Jesus confirms to His apostles what He told them to do in Luke 24:46–49. In Acts 1:8, Jesus tells His apostles, "But ye shall receive power, after that the Holy Ghost is come upon you: and ye shall be witnesses unto me both in Jerusalem, and in all Judaea, and in Samaria, and unto the uttermost part of the earth"—and that means where you live. Verse 9 says, "And when He had spoken these things, while they beheld, He was taken up; and a cloud received Him out of their sight." These scriptures let us know that Jesus left earth on or just after the fortieth day and went to heaven to stay in His bodily form.

The reason I said He went to heaven to stay in His bodily form is because He was soon to return to earth to lead and guide His church in Spirit form (Holy Ghost). And as you can see in verse 12, the apostles went back to Jerusalem just as Jesus instructed them to. Verses 13–14 say that they went up into an upper room, and then, Luke records some of the names who was present for the first day of the Lord's church.

Then, verse 15 says, "Peter stood up in the midst of the disciples, and said, (the number of names together were about an hundred and twenty)." Do you remember when I wrote about this earlier in this book? I wrote that the way I believe God's word is when Peter says about a hundred and twenty; it was not an hundred and twenty. If

Peter would have said a hundred and twenty, it would have been a hundred and twenty, but he said about. So I believe there were 119 or 121 people at church that day, but the number of people that made it to church is not what we are looking for. We are looking and learning how they were born-again so we can obey the scriptures, just as they did. As you now know, there are many false churches in this world, but there is only one true church, and they are the people who obey God's TRUTH. In verses 16–19, Apostle Peter tells them and us how Judas betrayed the Lord and then committed suicide. In verses 20–26, Peter teaches us that Matthias was added to the eleven apostles to complete the twelve.

Now, we have gotten to the fiftieth day (day of Pentecost) after His resurrection. Acts chapter 1 didn't mention whether Luke was there, but he had to be there because he starts writing what he saw and heard in Acts chapter 2. In Acts 2:1–11, Luke describes how the church (people) were born-again, and if you didn't achieve your salvation in the same manner as they did, you are not born-again no matter who you are. Notice that in chapter 1, Jesus' mother had to go to church that day and be born-again.

If you don't already know this, you are about to learn something that most people don't know. Acts 2:1 says, "And when the day of Pentecost was fully come, they were all with one accord in one place." When you read verses 2–4, I also want you to read John 3:1–8. Here is where you need to listen really closely with you spiritual ears. If you RIGHTLY DIVIDE these scriptures, you will see that what Jesus said to Nicodemus in John 3:1–8 was being fulfilled at church that day.

Jesus said in verse 8, "The wind bloweth where it listeth [will], and thou hearest the sound thereof, but canst not tell whence it cometh, and whither it goeth." Listen really closely to the end of this scripture, because Jesus says, "So is every one that is born of the Spirit." There are people who will try and tell you that speaking in tongues is of the devil, but I want you to read Acts 2:11 again.

Jesus plainly teaches us in John 3:8 that everyone is born of the Spirit will speak in tongues. God's word teaches us that when a person is born- again, they will speak in a known tongue, and these scriptures are really clear about this. Now, this is clear to me what Jesus taught, and if it's not clear to you, simply ask Jesus to reveal His TRUTH to you.

Read Luke 24:45 again. If Jesus had to open their (the apostles) understanding, He will have to open yours also.

The TRUTH is God's word comes to us by revelation—period. As we go through the second chapter of the book of Acts, the Lord will teach you His plan of salvation. But I must warn those who don't know about Acts chapter 2 that you are about to learn how the church started and you are going to read about one of the HOTTEST church services ever.

To my knowledge, there are four different kinds of tongues the Lord allows His church to use, when communicating with Him. Later in this chapter, I plan to explain those four different kinds of tongues. But for now, I must explain what I believe to be the second kind of tongues, and they are the tongues mentioned here in Acts 2:3–4.

> And there were dwelling at Jerusalem Jews, devout men, out of every nation under heaven. Now when this [them speaking in tongues] was noised a broad, the multitude came together, and were confounded, because that every man heard them speak in his own language. And they were all amazed and marveled, saying one to another, behold, are not all these which speak Galileans? And how hear we every man in our own tongue, wherein we were born? (Verses 5–8)

As you can see in verse 3, the "cloven tongues like as of fire, and it sat upon each of them." Verse 4 says, "And they were All filled with the Holy Ghost, and began to speak with other tongues, as the Spirit gave them utterance." Even though these scriptures are this clear, the Lord must reveal this TRUTH to you, or you will never hear it. In verses 9–11, Luke records the different nations that were there that day. And as I have said earlier, the end of verse 11 says that when these different nations heard them speaking in their own language, they said that it was the wonderful works of God.

All these nations came to Jerusalem for the Passover Feast, and they were caught up in one of the HOTTEST church services known to man. Verses 12–13 say, "And they were all amazed, and were in doubt, saying one to another, What meaneth this? Others mocking said, these men are full of new wine." Notice in the last sentence that they began to say that the church was drunk on new wine. And when they began to say that, those words got the apostles' attention.

Verses 14–15 say that Peter standing up "with the eleven, and lifted up his voice, and said unto them, Ye men of Judaea, and all that dwell at Jerusalem, be this known unto you, and hearken to my words. For these are not drunken, as ye suppose, seeing it is the third hour [9:00 a.m.] of the day." Now, notice in that scripture, Apostle Peter didn't say that they were not drunk. As a matter of fact, he told me that they were drunk when he said they "are not drunken, as ye suppose." Peter was simply saying that the church was drunk on the Spirit of God.

Now, I want to ask you a couple of questions. What did the multitude of people see and hear that made them think that they were drunk? I believe that they were loud, and as you now know, you can get loud with the Lord, and it's okay. I know for sure that they all were speaking with other tongues. What are the signs of being drunk? Maybe stumbling around, crying, and laughing! I believe that most of the people were shouting and dancing around, because God's Spirit just entered into them, and for the first time, they felt the love and power of God Almighty deep in their souls.

When you go to your first HOT church service, you too will think that they are all drunk—I know I did. But when you step out there by faith and join in with the move of God's Spirit, the next person who visits your church will think that you are drunk. And you will be, but not on wine. You can only imagine what you will do when the Holy Ghost enters into your body to live. It is truly unspeakable joy and full of glory. You must experience this to get to heaven. Read John 3:5 again. I want you to know this—the Lord has chosen the foolish things of this world to confound the wise. Read 1 Corinthians 1:27.

In Acts 2:16, Peter tells them, and us, "But this is what the Prophet Joel prophesied would happen." Then, in verses 17–20, Luke records what Joel wrote in his book. And as you now know, these onetime events will start when Jesus opens the sixth seal. Read Revelation 6:12–13. Then Peter begins to preach to them in Acts 2:22–41. Remember Jesus gave Apostle Peter the keys to heaven, and as you can see, Peter preaches the first message to the people in Jerusalem. As you RIGHTLY DIVIDE these scriptures, you will find that Peter was not just preaching to the 119–121 people who came to church that day. He was also preaching to the multitude outside of the building, and now to us, if we can hear him.

You need to read all of these scriptures, but I'm going to start explaining the scriptures, starting from verse 37.

Verses 37 tell us that when they heard what Apostle Peter was preaching, "They were pricked in their heart, and said unto Peter and to the rest of the apostles, Men, brethren, what shall we do?" Notice that in verse 37, the multitude asked all of the apostles how to receive forgiveness for their sinful ways.

In verse 38, Apostle Peter answers them because he has the keys to heaven. You are about to see in the scriptures that Peter is going to open the door of salvation for the Jews so they can go to heaven. Just remember that if they don't obey God's TRUTH after they hear it, their eternal home will be the other place (HELL). Peter tells the multitude in verse 38, "Repent, and be baptized every one of you in the name of Jesus Christ for the remission of sins, and ye shall receive the gift of the Holy Ghost." Here, Peter told them specific things to do to be saved (born-again). Even though Peter was speaking to the Jews, this same salvation (TRUTH) is what we (Gentiles) must obey, if we want to go to heaven.

Now, I know that I have written about Matthew 28:19 a few times in this book. But I must write about it one more time, because in this scripture, Jesus teaches a part of His salvation plan if you obey it. Again, I will say that I believe Matthew 28:19 is the most wrongfully used scripture from God's word. Jesus never told any preacher to repeat this scripture, when they baptize someone. As you study the book of Acts, you will see that every time someone is baptized, they were baptized in the name of Jesus.

As I have said before, billions have been wrongly baptized, because they don't understand these scriptures. God's TRUTH comes through revelation from the Spirit of God. When you RIGHTLY DIVIDE these scriptures (Matthew 28:19 and Acts 2:38), you will learn that Acts 2:38 is what Jesus told His apostles to DO in Matthew 28:19. In Acts 2:38, Apostle Peter tells the Jews that day "to repent, and be baptized every one of you in the name of Jesus Christ for the remission of sins." Please hear these four words (ever one of you).

The apostles knew that Jesus is the Father of creation. Read John 1:1–14 with spiritual ears. And they knew that Jesus is the Son of redemption. Read Matthew 1:21 with spiritual ears. And they also knew that Jesus was going to return to earth as the Holy Ghost to teach and guide us through this world victorious over Satan. Read John 14:26. God is the Father, the Son, and the Holy Ghost; and His name is Jesus. Just as I'm a father, a son, and an uncle, but my name is Jessie. I am not three separate persons, and God is not either. Read Romans 1:20. There will be no excuse for not knowing about the Godhead (Father, Son, and the Holy Ghost). Let's read

Colossians 2:8–10, and see what Apostle Paul teaches us about the Godhead. Verses 9–10 say, "For in Him [Christ] dwelleth all the fullness of the Godhead bodily. And ye are complete in Him, which is the head of all principality and power. Notice that in verse 10, the word says Him—it does not say them.

At this time, I want to give you a few examples from God's word that teach us Jesus is God when walking this earth and living the life of a man. My first example comes from a man who personally knew Jesus, and his name is Thomas. Read John 20:24–31. Through the years, Thomas has been called by most preachers as the "Doubting Thomas" because of this story. In verse 26, Thomas only doubted for eight days. But that is not what I want you to see from this story (TRUTH).

The scriptures before verse 24 teach us that Jesus came after His resurrection and met with the other disciples. As they tried to convince Thomas that they had seen the Lord, he plainly tells them, "Except I shall see in His hands the print of the nails, and put my finger into the print of the nails, and trust my hand into His side, I will not believe."

Verse 26 says, "And after eight days again His disciples were within, and Thomas with them." Notice that in this scripture, it says that Jesus was able to enter that room even though the doors were shut (locked) "and stood in the midst, and said, Peace unto you." Again, this is not what I want you to hear from this scripture, but I want to tell you what I believe about entering into a room while the doors are locked. I have already told you this before, about how the Lord has teleported me two different times in the past thirty-four years. I believe when we get to heaven, this will be the way we travel. You cannot tell me that the Lord doesn't teleport some of His people, because I have experienced this unexplainable method of travel twice in my life.

The dictionary defines teleport as "(esp. in science fiction) transport or be transported across space and distance instantly." In a couple of pages from now, I'm going to write about Philip baptizing the eunuch, but for now, I want you to only read Acts 8:39–40. I believe that Philip was teleported from the desert, where he had just baptized the eunuch to the city of Azotus.

In John 20:27, Jesus says to Thomas, "Reach hither thy finger, and behold my hands; and reach hither thy hand, and thrust into my side: and be not faithless, but believing." Now, the Bible never says this, but reading between the lines before Thomas says what is written in verse 28, I have always had a vision of Thomas falling on his knees and bowing before he said, "My Lord and my God." If Jesus is Apostle Thomas' God, we had better make Jesus our God. In verse 29, Jesus tells Thomas and us to believe. Jesus says, "Thomas, because thou hast seen me, thou hast believed: blessed they that have not seen, and have believed." If you don't believe that Jesus is God, you had better start.

Jesus gives this revelation to John in Revelation 1:8. Jesus tells John, "I AM Alpha and Omega, the beginning and the ending." Then, John finishes this verse by saying, "Which is, and which was, and which is to come, the Almighty." Here, John called Jesus the Almighty. Thomas and John knew who they served—we had better know who we serve.

I want to give you one more example before going back to God's plan of salvation, because until you know who Jesus is, you won't understand Matthew 28:19 (baptizing them in the name of the Father, and of the Son, and of the Holy Ghost.) Do you remember that I wrote about Job seeing God, and I couldn't explain how? I believe I know how because God is God, and He can reveal Himself to whomsoever He wants to. In this next set of scriptures, you will see (hear) what I'm talking about. Read Matthew 17:1–9. To most preachers, this mountain is called the Mount of Transfiguration. The dictionary defines transfiguration as "a complete change of form or appearance into a more beautiful or spiritual state." Here is a good question to you who don't know. What do you believe Jesus changed into that day? I will tell you what I don't believe. He didn't change into a German shepherd or a chicken. He revealed Himself (God) to His apostles. In John 10:30, Jesus said, "I and Father are one." You must learn this fact to be able to obey His word.

Now, if you believe that you can be baptized some other way than what the man who has the keys to heaven tells you, you are foolishly mistaken. Just as you learned that the Mormons, Muslims, and all the other false churches didn't have the right to change God's word, you don't either. It is as simple as this. Go to a church that teaches God's TRUTH, and be baptized in the name of Jesus and receive the baptism of the Holy Ghost with the evidence of speaking in other tongues. And you will be born-again, just as the Apostle Peter taught.

Now, speaking in other tongues is the initial evidence for man to know that a person has been baptized with the Holy Ghost. But living for the Lord is what man and God really looks at in a Christian. While reading this book, you (the reader) have heard God's true plan of salvation a few times, and it is up to you if you obey it or not. As you can clearly see, it takes all four steps for salvation—and they are to repent, be baptized in the name of Jesus, be reborn by the Holy Ghost, and serve the Lord and your fellow man. If you do these four steps toward the next life, you will find life, because Jesus is Life. And if you don't do these four steps toward the next life, you will find death (HELL). I can't say it any plainer than that, and that goes for every person who has walked this earth, since Jesus died on the cross. I don't mean to sound so harsh, but what I have written is the TRUTH. Believe it or not, I'm speaking the TRUTH in love, trying to get you to hear God's TRUTH. I didn't make these kingdom rules, but I must obey them, just as you have too, if you want to make heaven your eternal home.

Here is a good example about God's plan of salvation. In Acts 2:38–39, Apostle Peter told the multitude that day God's plan of salvation. In verses 40–47, you will find the example I referred to.

Verse 41 says, "Then they that gladly received his [Peter's] word were baptized: and the same day there were added about three thousand souls." Verse 42 says, "And they [the three thousand people] continued steadfastly in the apostles' doctrine." In the first part of verse 42, these three thousand people were born-again, just as the Apostle Peter taught them.

I want to ask you a question, and you don't even have to use your spiritual mind to answer it. Verse 47 says that the Lord added to the church daily such as should be saved. Do you honestly believe that the apostles taught another plan of salvation to be saved? You need to read Galatians 1:6–9 until you hear the TRUTH about who the teachers of God's plan of salvation are. As I have said so many times in this book, God's TRUTH comes by revelation, and you must ask Jesus for His TRUTH.

Man has changed God's TRUTH, but until the last person is born-again on this earth, Jesus will not change His plan of salvation. As a matter of fact, I believe His plan of salvation will be put in heaven's history book as the TRUTH and never be used again in the future. His plan of salvation is the same as on the first day of His church, until the end of this world. I just don't know why it's so hard to see this, but billions have died not knowing His TRUTH, and there is only one way to put it with my limited vocabulary. They were blind as a bat—again, harsh but true. The TRUTH is man has changed God's TRUTH to fit their lives, but we must change to fit God's TRUTH.

You have already read this scripture a couple of times from God's word, but I believe you need to read it again. Read 2 Corinthians 4:1–4. Just in case you have forgotten, Satan is the god of this world. If you don't believe this, just look and listen to what is going on around you each day. Just remember that you can rebuke Satan in the name of Jesus and begin praying and asking Jesus to reveal the glorious gospel of Christ who is the image of God to shine upon you and your family. And He will!

You should know God's plan of salvation by now, and I should be able to start writing about predestination and the Book of Life. But I am going to give you more scriptures to help you understand that God's plan of salvation is the same today as the first day it started. Next, you are going to learn a little about the Samaritans and how they received God's TRUTH (plan of salvation). I said in chapter 1 that I would explain in this chapter what I know about the Samaritans.

Now, what I have learned about the Samaritans is very little, but I do know how they were saved (born-again). Let's first find out what I learned in my studies about them. As you study their history, you can only read from what other people before us wrote. The Samaritans are a mix-breed between an Israelite/Jew and a Gentile. And if that is true, I see why the Jews would look at the Samaritans the way they do. What I found was that the Samaritans claimed to be a remnant of the kingdom of Israel. They claimed to have come from the tribes of Manasseh and Ephraim. If you will read Genesis 41:50–52, you will learn who Manasseh and Ephraim are. These scriptures teach us that Manasseh and Ephraim are the first two sons of Joseph, which would make them Jacob's (Israel's) grandsons.

Now, if the Samaritans are from the tribes of Manasseh and Ephraim, their claim to be a remnant of the kingdom of Israel would be true, because their grandfather was Jacob. John 4:3–29 tells us that Jesus goes through Samaria and talks to a woman of that city. In verse 5, Jesus came to the city of Sychar, near a parcel of ground that Jacob gave to his son Joseph. Verse 6 says that Jacob had a well there. And as you would know, there would be the place that Jesus would meet this Samaritan woman.

In verse 7, Jesus asked the woman for a drink. In verse 9, she says to Jesus, "How is it that thou, being a Jew, asketh drink of me, which am a woman of Samaria? For the Jews have no dealings with the Samaritans." She knew that there was something standing between the Jews and the Samaritans. As you can see, I'm skipping through these scriptures trying to help you understand that this Samaritan woman was claiming to be the descendants of Jacob.

I'm going to come back to verse 10, but first I want to tell you about verse 12. After Jesus finishes telling her about giving her Living Water, in verse 12, she says to Him, "Art thou greater than our father Jacob, which gave us the well, and drank thereof himself, and his children, and his cattle?" Now, in this stage of your studying of God's word, you know that Jesus knows about everyone and everything. As you read this story, you will see that Jesus knew all about her.

I believe that Jesus would have corrected her in verse 12 if she was not a descendant of Jacob, when she made that claim. Because if you will remember, Jesus is a descendant of Jacob. Read Matthew 1:1–16. If you will look at the end of verse 2, you will see that it says, "And Jacob begat Judas and his brethren." Remember what you learned about the twelve tribes of Israel (Jacob) and that there will be twelve thousand from each tribe that will be saved during the tribulation period. In verse 2, you can see that Jesus come from the tribe of Judas, but you had better believe He knows who His kinfolks are. Jesus would have known if this Samaritan woman was his kin.

Look in John 4:10 and see what Jesus asked her, "If thou knewest the gift of God, and who it is that saith to thee." In the next few scriptures, she is about to find out who Jesus is. After He tells her in verse 18 about her five husbands, she says to Him in verse 19, "Sir, I perceive that thou art a prophet." She just didn't know who she was talking to, but she is about to. Her Creator was staring at her in the face. Verse 25 tells us that the Samaritans believed in the coming of the Messiah. In verse 26, Jesus plainly tells her that He is the Messiah. As you can see by the beliefs of this Samaritan woman that the Samaritans were taught some of the Jewish beliefs.

Being a mix-breed is what separated the Jews and the Samaritans, look what Jesus tells her in verse 22, "Ye worship ye know not what.

We know what we worship for salvation is of the Jews." Read Matthew 10:1–6. Jesus looked upon the Samaritans differently than the Jews, even though they claimed to be of the tribe of Israel (Jacob). Read John 8:48, and you will see that the Jewish leaders of that time even called Jesus a Samaritan.

To tell you the TRUTH, I have not studied a whole lot about the Samaritans. If you want to study about them, I'm sure you can find the TRUTH about them in God's word. I already know what I want to know about them. What really matters to me is I know how they were born-again. In Acts chapter 8, Luke recorded how, when, and where, the Samaritans were born-again.

At the end of Acts chapter 7, you will find that a disciple named Stephen was stoned to death. He was killed by the crowd that day, because the message that he was preaching was the TRUTH and they could not stand it. At the end of verse 58, you will see that the name Saul was mentioned. Read Acts 8:1 where you will see that Saul consented (agreed) unto his death. We are going to come back and read from chapter 8, but first I want you to read Acts 9:1–2. As you read these two scriptures, you will see that Saul was persecuting the church.

You have already learned about Saul earlier in this book and how the Lord changed his name to Paul, who wrote more than half of the New Testament. Just remember that it's not what you used to be—it is what you allow the Lord to make you that counts. To know how Saul (Paul) was saved, you need to read Acts 9:1–22. As you read these scriptures, you will not find in them where Apostle Paul was baptized in Jesus name or spoke in other tongues when he was filled with the Holy Ghost. But he did, because it is God's plan of salvation. Soon, I am going to give you some scriptures where Apostle Paul teaches God's plan of salvation, and the only way he would know what he was teaching, he had to experience it (God's plan of salvation) himself. I can't teach you how to fly an airplane because I've never flew one, but I can show you where to find the scriptures that teach God's plan of salvation.

Now, let's go back to Acts 8:3–4 and learn a little more about Saul. As you can see in these scriptures, there was so much persecution in Jerusalem, and the apostles were scattered abroad and went everywhere preaching the word. Verse 5 says, "Then Philip went down to the city of Samaria, and preached Christ unto them." If you will read verses 6–13, you will learn of the miracles that the Lord did through Philip. You will also learn about a man named Simon, who had a change of heart.

> Now, when the apostles which were at Jerusalem heard that Samaria had received the word of God, they sent unto them Peter and John. [Here comes Apostle Peter with the keys to heaven.] Who, when they were come down, prayed for them, that they might receive the Holy Ghost. (For as yet he [the Holy Ghost] was fallen upon none of them: only they were baptized in the name of the Lord Jesus.) Then laid they hands on them, and they received the Holy Ghost. (Acts 8:14–17)

In verse 18, you will see that Simon saw that through laying on of the apostles' hands, the Holy Ghost was given, he offered them money. He began to see a way to make some money, coupled with his business of sorcery. These scriptures never say that the Samaritans spoke in other tongues. But notice that when they received the Holy Ghost, Simon pulled out his billfold and offered Peter and John money to show him how to do this to others.

Now, here is the TRUTH that I see in this scripture. What Simon saw that day was an outward manifestation of the Holy Ghost. Just as what happened on the first day of God's church, the Samaritans who received the Holy Ghost were speaking in other tongues, as God gave them utterance, besides some other acts they might have been displaying. I know that this is what happened that day, because I know God's word and I know that He would not have His apostles teach any other teaching than what they started teaching.

If you will read the rest of chapter 8, you will learn about another born- again experience. But as you are going to learn, it is conjecture, because we do not have all of the story. We must believe the Lord is not going to start something that He does not finish. Read Acts 8:26–40, and you will see that the Lord sent Philip on another mission. In verse 26, the Lord sent him to the desert. In verse 27, Philip listened to the angel, because he arose and went. The Lord had a man that was traveling through the desert, and He wanted His TRUTH to spread to Ethiopia and beyond.

Notice that at the end of verse 27, the Ethiopian eunuch had come to Jerusalem to worship. Not even using spiritual discernment, just common sense tells me that if he had been in Jerusalem to worship, he saw and heard about Jesus. When reading these scriptures, you can clearly see that the Lord put all of this in action to save the Ethiopian eunuch.

In verse 34, the eunuch asked Philip an important question. Who is the Prophet Isaiah talking about, himself or some other man, for the eunuch was reading Isaiah 53:7.

Acts 8:35 says, "Then Philip opened his mouth, and began at the same scripture, and preached unto him Jesus." In verse 36, you can see that the Lord even provided the eunuch the water in the desert so he could be baptized. The end of verse 38 says that Philip baptized the eunuch. These scriptures never mention that the eunuch was baptized in the name of Jesus, nor did they teach that he was born of the Holy Ghost with the evidence of speaking with other tongues. This is just the way the Lord had the apostles write His word so we would have to seek Him for the TRUTH.

I just can't believe that the Lord would put all these actions in place to save the eunuch and not give him His Spirit. The Lord would not have left this eunuch half born; He would have completed his birth.

Verse 39 says, "When they were come up out of the water, the Spirit of the Lord caught away [teleported] Philip, that the eunuch saw him no more: and he went on his way rejoicing." I believe the key word in the last sentence is rejoicing. I believe the eunuch had a reason to rejoice, because he had been born-again.

Now, let's find out how the Gentiles were born-again. You will find how the Gentiles were saved in Acts chapter 10. Verse 1 teaches us the name of the first Gentile man to receive God's plan of salvation, and his name was Cornelius. Verse 2 tells us why the Lord chose him. This scripture says that Cornelius was devout, and him and his whole house feared God. And he also gave much alms (money) to the people, and he prayed to God alway.

In verse 3, you will learn what praying always to God can get you. Cornelius was blessed with a vision and saw an angel of God that the Lord sent to instruct him what he and his family must do to be saved. When reading verse 4, I want to bring this point out of this scripture. The angel tells Cornelius, "Thy prayers and thine alms are come up for a memorial before God." The point I want to make is if being good could get us to heaven, Cornelius would have made heaven with flying colors. But you are about to find out that Cornelius has to be born-again, just like everyone else who lives during the New Testament era.

In verse 5, you will learn that the angel tells Cornelius to send men to Joppa and ask for Peter. In verse 6, the angel tells Cornelius, "He [Peter] shall tell thee what thou oughtest to do." Before I go any further with this story (TRUTH), I want to inform you what I haven't done in this book. I haven't told you to go to any certain church (assembly), because that has nothing to do with me—that is the Lord's business, and He will put you where He wants you. I have only told you to ask Jesus to send you to an apostolic church so you can be fed with the milk and meat of His word. But if you ever find yourself in a church that doesn't teach what you have learned from God's word, LEAVE IMMEDIATELY.

As you continue reading Acts chapter 10, it is so clear how the Lord puts into motion the right people, or angel, to put Cornelius on the right path to His plan of salvation. I want to share with you how the Lord visited me for the first time and set in motion his plan of salvation for me and my family. I'm going to tell you some things that I haven't talked about very much through the years, and some of it may sound funny to some of you, but it was not funny to me that day.

One summer day in 1976, James Taylor (not the singer) came to where I was staying. At that time, I was staying with my sister, brother-in-law, and Amy. James was my brother-in-law's brother, and during that time (1976), the Lord was truly working in their lives. When James and his wife came to our apartment that day, he simply asked me and my girlfriend (now wife) if we wanted to pray. I didn't know about Cindy, but I was not used to praying. But we agreed to kneel down at the coffee table, and they prayed and laid hands on us for the first time.

That day, I experienced a move of God's Spirit that I had never felt before. Although it has been so many years later and it's hard to remember all that went on that day, I do remember what I did. After they prayed—notice that I said after they prayed—we got up, and I went to the bathroom. Not only did I need to compose myself, but also I needed to use the bathroom. It's always been my habit to lock the door, and I did. Not long ago, I wrote about Jesus and His meeting with Thomas, and if you will recall, the doors were locked also; but those locked doors didn't stop Jesus from coming in to Thomas. I learned about Jesus and locked doors when I was twenty-one years old. Jesus didn't appear in human form, as he did to Thomas, but that same Jesus came into the bathroom with me in Spirit form. No locked door or sheetrock could stop Him!

I'm about to admit to something that very few people know. As I was trying to use the bathroom (urinate), the Holy Ghost filled the bathroom. I don't never use the word urinate, so I'm going to say what I did. As I was trying to see behind me, I peed all over the toilet and floor. To tell you the TRUTH, the Lord scared the piss out of me. After I got a little bit control of myself, I cleaned up the mess that I made and got out of there. I don't remember all that went on that day, but we did leave and moved to Louisiana. The Lord continued dealing with me, and finally, seven years later (1983), I surrendered. I don't know why, but I just had to do it the hard way. I should have been like Cornelius and followed the Lord from the beginning. I am so thankful the Lord didn't give up on me.

What I want you to learn from this and Cornelius' story is that the Lord will put in motion the right people for you to hear His plan of salvation (TRUTH). If you will just look at what you are reading, God has already started working on you, trying to show you His TRUTH. God's TRUTH has come to your eyes, ears, and mind and will be in your heart, if you will obey it.

Now, let's go back to Acts chapter 10 and see how the Lord puts everything in motion to bring salvation to Cornelius (us the Gentiles). Verses 7–8 say that after the angel left Cornelius, he called two of his servants and a devout soldier and told them what they should say and do and then sent them to Joppa to find Peter.

Verse 9 says, the next day as they went on their journey, they drew near to Joppa. And as you can see at the end of verse 9, the Lord was getting Peter ready spiritually. Peter went to pray about the sixth hour (12:00 p.m.). In verse 10, Peter became very hungry and would have eaten, but while they made ready, he fell into a trance. In verses 11–16, the Lord shows Peter three times in the vision "all manner of fourfooted beasts of the earth, and wild beasts, and creeping things, and fowls of the air." Then the Lord tells Peter, "Kill, and eat." But Peter said, "Not so, Lord; for I have never eaten anything that is common or unclean." Verse 15 says that the voice unto him again the second time, "What God hath cleansed, call not thou common."

Verse 16 says that this was done three times. To someone who doesn't read and study God's word and don't know the TRUTH, they will think that the Lord was showing Peter a menu. The Lord already knew that the Jews only ate certain food and how the Jews felt about the Gentiles. The TRUTH is the Lord was preparing Peter to share His TRUTH with the Gentiles, and the Lord knew that Peter had to be taught all men are equal. Meanwhile as Peter thought about what the vision should mean, the three men that Cornelius sent were knocking on the gate where Peter was staying. In verse 19, the Lord informs Peter that these three men seek thee.

The Lord tells Peter in verse 20, "Arise therefore, and get down thee, and go with them, doubting nothing, for I have sent them." In verses 21–23, Peter and some of his friends went with these three men back to Cornelius' house. Verses 24–26 say that Cornelius waited for them and had called together his kinsmen and near friends. And as Peter was coming in, Cornelius met him and fell down at his feet and worshipped. But Peter took him up, saying, "Stand up; I myself also am a man." In verse 28, Peter learned what the Lord wanted him to learn about non-Jewish people. Peter tells Cornelius in verse 28, "Ye know how that it is an unlawful thing for a man that is a Jew to keep company, or come unto one of another nation; but God hath shewed me that I should not call any man common or unclean."

In verses 29–33, Peter and Cornelius tell each other how they were brought to each other. At the end of verse 33, Cornelius says to Peter, "We are here to hear all things that are commanded thee of God." Now, that is what Peter had been wanting to hear, and he begins to preach God's TRUTH to them. In verses 34–35, the first thing Peter tells them is "of a TRUTH, I perceive that God is no respecter of persons." Then, Peter says, "But in every nation he that feareth Him, and worketh righteousness, is accepted with Him."

In verses 39–40, as Apostle Peter preached, he came to where he began telling them about Jesus being crucified and being raised on the third day from the grave. Then, in verse 43, Peter says, "To him give all the prophets witness, that through His name whosoever believeth in Him shall receive remission of sins." Verses 44–45 say, "While Peter yet spake these words, the Holy Ghost fell on all of them which heard the word. And they of the circumcision [Jews] which believed were astonished, as many as came with Peter, because that on the Gentiles also was poured out the gift of the Holy Ghost."

You can find the answer to the question in verse 46 as to how they knew that Cornelius, his family, and friends received the Holy Ghost. Verse 46 says, "For they heard them speak with tongues, and magnify God." Then Peter said in verse 47, "Can any man forbid water, that these should not be baptized, which have received the Holy Ghost as well as we?" You can clearly see in verse 48 that Peter commanded them to be baptized in the name of the Lord to complete their born-again experience. I want you to see in verse 47 that Apostle Peter says, "These Gentiles have received the Holy Ghost, just as we did on the day of Pentecost."

Read Acts 11:1–18, and you can hear this TRUTH again, because when Peter went back to Jerusalem, he had to explain what he and the Lord had accomplished with the Gentiles. I'm going to say this as clear as I can.

Verses 14–15 say, "Who [Peter] shall tell thee words, whereby thou and all thy house shall be saved. And as I began to speak, the Holy Ghost fell on them, as on us at the beginning." Peter just clearly told everyone who can understand the scriptures that this is God's plan of salvation for everyone. If you believe that you have been saved, and you have not been born-again according to God's plan of salvation, you're not saved. In chapter 1, I let you fill in the blank spaces, but I will fill in the blanks this time. You *are not* born-again.

Here is something that happened back in 1989. We lived about a quarter of a mile off the main road, and our two children were in the second and third grades. I hardly ever went to pick them up, but this day, I did. At the end of our driveway was the Bethel Road Assembly of God, which is now called the Branch Assembly of God, in Olive Branch, Mississippi.

I have forgotten the pastor's name, but as I sat in my truck waiting for my son and daughter's bus, the pastor came out of the church and talked with me. I don't mean to sound arrogant or boastful in any way, but that pastor didn't get to say too much, because I was speaking the TRUTH and telling him about how Peter was given the keys to heaven. He already knew that Jesus gave Apostle Peter the keys to the kingdom of heaven.

But he had never RIGHTLY DIVIDED the scriptures and heard how Peter opened up the doors for the Jews in Acts chapter 2, the Samaritans in Acts chapter 8, and the Gentiles in Acts chapter 10.

As I told him how Peter had to be there to open those three doors, the Spirit moved on him, and he heard God's TRUTH for the first time. He simply said, "I have never heard the word of God explained to me like that." I never seen or talked to him again, but I believe he taught what he learned that day to his congregation. I hope he gets the chance to read this book, because there is so much more written in this book that he needs to learn. If he ever reads this book, he will remember our talk that day.

He invited me to come to their church, but I told him that I was already going to a church. To tell you the TRUTH, I would not have gone to their church, because they don't teach God's TRUTH, referring to God's plan of salvation. Now, don't get me wrong—I believe that there are some people in that assembly who will eventually come to the knowledge of God's TRUTH. But as of that day, that church was still blinded by Satan. Read again 2 Corinthians 4:4.

Now, they believe in speaking in tongues when a person receives the Holy Ghost, and they worship the Lord just as the apostolic churches do. But they believe in the Trinity; and they, just like all the other false-doctrine churches, baptize their members by quoting Matthew 28:19 instead of doing what that scripture says to do. Most all of, the false-doctrine churches pray over their food in the name of Jesus. They will pray for their sick in the name of Jesus. As a matter of fact, most of them do everything in the name of Jesus, but when they come to baptism, they all begin to crawfish. Jesus says in John 4:23, "But the hour cometh, and now is, when the true worshippers shall worship the Father in Spirit and in TRUTH for the Father seeketh such to worship Him." There is a TRUTH to learn from this verse.

I am not speaking about all the false churches, but I am speaking of the Assembly of God and the Church of God churches. I believe that there are some members of those churches who have been baptized in the Holy Ghost with the evidence of speaking in other tongues, but they still need to be baptized in the name of Jesus to complete their born-again experience. But until they come to the knowledge (God reveals it to them) that Jesus is the Father, and the Son, and the Holy Ghost, they will continue in what they believe. But I know that the Lord is calling His people from these churches because He is not going to have some half-born Christians. Believe me, when the Lord starts something, He finishes it. The Assembly of God and the Church of God members must seek the Lord for His TRUTH. If you belong to one of these churches, I believe that you are over halfway there, but you must seek Jesus to reveal Himself to you and your assemblies.

I have written about some things in God's word that are conjecture, because we don't have enough TRUTH (scriptures) to make an infallible proof, about that particular subject. Here is a good example of what I'm talking about. If you will read Revelation 10:1–4, you will find a conjecture. Notice that in verse 4, as John started to write, a voice came from heaven and said, "Seal up those things which the seven thunders uttered, and write them not." I believe that there are very few people, if any, who know what the thunders uttered that day. There are no other scriptures to refer to, to make an infallible proof of what they said.

There are just some things that the Lord didn't want us to know. And as you now know, the Bible is written in such a way that we must read and study God's word and RIGHTLY DIVIDE it to find TRUTH. And only the Holy Ghost can teach us TRUTH and reveal to us the things concerning Himself, heaven, and the church, because He is the TRUTH. Through His word, and by His Spirit, only He can teach us what happened in the past and what is happening in our present. And anyone will tell you that only the Lord can teach us about our future. I just have to say it one more time, before I finish writing this book. Read John 14:26.

In this chapter, I have been writing how God's word teaches us to be born-again. And I have given you plenty of scriptures with infallible proof, proving that God's plan of salvation is not conjecture. Now, Satan has deceived man in believing a false doctrine, but the Lord has clearly given the whole world His plan of salvation. And it is up to you to receive it or reject it, when His TRUTH comes to you. I'm about to say something that is harsh, but it is true. I'm going to give you one more example about how God's plan of salvation is achieved, and if you don't hear it this time, you just might never hear it.

Before I give you the last example, I want to share something with all the John 3:16 salvation believers.

In the last example of how to achieve God's plan of salvation, you will learn that there is way more than just believing. I shouldn't have to quote this scripture, but there could be some people who never heard of it. In John 3:16, Jesus says, "For God so loved the world that He gave His only begotten Son that, whosoever believeth in Him should not perish but have everlasting life." As I have said a few times in this book, I believe that Matthew 28:19 is the most wrongfully used (taught) scripture from God's word as preachers baptize their members by quoting Matthew 28:19 and not actually obeying it. And I also believe that John 3:16 is the second most falsely taught (used) scripture from God's word.

For the John 3:16 salvation believers, you can lift a drunken street bum's head from off the street and ask him or her if they believe in Jesus, and nine times out of ten, they would say yes. But I'm here to tell you God's TRUTH; there is way more to do than just believe. I want you to remember what you read in 2 Corinthians 4:4 about Satan being the god of this world. When the John 3:16 salvation believers believed that all they had to do is believe, I believe Satan blinded them, because if they would have kept reading the gospel of John, they would have heard God's TRUTH.

I truly know how you feel. When I was a teenager, I believed myself to be a Baptist. And at that Baptist church, not only did they teach the John 3:16 salvation (just believe), but also they taught that when a person was baptized, they were making an outward confession of their faith. Some man or Satan made up that lie, because that teaching does not come from God's word. Thank God He called me out of that false teaching and taught me His TRUTH. When I heard God's plan of salvation, I just had to obey it, and so does everyone else, IF you want to be a part of God's church.

IF you will continue reading John's gospel, you will find God's TRUTH about just believing. In John 7:38, Jesus says a mouthful, "He that believeth on me, as the scripture hath said, out of his belly shall flow rivers of Living Water." In verse 38, Jesus was speaking of the future (when the church would receive His Spirit). In verse 39, John explains (brakes it down) what Jesus was teaching us in verse 38, saying, "But this spake He of the Spirit, which they that believe on Him should receive, for the Holy Ghost was not yet; because that Jesus was not yet glorified." Read Ephesians 1:13. You can believe all you want to, but until you are born-again according to God's plan of salvation, you are not saved. I know that this may sound harsh, but truly, I'm speaking God's TRUTH in love for your soul.

And as I have said before, God's salvation is just the beginning of our race to heaven. We all must grow in the Lord as we learn His word, and we can only grow in the Lord if we obey His word. You must remember this—God and Satan are the main two SUPPER POWERS of this world. Satan will do anything to deceive us. If he deceives us by blinding us from obeying God's plan of salvation, he has got us. A person who believes that they are saved because they just believe in Jesus, Satan has deceived you, and you don't even know it. Again, I'm speaking the TRUTH in love.

I don't care who you are, but if you don't get God's salvation right, what you believe to be your walk with the Lord is vain. I want you to see something else from John chapter 7, and it is in verse 43. Just as there was division in those days, there is even more division in 2017. As you now know, Satan has blinded all the false churches, and that is why there are so many of them throughout the world. And while I'm speaking the TRUTH in love, that's all I have to say about that.

In this last example of how to be born-again, you will be able to see that just believing is not going to get you to heaven. What John recorded in John 7:38–39 is going to come to pass in these men's lives. The last example that I want to share with you is found in Acts 19:1–7. I believe that we have already read this TRUTH before, but it never hurts to read God's TRUTH again. We must get His word into our minds and know it so we can obey His TRUTH from our hearts. Read Romans 12:1–2. In Acts 19:1–7, you are going to see God's plan of salvation being achieved by these men, by the Lord, and the mouth and hands of Apostle Paul.

If you will listen really closely in verse 1, you will see that Paul went to Ephesus and saw some men who were evidently living right. The reason I say that is because in verse 2, he asked them a question as if he saw some godly men, "Have ye received the Holy Ghost since ye believed?" And they answered him and said, "We have not so much as heard whether there be any Holy Ghost. And just maybe, that could be your problem, you might have never heard about the Holy Ghost." When they told Paul that they didn't know about the Holy Ghost, Paul asked them another important question in verse 3, "How were you baptized?" And they said, "Unto John's baptism." Paul tells them in verse 4, "John truly baptized with the baptism of repentance, saying unto the people, that they should believe on Him which should come after him, that is, on Christ Jesus."

You should be hearing all these scriptures, but I want you to listen again with your spiritual ears to verses 5–6. You are going to hear God's plan of salvation as it comes to these men, and they were born-again according to the word of God. Paraphrasing verse 5, when they heard what Apostle Paul was teaching, they were baptized in the name of the Father, and of the Son, and of the Holy Ghost, when they were baptized in the name of Jesus. When these men were baptized in the name of Jesus, they fulfilled what Jesus told His apostles to teach in Matthew 28:19. If you just heard that, the Holy Ghost is teaching you His TRUTH.

Verse 6 says, "When Paul had laid hands upon them; the Holy Ghost came on them; and they spake with tongues, and prophesied." These men had just received the Holy Ghost and was born-again just as they were on the day of Pentecost, when the church was started.

We all must learn to RIGHTLY DIVIDE these scriptures to know that when a person is baptized of the Holy Ghost, they will speak in other tongues as the Spirit of God gives them utterance. If your preacher doesn't teach this plan of salvation, he is blind. Read Matthew 15:14. The ditch that Jesus was referring to is HELL. According to Matthew 15:14, the student will follow the preacher into HELL, if they continue to follow his false teachings.

Through the years, I have learned some very important lessons, and one of them is that when you find yourself digging a hole and you have dug it so deep you can't get out, keep digging. Now, that just doesn't make a lot of sense; but listen, you must change the direction in which you are digging. If you will begin digging on the side of the hole, you will fill the hole under your feet, and eventually, you will be able to step out of the hole, which made you a prisoner. If you have not been born-again according to God's word, change your direction and come out of the hole that you're in. Seek Jesus for the TRUTH, ask Him for the TRUTH, and live His TRUTH as you learn. I'm not trying to offend anyone, but if you are offended, you must get over it and obey God's TRUTH.

At this time, I want to share with you what I know about how and why God uses our tongues to communicate with Him. In 1 Corinthians chapter 12, Apostle Paul teaches the Corinthians and us about the spiritual gifts that the Lord has given to His church for our benefit and to whosoever can believe. As you read 1 Corinthians 12:1–18, the Lord gives His church spiritual gifts. And in those gifts, God gives some members kinds of tongues for their gift. The Lord uses tongues to edify (strengthen) His church. You can also learn about how the Lord uses tongues in 1 Corinthians chapter 14. Now, I want to be crystal clear about this—the gift of tongues that Apostle Paul taught about in 1 Corinthians chapters 12 and 14 are not the other tongues that a person speaks when they receive the Holy Ghost. Study these two chapters, and ask the Lord to reveal His TRUTH to you.

I will try to clarify what I know about the different kinds of tongues that are taught about in God's word.

To my knowledge, there are four different kinds of tongues mentioned in God's word, which the Lord uses to communicate with His people. The first tongue the Lord uses is our own dialect. When we first come to the Lord, we all speak to Him in our own language. This is when we ask the Lord to forgive us (repent) of our sins. I truly believe when we begin asking the Lord for His forgiveness, we begin telling Him that we are turning everything over to Him.

"Lord, I give you the rest of my life to serve you and my fellow man. My family is yours, Lord. My car and my dog are yours." When we reach the Lord with a sincere prayer, this brings us to the second kind of tongues (other tongues). You are about to hear what I believe to be the TRUTH about why we speak in tongues when we receive the Holy Ghost. There is something in every person that the Lord wants to control, and it just makes sense for Him to take control of this, when you are born-again. Read James 3:1–13, and you can find this TRUTH about why we speak in other tongues, when we are born-again. These scriptures teach us how poisonous and deadly our tongues are. Verse 8 says, "But the tongue can no man tame; an unruly evil, full of deadly poison. The tongue can no man tame, but God can and will." I believe these scriptures have been RIGHTLY DIVIDED, revealing the TRUTH to you about why God has to tame our tongues. Having to speak in other tongues when you receive the Holy Ghost is an unpopular belief by most so- called Christians, but the history of the church (Acts 2:1–8) is really clear about this.

There is no set order in which these next two kinds of tongues would come to someone. It would be determined by your prayer life and the Lord choosing to give you the gift of tongues. In 1 Corinthians 14:1–28, you can learn about speaking in tongues, which are used to edify (strengthen) God's church. The church will be edified (strengthened) if there is an interpreter, when these kinds of tongues are spoken. There is that big word IF again.

Paul teaches us in verse 5, "I would that ye all spoke with tongues, but rather that ye prophesied [God's Spirit can reveal what is going to happen in the future]. For greater he that prophesies than he that speaks with tongues, except he interpret, that the church may receive edifying." I want you to read the last sentence again so you won't miss the key words "except he interpret." Here in this chapter, Apostle Paul is teaching them and us the right way to communicate with Him and His church, how to be in order when we come together as the body of Christ. Prophesy is a clear way to hear God speak to us (the church), and so is speaking in tongues, IF there is an interpreter. Read verses 7–13, and you will hear a clear explanation of this kind of tongues.

The fourth way the Lord uses tongues for our benefit is when a person prays in the Spirit. Jude teaches us (the church) in verse 20 that we are to build up ourselves on our most Holy faith, praying in the Holy Ghost. Praying in the Holy Ghost is simply Jesus speaking through you, and you will be speaking in a prayer tongue, which only benefits that person at that moment.

But, as you grow in the Lord by praying in the Spirit, it will eventually benefit others in the future. As a person prays in the Spirit, they become more spiritual, and they can help others spiritually, because they will be more in tune with Jesus. Read Romans 8:26. The best way that I can explain it is to get lost in the Spirit and let Jesus have His way with you. I believe praying in the Spirit is how Jesus makes Love with His church. I'm not talking about sex. A carnal-minded person cannot hear this; you must have spiritual ears to hear what I just wrote.

Just in case you missed it, I want to share with you what Apostle Paul has to say about spiritual gifts. I want you to hear the importance he puts on loving God and our fellow man. You can find this TRUTH in between 1 Corinthians chapters 12 and 14, and that would be, 1 Corinthians chapter 13. First, we must read 1 Corinthians 12:31. Paul says, "The church needs to covet earnestly the best gifts, and yet show I unto you a more excellent way."

I'm about to preach to you, but I'm preaching to myself also. Paul continues with that same thought into chapter 13, and he proclaims a TRUTH, which is beneficial for all of us if we learn from it. Paul says in verse 1, "Though I speak with tongues of men and of angels, and have not charity [Love], I am become sounding brass, or a tinkling cymbal."

As I was just writing these words "and have not charity," I could not write charity, because Satan showed up and put pressure on my shoulders and neck. And when I say pressure, I mean pressure. For about fifteen seconds, it was if I had two hundred pounds on each shoulder. I broke into a cold sweat, and it zapped me of my strength. I did have enough strength to reach over and grab a bottle of oil. As I anointed my shoulders and head, I rebuked Satan and asked the Lord for help. I'm so glad that I know the power that is in calling the name of Jesus.

I don't want to die today, because I want to finish writing this book, and I believe that I have other things to accomplish on this earth. But it sure would have been a good way to pass from this life. As I write about and sharing God's TRUTH about charity. When I die, I truly want to be doing something pertaining to the Lord and my Christian family. It has been between thirty minutes and an hour since Satan attacked me. I still feel a little drained, but I'm not letting that stop me from writing God's TRUTH. Like I said before, I want to help others find the TRUTH, which the Lord shared with me.

Now, I feel a little better, so I will continue writing about what Paul was teaching us in 1 Corinthians chapter 13. Paul says, "Though I have prophecy, and understand all mysteries, and all knowledge; and though I have all faith, so that I could remove mountains, and have not charity, I am nothing. And though I bestow all my goods to feed, and though I give my body to be burned, and have not charity, it profiteth me nothing" (1 Corinthians 13:2–3). I believe in verse 11, Paul is telling us that when he found the Love of God, he became a man. Read and study these three chapters (1 Corinthians 12, 13, and 14), and seek the Lord and ask Him for wisdom and understanding. You will be blessed.

I hope you have learned the TRUTH about the different kinds of tongues that the Lord uses to communicate with His church. If so, now you know about how the Lord uses different kinds of tongues to teach us and to strengthen His people. As you talk to other so-called Christians, you will find that most don't believe in tongues and some will even say that speaking in tongues are of the devil. I know and believe that what I have read in 1 Corinthians chapters 12, 13, and 14 are the TRUTH. I also know and believe that what Luke writes in Acts 2:11 is the TRUTH. Read Acts 2:11, and see for yourself who he says that is using tongues for His purpose. No matter what anyone may try to tell you now, you know the TRUTH, and you will be able to see (hear) their blindness of the TRUTH.

The false churches must learn how Satan has blinded them, but we (the church) must not allow him to blind us (the church). When Jesus said in John 3:5, "Verily, verily, I say unto thee, Except a man be born of water and the Spirit, he cannot enter into the kingdom of God," I don't see how it can get any plainer; but some of the false teachers who are in world churches teach that Jesus was speaking about when a person is born from their mother's womb. But any second grader who reads this scripture knows that it says born-again. In this scripture, Jesus is teaching us that we all must be baptized by water and be baptized by His Spirit to go to heaven.

The reasons why we must be baptized (born) of the Spirit are many, but I will list a few. First, the Spirit gives us life. Jesus' Spirit is our teacher and our guide here on earth, helping us on our journey to heaven. He is our Comforter and our strength. He is our protector and our provider. And we can't forget that He is our GREAT PHYSICIAN. And I can't say it any better than Apostle Paul did in Galatians 5:22–23. These two scriptures teach us that the Holy Ghost shares Himself with us.

I said earlier in this book that I was going to list all the benefits that I know of being baptized in water, and this looks like a good place to share this TRUTH with you. And as you should know by now that if you are not baptized in the name of Jesus, these benefits will not apply to you. Acts 4:12 says, "Neither is there salvation in any other, for there is none other name under heaven given among men, whereby we must be saved."

Now, when you are baptized in the name of Jesus, you receive all the benefits at the same time. First, let's read what Ananias teaches Apostle Paul what water baptism accomplishes. Paraphrasing Acts 22:16, Ananias tells Paul, "What are you waiting on, arise, and be baptized, and wash away thy sins, calling on the name of the Lord." Here, Ananias taught Paul to be baptized in the name of Jesus, and his sins would be washed away. And as you already know, Apostle Paul taught that same message. Read Ephesians 5:25–27, and hear what Apostle Paul teaches about water baptism. In verse 26, he says, "He [Jesus] might sanctify [set the church apart] and cleanse it [the church] with the washing of water by the word [according to the word].

Here is another benefit of water baptism. Most of the false-teaching preachers teach the opposite of what God's word teaches. But I say God's word is true, and the false teachers are wrong. For those who don't know the TRUTH about this, I'm going to say what the false teachers don't believe and teach, before I give you the scriptures that teach this TRUTH—water baptism saves us. Now, don't get your feathers all rustled up, because of what I just wrote. Read 1 Peter 3:20–21 and you will hear the TRUTH about water baptism saving us.

Back in the days of Noah, there were large cities, and there could have been millions of people back then. The reason I mentioned this is I want you to hear this TRUTH! From verse 20, Peter was inspired by God to write this scripture, and it is the TRUTH. Peter says that there were only a few, that is, eight souls, that were saved by water in the days of Noah. Today, there are about seven billion people living on this earth. Now, I'm not trying to give you a prediction of how many people that will be saved. But let's look in the scriptures and see what Jesus says about this. Read Matthew 7:13–14 and you will see that Jesus uses that same word (few) when He describes the number of people that will find their way to heaven. Now, that same Jesus inspired Peter to warn us in 1 Peter 3:21 that in the last days, baptism (water) will save us just as it saved Noah and his family. Again, that is the TRUTH. And you just need to believe it as the TRUTH, and obey God's word.

Most preachers teach this TRUTH (Ephesians 2:8–9), and it is the TRUTH. Ephesians 2:8–9 is one of the first scriptures I learned, thirty-four years ago, and it is still the TRUTH today. Verse 8 says, "For by grace are ye saved through faith, and not of yourselves." The end of verse 8 says, "Grace is a gift of God." Verse 9 teaches us that we're not saved by works, because if it be by God's grace, we could not boast (brag about what we have done).

These scriptures are true, but it takes God and our actions in obeying His TRUTH to be born-again. A person is saved by grace when he or she has faith in the TRUTH the Lord has taught him or her.

Here is another benefit of water baptism. Baptism is for the death and the burial of our old man so we can resurrect out of the water in newness of life. Read Romans 6:1–23. There is a teaching that comes from some of the false churches, and it is everyone sins every day. That teaching is false! That teaching is the opposite of what Paul taught in Romans chapter 6. According to Apostle Paul, after we are baptized, we are to live a sinless life. I am going to paraphrase verse 7, but I believe you will hear this TRUTH. In verse 7, Paul says, "If you will look in the casket at Uncle Joe, he will never sin again. If you truly die to Jesus, and bury your old self by baptism in Jesus name, you can walk with Jesus, and live a sinless life." IF, what a big word. I will say this with full assurance of no kind of correction from the Lord—IF you sin every day, you're not of God. Read 1 Peter 4:18. I must say this again, I am speaking God's TRUTH in love.

Here is another benefit of Jesus' name baptism. The church is known in God's word as the Bride of Christ.

And as you know, when a woman becomes a bride, most women take on their husband's name. Read Ephesians 3:14–15. If you want to be a part of Jesus' Bride, you must take on His name. There is only one place in God's word that I know of where the church takes on the name of Jesus. And we take on Jesus' name when we are baptized in His name. I would not want to stand before Him having been baptized in some other name (method) than Jesus name. Read again Acts 4:12 and Philippians 2:9–11. You had better learn to bend your knees and confess with your tongue that Jesus is Lord now and not to be made to later.

Read Hebrews 8:1–13, and you will learn how the Old Testament was done away with so the New Testament could begin. Verse 6 says, "But now hath He [Jesus] obtained a more excellent ministry, by how much also He is the mediator of a better covenant, which was established upon better promises." Verse 7 teaches us that if the Old covenant (Testament) had been faultless, the Lord would not have needed a New Testament. Verse 10 says, "For this the covenant that I will make with the house of Israel after those days [when the Lord ends the Old Testament], saith the Lord; I will put my laws into their mind, and write them in their hearts, and I will be to them a God, and they shall be to me a people."

Verse 13 teaches us concerning the Old Testament with words like which decayeth and waxeth old, ready to vanish away. There are preachers who teach that we still live under the law that the Lord gave to Moses. I want to say this as clear as I can—we do not live under the Law of Moses. But we do live under a law. Read James 1:25.

Now read James 2:1–12, and you will hear some teaching from James about the law of liberty.

After the Lord teaches you His TRUTH, you will not go around killing, stealing, and breaking all the Old Testament laws, because under the law of liberty, it still covers all the Old Testament laws. I believe everyone needs to learn about how the Lord called and used Moses to bring His people out of Egypt and how the Lord instructed him to build the first tabernacle. Read Exodus chapters 24, 25, 26, and 27, and you will learn how the Lord instructed Moses to instruct the people to build the first tabernacle and how to build all the furniture.

While I'm on this subject, I want to share with you what I believe to be the TRUTH. As you read and study these chapters in the book of Exodus, you will learn that the tabernacle was partitioned into two separate areas. Exodus 26:30–34 teaches us about the area of the tabernacle that is called the most holy. In the most holy area was placed the Ark of the Covenant, which was what Indiana Jones was looking for in his movie *Raiders of the Lost Ark*. In this area of the tabernacle, only the high priest was allowed to enter and communicate with the Lord. He would enter the most holy area once each year and offer a blood sacrifice for himself and the errors of the people. Read Hebrews 9:1–7.

Now, the first tabernacle was built out of material much like a tent. But many years later, the Lord wanted King David to build the first temple in Jerusalem for a permanent home for the Ark of the Covenant, but David never got to build it. If you will read 1 Chronicles 28:1–3, you will learn why David was not allowed to build the first temple. Now read 2 Samuel 7:1–13. Verses 12–13 teach us that after David dies, his son Solomon has been chosen by the Lord to build the temple. And the Lord allowed Solomon to build the first Jewish temple in the tenth century BC.

At this time, I must refresh your memory about the four beast (kingdoms) that Daniel saw. As you already know from chapter 6, the temple that Solomon built was destroyed, when the Babylonians captured and took control of Jerusalem in 586 BC. The Babylonians kept Jerusalem under their thumb, for almost fifty years. Then, the Medes and Persians captured and killed Belshazzar, the king of Babylon, in 539 BC. During the reign of the Medes and Persians, Cyrus, king of Persia, permitted the exiles

(Jews) to return to their homes and allowed them to rebuild the temple for the second time.

For the next 208 years, the Medes and the Persians ruled the world, until the Greek leader Alexander the Great defeated them in 331 BC in the battle of Arbela. During the reign of Alexander the Great, the second Jewish temple was left alone and was not destroyed. The Greek Empire lasted for 163 years and was overthrown by the Roman Empire in 168 BC. So in the second century BC, the Jewish state came under the power of the Romans.

For 238 years, the Romans left the second temple alone, but when the Romans started exercising their power in a cruel and arbitrary (heavy- handed) way, a Jewish revolt began in Jerusalem in AD 66. After a long and fierce Jewish resistance, the Roman legions conquered Jerusalem in AD 70. They executed the Jewish leaders and exiled the whole people. In AD 70, the Romans destroyed the second temple, and they left only the western wall standing. This wall became known as the Wailing Wall and has remained the holiest place of prayer for Jews to this day.

As I was proofreading my book today (May 14, 2018), Fox News reported from Jerusalem that the United States President (Donald Trump) opened our new embassy there and confirmed what King David did 3,000 years ago, that is, Jerusalem is recognized as the capital of Israel again. I believe this is just another step to the rebuilding of the new temple. If I were you, I would start paying close attention to what is happening in Jerusalem. The Lord's temple must be rebuilt one more time so the Beast can make his stand. You have already learned a little about this temple earlier in this book, when I wrote about the Beast taking over the new temple, which will be built in our future. The first two temples were built in the same fashion as the old tabernacle Moses had built, referring to the two separate rooms (holy and most holy areas).

Here is the TRUTH that I want to share with you about the area called the most holy. The day when Jesus sacrificed Himself on the cross and shed His blood for our sins, He changed the way to come to Him and get forgiveness of our sins. There were many significant things that happened that day. There is no doubt to most people that He died for us and His blood was shed for our sins. There were many hearts change, and many people began following Jesus that day, but like I said, Jesus changed the way we come to Him and get forgiveness of our sins.

In Matthew 27:24–53, you can learn about His death on the cross. But what I want you to hear comes from verse 51. Matthew records that when Jesus died, the veil of the temple (the veil that divided the holy from the most holy) was "rent in twain from the top to the bottom." Here is the TRUTH that this scripture is teaching us. When the Lord ripped the veil in half, He was teaching us that we no longer need a priest to enter the most holy area for us; we can come to the Lord ourselves and find forgiveness. Read Hebrews 10:19–20. These scriptures teach us that Jesus' body became the veil for each one of us.

Now, for the new temple that will be built in the future. I'm sure that it will have a veil dividing these two areas, because of the old Jewish beliefs. I believe it will be a waste of money and time to hang the veil, but the powers that be, they will most likely hang a veil. But for you who still believe in going to your priest, my prayer is that you listen to the lesson the Lord taught about the veil being torn in half and His sacrifice of Himself, becoming the veil for us.

Hebrews 9:1–7 starts off by teaching us about the first tabernacle that Moses had built. Now, let's read the rest of Hebrews 9:8–28. In those scriptures, you will also learn how the animal's blood was not good enough to redeem man from their sins. And just as the Old covenant was done away with, the blood sacrifice of animals was also done away with. In this New Testament, the Lord has given man a better covenant, because He gave Himself as a blood sacrifice for our sins.

During the Old Testament times, the Lord wrote His laws in stone to tell His people how they should live, but in the New Testament era, He puts His laws in our mind, and He writes His laws in our hearts. The New Testament is truly a better covenant, and I am so glad to live in this dispensation of time. Now, read Hebrews chapter 10, because it goes along with and will help explain what you have learned from Hebrews chapter 9.

This is the problem with most so-called Christians, they don't know that God came to earth in the form of man and shed His own blood for our sins. Read Acts 20:28. Here are a few scriptures that teach us who Jesus is. Read Philippians 2:4–11. Now, I want you to read John 1:1 and verse 14. Verse 14 plainly teaches us, "The word [God] was made flesh, and dwelt among us." To make this New Testament salvation plan complete, it took the blood of a sinless Lamb, to redeem man back to God, from Adam and Eve's fall from God's grace. Read John 1:29 and hear what John the Baptist says about Jesus when Jesus comes to where he is baptizing some people one day. I also want you to read 1 Peter 1:18–23. "Jesus' [God's] blood was shed for us, that we might live unto Him."

Here is another benefit of being baptized in Jesus' name. I believe the scriptures teach us that the blood of Jesus is applied to our lives in water baptism. From the scriptures, let's read and find out what they say about the Lord giving His blood for us and find out how His blood is applied to our lives. First, read Revelation 5:9. We now know from this scripture that when the Lord was hung on the cross and died for all of us, when His blood was shed, the purpose was to redeem us back to our Creator. But the big question is, when or where is His blood applied to our lives? Again, we haven't found any certain scripture that plainly tells us when or where the Lord's blood is applied to our lives, but we do have a few scriptures that tell that the Lord's blood cleanses us of our sins. So that tells me to find out the answer to when or where the Lord's blood is applied to our lives; we must study the scriptures that teach us about water baptism.

Let's RIGHTLY DIVIDE these scriptures and see how this TRUTH sound to you. First, we need to read 1 John 1:7. This scripture teaches us, "If we walk in the light, as He is in the light, we have fellowship one with another, and the blood of Jesus Christ His Son cleanseth us from all sin." Now, this scripture teaches me that after a person is born-again, we can walk in the light (TRUTH), and we can have fellowship with our Christian brothers and sisters. However, this still doesn't tell us when or where His blood is applied to our lives.

I believe this next scripture will reveal some of the light (TRUTH) that we are looking for. 1 John 5:8 says, "There are three that bear witness in earth, the Spirit, and the water, and the blood, and these three agree in one." Based on all the studying of God's word that I have done through the years, I know that this scripture is teaching us about the born-again experience. Now, if that is the TRUTH, the Lord's blood is applied to our lives when we are born-again. Now, this scripture (1 John 5:8) narrows it down to two certain times that the Lord's blood could be applied to our lives, and they are when a person is baptized of God's Spirit or when a person is baptized in water in the name of Jesus.

This next scripture will even shine more light (TRUTH) about when the Lord applies His blood to our lives. Revelation 1:5 says, "And from Jesus Christ, the faithful witness, the first begotten of the dead, and the Prince of the kings of the earth. Unto Him that loved us, and washed us from our sins in His own blood." According to this scripture, the Lord applies His blood to our lives when we are baptized in water in the name of Jesus.

God's word teaches us that our sins are washed away from our lives when we are baptized in the name of Jesus. Remember in Acts 22:16 when the Lord's blood was applied to Apostle Paul's life and washed away his sins? Having the Lord's blood applied to our lives is one more benefit we get by being baptized in water in the name of Jesus. Here is a bold statement, but true. If you are baptized any other way than in the name of Jesus, the Lord's blood is not applied to your life.

Read Ephesians 2:11–22 and you will learn that the shedding of the Lord's blood, IF it is applied to our lives, makes us (Gentiles) brothers and sisters with the Jewish nation. In other words, when we are born-again and God washes us in His blood, we are grafted into the Jewish nation, and we become Jewish. Now, that's what I believe to be the TRUTH.

Ephesians 2:13–16 says, "But now in Christ Jesus ye [us Gentiles] who sometimes were far off are made nigh by the blood of Christ. For He is our peace, who hath made both one, and hath broken down the middle wall of partition. Having abolished in His flesh the enmity, the law of commandments in ordinances; [in other words, through Jesus' death upon the cross, He did away with the Old Testament laws so grace could begin] for to make in Himself of twain one new man, making peace. And that He might reconcile both unto God in one body by the cross, having slain the enmity thereby." You must read and study Romans chapter 11 to learn about the Gentiles being grafted into the Jewish nation. In this chapter, you will learn how we become one, so we all can be presented to God as one people. As you now know, we all came from Adam and Eve, and the Lord wants to make us one people again no matter what color or what nationality we might be. Now this is just my belief, but I believe, when the Lord washes us in His blood is when He gives us a blood transfusion, and turns our blood into royal blood!

During the time that I was writing about this next benefit, I had been thinking about investing a little money in silver. In 2017, silver was at a good price, but I remembered what Jesus said in Matthew chapter 6, so I changed my mind. Now, you know that when you are baptized in Jesus' name, He completely removes every sin from your past. The only things the Lord remembers from our past are the good things that we have done. I truly believe at that moment, God opens us a bank account in heaven. I believe He makes our first deposit for us of all the good that we have ever done. Now, it is up to us to fill our bank accounts. Just imagine having a bank account in heaven that you can withdraw from in time of need. It is your account, and God will allow you to withdraw if you are in need. Read Matthew 6:19–21.

If we (Gentiles) are to be a part of the tribes of Israel, I believe we should know what tribe the church comes from. To find out what tribe the Gentiles are grafted (born) into, we must learn about Abraham and his descendants. Read Matthew 1:1–2 and you can find the TRUTH about what tribe the Gentiles are grafted into. Verse 2 reveals that Judas (Juda) is the tribe that we are born into. The tribe of Juda is the tribe the Lord chose to come to earth as the sacrifice for the world's sins. At the end of verse 2, "Jacob begat Judas and his brethren." As far as I can find in the scriptures, Jacob had twelve sons and one daughter, and her name was Dinah. You have already learned the TRUTH about how the Lord will make a new covenant with the tribe of Judah in Hebrews 8:7–8.

Read Genesis chapter 32 and you will learn that Jacob had a need, and to achieve that need, he wrestled with the Lord all night until he prevailed. As you read, you will see that Jacob was injured that night as he wrestled with the Lord. So beware if you try wrestling with the Lord about some special need, because you could receive your need, but be injured for life, as Jacob was. I believe that Israel walked with a limp for the rest of his life, and it was a constant reminder of the night that he wrestled with God, but he was blessed.

Not only did the Lord meet Jacob's need that night, but also the Lord changed Jacob's name to Israel. Jacob's (Israel's) twelve sons and their descendants are known as the twelve tribes of Israel. Read Genesis chapter 49, and you will find the names of Israel's twelve sons, as he prophesied to them about their future. You can also find the names of Israel's sons in Revelation chapter 7. As you read Revelation 7:5, I want you to know that this scripture gives the number of Jews that will be saved during the tribulation period, from the tribe of Juda. As you continue reading Revelation chapter 7, you will learn that the Lord is going to seal (save) twelve thousand from each tribe, which equals to 144,000 Jews saved during the tribulation period. To tell you the TRUTH, I have only scratched the surface concerning our forefathers, and now, it is up to you to learn more TRUTH about them.

As you read and study God's word, you will come across this terminology circumcision and uncircumcision. These two words are some of the easiest of God's word to understand. Circumcision are the Jews, and uncircumcision are non-Jewish people. There could be others, but the final benefit of water baptism that I know of is circumcision. Most people don't know the importance of circumcision. You can't learn about circumcision without learning about Abraham, because circumcision started with him and his son Isaac. Read Genesis chapter 17 and you will find the TRUTH how circumcision started.

Genesis 17:10–11 says, "This my (God's) covenant, which ye shall keep, between me and you and thy seed after thee. Every man child among you shall be circumcised. And ye shall circumcise the flesh of your foreskin; and it shall be a token of the covenant betwixt me and you." As you read and study Genesis 17:12–14, you will see the importance of being circumcised, and you will also see that the Lord says that this will be an everlasting covenant between Him and Abraham and his seed after him.

A little earlier, I had you read Matthew 1:2 so you would know what tribe of Israel the church is born into. Now, I want you to read Matthew 1:16 and you will learn that Jesus was born in the lineage of Abraham, Isaac, and Jacob.

It only makes sense to me that the Lord from heaven would come to earth through the lineage of Abraham.

Soon, I am going to write and teach what I know about predestination, and when I do, I want you to remember what you have learned in Matthew chapter 1. There is no way that anyone can convince me that the Lord didn't know who His earthly forefathers and His descendants (the church) were going to be.

Read Luke 2:21 and you will learn, that Jesus' parents kept that same covenant of circumcision that was started by God and Abraham. Now in Genesis chapter 17, when the Lord made His covenant of circumcision with Abraham, He was only making that covenant with the Jewish nation. The Lord had other plans for all of us non-Jewish people, and I will soon explain that last statement. Now, I believe if you are born a Jew by natural birth, you will remain in the tribe of Israel that you are born into, until they are born- again. You already know what I believe about Apostle Paul, but Paul does let us all know from what tribe of Israel he came from. Read Philippians 3:3–5. These scriptures teach us that Apostle Paul was of the tribe of Benjamin. Notice that I said that "Apostle Paul was" because I believe the scriptures teach, that when Paul was born-again, he became a son of God into the tribe of Juda.

Now, if the non-Jews are going to be grafted into the descendants of Abraham, we must be circumcised. Like I said earlier, the Lord had a different plan of circumcision for the Gentiles, but either way, we must be circumcised to be a part of His church. Let's look in the scriptures and see what they teach about us being circumcised.

You can find out how Jesus circumcises the Gentiles in Colossians 2:8–14. In verse 8, Paul warns us about being deceived by false teachers, while verses 9–10 tell us about a GREAT TRUTH, if you can hear them. Now, in verses 11–12, Paul teaches us how the Gentiles are circumcised and that it is Jesus who circumcises them. Verse 11 says, "In whom also ye are circumcised with the circumcision made without hands, in putting off the body of the sins of the flesh by the circumcision of Christ." From what you have learned from God's word, our sins are removed from us in water baptism in the name of Jesus. In the beginning of verse 12, Paul says that "buried with Him in baptism," so baptism in water is our circumcision. Here is another bold statement, but it is God's TRUTH. If you are a Gentile, and you are not circumcised according to God's word, you are not grafted into the Jewish nation.

Here is some more TRUTH that I want to share with you that has been taught as the TRUTH, but is false. Some preachers teach that you don't have to be baptized, because of something Jesus said and did. Luke 23:39–43 teaches us the TRUTH of what Jesus said while hanging on the cross. This controversial statement is found in verse 43. Jesus says to one of the thieves that hung beside Him, "Today, shalt thou be with me in paradise."

In Matthew 27:38, he records that the two men who were crucified with Jesus that day were thieves. And we all know that a thief can't go to heaven without being baptized in the New Testament era. But you are about to learn from the scriptures that when Jesus spoke those words to the thief, the New Testament salvation plan had not yet started. The simple fact is that while Jesus was hanging on the cross and still talking, this tells me He had not yet died.

Let's look into the scriptures and find God's TRUTH about what it took for the New Testament to become officially started. You will hear why Jesus could say to the thief, "Today shalt thou be with me in paradise," in Hebrews 9:16–17. Jesus could have taken everyone that day to heaven, because at that time, they were all still under the law, and the New Testament had not yet begun. It took Jesus' death to accomplish what He started. In John 19:30, you can find Jesus' last words while hanging on the cross. Jesus said, "It is finished: and He bowed His head, and gave up the ghost [died]." Now, that is the TRUTH about the thief on the cross going to heaven without being baptized. After Jesus died, from that day forward, everyone must be baptized in the name of Jesus to receive the benefits that I have been writing about. I believe that I have told you as clear as I can, so it is up to you to seek Jesus' words and obey God's TRUTH.

Now, for the last two subjects (TRUTHS) that I want to share with you, which are controversial, because most people don't know the TRUTH about them. These last two TRUTHS are about the

Book of Life and predestination. It's hard to write about the Book of Life without writing about predestination, because they both go together. I just want to start by saying there is no way that anyone can convince me that the Lord didn't know who His Bride (the church) was going to be.

As you now know, Jesus is the Alpha and Omega, which means the Beginning and the Ending. I believe it would be foolish on our part if we thought that God didn't know who His leaders in this war against Satan were going to be. I hope you will always remember this. Jesus is omnipresent; He is an all-seeing and an all-knowing God. Read Hebrews 4:12 and you will see that there is no way to escape His abilities. He knows your thoughts and the intentions of your heart.

"In the beginning was the Word, and the Word was with God, and the Word was God" (John 1:1). John 1:14 starts off by saying, "And the word was made flesh." As you read this next scripture, just remember that the words you are reading are God, and He knows what He's talking about. Revelation 13:8 tells us that He knew He had to die for mankind from the foundation of the world. 1 Peter 1:19–20 teaches us that we are not redeemed from the things Peter listed in verse 18, but it was the precious blood of Christ "who verily [truly] was foreordained BEFORE THE FOUNDATION OF THE WORLD, but was manifest [revealed] in these last times for you."

Next, Romans 9:4–5 tells us of the "human ancestry of Jesus" on earth. This is a fact! When God wrote the Book of Life, He knew that He was going to come to this earth as a baby and grow into a man. He also knew who His parents were going to be and what He must do to bring man back from our fallen state. Even Jesus was predestinated.

Now, I want to show you how the Lord chose certain people to carry out His plan for humanity. He could have done all this by himself, but He chose to use man as His hands and mouth here on earth. And as you now know, I believe that this relationship between God and man was the fall of Lucifer. If the Lord is the Alpha and Omega and if He is an all-seeing and an all- knowing God, He knew that Adam and Eve were going to be the first two people to live on earth. He even knew that Lucifer was going to start his rebellious move in heaven and that Satan was going to lose and eventually wind up in HELL.

In Romans chapter 9, you can find some examples of how the Lord has put certain people on this earth to help populate it, which is where His Bride comes from. In other words, He predestinated them for His purpose in order to bring in His everlasting kingdom. In verse 4, Apostle Paul explains how the Israelites received "the adoption, and the glory, and the covenants, and the giving of the law, and the service of God, and the promises." In verses 6–11, Paul teaches us about the promises He made to Abraham and his descendants and how the church would be formed through the lineage of Abraham. The only word I can think of is predestination. To tell you the TRUTH, I don't know why some people have a problem with the Lord predestinating us.

In Romans chapter 9, you will find a couple more people the Lord put here on earth for His purpose. These two people are well known to the church world, and they are Moses and the Pharaoh, the leader of Egypt. Apostle Paul mentions Moses and the Pharaoh in Romans 9:15–18:

> For He [the Lord] saith to Moses, I will have mercy on whom I will have mercy, and I will have compassion on whom I will have compassion. So then not of him that willeth, nor of him that runneth, but of God that sheweth mercy. For the scripture saith unto Pharaoh, Even for this same purpose have I raised thee up [in a leader position], that I might shew my power in thee, and that my name might be declared throughout all the

earth. Therefore hath He mercy on whom He will, and whom He will He hardeneth.

This is what the Lord has taught me, and I want to share this TRUTH with you. Moses wrote the first five books of the Old Testament—Genesis, Exodus, Leviticus, Numbers, and Deuteronomy. When you read these five books, you will see that Moses didn't even come into the world until the second book, which he wrote. This tells me that the Lord Himself taught Moses and gave him the words (TRUTH) to write in the book of Genesis and the first part of Exodus. The reason I said the first part of Exodus is that Moses was just born, and he didn't leave the Egyptians until he became a man. The rest of his books were written according to what he experienced as he grew into an old man.

Before Moses was born, the Israelites/Hebrews/Jews were slaves and under the bondage of the Egyptians. For many years, the Hebrews prayed and bombarded the Lord's ears for help. What the Hebrews didn't know was that the Lord was going to send them a deliverer named Moses. As you read about Moses, you will see how he was put in the right place at the right time by God. The Lord had Moses' mother to put him in the river so he would be taken by the Pharaoh's daughter and raised as her son. As the Hebrews prayed for their deliverer, he was already ruling over them as an Egyptian. Exodus 2:10–15 teaches us that after Moses became a man, he saw the Israelites for the first time as his people. These scriptures also teach us that Moses killed an Egyptian who was mistreating an Israelite. I believe that was the start of his walk with God, because before that day, he believed himself to be an Egyptian and had other gods.

While I'm writing about Moses being predestinated, I will have to write about the Book of Life, because he mentions the Book of Life in this set of scriptures. Moses leads the Israelites through the sea (on dry land) and then across the desert as he led them to the

Promised Land that the Lord instructed him to do. You will find out more about the TRUTH of the Book of Life in Exodus 32:32–35. These scriptures teach us about when Moses is standing up to God for the children of Israel. When Moses comes down from Mount Sinai, after receiving the Ten Commandments from the Lord, he finds the Israelites have fallen back into sin. You are about to hear something the Lord had to teach Moses. In verse 32, Moses asked the Lord to forgive their sin, and "if not, blot me, I pray thee, out of thy Book [Book of Life] which thou hast written." Then, the Lord tells Moses in verse 33, "Whosoever hath sinned against me, him will I blot out of My Book."

I wrote earlier in this book about the word blot, and it looks like you have found it in the scriptures. As you can see for yourself from these scriptures, the Lord chose Moses to do His work on earth. And I believe the Lord chose him from the foundation of the world when He was writing the Book of Life. And as I have said, while writing about predestination and the Book of Life, they are intertwined with each other, because they go together. I do know this—you do not want your name erased (blotted) from the Book of Life. Because I have never heard about the Lord writing someone's name back in the Book of Life after He blotted their name out. This is not the only scripture that says this, but it is a good one. In Revelation 20:15, the Lord instructed John to record, "Whosoever was not found written in the Book of Life was cast into the lake of fire." He told Moses the same thing. I must say again—you do not want your name erased from God's Book of Life.

I believe the Lord invented the eraser while He was writing the Book of Life. Read Revelation 3:5, and you will see that the Lord has an eraser. If you will look closely at that scripture, you will see that the Lord will not erase your name, IF you overcome (I believe He means Satan). There are other things that will cause the Lord to erase a person's name, but Revelation 22:19 teaches that the Lord will erase your name, IF you take away from His word.

Most false churches teach that when a person is saved at that time, God writes their name in the Book of Life. We need to look in the scriptures and see what they say about the Book of Life. You can find this TRUTH in Revelation 17:8. "Whose names were not written in the Book of Life FROM THE FOUNDATION OF THE WORLD." Now, this teaches us that the Book of Life was written when the Lord was building the foundation of this world. As you are about to find out in this chapter, the Lord recorded everyone's name that was going to be born on this earth in the Book of Life as this world was created. I must say this. The preachers who teach that your name is written down in the Book of Life when you are saved, they don't have a clear understanding of the scriptures.

After reading and studying these scriptures, what few there are that teach us about the Book of Life tells me that the Book of Life was written in the beginning. As you know, the book of Revelation is at the end of God's word, and we have Revelation 17:8 that teach us that the Book of Life was written from the foundation of the world. But what about the scriptures that we have read from Exodus chapter 32? Remember that in verse 32, Moses asked God, "Blot me I pray thee, out thy Book which thou hast written." When Moses asked God to blot him out of His Book, it was thousands of years ago, closer to the beginning of this world. You need to hear this TRUTH.

The Book of Life has been around for a long time, way before the New Testament church started. This is something that doesn't really matter, but here is a good question—how did Moses even know that God wrote a book with our names in it? As far as I know, Revelation 17:8 and Exodus 32:32 are the only two scriptures in God's word that teaches us about the Book of Life, being written in the beginning of the world. If you will notice in Exodus 32:32, Moses' last three words are "thou hast written" (in the past tense.) Not writing names for six thousand years, as people are naturally born or born- again. And for the first four thousand years, no one was born-again. And I would bet my left again, that Moses' and Abraham's name will be written in the Book of Life. And I believe, "When the roll is called up yonder." And the Book of Life are the same. Read Revelation 20:15. But all the other scriptures that speak about the Book of Life, always talks about blotting (erasing) names. Don't believe their lies, about Jesus writing your names in the Book of Life, when you are born-again. Simply ask Jesus to teach you, and He will. Another great teaching! Thank you Lord! In the next few paragraphs, you will see the four times that the word predestinate is written in God's word.

Let's read what Apostle Paul has to say about predestination, and then, we will find in the scriptures the actual account of what Paul was writing about. We are going to have to cover a few scriptures, so please bear with me. In Romans 8:28–30, Paul says, "And we know that all things work together for good to them that love God, to them who are the called according to purpose. For whom He did foreknow. He also did predestinate, conformed to the image of His Son, that He might be the firstborn among many brethren. "Moreover whom He did predestinate, them He also called and whom He called, them He also justified and whom He justified, them He also glorified."

In verse 28, Paul speaks of people whom God called for a certain purpose. What I get out of this scripture is God called certain people to do His work on earth to complete His master plan for the human race. In verse 29, Paul says, "For whom He did foreknow, He also did predestinate." This scripture lets me know that God already knew certain people before the beginning of the world that He was going to use to help Him complete His work. Verse 30 says, "Moreover whom He did predestinate, them He also called."

No one will ever know everything that the Lord has done or why. I do know this—the Lord Jesus is "KING of kings, and LORD of lords," and He knows any and everything. I believe when God was creating this world, He could see how most would not come and serve Him, and even some would turn from Him. I also believe that the foreknowledge the Lord had of the war to come with evil gave Him the opportunity to alter His plan for humanity. After all of the things that I have learned about the Lord, it's hard for me to believe that the KING of Glory would go to war with Satan without knowing and having His leaders in place to win the war.

You can find the list of leaders in Ephesians 4:11. It's not hard for me to believe the Lord predestinated the apostles, prophets, Evangelist, pastors, and teachers. Read verses 12–14, and you will see why the Lord has put them as our leaders. Let's read Ephesians 1:1–14 and find the last two times Apostle Paul spoke about predestination. In these scriptures, you will learn about the Lord predestinating His apostles. In Ephesians chapter 1, Apostle Paul teaches us the Lord predestinated the apostles before the world was created, and when the time came, He called them to do His work. In verse 1, Paul acknowledges that he is an apostle of Jesus Christ. However, note that Paul acknowledged he is an apostle by the will of God.

Notice what Apostle Paul says at the end of verse 1. Paul says that he is not only an apostle to the saints, which are in Ephesus, but also he is an apostle to you and me. If we are faithful in Christ Jesus, if you are faithful in Christ Jesus, I want you to hear the blessings that Apostle Paul wants God to send to us in verse 2—grace and peace. What better blessings are there than grace and peace? In verse 3, you will see (hear) that Apostle Paul praises God for blessing us with all spiritual blessings.

To find the TRUTH that I'm trying to share with you from these scriptures, I must say again what I said in chapter 1 of this book. When you read the words we, our, or us, 99.9% of the time, the scriptures are referring to the apostles, because they wrote the New Testament, with the exceptions of Mark, Jude, and Luke. Ephesians 1:4 tells us when the Lord chose (predestinated) the apostles. Verse 4 plainly tells us that God chose the apostles before the foundation of the world.

Verse 5 clearly states that God "having predestinated us (the apostles) unto the adoption of children by Jesus Christ to Himself, according to the good pleasure of His will." As you continue reading Ephesians chapter 1, when you get to verse 11, you will find the fourth and final time that Apostle Paul uses the word predestinate. In verse 11, Paul says for the second time that we (the apostles) were "predestinated according to the purpose of Him [God], who worketh all things after the counsel of His own will." Verse 12 says, "That we [the apostles] should be to the praise of His Glory, who first trusted in Christ."

We are about to look in the scriptures and find when the Lord called His apostles to start His work on earth. But first, I want to share this with you. After I read and studied the first chapter of Ephesians, I found in it the reason I wrote this book. Read verse 16–17 and you will find that Apostle Paul has been praying for us (the people who are faithful in Christ Jesus). Verse 17 tells us that Paul has been seeking the Lord for us—"That the God of our Lord Jesus Christ, the Father of glory, may give unto you the spirit of wisdom and revelation in the knowledge of Him." Now, that is why I wrote this book that God would give you the Spirit of wisdom and revelation in the knowledge of Him.

Now, let's look in the scriptures and find where the Lord began to call His apostles. The Lord had Isaiah prophesy about the Great Light (Jesus) coming into this world. In Isaiah 9:1–2, you will learn about the Great Light coming to the apostles so they could begin their work for the Lord. In Matthew 4:12–19, you will find where Isaiah's prophecy come to pass and also that the Lord begins calling His apostles. I believe that the Lord knew from the beginning of time that He was going to come on that day and preach His message to the people. Verse 17 says, "From that time Jesus began to preach, and to say, Repent: for the kingdom of heaven is at hand."

Matthew teaches us in verse 18 that Jesus first came to Peter and Andrew. In verse 19, Jesus tells them, "Follow Me and I will make you fishers of men." Here is something to think about, if you will notice at the end of verse 18 says "…for they were fishers." I believe this is where fishermen started, because before this day, they were called fishers. Fishermen! If you will continue reading, verse 21 says that the Lord called James and John that same day. And the Lord calls Matthew in Matthew 9:9. John 1:43 says that the Lord found Philip the day after He found Peter and Andrew. Now, the word doesn't reveal to us how the Lord found and called every apostle, but Luke 6:13 says that Jesus called His disciples, and of them, He chose twelve to be His apostles. In verses 14–16, Luke records the names of the twelve apostles, whom He chose. And these twelve apostles were predestinated from the foundation of the world, according to Apostle Paul.

Now, I want to share with you what I believe about how the Lord predestinated my family's lives. I first want to tell you I know that I'm working for our kingdom, and I am positive that my name is still written in the Book of Life. I believe if you are reading and studying this book with your Bible seeking for the TRUTH, your name is still written in the Book of Life also.

Here is something else I know to be the TRUTH. God wrote my name in the Book of Life as He laid down the foundations of this world. The Lord has had His hand on my life since before I was born (1955). Even though I didn't know it for a long time, God has taken care of me my whole life. He was watching over me when I was just six years old, and I would swim across a swollen (over flowing the banks) Coldwater River. The Coldwater River and a lake that was behind our house were mine and my two brothers' playground during the summer months of the early 1960s.

Looking back now, I can see how the Lord brought me and my wife together, and it was His plan. I met Cindy when she was twelve years old, and by the time she turned thirteen, we were what most call going steady. When Cindy was thirteen, I was seventeen. Over the years when I tell our story, how I met Cindy, some have said that

I robbed the cradle. Maybe so, but I know that mine and Cindy's life (family) are in God's master plan. As you know, hindsight is 20/20, and they didn't understand the Lord's plan, and neither did we. But it has been forty-five years, and we are still together.

Let me tell you a few things that I learned from my studies about the Book of Life concerning my family. I found out that parents don't give their children their names as they think they do. When my daughter Chasity was pregnant with her first son, the family went through a baby book that had 10,000 names in it. Remembering back, I did put my two cents in about it, but that was all it was, my two cents. Chasity and Jeff thought that they were naming their son Braxton Alan Gilliland. Jeff is the guy's name that Chasity had Braxton with, but he decided he wanted to live his life with another family, besides ours. And that's all I'm going to say about that.

I believe Hattie, as most people call him, will like this. After a couple of years passed, Chasity met her mister right. They too were having a son, and here, they go again, looking through the baby book for the perfect name.

Again I put my two cents in, but that's all it was. They asked for our opinion, but they finally announced to the world that their son's name would be Gunner Scott-Ronin Hatfield. My son Jason came up with the hyphen, but there has been talk about removing the hyphen. The hyphen has not been removed from Gunner's name as of the day I wrote this. Gunner is one and a half years old now, and only God knows if the hyphen is supposed to be in his name. If the hyphen stays in his name, Jason will have helped named Gunner, as it is written in the Book of Life.

I have come to know that when me and my wife Cindy named our children (Jason and Chasity), it was not us that named them. The Lord allowed us to announce their names that He had chosen for them, as He laid the foundation of the world. For those who are parents to-be, don't think you are going to name your child what you want it to be; the Lord will give you his or her name to announce to the world, just as the Lord brought me, and Cindy together forty-five years ago so we could bring Jason and Chasity to this world and so on. After learning the scriptures that teach us about the Book of Life, I don't see how you could not believe in predestination.

Here is one more set of scriptures that teach us about predestination. You need to read and study Hebrews 4:1–3, until you hear what these scriptures teach. Now, I have only written about the scriptures I know that teach us about predestination and the Book of Life, but I'm sure there are others that you will find in God's word. You can study God's word and make up your own mind to whatever you believe concerning the Book of Life. I believe I have covered when and why the Book of Life was written. But why and when the Book of Life was written is something that really doesn't matter. The main thing you need to know is that your name is written in the Book and that it remains there.

This is a fact. The only way anyone can get into heaven from the New Testament era is if you are born-again. Being born-again and living right by serving God and our fellow man are going to keep your name in the Book of Life. I believe the name Book of Life explains it all. Now you know about the word blot and that the Lord has an eraser, and He will use it. There are 142,300 words written in this book, and I know and believe every one of them. I just want you to know that if there is anything that is not true in this book, it is my fault and not God's. I should have listened better with my spiritual ears. And I will accept any consequences from the Lord for my lack of ability to hear Him and what I have shared with you as TRUTH.

Apostle Paul teaches us in 2 Timothy 3:7 that there are people who are ever learning and never able to come to the knowledge of the TRUTH. Just remember, it's not good enough to know the TRUTH—we all must live God's TRUTH. We must listen for the Spirit of God to speak to us, because Jesus says a few times in the scriptures, "Hear what the Spirit is saying to the church." To sum up what the Lord and I are trying to convey to you in this book is found in Matthew 24:14, "AND THIS GOSPEL OF THE KINGDOM SHALL BE PREACHED IN ALL THE WORLD FOR A WITNESS UNTO ALL NATIONS; AND THEN SHALL THE END COME."

I have wondered for years how I was going to end this book. But I didn't know about my future. So when I got to this part of our book, I want to tell you something I wrote about in the first chapter. At that time, I was sharing with you how THE GREAT PHYSICIAN operated on my heart and didn't even leave a scar. And He did. I used to pull up my shirt while witnessing and show them my scarless chest. I can't do that anymore, because on December 20, 2017, I had to have a heart surgery. Now, I'm scarred as if I had been in a Mississippi Juke Joint knife fight. I had to stay for twenty-nine days in that hospital. In sixty-two years, I have never had to stay at a hospital before, and twenty-nine days is a long time to be there.

This is how I made it through this operation. A couple of days before I went to the hospital, I was upstairs praying, and I remember asking the Lord to pick me up and hold me in His arms. In the past thirty-five years, I have asked the Lord for His help on many occasions. But asking the Lord to hold me in His arms is one of the most important things that I have ever asked Him. When my physician asked me if I wanted to have this operation, I remember telling him yes and that the Lord would guide his hands and I will make it through this operation if it is His will. The Lord truly held me in His arms.

When finding out that you have to go through something like this, you will get a reality check like no other. I was in the hospital for a couple of weeks before my surgery because of other complications. That gave me time to witness to some of the doctors and most of the nurses. I told most of them how the Lord has allowed me to write a book to help my fellow man find His TRUTH. But there was only one problem—my book was not complete. I still had about five more pages to complete it. And as you can see by the words written on this page, it was the Lord's will for me to finish this book.

Before I run out of room on these pages, I must take this space to confirm a TRUTH I shared with one of my nurses. This nurse's name is Anna. I just want Anna to know even though I was on drugs, I saw what I saw that day. The first day that I met Anna, I began asking her some questions about God's word. I would quote a scripture and ask her if she had ever heard that before. As far as I can remember, we talked for thirty minutes or more, and every time I would ask her if she had ever heard that scripture before, she would say yes, but not like that.

God's Spirit was really moving that day in my hospital room. I could see and hear her receiving God's TRUTH. Now, you know from reading this book, the Lord has showed me and done some strange things in my life. And this day was one of them. After we talked for a while, the Lord began anointing in such a way that I have never seen before. Anna's body began to smoke. From her waist up, a fog-type substance was coming from her body and rising to the ceiling. She could not see this fog, but I began telling her how it was coming from her face and arms, and it was covering the ceiling. At first, she must have believed it was the drugs or that I was just crazy.

I remember crying out to the Lord and asking Him what all of this means, but He didn't reveal to me what He was doing. And when I say crying out, I mean, I began weeping. The reason I was weeping is I wanted to know what the Lord was doing for Anna and what this meant. I have been off those drugs for three months, and the Lord has still not revealed to me what He was doing that day. I just want Anna to know that I'm not on drugs and I'm not crazy, at least I don't believe I am. Everything I saw and said that day was the TRUTH. All I can say about this is that she had to believe it was God, because she gave me her phone number, because she wanted a book and she knew that she had heard God's TRUTH that day.

As I write these words, I want Anna to know I am experiencing that same Spirit moving upon me today. For some reason, I lost her phone number. A couple of days later, I saw her in the hall and I waved for her to come in, and she gave me her phone number again. I immediately put her number in my phone so I wouldn't lose it. Lord willing, as soon as I finish writing, Anna will get a book. If Anna has read this book to this point, she has heard more than she heard that day, and it is up to her to obey God's TRUTH. That is my prayer for you, Anna, and may God bless you and your family.

I'm about to say something, and you may think I'm crazy. So before I say what I'm about to say, I want to give you an example of how the Lord allows Satan to give Apostle Paul a thorn in his flesh. As you read these scriptures, you will learn that Apostle Paul was afflicted by Satan so he would not be boastful about what he has done for the kingdom. Read 2 Corinthians 12:1–10. I know that this is going to sound stupid to some of you who reads this book, but it is true. My heart attack was a blessing to keep me humble before the Lord. Any and everything that I know and done for our kingdom, Jesus taught and helped me do the work.

Here is a good example of what was going on in my life to get my attention. Do you remember in Matthew 14:22–33 how Apostle Peter walked on the water, but when he began to look at the wind and waves, he began to sink? Well, I too found myself beginning to sink. I did as Apostle Peter had done. I found myself not focusing on the Lord, as I know I should.

Here is something else I believe, but I want you to understand this. I'm in no way comparing myself with Job. If you can remember when I wrote about how Job was attacked by Satan, Satan did not come to the Lord seeking Job. Satan was seeking anyone that he could deceive. Remember that it was the Lord that said, "Have you considered My servant Job?" Simply put, the Lord just handed Job and his possessions to Satan.

I have written in this book how Satan doesn't like me sharing God's TRUTH with the world. But I also know that the Lord loves what I'm doing, because I'm working for our kingdom. I didn't know or believe what I'm about to say, but I now believe it is true. I believe as Satan came to God looking for a soul to steal, the Lord asked Satan, "Have you considered My servant Jessie?" Now, I didn't have to go through what Job did, but what I went through was bad, but I am still standing for the Lord. The Lord will lift you up if you begin to sink if you will just call on His name. Now my prayer is, Lord pick me up and hold me in your arms. You never know what you are about to go through, so I suggest that that would be your prayer also. I also pray that you have received this TRUTH and that you will obey it.

I have read and studied this book with my Bible four times, trying to find God's TRUTH for you. And every time I studied it, I would learn something else. I suggest for you to read and study it a few more times. And go find the church that the Lord wants you to go to so you can be fed His word. I also pray that the Lord will reveal His name to you and the power that is in His name.

I believe the Lord is going to anoint my work, and millions will read this book and find His TRUTH. I asked the Lord to help me be a soul winner, and as you can see, the Lord has truly blessed me with the desires of my heart. But you had better chose your words carefully when you ask the Lord for the desires of your heart. Since I started writing this book, I became bald, had to start wearing glasses, and had to have heart surgery, among many other things. Through all of that, the Lord has taken care of me, and I know that the Lord gave me my first breath, so I want to give Him my last. I have worked a long time on this book, but it would be worth everything I went through if only one person heard and obeyed God's TRUTH. Cliché but true! I don't know what you have learned from this book, but the Lord has been feeding me with a snow scoop every time I study it with my Bible.

It has taken me ten years to write this book, and I'm going to finish it on April 21, 2018, which is my grandson's (Braxton's) birthday. This will help me to remember the day I finished it. Through the years, I have always believed that I was going to give this book away for free, because I don't believe in charging for something that the Lord has given me. But the publishers that I'm using to publish this book want to make money, so it had to be sold. So I decided to start a charity named Any Charity Ministries Foundation.

I have always believed that I would be an entrepreneur, but I have learned a new word in the last few years that I want to be, and it is being a philanthropist. October 19, 2025, I edited our book and I'm now an entrepreneur and a philanthropist. Whatever you donate to the Any Charity Ministries Foundation will be distributed to the needy. I will spend the rest of my life here on earth serving the rich and giving to the poor. They truly need our help, and if the Lord puts it in your heart to give, give accordingly to the knowledge you have received. Your donation to Any Charity Ministries Foundation will be spent wisely. Donations can be made at anycharityministriesfoundation. org and they will be greatly appreciated by the poor and needy. I have three more requests. I need you to help me spread God's TRUTH and I need you to buy a few books and give them to your friends and family. If you share this TRUTH with others, you will be BLESSED. Thank you for your help, and may God BLESS you and your family with more TRUTH.

Donate to: anycharityministriesfoundation.org

ABOUT THE AUTHOR

This is Jessie Dunson's first book. Although the author had very little schooling, because he failed the first, fifth, and seventh grades and he dropped out of school after the eighth grade, the Lord has been teaching him His word for thirty-five years and allowed him to RIGHTLY DIVIDE His word.

The Lord has spoken to him in English seven times during those thirty-five years. In 1991, the Lord spoke and told him a specific thing to do. But it took the author seventeen years to start writing what the Lord was trying to teach him.

Whenever these so-called Christians come witnessing in the author's neighborhood, he would open both garage doors so they will not miss him and so he would not miss them. In 2008, two young men came by and talked to him, and when they were ready to leave, they tried to give him some literature. However, he didn't take their literature, because he didn't believe what they were selling.

It bothered him that he didn't have any TRUTH to share with them. When they left, the Lord began giving him the words to write. These writings started off being a tract, but soon turned into a book. It took him ten years to write this book, because of his lack of education, and the job of RIGHTLY DIVIDING God's word. Without Jesus, this book would not have been written, so he believes Jesus is the real author, but He used his hands and mind to write this book.

My Personal Warning

I am about to do something, that I am not really sure of, and I will be held accountable by Jesus, if I am wrong. I don't know if anyone else did this besides me, but I am reaching out past the tribulation period, because there must be some decent people on earth, because Satan is locked up in HELL during this time, and can't influence anyone with his evilness, as he did us. The reason I wanted my book in hardback copy, is so it would last hundreds of years after Jesus came back to earth to get His Church (Bride.) There was nothing ever written in God's word that teaches about someone being saved during this time period, but just maybe, Jesus is trying to reach you.

If you are reading this book during this time period, I would suggest, start seeking Jesus with all your heart and might. Cry out, snot, beg, or whatever it takes, because you must touch Jesus' heart to accomplish this, if it is even possible. And start studying God's word, by using this book as a guide to the scriptures, of the King James Version Bible, that you MUST OBEY to go to Heaven.

I am in no way, trying to take God's word out of context, because this scripture is referring to the 144,000 Jews that will be born-again during the tribulation period, and any other Jew that will hear it, but Revelation 14:6, John calls God's word, the everlasting gospel. And in June 13, 2023 when I wrote this, everlasting still means everlasting! Remember in Romans 11:25, that Apostle Paul said

"...that blindness in part is happened to Israel, until the fullness of the Gentiles be come in." God's word teaches us, that when the tribulation period comes, Jesus has completed His time with the Gentiles, and turned back to the Jewish people. You will know that this book is TRUTH, because ALL of this will have already happened, and be in your past. Boy, this is like a movie back in 1985 named, BACK TO THE FUTURE, because they went back in time and wrote a letter warning themselves about their future. I pray that you seek Jesus with all that is within you, and He grants you your prayers of salvation.

May Jesus Bless you with eternal Life. In Jesus mighty name I pray.

www.ingramcontent.com/pod-product-compliance
Lightning Source LLC
Chambersburg PA
CBHW051505120626
46551CB00012B/777